Volume 3
of an Analytic Commentary on
the *Philosophical Investigations*

Wittgenstein
Meaning and Mind

Part II: Exegesis §§243 – 427

P. M. S. Hacker

Fellow of St John's College · Oxford

BLACKWELL
Oxford UK & Cambridge USA

Copyright © P. M. S. Hacker 1990, 1993

The right of P. M. S. Hacker to be identified as author of this work has been asserted in accordance with the Copyright, Designs and Patents Act 1988.

First published in paperback 1993

Blackwell Publishers
108 Cowley Road, Oxford OX4 1JF, UK

238 Main Street
Cambridge, Massachusetts 02142, USA

All rights reserved. Except for the quotation of short passages for the purposes of criticism and review, no part of this publication may be reproduced, stored in a retrieval system, or transmitted, in any form or by any means, electronic, mechanical, photocopying, recording or otherwise, without the prior permission of the publisher.

Except in the United States of America, this book is sold subject to the condition that it shall not, by way of trade or otherwise, be lent, resold, hired out, or otherwise circulated without the publisher's prior consent in any form of binding or cover other than that in which it is published and without a similar condition including this condition being imposed on the subsequent purchaser.

British Library Cataloguing in Publication Data

A CIP catalogue record for this book is available from the British Library.

Library of Congress Cataloging-in-Publication Data

Hacker, P. M. S. (Peter Michael Stephan)
Wittgenstein, meaning and mind / P.M.S. Hacker.
p.   cm
"Volume 3 of An analytical commentary on the Philosophical investigations." Slightly rev. and reissued separately in 2 vols.
Includes bibliographical references and index.
Contents: pt. 1. Essays — pt. 2. Exegesis.
ISBN 0–631–18934–3 (pt. 1 : alk. paper).—ISBN 0–631–19064–3 (pt. 2 : alk. paper)
1. Wittgenstein, Ludwig, 1889–1951. Philosophische Untersuchungen. 2. Philosophy. 3. Language and languages––Philosophy. 4. Semantics (Philosophy) I. Title.
B3376.W563P53244   1993
192—dc20   93–19474
                                                                          CIP

Typeset in 10 on 12 pt Bembo by TecSet Ltd, Wallington, Surrey
Printed in Great Britain by TJ Press Ltd, Padstow, Cornwall

This book is printed on acid-free paper

For Sylvia

CAPILANO COLLEGE LIBRARY

B3376W563P53244Y93PT2

WITTGENSTEIN MEANING A

HACKER P M S

DATE DUE

Brodart Co.   Cat. # 55 137 001   Printed in USA

Wittgenstein: Meaning and Mind

Part II: Exegesis §§243 – 427

B

Previous volumes of this Commentary in paperback

Wittgenstein: Meaning and Understanding, essays on the *Philosophical Investigations* (Volume 1)

G. P. Baker and P. M. S. Hacker

An Analytical Commentary on Wittgenstein's *Philosophical Investigations* (Volume 1)

G. P. Baker and P. M. S. Hacker

Wittgenstein: Rules, Grammar and Necessity, Volume 2 of an Analytical Commentary on the *Philosophical Investigations*

G. P. Baker and P. M. S. Hacker

Companion to this volume

Wittgenstein: Meaning and Mind, Volume 3 of an Analytical Commentary on the *Philosophical Investigations*, Part I: Essays

P. M. S. Hacker

Contents

Note to the paperback edition

In 1990 I published a 575-page volume entitled *Wittgenstein: Meaning and Mind, an Analytical Commentary on the* PHILOSOPHICAL INVESTIGATIONS. It was the sequel to two previous volumes of commentary on Wittgenstein's masterpiece which I had written together with my colleague Dr G. P. Baker. The first volume, published in 1980, was entitled *Wittgenstein: Understanding and Meaning*. It covered §§1 – 184 of the *Investigations*, and consisted of analytical essays on the main topics discussed in these sections of Wittgenstein's book and detailed textual exegesis of the numbered remarks, examining the argument of each remark, explaining its role in the overall strategy, and, where it was illuminating to do so, tracing its ancestry to Wittgenstein's voluminous *Nachlass*. The seventeen essays in that volume were interspersed at appropriate places in the exegesis. The second volume, published in 1985, was a 375-page book entitled *Wittgenstein: Rules, Grammar and Necessity*. It covered §§185 – 242 of the *Investigations*. Its structure was modelled on that of Volume 1, consisting of detailed exegesis accompanied by six analytical essays. When the time came for the publication of a paperback edition, Volume 1 had to be split into two, one volume consisting of the seventeen essays and entitled *Wittgenstein: Meaning and Understanding, Essays on the* PHILOSOPHICAL INVESTIGATIONS (Volume 1), and the second consisting of the original exegesis of §§1 – 184 and entitled *An Analytical Commentary on Wittgenstein's* PHILOSOPHICAL INVESTIGATIONS (Volume 1). Volume 2, being shorter, was published in paperback in the same form as the original hardback and under the same title.

Like Volume 1, Volume 3 has had to be split into two, this paperback, consisting of the original exegesis, and a companion paperback, *Wittgenstein: Meaning and Mind*, Part I, consisting of the essays. Each can be read and used independently of the other, although they are, of course, complementary.

Apart from the structural alterations essential for the bifurcation of the original volume, the changes introduced are minimal. First, the few internal cross-references within the original text have now been replaced by cross-references to the companion volume. In this volume references in the exegesis to themes developed at length in the philosophical essays of the companion volume (*Wittgenstein: Meaning and Mind*, Part I: Essays) are signified (as in the original) by a quoted essay title and section number. The original locus in the exegesis of the essay and the contents of each essay are here indicated by printing each essay title and its section headings in a box frame at the appropriate place in the text. Secondly, the original Preface has been adapted to match it to each of the two paperback volumes. Thirdly, minor errors and typographical mistakes in the hard cover edition have been corrected. In this volume, a few additional references to the *Nachlass* have been added to the tables of correlation that occur at the end of the introductions to each chapter of exegesis.

Since I completed Volume 3, Wittgenstein's *Last Writings on the Philosophy of Psychology, Volume 2* has been published. It contains much that is of importance to the themes discussed here, but nothing that was not available to me and, when relevant, used, with references to his manuscript volumes, in the original publication. Consequently, I have left those references as they were.

P. M. S. H.
Oxford, 1992

Acknowledgements

While writing this book I have been generously assisted by institutions, friends, and colleagues.

By electing me to a two-year Research Readership, which relieved me of teaching, the British Academy made the initial research on the Wittgenstein manuscripts easier and more efficient than it would otherwise have been. I am grateful to my college, St John's, for the many facilities it offers to its Fellows. Its support for research and the pursuit of scholarship is heart-warming. I am indebted to the Bodleian Library, in particular to the staff of the Western Manuscript Department, for many services. The publishing team at Basil Blackwell Ltd, especially Mr S. Chambers and Mr A. McNeillie, have been most helpful in planning and executing this difficult publishing project. As in the past, so too now, it has been a pleasure to work with them in close cooperation. I am most grateful to Miss Jean van Altena for the excellence of her copy-editing.

Professor N. Malcolm, Dr S. Mulhall, Professor H. Philipse, Professor J. Raz, Mr B. Rundle, Professor S. Shanker, Mr T. Spitzley, and Professor T. Taylor kindly read and commented on various drafts of essays or exegesis. Their criticisms, queries, and suggestions were of great assistance. I am especially indebted to Dr H. J. Glock and to Dr J. Hyman, whose comments on essays and exegesis alike were invaluable. Dr Glock and Mr Spitzley kindly checked my German transcriptions and translations. Participants in the university seminars which I have given together with Dr G. P. Baker over the past three years have contributed greatly to the clarification of my thoughts. Their questions were challenging and a stimulus to further efforts. I am most grateful to them all, but especially to Dr O. Hanfling, who both curbed some of my excesses and spurred me on to improve my arguments.

For various reasons it was not feasible for Dr Baker to join me in writing this third volume of Analytical Commentary. However, despite occasional disagreement in interpretation and deeper disagreement over nuance (and it is the chiaroscuro that finally makes the sketch), he read the whole manuscript and joined me in giving the university seminars. His painstaking and helpful criticisms as well as his constructive suggestions saved me from error again and again.

Finally, I am, as before, indebted to the Wittgenstein executors for permission to quote from the unpublished *Nachlass*. Professor G. H. von Wright has, as always, been unstintingly generous in putting at my disposal the results of his extensive bibliographical research on the *Nachlass*.

P. M. S. H.
St John's College, Oxford
1989

Thoughts reduced to paper are generally nothing
more than the footprints of a man walking in
the sand. It is true that we see the path he
has taken; but to know what he saw on the way,
we must use our own eyes.

Schopenhauer

Preface

The first volume of this Analytical Commentary was begun in 1976. Little did I then dream that a decade later I should still be struggling through the thousands of pages of the *Nachlass*, attempting to piece together a surveyable representation of the most fascinating array of philosophical arguments of the twentieth century. The task proved far more difficult and controversial, and certainly involved much greater labour, than originally envisaged. With hindsight, this is hardly surprising. For on every major issue about which he wrote, Wittgenstein undermined the fundamental presuppositions of the debate. The landscape he traversed is familiar; but the routes he took were always new, and his footsteps are not easy to follow. New solutions to received questions are difficult enough to come to terms with. New questions regarding well-worn subjects are difficult to put into fruitful perspective. But a challenge to the very presuppositions of the questions, old and new, which characterize philosophical reflection is far harder to understand and accommodate. There is no short-cut to Wittgenstein's viewpoint: one must follow his trail and look afresh at each landmark. The *Philosophical Investigations* does not aim to add a fresh theory — about meaning and understanding, about necessity or the nature of the mind — to the array of established ones. Nor is its purpose to examine opposing positions in centuries-old debates — such as realism versus nominalism, mentalism versus behaviourism, or Platonism versus formalism — in order to side with those supported by superior arguments. Its goal is to dissolve the questions themselves by showing that they rest upon illegitimate presuppositions and misguided expectations. What is legitimate about philosophical questions can be resolved by a careful description of the uses of words; the rest is illusion. As Wittgenstein observed in one of his more startling remarks. 'In philosophy, all that isn't gas is grammar' (LWL 112).

Wittgenstein: Understanding and Meaning (Volume 1 of this Analytical Commentary) laid the groundwork for understanding the trajectory of his thought. It gave due prominence to the Augustinian picture of language as an *Urbild* informing a multitude of philosophical theories about the nature of language, all of which Wittgenstein aimed to undermine. Misconceptions about the essential nature of words as names and of sentences as descriptions stand in the way of an unprejudiced view of the manifold techniques of using words and of the diverse functions of sentences in the stream of life. These misconceptions give rise to philosophical mythologies about 'the name-relation', logically proper names, sentence-radicals and semantic-mood operators, determinacy of sense, and 'the general propositional form'. They generate misguided pictures of the relationship between language and reality, and of ostensive definition as forging a connection between the two. This in turn contributes to the pervasive illusion that grammar is answerable to reality or that it reflects, and must reflect, the essential structure of the world. Against the background of Wittgenstein's demythologizing, his radical conception of philosophy was displayed. He held philosophy to be therapeutic, not theoretical. It destroys idols, but does not replace them. It is a quest for a surview of grammar, not for an armchair preview of future science. Achievement in philosophy consists in dissolution of philosophical questions, not in acquisition of new information that provides answers to them. Understanding is indeed attained; but it consists in arriving at a clear vision of what is known and familiar, rather than in grasping the articulations of a new theory about the nature of things. Theory construction lies within the province of science, and philosophy — in its questions, methods, and results — is wholly distinct from science.

Once this had been clarified, it was possible to put Wittgenstein's discussion of understanding in the right perspective. Meaning, explanation of what something means, and understanding constitute a triad of key concepts in philosophical investigations into language and the nature of linguistic representation. Reversing the direction of fit between these concepts that is presupposed by the prevailing philosophical tradition, Wittgenstein elaborated the consequences of the grammatical propositions that meaning is what is given by an explanation of meaning, and that it is what is understood when the meaning of an utterance is understood. Understanding (which is akin to an ability rather than a mental state) and the criteria of understanding assume a dominant role in his descriptions of the network of grammar in this domain. Clarification of the internal relations between meaning, understanding, and explanation also illuminates their complex connections with truth, evidence, justification, definition, rules of use, grammatical proposition, and so forth.

Wittgenstein: Rules, Grammar and Necessity, Volume 2 of the Analytical Commentary, constituted an alteration to the original plans. The complexities of §§185 – 242 of the *Investigations* needed very detailed analysis, the extensive controversies over the interpretation of Wittgenstein's intentions required the presentation of much background material from the *Nachlass*, and the generally ill-understood consequences of his account of grammar and rule-following demanded at least a fragmentary investigation of his philosophy of logic and mathematics. Hence the whole of Volume 2 was dedicated to the clarification of Wittgenstein's discussion of rules, acting in accord with a rule, and following a rule. This led to an examination of his discussion of the autonomy of grammar and of his remarks on the nature of necessity in the domains of logic, mathematics, and metaphysics.

The present paperback volume of exegesis takes the Analytical Commentary forward from §243 to §427. These sections are no less controversial than the preceding ones. To be sure, the rocky ground already traversed should have taught one much. But as one plunges into the tropical undergrowth of the great private language arguments, it is all too easy to lose one's bearings. The path is overgrown with prevalent misinterpretations, and dark distorting shadows are cast across it by our disposition to extract theories from Wittgenstein's descriptions. The position of these arguments in the overall structure of the book needs to be clarified. Why, at this particular point, is the question of whether a private language is possible raised? To what extent are the previous remarks presupposed? Is Wittgenstein simply moving on to yet another of the 'great questions of philosophy', or is there a natural progression from the preceding argument? Why is the discussion of a private language followed by an investigation of thinking and imagining — and why is there no discussion of remembering and other faculties of the mind?

Not only is the rationale of the locus of these sections in the grand strategy controversial, but the very subject of debate in §§243ff. is disputed. What is a 'private' language? And why should anyone be interested in whether there could be a language which, unlike ordinary languages, only its speaker can, logically, understand? What is Wittgenstein's purpose? Is he trying to demonstrate the essential *social* nature of language, to show that it is an *a priori* truth that only a social creature can speak or use symbols? Is he aiming to refute a *recherché* form of scepticism about knowing what one means by one's words? Or is his target quite different?

If the subject is disputed, so too is the conclusion. Is he arguing that there can be no such thing as a 'private' ostensive definition, or rather that such a mode of assigning meaning to an expression is possible only within the context of mastery of a shared, public language? How can a philosopher who repudiates theses and proofs in philosophy go on to try to *prove* that there cannot be a private language? Or was he not trying to prove this at all?

The tactical moves are equally subject to divergent interpretation. Does Wittgenstein implicitly rely on a verification principle? Is his denial of the possibility of a private language dependent on worries about the reliability of memory? And if there is such a philosophical, as opposed to practical, worry, how could it possibly disappear in company? It is evident that he denies that sensations are 'inner objects'; but does he contend instead that they are nothing at all? He explicitly denied that he was propounding any form of behaviourism, but many have argued that his philosophy of psychology is a version of logical behaviourism. This too needs elucidation.

If the path through this terrain is shrouded in gloom, its direction is no less difficult to discern. It is clear that Wittgenstein thought that the matter of a private language bears directly on solipsism and idealism. But why is this never explicitly shown? Is the argument meant to be an implicit refutation of idealism? But is the issue not too important for such cursory treatment? Or are these venerable philosophical doctrines merely ancient idols in the jungle which are briefly illuminated as he passes by, intent upon an altogether different goal? Was Wittgenstein trying to re-órient completely our picture of the mind, so that *everything* would appear in a new light? Certainly the relation between the 'inner' and the 'outer' is as philosophically problematic, especially when viewed from the perspective of the Augustinian picture of language, as the relation between proof and truth in mathematics. Wittgenstein's treatment of the latter theme involved a radical break with all traditional approaches. It is not unreasonable to expect his discussion of the former to involve an equally startling repudiation of the very presuppositions of the debates between idealism and realism, dualism and monism, mentalism and behaviourism. Surely we should take seriously his avowal that he was destroying 'houses of cards' and 'clearing up the ground of language on which they stand' (PI §118).

The exegesis follows the pattern established by the previous volumes. It aims to elucidate Wittgenstein's individual remarks and their role in his progressive argument. Since many of the remarks in this part of the *Investigations* have been the source of heated interpretative controversy, extensive material from the *Nachlass* has sometimes been presented. Although a particular reading has typically been favoured, it seemed desirable, in cases where substantially different interpretations are reasonable, to display all the relevant evidence. An overview of Wittgenstein's ideas on the central themes dealt with in this part of the *Investigations* is given by the thirteen essays in the complementary paperback volume *Wittgenstein: Meaning and Mind, Part 1: Essays*.

The arguments of §§243–427 do not constitute the 'foundations' of, let alone the whole of, Wittgenstein's philosophy of mind. But they provide essential methodical guidelines and fundamental insights. They are the route to 'the correct logical point of view' — but to achieve it, one must follow the arduous trail he blazed. In the following pages I have tried to plot it as best I could. Doubtless I have erred in places, but I hope that I have captured the direction of his thought. If he is right, then the mainstream of philosophical psychology, past and present, is misguided — flowing from misconceived questions to quagmires of confused pseudo-theories. Of course, his ideas run counter to the spirit of the age, and today the will to illusion is stronger than ever. Only when philosophers wish to be cured of the sicknesses of the understanding that beset them, will they be in a position to take up the legacy of Wittgenstein.

Abbreviations

1. Published works

The following abbreviations are used to refer to Wittgenstein's published works, listed in chronological order (where possible; some works straddle many years). The list includes derivative primary sources and lecture notes taken by others.

NB   *Notebooks 1914–16*, ed. G. H. von Wright and G. E. M. Anscombe, tr. G. E. M. Anscombe (Blackwell, Oxford, 1961).

TLP   *Tractatus Logico-Philosophicus*, tr. D. F. Pears and B. F. McGuinness (Routledge and Kegan Paul, London, 1961).

RLF   'Some Remarks on Logical Form', *Proceedings of the Aristotelian Society*, suppl. vol. ix (1929), pp. 162–71.

WWK   *Ludwig Wittgenstein und der Wiener Kreis*, shorthand notes recorded by F. Waismann, ed. B. F. McGuinness (Blackwell, Oxford, 1967). The English translation, *Wittgenstein and the Vienna Circle* (Blackwell, Oxford, 1979), matches the pagination of the original edition.

PR   *Philosophical Remarks*, ed. R. Rhees, tr. R. Hargreaves and R. White (Blackwell, Oxford, 1975).

M   'Wittgenstein's Lectures in 1930–33', in G. E. Moore, *Philosophical Papers* (Allen and Unwin, London, 1959)

LWL   *Wittgenstein's Lectures, Cambridge 1930–32, from the Notes of John King and Desmond Lee*, ed. Desmond Lee (Blackwell, Oxford, 1980).

PG   *Philosophical Grammar*, ed. R. Rhees, tr. A. J. P. Kenny (Blackwell, Oxford, 1974).

GB   'Remarks on Frazer's "Golden Bough"', tr. J. Beversluis, repr. in C. G. Luckhardt (ed.), *Wittgenstein: Sources and Perspectives* (Cornell University Press, Ithaca, 1979), pp. 61–81.

AWL   *Wittgenstein's Lectures, Cambridge 1932–35, from the Notes of Alice Ambrose and Margaret MacDonald*, ed. Alice Ambrose (Blackwell, Oxford, 1979).

BB   *The Blue and Brown Books* (Blackwell, Oxford, 1958).

LPE   'Wittgenstein's Notes for Lectures on "Private Experience" and "Sense Data"', ed. R. Rhees, *Philosophical Review*, 77 (1968), pp. 275–320.

LSD   'The Language of Sense Data and Private Experience' (Notes taken by R. Rhees of Wittgenstein's lectures, 1936), *Philosophical Investigations*, 7 (1984), pp. 1–45, 10–40.

RFM   *Remarks on the Foundations of Mathematics*, ed. G. H. von Wright, R. Rhees, G. E. M. Anscombe, revised edition (Blackwell, Oxford, 1978).

LA   *Lectures and Conversations on Aesthetics, Psychology and Religious Beliefs*, ed. C. Barrett (Blackwell, Oxford, 1970).

LFM   *Wittgenstein's Lectures on the Foundations of Mathematics, Cambridge 1939*, ed. C. Diamond (Harvester Press, Sussex, 1976).

PI   *Philosophical Investigations*, ed. G. E. M. Anscombe and R. Rhees, tr. G. E. M. Anscombe, 2nd edition (Blackwell, Oxford, 1958).

Z   *Zettel*, ed. G. E. M. Anscombe and G. H. von Wright, tr. G. E. M. Anscombe (Blackwell, Oxford, 1967).

RPP I *Remarks on the Philosophy of Psychology*, Volume I, ed. G. E. M. Anscombe and G. H. von Wright, tr. G. E. M. Anscombe (Blackwell, Oxford, 1980).

RPP II *Remarks on the Philosophy of Psychology*, Volume II, ed. G. H. von Wright and H. Nyman, tr. C. G. Luckhardt and M. A. E. Aue (Blackwell, Oxford, 1980).

LPP   *Wittgenstein's Lectures on Philosophy of Psychology 1946–7*, notes by P. T. Geach, K. J. Shah, A. C. Jackson, ed. P. T. Geach (Harvester · Wheatsheaf, Hemel Hempstead, 1988).

LW   *Last Writings on the Philosophy of Psychology*, Volume I, ed. G. H. von Wright and H. Nyman, tr. C. G. Luckhardt and M. A. E. Aue (Blackwell, Oxford, 1982).

C   *On Certainty*, ed. G. E. M. Anscombe and G. H. von Wright, tr. D. Paul and G. E. M. Anscombe (Blackwell, Oxford, 1969).

CV   *Culture and Value*, ed. G. H. von Wright in collaboration with H. Nyman, tr. P. Winch (Blackwell, Oxford, 1980).

PLP   *The Principles of Linguistic Philosophy*, F. Waismann, ed. R. Harré (Macmillan and St Martin's Press, London and New York, 1965).

R   *Ludwig Wittgenstein: Letters to Russell, Keynes and Moore*, ed. G. H. von Wright (Blackwell, Oxford, 1974).

Reference style: all references to *Philosophical Investigations*, Part I, are to sections (e.g. PI §1), except those to notes below the line on various pages. References to Part II are to pages (e.g. PI p. 202). References to other printed works are either to numbered remarks (TLP) or to sections signified '§' (Z, RPP, LW); in all other cases references are to pages (e.g. LFM 21 = LFM, page 21) or to numbered letters (R).

2. *Nachlass*

All references to unpublished material cited in the von Wright catalogue (G. H. von Wright, *Wittgenstein* (Blackwell, Oxford, 1982), pp. 35ff.) are by MS. or TS. number followed by page number. Wherever possible, the pagination entered in the original document has been used. The Cornell xeroxes in the Bodleian are defective; sometimes a dozen or more pages have been omitted. Consequently, where access to the originals or to complete xeroxes has not been possible, some errors of page reference will unavoidably have occurred. For memorability, the following special abbreviations are used.

Manuscripts
Vol. I, Vol. II, etc. refer to the eighteen large manuscript volumes (= MSS. 105–22) written between 2 February 1929 and 1944. The reference style Vol. VI, 241 is to Volume VI, page 241.

Typescripts
BT   The 'Big Typescript' (TS. 213): a rearrangement, with modifications, written additions and deletions, of TS. 211, 1933, vi pp. table of contents, 768 pp. All references are to page numbers. Where the page number is followed by 'v.', this indicates a handwritten addition on the reverse side of the TS. page.

PPI   'Proto-Philosophical Investigations'[1] (TS. 220): a typescript of the first half of the pre-war version of the *Philosophical Investigations* (up to §189 of the final version, but with many differences); 1937 to 1938, 137 pp. The shortened title form 'Proto-Investigations' is used freely. All references are to sections (§).

3. *Abbreviations for works by Frege*

FA   *The Foundations of Arithmetic*, tr. J. L. Austin, 2nd edition (Blackwell, Oxford, 1959).

GA   *Grundgesetze der Arithmetik, begriffsschriftlich abgeleitet*, Band I, (Hermann Pohle, Jena, 1893).

---

[1]This is not Wittgenstein's title.

PW *Posthumous Writings*, ed. H. Hermes, F. Kambartel, F. Kaulbach, tr. P. Long, R. White (Blackwell, Oxford, 1979).

4. *Abbreviations for works by Russell*

AM *The Analysis of Mind* (George Allen and Unwin, London, 1921).
LK *Logic and Knowledge, Essays 1901–1950*, ed. R. C. Marsh (Allen and Unwin, London, 1956).

5. *References to previous volumes of this Analytical Commentary*.

References to Volume 1 are flagged 'Volume 1' with a page number referring to the hardback edition. Where necessary the abbreviation MU (with a page number) is used, referring to the paperback volume of essays entitled *Wittgenstein: Meaning and Understanding* (Blackwell, Oxford, 1983). References to Volume 2, *Wittgenstein: Rules, Grammar and Necessity*, are flagged 'Volume 2'.

Analytical
Commentary

CHAPTER 1

The private language arguments
(§§243 – 315)

INTRODUCTION

§§243–315 constitute the eighth 'chapter' of the book. Its point of departure is a natural query with respect to the conclusion of the immediately preceding argument, viz. that for a language to be a means of communication, there must be agreement not only in definitions but also in judgements. Could there not be a language which was wholly independent of such interpersonal agreement or even any possibility of such agreement? Can we not imagine a language the words of which cannot be explained to other people, although the speaker of such a language knows perfectly well what they mean? Indeed, on certain natural philosophical assumptions, is the language each person uses to talk about his inner experiences not, in some deep and important sense, such a private language?

Part A (§§243–55) opens by clarifying what a 'private' language is supposed to be — not a contingently private language which no one else happens to understand, but an essentially private language which it is logically impossible for another to understand. What the words of such a language refer to are the speaker's immediate private sensations and experiences, which only he can know. §244 clarifies what it is for a word to refer to or name a sensation such as pain. 'S' names a sensation of pain if the first-person use of 'S' in an utterance replaces the natural behavioural expression of the sensation. This verbal expression of a sensation, however, is not a description of the behaviour it replaces or of the sensation itself; for it is incoherent to suppose that one might even want to insert language (in this case, a description) between pain and its expression (§245). §§246–8 subject the supposition of epistemic privacy to critical scrutiny. 'Only I can know whether I am in pain' is in one sense simply wrong, in another nonsense. The only truth here is that it makes no sense for me to doubt whether I am in pain. The epistemic

privacy of sensations is a grammatical proposition dressed up in the guise
of an epistemic truth. §§249–50 can be connected to §246 in as much as
they exemplify cases where doubts about the experiences of others based
on the possibility of pretence are excluded. They can also be viewed as
raising an objection to the argument of §244: if verbal expressions of pain
are learnt as replacements for natural pain-behaviour, might the infant's
natural pain-behaviour not be mere pretence? The possibility of pretence
would cast a cloud of scepticism over judgements of others' experiences,
just as the possibility of illusion enshrouds in doubt our knowledge of
objects. But one's scruples are groundless. §§251–2 pick up the theme of
§248, viz. that 'sensations are private' is a grammatical proposition in
metaphysical guise — one cannot imagine the opposite, but not because
of limitations on one's powers of imagination — rather because there is
here nothing to imagine. For the negation of a grammatical proposition
is not a description of an impossibility, any more than a grammatical
proposition is a description of a (necessary) actuality. §§253–5 examine
the idea that another person cannot have my pain, but only a similar one.
What looks like a metaphysical limitation on sharing or transferring
mental objects merely conceals a grammatical confusion. For different
people can have the same pain. It appears otherwise only because we
misguidedly project the grammar of 'same object' onto 'same pain', and
hence misconstrue the criteria of identity for pain. §255 closes this set of
remarks with a methodological observation on the therapeutic character
of philosophical investigation.

The structure of Part A:

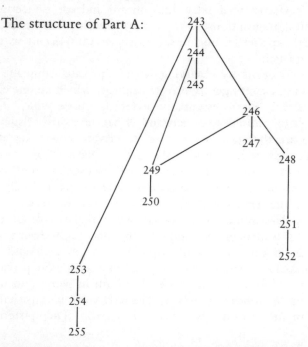

Part B (§§256–71) reverts to §243: having clarified 'private ownership' and epistemic privacy, W. examines the hypothesis that a 'private' language as envisaged in §243 is intelligible to its alleged speaker. The words for sensations cannot be tied up with the natural expression of sensation, for then the language would not be 'private'. So the speaker must be conceived to *associate* names with sensations and to use them in descriptions (§256). The intelligibility of this conception is the subject of Part B. That such a name of an unexpressed sensation could not be taught is brushed aside as irrelevant, for W. concentrates on the question of what it is to *name* a sensation (§257). Naming, as argued (§§26–37), presupposes stage-setting. The moot question is whether the mind can supply the appropriate stage, and whether its furniture can constitute a serviceable set. The example of a private diary (§258) is introduced to demonstrate the unintelligibility of private ostensive definition. For here there would be no distinction between remembering correctly the connection between the sign 'S' and the sensation that defines it, and seeming to remember it. But the rules of a private language cannot be merely impressions of rules, for one cannot determine whether one has what is to be called 'S' by reference to an *apparent* rule relative to which there is no distinction between being right and seeming right (§259). Falling back on the pious hope that one may *believe* that one has reidentified S correctly is useless, since nothing has been fixed to determine what *counts* as S — that was what was intended to be effected by the private ostensive definition (§260).

§261 is a pivotal remark: an ostensive definition, e.g. of 'red', presupposes the grammar of the definiendum, viz. that it is a colour word. Hence a 'private' ostensive definition of 'pain' must presuppose that it is the name of a *sensation*. But 'sensation' is a word in our common (public) language, and sensations have perceptible expression in behaviour. Hence the private ostensive definition of the word 'S' in the private language cannot be identified as a definition of a sensation-word by invoking the grammar of 'sensation' in the public language to determine the grammatical post at which 'S' is to stand (cf. §257). Nor does it help to reduce one's commitments by saying that 'S' names *something* the private linguist *has*. For these expressions too have a fixed (public) grammar. §§262–4 examine the futility of the supposition that one can invent the technique of using 'S' (i.e., what corresponds in the private language to the technique of using sensation-words in our public language) merely by concentrating on one's private experience and undertaking to call it 'S' in the future. The myth behind this misguided thought is the Augustinian picture of language.

§§265–9 introduce a mental table (a kind of dictionary that supposedly exists only in the mind) that is intended to function as a subjective justification for the use of the words of a private language. This is unintelligible, for it provides no independent justification for the use of a word, hence no distinction between correct application and an application that only seems correct. §§266–8 give three co-ordinate examples of similarly futile manoeuvres. §269 rounds off this subset of remarks by reminding us of the criteria for understanding, not understanding, and thinking one understands an expression. §§270–1 introduce a genuine use for 'S' as a sensation-name in a diary entry, making it clear that the supposition of the possibility of misidentification of a sensation, which must arise in a private language, is vacuous in a public one. The 'private object' is only a free-wheeling cog in the mechanism of a genuine language.

The structure of Part B:

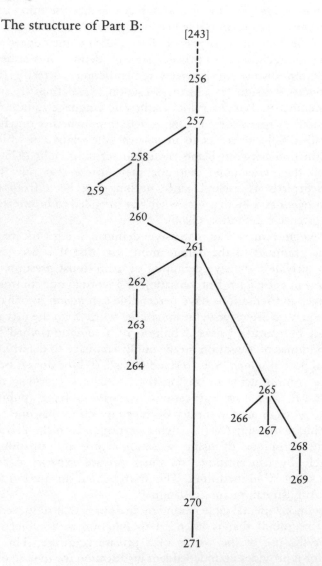

Part C (§§272–80) switches from the concept of pain to that of the colour red. When mesmerized by the ideas involved in a 'private' language, philosophers construe the grammar of 'pain' as analogous to the grammar of colour-words such as 'red' — only 'in private'. But it is only natural that they should then construe the grammar of colour-words on the model of the grammar of 'pain' thus misconstrued. The immediate consequence (§272) is that the assumption of an 'inverted spectrum' becomes intelligible, for no one has 'access' to another person's 'private' samples. That in turn suggests, absurdly, that colour-words are ambiguous, signifying now something publicly perceptible, now something private to each perceiver (§273). We are inclined to say that 'red' *refers* to something 'private': this does not clarify matters, but is importantly symptomatic of the confusion under which one labours here (§274), a confusion that besets us only when language 'goes on holiday' (§275). The following two sections focus on a feature of the phenomenology of these philosophical confusions (§§276–7), and the next remarks stress the vacuity of one's insistence in this context that one *knows* how a certain colour looks to one (§§278–9). The concluding remark (§280) makes it clear that it is an illusion to think that when one imagines something, one's mental image clarifies to oneself, in a unique way inaccessible to others, precisely what one imagines. Similarly, the mental image one might have when one imagines something red cannot serve to inform oneself what one means by 'red'.

The structure of Part C:

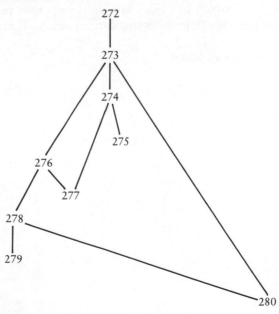

Part D (§§281–7) examines the restriction of experiential predicates to human beings and to what behaves like them. W. is not insisting, as a behaviourist might, that there is no pain without pain-behaviour, but rather that it only makes sense to attribute pain to something that can manifest it in behaviour (§281). It is no objection that in fairy-tales inanimate things are said to have pains, for this is essentially a secondary use of 'pain' (§282). One is inclined to think that one acquires the concept of pain by concentrating on one's own pains (i.e. something 'mental' and wholly 'private'), and that one then transfers the idea of pain to external objects (i.e. other living creatures) — although not to stones, etc. The pain then is surely attributed either to the body or to the mind associated with it! §§283–7 undermine this thought by focusing on the supposition that it is logically possible that I might turn to stone yet my pain continue, i.e. that 'for me', my pain is independent of my body and my behaviour. It makes no sense to attribute pain to a stone, and it is of no avail to suppose that it is the soul or mind, which the stone has if I turn to stone, that has the pain. For that too makes no sense, because it is senseless to suppose that a stone might 'have' a soul or mind. Grammar restricts the attribution of psychological predicates to what *behaves* in appropriate ways. It is not the body *or* the soul which the body 'has' that is the bearer of pain, but the *living human being* who has a soul. Only of what behaves like a human being can one say that it *has* pains. §§284–5 examine the absurdity of attributing pain to the inanimate or dead. The living move, behave, and that is a categorial difference — a case of the transition 'from quantity to quality'. §§286–7 argue that it is grammar, not the facts, which precludes ascribing pain to a person's body. But grammar here has facts about our natural reactions as its background.

The structure of Part D:

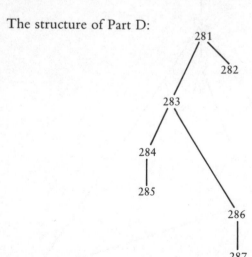

Part E (§§288–92) picks up the petrification example of §283 in order to examine afresh avowals (*Äusserungen*) of pain. Following §246, W. repeats that doubt or error about whether one has a pain is senseless; the expression of doubt would be a criterion for not knowing what the word 'pain' means. An avowal of pain is a criterion for the speaker's being in pain, but he avows pain without any criteria. However, if one cuts out the behavioural expression of pain, if one assumes the abrogation of the normal language-game (as in the petrification case), then, *per absurdum*, a criterion of identity for the 'sensation' would be necessary in one's own case, and the possibility of error would exist. §§289–90 emphasize the absence of justifying grounds for saying 'I am in pain', clarifying the fact that this is no epistemic *defect*. One is misled here by the assumption that all sentences serve to describe, and also by an unwarranted assumption of the grammatical uniformity of descriptions (§§291–2).

The structure of Part E:

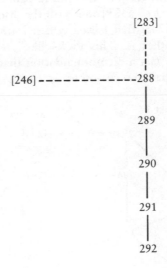

Part F (§§293–303) picks up the supposition of §283 that one knows what the word 'pain' means only from one's own case. If so, one must say something similar of others. The example of the beetle in the private box is invoked to show that *if* one construes the grammar of the expression of sensation on the model of name and object (e.g. 'beetle' and the insect named), then the 'object' *would* drop out of consideration as irrelevant to the shared language-game. (But the actual grammar of 'pain' is the grammar of a sensation-word, the characteristic first-person present-tense use of which is a manifestation (*Äusserung*) of a sensation.) §294 explores the claim that the 'private object' cannot even be said to be a something (cf. §261), for 'something' holds a place for a determinate category, which, in the private linguist's case, has not been determined. §295 reverts to the confused claim in §293 that one knows what 'pain' means only from one's own case. This is neither an empirical proposition nor a grammatical one, but one might view it as an allegorical picture. §296 introduces a similarly uninformative proposition, viz. that there is *something* accompanying one's cry of pain. This too could be said to be a pictorial representation of our grammar. §297 gives an analogy for the misconceived 'something' that is held to accompany pain (cf. §§294, 296): the pain one has does not play the role in the language-game that one is inclined to attribute to it, viz. the role of a paradigm or 'picture' of pain. §§298–9 emphasize the vacuity of the claim that there is *something* accompanying the cry of pain. §§300–2 make clear that the language-game with 'pain' involves no inner paradigm of pain, that to imagine pain is not to conjure up a 'private sample' of pain. One can, of course, imagine someone else's pain, but not on the model of a putative 'private language', for that would require imagining pain one does *not feel* on the model of pain one *does feel*. §303 rounds off the discussion by reverting to the supposition (cf. §246) that I *know* when I am in pain but can only surmise whether another is. This looks like a claim about epistemic possibilities, but is in fact a recommendation that we adopt a different grammar — and we have no reason to accept it.

The structure of part F:

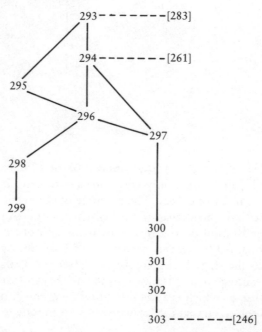

Part G (§§304 – 15) clarifies why W.'s grammatical elucidations do not commit him to a form of behaviourism. Indeed, to the extent that they might appear to do so, to that extent one has misunderstood his remarks. The interlocutor insists on the difference between pain-behaviour without pain and pain-behaviour with pain. W. concedes that there could be no greater difference. But, reverting to §294 and §261, it seems that W. is arguing that the pain is a nothing. But this is an illusion; pain is neither a something nor a nothing. That appears paradoxical only as long as one conceives of the grammar of the expression of pain on the pattern of object and name (cf. §293). One must break with the Augustinian picture of language according to which language has the uniform function of conveying thoughts concerning how things are (§304). The interlocutor insists that inner processes take place, e.g., when remembering. W. replies that he denies nothing other than the misleading picture we associate with the expression 'inner process' (§§305–6). It seems that W. is a behaviourist, that he is arguing that everything apart from behaviour is a fiction. But this misconstrues his argument: it is the *grammatical* fiction about 'inner processes' that he denies (§§307–8). And his aim is not to deny *facts*, but to show the fly the way out of the (grammatical) fly-bottle (§309).

The interlocutor reverts to his (correct) point that there is a difference between pain-behaviour with and without pain: do not our attitudes to the sufferer *show* that in the former cases we *believe* that there is something behind the manifestations of pain (§310)? No; our attitudes prove that we commiserate with the sufferer's suffering, believe that he is in pain — not that we believe a misguided philosophical thesis according to which pain is a 'private object' hidden behind pain-behaviour. The final remarks (§§311–15) demolish a last objection: is not the difference between pain-behaviour with pain and pain-behaviour without pain precisely one which a person can privately exhibit to himself? This too is an illusion. One can imagine pain, but to imagine pain is not to give oneself a private exhibition of pain (§§311–12). One can exhibit pain, but not 'privately' (§313). It is a misunderstanding to believe that the philosophical problems concerning psychological concepts can be clarified by concentrating upon one's experiences (§314), and a confusion to think that a person cannot master the use of a psychological concept, e.g. pain, unless he has experienced pain (§315).

The structure of Part G:

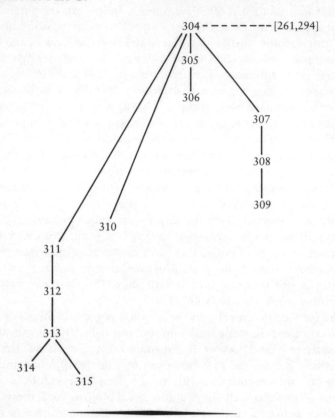

Correlations

The early version of the *Investigations*, which, as in previous volumes is referred to as the 'Proto-Philosophical Investigations' (PPI), is TS. 220, compiled in 1937 or 1938 on the basis of the now lost MS. 142. It corresponds roughly to §§1–188 of the final version, and was continued in TS. 221 into a version of Part I of the *Remarks on the Foundations of Mathematics*. In 1944 and early 1945, Wittgenstein compiled the so-called Intermediate Version (*Mittelversion*) of the *Investigations* (PPI(I)), which has been reconstructed by von Wright. This modified and extended the early version. It consists of 300 numbered remarks, the last of which corresponds to *Investigations* §421. Pages 1–143 of the Intermediate Version are identical with the pages of the final typescript, save for MS. modifications. Pages 144–91 (where the Intermediate Version ends) are derived from a preliminary typescript (TS. 241) compiled in 1944 or early 1945. The immediate MS. source of these remarks is the first 89 pages of MS. 129, begun 17 August 1944.

From Easter 1945 Wittgenstein worked on yet a further revision of his material. He compiled the typescript known as *Bemerkungen I*, consisting of 698 remarks derived primarily from Manuscript Volumes X–XII (MSS. 114–16) and MSS. 129–30. Four hundred of these remarks were selected for inclusion in the final typescript, some dovetailed into the Intermediate Version, and the majority contributing to its extension from §422 to §691.

The following list correlates remarks on the *Investigations* with, in the first instance, the numbered remarks of the Intermediate Version (PPI(I)). The 'gaps' in the column indicate remarks inserted (largely) from *Bemerkungen I* in the course of reworking PPI(I). The next column gives the immediate MS. source of PPI(I), viz. MS. 129. The remaining columns give more remote MS. sources that were copied into MS. 129, as well as MS sources, immediate and remote, of remarks in *Bemerkungen I* which do not occur in PPI(I).

PI§	PPI(I)§	MS. 129	MS. 124	MS. 165	Vol. XII	Others
243	213	36 – 7	213 – 14[1] 222[2]			MS. 180(a), 13 – 14[1], 20 – 1[2]
244	214	38	222 – 4			MS. 180(a), 21 – 2
245			270			
246	215	39 – 40	224 – 5			MS. 180(a), 22 – 4
247		152				MS. 128, 16
248					179	Vol. XVI, 241
249					336[3]	Vol. XV, 84[4]
250		111	269	66		
251					75 – 6	MS. 153(a), 102 – 4; Vol. VI, 290 – 2; Vol. X, 121 – 2
252					78	
253	216	40 – 1				
254	217	41 – 2				
255					323	MS. 163, 124
256	218(a)	42 – 3	225 – 6			MS. 180(a), 24 – 5
257						Vol. XI, 91; BT 209v.
258	218(b)	43 – 4	226			MS. 180(a), 25 – 7; MS. 179, 47; Vol. XV, 256 – 9
259	218.1[5]	24				MS. 163, 136
260	219[6]	44 – 5	227[7]	225[8]		
261	220	45 – 6	227	230, 42[9]		
262					338	
263					251	
264					118	
265					249 – 50	Vol. XVI, 125 – 6, 148 – 9
266					337	
267					250 – 1	Vol. XVI, 150
268					251 – 2	
269						MS. 130, 15
270	221	46 – 7	283 – 3	145 – 8 226 – 30		
271	222	48	271			MS. 179, 36
272	224	51	291	179 – 80		
273	225	50 – 1	290 – 1	178 – 9		
274	226	52 – 3	291 – 2	43 – 4, 180 – 1		
275	227	51 – 2	292	181 – 2		
276	228	22				MS. 163, 129
277	229	1		183 – 6		
278	230	23				MS. 163, 131
279					339	
280	231	23 – 4				MS. 163, 131 – 3
281	232	53 – 4	238			
282	233	54 – 5	239	95[10] 188 – 9[11]		
283	234	19 – 20	240 – 2 284 – 5	152 – 6		MS. 179, 68 – 9
284	235	55 – 6	242 – 4			
285	236	56	244			
286	237	20 – 1				MS. 179, 69 – 71
287	238	1 – 2		188		
288	239	56 – 8	245 – 7	140 – 4		
289	239.1[12]	49[13] 89[14]	132[14] 272[13]			

PI§	PPI(I)§	MS. 129	MS. 124	MS. 165	Vol. XII	Others
290	240	67	286	160 – 1		
291	241	22				MS. 163, 129 – 30
292		155 – 6				MS. 180(b), 47 – 8
293	242	58 – 60	256 – 7			
294					209 – 10	
295	243	60 – 1	258 – 9			
296	244	61	259			
297					207	Vol. XVI, 56 – 7
298	245	61 – 2	259 – 60			
299					316	
300						MS. 162(b), 66 – 8
301						MS, 130, 33
302	246	18				MS. 179, 66
303	247	62 – 3	269[15]			MS. 179, 32 – 3
304	248	63 – 4		163		
305					252	Vol. XVI, 249–70
306					246	
307		114	5 – 6			MS. 161, 80 – 1
308					332, 335	
309						Vol. XIII, 92; Vol. XIV, 142 – 3
310	249	64 – 5	288	170 – 2		
311	250	65 – 6	288 – 9	173 – 4		
312	251	66 – 7	289 – 90	175 – 7		
313	252	67	290	178		
314	253	68	271			
315	254	67 – 8	286	162		

[1]PI §243(a) only.
[2]PI §243(b) only.
[3]PI §249(a) only.
[4]The first sentence corresponds roughly to PI §249(b).
[5]Transposed from p. 160 of this typescript.
[6]PI §260(a)–(b) only.
[7]PI §260(a) only.
[8]PI §260(b) only.
[9]MS. 165, p. 230, continues onto p. 42.
[10]A variant of PI §282(a) (see also MS. 165, 126 –7).
[11]PI §282(c) only.
[12]Transposed from p. 165 of the typescript, where it was the sequel to PPI(I) §223.

[13]PI §289(a) only.
[14]PI §289(b) only.
[15]PI §303(a) only.

The private language arguments
  1. Preliminaries   2. From grammatical truth to metaphysical theory
  3. Deviations and dialectic

SECTION 243

1   The long trek of clarifying the concept of following a rule concluded with the claim that if language is to be a means of communication there must be agreement not only in definitions but also in judgements. At this point one is inclined to insist that the concept of *a language* is not thus bound up with agreement. Is it not possible for a person to have a language which he employs only to communciate *with himself*, to tell himself things? Here, it seems, neither agreement nor even the possibility of agreement with others is requisite.

§243(a) opens with the truism that there is a multitude of reflexive speech-acts and speech-related activities. We can even imagine people *all* of whose uses of language are thus reflexive, i.e. they speak *only* to themselves. (Note that W. does *not* claim that such reflexive speech-acts are parasitic on non-reflexive ones.) Does this not show that the concepts of language and of agreement are *not* internally related? No, for the necessity is for *possible* agreement. In order to communicate, people must actually agree in definitions and judgements. For communication to be possible, it must be intelligible that people should agree. For an activity to count as the use of a language, it must be possible that another person should come to understand the signs employed. This requirement *is* secured in the case of the imaginary monologuists. They accompany their activities by talking to themselves, and there is sufficient regularity in their behaviour in given circumstances, i.e. between the sounds they emit and what they do or experience, for an explorer to translate their language into ours. 'The common behaviour of mankind is the system of reference by means of which we interpret an unknown language' (PI §206). But this means precisely that the explorer *can* come into accord with the monologuists' judgements, can achieve the requisite 'constancy in results of measurement' (PI §242). For the possibility of interpreting (translating) an unknown language presupposes a large measure of consensus in judgement (expressed in the monologuists' 'units of measurement', which need not coincide in any simple way with the explorer's). This is further emphasized by the parenthetical remark that the explorer would be able to *predict* the monologuists' actions from their expressions of intention. As has been noted previously, understanding rule-governed techniques (in this case, reflexive speech-acts) provides foundations for predictions (Volume 2, pp. 46, 162), *a fortiori* interpreting correctly their expressions of decisions and intentions does so.

(b) clarifies what supposition would undermine the claim that there is an internal relation between the concept of a language and the possibility of agreement. This would be the supposition of the conceivability of a language which, unlike the monologuists', is used to register or voice for oneself features of one's inner life. W.'s interlocutor retorts correctly that one can do just this in our ordinary language. But this is not what W. has in mind. Rather, the supposed language, a *private language*, must be conceived of as consisting exclusively of words which refer to what can be known only to the speaker. On one widespread (mis)conception of sensations (or, more generally, 'inner experiences — feelings, moods, and the rest'), these are indeed known only to their owner. If this were so, and if the supposition of such a private language made sense, then no one else could understand the language. It would be essentially private, unlike the language of a solitary monologuist, caveman, or Robinson Crusoe. For in this case, unlike the others, the explorer could not attain 'agreement in results of measurement', for neither what measures nor what is measured would be accessible to him. If this makes sense, then agreement (or rather even the mere possibility of agreement) in definitions and judgements is not internally related to the very concept of a language.

1.1   (i) 'by talking to themselves': (cf. PI §260) speaking when no one else is present ('Is anyone here?'; 'Blow, winds and crack your cheeks!') is not necessarily talking to oneself, and one can talk to oneself even in company.

(ii) 'für den eigenen Gebrauch': 'for his own use'.

(iii) 'aufschreiben, oder aussprechen': 'give vocal expression' is too close to 'Äusserung', so better 'write down or voice'. The introduction of *writing* things down for oneself prepares the way for the 'private diary' example (§258). It also strengthens the putative counter-example. It is not obvious that saying to oneself 'I have a pain' is a case of telling oneself something (communicating something to oneself), although saying to oneself 'I have a toothache, so I had better skip lunch and ring up the dentist' might be said to be. But writing 'I have a pain' in one's diary can obviously be recording one's experiences for one's subsequent use, and might be called 'communicating with oneself'.

(iv) 'wovon nur der Sprechende wissen kann': 'to what can be known only to the speaker'. This idea is examined in PI §§246f.

(v) 'are to refer to': cf. §244 and, more critically, §§273f. One *can* say that 'pain' is the name of a sensation or even that it refers to a sensation, but in a philosophical discussion this is likely to incorporate the wrong picture, namely that of 'object and name' (cf. §293).

(vi) 'So another person cannot understand the language': if meaning is a matter of correlating words with things which are their meanings (or defining samples) and if immediate private sensations can be known only to their subject, then a language the words of which refer to private experiences cannot be understood by anyone other than the speaker. But, these premises are incoherent, and the concept of privacy is here abused.

2   The ideas embodied in this remark had somewhat different roles in earlier manuscripts. Their initial emergence seems to have been in 1936 reflections (Vol. XII, 117) on *contingently* private uses of signs and a corresponding contrast between objective and subjective understanding of signs. A language, in so far as it is only subjectively understood, is not a means of communicating with others, but rather a set of tools for one's own private use. Should such utterances of sounds, writing of signs, still be called 'a language' or 'tools'? Only if one plays language-games with them. But this one surely can do! Just think of Robinson Crusoe, who employs a language (signs) for his private use. You see him (without his knowing it) in a multiplicity of circumstances making marks on wood or emitting sounds. If you can discern a certain kind of regularity here, you would rightly say that this is a use of signs. But if we detect *no* regularity, should we conclude that he is speaking a purely private language, in which the same sounds are always associated with the same mental image?

Subsequently (Vol. XII, 138) we find W.'s first observations on self-addressed speech-acts that are the ancestry of PI §243(a). One can engage in such activities, as indeed one can play chess against oneself or win money from oneself.[1] 'One can' in such cases means, W. remarks, 'one does such-and-such, and does one not call that thus-and-so?' What then is communicating with oneself, talking to oneself? Not looking at a piece of paper and saying 'This paper is white', or coming into an empty room in which one expected to meet someone and saying 'I am alone'; for in such cases one does not use this sentence to tell oneself something (*Mitteilung*), but rather as an exclamation. But if I come in and look around in surprise, saying 'It is empty. I can do what I like here,' and proceed to do this or that, then we have here a case of telling oneself something (Vol. XV, 201).

MS. 165, 88–124 explores adjacent territory at length, and the criss-cross route illuminates the web of remarks in *Philosophical Investigations*. Beginning from the puzzle of PI §198(a), viz. how can a rule which can be variously interpreted show me what I have to do at a given point, the discussion moves (MS. 165, 90) to PI §217(a)–(b): how I can follow a rule is explained by either causes or reasons; if causes are not in question, then one is concerned with justifications; but justifications come to an end in

---

[1] It is less than obvious what would be called 'winning money from oneself' (cf. PI §268); but it is noteworthy that Pepys, amusingly, used to promise himself not to frequent the theatre too often, and to threaten himself with a fine; when he broke his promise, as he often did, he fined himself and paid the fine into the poorbox!

the practice of following the rule; acting thus is what is called 'following this rule'. But that presupposes agreement (PI §206(a) ≃ MS. 165, 92); following a rule is akin to obeying orders: lack of agreement over what counts as accord with a rule would be akin to lack of agreement over the meaning of orders. There would in such cases be a 'confusion of tongues'. An explorer coming to an unknown country identifies the people's utterances as orders, questions, answers, etc. by reference to their behaviour in the given circumstances (MS. 165, 97; PI §206(b)). Yet are not these behavioural 'externalities' necessary only for *others to recognize* that, say, an order has been given? He who issues the order knows what he means even if the others do not! (Here lies the connection between PI §206 and PI §243.) No; this conception of mere 'externalities' is misleading, for there is an imperative form in a language only in the context of a family of modes of *action*. Orders can sometimes be disobeyed, but not always. One can mean what one says as an order, but only against the background of a practice of using words thus and of responding to this use appropriately. Then follows the core of the idea of a private language:

Und hier sind wir am Rande einer Diskussion über die Sprache in der Einer nur zu sich, nur für ihn selber verständlich, über seine privaten Erlebnisse spricht. In diese Diskussion, die zu den Problemen des Idealismus and Solipsismus gehört, werde ich an dieser Stelle hier nicht eintreten. Nur soviel will ich sagen, dass hier keine Sprache beschrieben wurde, obwohl es so scheint. Es verbürgt uns nichts, dass ein Wort dieser Sprache zweimal in gleicher Bedeutung verwendet wird. Denn, sagst Du, die Gegenstände sind hier gleich, wenn sie dir gleich scheinen, so frage ich: 'Wenn sie Dir *wie* scheinen?' 'Gleich' ist ja ein Wort der *allgemeinen* Sprache. (MS. 165, 101ff.)

(And here we are on the brink of a discussion about the language in which someone speaks to himself about his own private experiences and is intelligible only to himself. This discussion, which belongs to the problems of idealism and solipsism, will not be broached here. I want to say only this much, that here no language is actually described, even though it appears to be. There is no warrant here that a word of such a language is used twice with the same meaning. For if you say, the objects here are the same when they appear the same to you, then I ask: 'When they appear *how* to you?' 'The same' is surely a word of *common* language.)

In another sense, W. continues, there is, of course, such a thing as a private language, e.g. the one which a Crusoe uses to talk to himself, although to be sure talking to oneself does not mean: being alone and talking (MS. 165, 103 ≃ PI §260(c)). One need not be alone, and just talking is not enough. Then follows an early draft of PI §243(a): we can imagine a person who encourages himself, asks himself questions and answers them, reproaches himself, etc. We would call such a pheno-menon 'a language' if the modes of action of such a person resembled corresponding human actions embedded in normal human contexts and if we could understand his gestures and mien as expressions of sadness, joy, reluctance, etc. After all, we can imagine someone living alone who draws pictures of objects on the wall of his cave, and such a picture-language would be readily understood. On the other hand, mastery of a language one speaks only to oneself no more implies mastery of a language one speaks to others than mastery of patience implies mastery of bridge. Then follows the remark that languages are first and foremost the languages spoken by the peoples of the world; i.e. English, Russian, Chinese, etc. are languages, and we call other things 'languages' because of their similarity to these (cf. PG 190). Thus ordering is a technique of our language, and it is none too difficult for an explorer to realize that he is being given an order even though he does not understand the alien tongue. It would be more difficult, however, to recognize a Crusoe's self-addressed orders.

The theme of the explorer (PI §206) is pursued further, as is the possibility of a solitary caveman who speaks only to himself (cf. Volume 2, pp. 174ff.). It is possible to imagine this, and we could come to understand his reflexive speech-acts if he used only simple signs. What is more problematic, however, is the idea of a language which one speaks to oneself only in the imagination. For though we can speak to ourselves *in foro interno*, is it intelligible that such a phenomenon obtain *independently* of the patterns of *behaviour* into which speech is woven? Note that W.'s point is not epistemological. The issue does not concern the conditions under which we can come to *know* whether someone speaks to himself in his imagination, but rather the conditions and presuppositions under which something *counts* as so doing (whether we know that a person is doing so is a further question). Even one's silent and unrevealed talk must be interwoven in complex ways with one's actions and reactions. To describe the language of a people is to describe a regularity of their behaviour; and to describe a language which someone speaks only to himself is to describe a regularity of his behaviour, not something which happens only once (cf. RFM 334f.; MS. 124, 279). Something constitutes speaking a language only in so far as it is analogous to what we do when we speak our language.

It is noteworthy that much earlier in MS. 165 a further thread was spun that connects with these reflections:

Aber ist es nicht das//unser//*Meinen*, das dem Satz Sinn gibt? (Und dazu gehört natürlich: sinnlose Wortreihen kann man nicht meinen.) Und das Meinen ist etwas im Reich der Seele.//im seelischen Bereich.// Aber es ist auch etwas Privates! Es ist das *ungreifbare* Etwas; vergleichbar nur dem Bewusstein selbst.

Man könnte es einen Traum unserer Sprache nennen . . . (MS. 165, 5)

(But isn't it the //our// *meaning it* that gives sense to the sentence? (And along with this, of course, goes: one cannot mean senseless strings of words.) And meaning it is something in the realm of the mind //mental domain.// But it is also something private! It is the ungraspable something comparable only to consciousness itself. One could call this a dream of our language . . .)

MS. 124, 213ff. develops these ideas further. Following a draft of PI §241, W. wrote:

Wäre es denn aber nicht denkbar, dass jeder Mensch nur für sich selbst dächte, nur zu sich selbst redete? (In diesem Fall könnte dann auch jeder seine eigene Sprache haben.)

Es gibt Fälle, in welchen wir sagen, Einer//jemand//ermahne sich selbst; befehle, gehorche, bestrafe, tadle, frage und antworte sich selber. Dann kann es also Menschen geben, die nur die Sprachspiele kennen, die jeder mit sich selbst spielt. Ja, es wäre denkbar, dass solche Menschen ein reiches Vokabular hätten. Wir können uns denken, dass ein Forscher in ihr Land käme und beobachtete wie jeder von ihnen seine Tätigkeiten mit artikulierten Lauten begleitet, sich aber dabei nicht an Andere wendet. Der Forscher kommt irgendwie auf den Gedanken, dass diese Leute Selbstgespräche führen, belauscht sie bei ihren Tätigkeiten, und es gelingt ihm ein wahrscheinliche Übersetzung ihrer Reden in unsere Sprache. Er ist durch das Lernen ihrer Sprache auch in den Stand gesetzt, Handlungen vorauszusagen, welche die Leute später ausführen, denn manches was sie sagen ist der Ausdruck von Entschlüssen oder Vorsätzen. (Wie diese Leute ihre Sprache haben lernen können ist hier gleichgültig.)

Aber wenn nun so ein Mensch sich selbst befiehlt auf diesen Baum zu klettern und wenn anderseits ich es mir befehle, der diesen Befehl nicht nur sich//mir//selbst, sondern auch einem//dem/Andern geben kann: ist *der Gedanke* dieses Befehls in beiden Fällen der gleiche?

Das kannst Du beantworten, wie Du willst. Stell Dir nur nicht vor, dass der Gedanke eine Begleitung des Sprechens ist.

(Is it not imaginable, that each human being should think only for himself, speak only to himself? (In this case each person could even have his own language.)

There are cases in which we say, someone has admonished himself, ordered, obeyed, punished, blamed, asked, and answered himself. So then there can be human beings who are acquainted only with language-games which one plays by oneself. Indeed, it is imaginable that these human beings should have a rich vocabulary. We could imagine that an explorer came to this country and observed how each one of them accompanied his activities with articulate sounds, but did not address others. Somehow the explorer gets the idea that these people are talking to themselves, listens to them in the course of their activities, and succeeds in producing a probable translation of their talk into our language. By learning their language, he reaches the position in which he can predict actions which the people subsequently perform, for some of their utterances are expressions of decisions or plans. (How these people were able to learn their language is here irrelevant.)

But now, when such a person orders himself to climb up this tree and when, on the other hand, I, who can give this order not only to myself but also to the others, order myself to climb up the tree, is *the thought* of this order the same in both cases?

You may answer that as you please. Only don't imagine that the thought is an accompaniment of the speaking.)

It is important to note here the following features: (i) The explicitly stated irrelevance of the genesis of linguistic abilities to their identification and to the intelligibility of the tale. (ii) That the imagined human beings are not conceived of as having *previously* spoken a shared language. On the contrary: (a) they are *acquainted* only with language-games one plays alone; and (b) one could even imagine each of them speaking a different language. (iii) The question of whether their self-addressed orders mean the same as our corresponding self-addressed orders would not even arise if their language was being conceived to be a degenerate fragment of an ordinary shared language (e.g. like the language of a monastic community sworn not to talk to each other, but where each monk has learnt to speak the language in an ordinary social setting before joining the order).

W. then pursues the issue of the relation of thought to utterance, and returns to our theme only on page 221:

Die Private Sprache, die ich oben beschrieben habe, ist eine solche, wie sie etwa Robinson auf seiner Insel hätte mit sich selbst sprechen können. Hätte ihn jemand belauscht und beobachtet, er hätte diese Sprache Robinsons lernen können. Denn die Bedeutungen der Worte zeigten sich im Verhalten Robinsons.

Wäre aber nicht eine Sprache denkbar in der Einer für seinen eigenen Gebrauch seine privaten Empfindungen, seine inneren Erlebnisse ausspricht oder aufschreibt? Diese Sprache wäre dann natürlich nur für ihn selbst verständlich, denn niemand als er könnte je wissen, worauf sich die Worte, Zeichen, der Sprache beziehen.

(The Private Language which I have described above is like the one Robinson had on his desert island in which he was able to talk to himself. Had someone heard and observed him, he would have been able to learn Robinson's language. For the meanings of the words are apparent in Robinson's behaviour.

But couldn't we imagine a language in which a person could voice or write down his private sensations, his inner experiences, for his own use. Of course, this language would then be intelligible only to himself, for no one else could ever know to what the words, signs, of the language refer.)

From this remark we can extract the further points: (iv) The monologuists' languages are not, in respect of the present concern, essentially different from Crusoe's. Hence (a) the fact that Crusoe learnt English in London, whereas the manner of the monologuists' language acquisition is irrelevant, is here unimportant; and (b) the fact that Crusoe was acquainted with language-games with two or more people, whereas the monologuists were not, is here likewise unimportant. What *is* crucial is (v) the fact that a language is being spoken is manifest in *behaviour* — how that behaviour pattern was acquired is *not* relevant to determining whether a language is in use. And (vi) that the contrast W. is concerned with is not between a shared language which can be employed in solitude (on a desert island) and an unshared, non-social language (which is nevertheless translatable), but rather between a sharable, translatable language on the one hand and an unsharable, untranslatable one on the other.

It is perspicuous from this discussion that W. is not concerned here with claims about the social genesis of a language or of an individual's linguistic abilities. Nor is his argument aimed at establishing that an unshared language is conceivable only in so far as it is derived, by accident (the last Mohican), degeneration (monks who speak only to themselves), or invention (Esperanto before it was taught to others), from a shared one. He is not claiming that reflexive speech-acts are essentially parasitic on non-reflexive, communicative ones. Consequently he is not trying to show that the phenomenon of language is essentially, logically, social — like trade and barter. Rather, his target is the idea of an unsharable language, one which cannot, in principle, be made intelligible to anyone other than its speaker. For the idea that such a language is not merely possible but actual is an unnoticed presupposition tacit in the reasoning underlying idealism (both problematic and dogmatic) and solipsism. It has also, unwittingly, dominated philosophical and theoretical linguistic reflections on language and communication for centuries.

MS. 180(a), 13ff. is derived from MS. 124 with further variations; the final MS. draft is MS. 129, 36ff., where PI §243 occurs after the following sequence: PI §§211, 217, 212–13, 209(a)–(b), 208(g), RFM 417(b)–(c), PI §§208(f), 208(e).

SECTION 244

1   Of course, we do talk about our sensations and use sensation-words to refer to them. (Whether the sensations thus named are known only to the speaker is deferred until §246; what is potentially misleading about talking of *referring* here is discussed in §§273f., 293.) But the crucial question to be clarified (cf. PI §51) is what it means for a word to correspond to, be the name of, a sensation *in the practice of speaking a language*. One cannot hang a name-plate on the sensation (MS. 124, 122), so how is the connection between name and sensation established? How is the practice of employing 'pain' as a sensation-word set up? To answer this, we must look to how the technique of its use is learnt,[2] how we teach or train a person to use such words correctly — for there we shall see what it is that one who has learnt to use the word has thereby learnt

---

[2] This is perfectly consistent with the principle that what a conceptual capacity is, what technique has been mastered in acquiring it, is independent of its genesis (cf. 'Explanation', Volume 1 pp. 70ff.; MU pp. 30ff.).

to *do*. W. canvasses what he here calls 'one possibility', viz. that
sensation-words are taught as substitutes for natural expressive behaviour. It is natural for children to cry when they fall and hit their knee,
when they touch something hot and burn themselves. Their parents
teach them to exclaim 'Ow!', later 'Hurts, hurts!' and then 'I have hurt
myself', 'I have a pain'. These utterances are new pain-*behaviour*, grafted
onto and partially replacing the natural pain-behaviour in circumstances
of injuring oneself. But this is not to say that they do not *also* have other
uses, subsequently learnt, e.g. in reporting one's pains to the doctor.

The initial question was: how are sensation-words connected with the
sensations they name? In the case of pain, W.'s reply is that it is
connected, *qua* replacement, with natural expressive behaviour. This
seems to imply that 'pain' means not pain, but pain-*behaviour* — for it is
connected thus to the *behaviour*, not to the sensation which that behaviour manifests. Hence the interlocutor's question in §244(b). But the
apparent implication does not hold. 'Pain' does not mean crying; it
means pain. The fact that 'I have a pain' is a learnt replacement for
moaning or crying is *not* comparable to the fact that the word 'bachelor'
is a substitute for the phrase 'unmarried man' and means an unmarried
man. The word 'pain' does not mean the same as the *word* 'moan'; rather,
groaning 'It hurts' or 'I am in pain' replaces moaning and crying out in
pain. To móan is not to say 'I moan', and saying, 'I am in pain' is not a
learnt substitute for *saying* 'I moan', but for *moaning* (cf. LSD 11). 'I have
a toothache' (unlike 'I am holding my cheek') is not a description of
behaviour.

1.1   (i) 'und benennen sie': 'and name them', i.e. refer to them by name;
assigning them a name (giving them a name) is not in question in this
sentence.

(ii) 'This question is the same as . . . ': what of the case, which W.
countenances (PG 188; BB 12, 97; PI §495), of a being born with an
innate propensity to react to uses of language as we do? Here there would
be no question of how the connection between the name and the thing
named is *set up*, and that connection could not be clarified by describing
how one *learns* the meaning of names of sensation. Nevertheless, this
kind of case does not conflict with W.'s argument. For here too the
articulate avowal of pain is a substitute for an inarticulate groan of pain; it
is a piece of linguistic pain-*behaviour*, and, like inarticulate pain-
behaviour, it constitutes a criterion for third-person ascriptions of pain.

(iii) 'Here is one possibility': i.e. one way in which a human being
learns the meaning of names of sensation, such as the word 'pain'. The
possibility here canvassed is by way of training a child to replace its
primitive, natural expressive pain-behaviour first with exclamations and
later with sentences such as 'I have a toothache'. Are there other
possibilities? Yes, indeed. §288 introduces one: if we have grounds for

thinking that an adult does not know what the English word 'pain' means, we should explain it to him, perhaps by gestures, or by pricking him with a pin and saying 'See, that's what pain is!' Here we have a case not of training, but of explaining, and — as with any other explanation — it may be understood rightly, wrongly, or not at all. One might likewise point at someone who is manifestly in pain and say, 'There, that is what it is to be in pain', or even 'That is pain' (cf. LPP 238–40, see 2.1(vi)(b) below). Whether these different possibilities for teaching the use of the word 'pain' have been successful in a particular case will be evident in how the learner goes on to use the word.

Are all sensation-names thus bound up with primitive expressive behaviour? After all, there are many cases in which there is no distinctive natural mode of expressive behaviour which is pre-linguistic, e.g. sensations of pressure, of tingling, and throbbing sensations. So the expression 'a throbbing sensation' cannot be viewed simply as a learnt replacement for natural expressive behaviour. This may be granted; but in all these cases the concept of *sensation* is invoked; and *that* concept is bound up with the natural manifestations of sensation, such as groaning with pain, scratching itches, laughing or wriggling when tickled, etc. (cf. 2.1(vi)(a) below.

(iv) 'the primitive, the natural, expression': not symbols but expressive behaviour, as laughter is an expression of amusement.

2   The picture of the relation between experience and its first-person linguistic expression that W. strove to displace is immensely powerful, and his suggestion that we view typical verbal expressions of sensation as learnt forms of sensation-behaviour is still pregnant with a multitude of possible misunderstandings stemming from the classical picture. Some of these are:

(i) LSD 41f.: one is inclined to object that whereas 'I have a pain' is articulate and says something definite, moaning with pain is not. He who moans does not *say* that he is in pain. So how can the avowal of pain be said to resemble a groan of pain? ('Resemble', not 'be the same as'; cf. LSD 11.) The objection is misleading, for a groan is as direct and clear an expression of pain as there is, i.e. the avowal 'I have a pain' is *no closer* to the pain than the groan (cf. PI §245). A person's inarticulate moans manifest his suffering no less than his groaning 'It hurts' or 'I have a pain'.

(ii) LSD 42: We are inclined to say that 'pain' in 'I have a pain' *refers* to a certain phenomenon. This is not incorrect, but it can mislead in this context; for we are inclined to construe it on the model of '"chair" in "I have a chair" refers to something'. But in the former case one cannot *point* to the pain to explain to what the word refers; and in so far as we wish to talk of the 'phenomenon' of pain, then, what we call 'pointing to the phenomenon of pain' is to point at a sufferer's groaning. But that does not mean that 'pain' signifies groaning; rather, that 'pain is a certain phenomenon' is philosophically misleading here, for it looks analogous to 'lightning is a certain phenomenon' (viz. this ↗), but is not.

(iii) RPP I §146 elaborates the classical picture. We are inclined to think that a child learns to use the word 'pain' correctly in as much as in such-and-such circumstances it acts thus-and-so, and we think it feels what we too feel in similar circumstances. We teach it to say 'I have a pain', and if our supposition is correct, it learns to associate 'pain' with its feeling and uses it when that feeling recurs. Rather than attacking this associative picture, W. milks what he can from it. What kinds of errors does it correctly exclude? That the word 'pain' is not the name of the pain-behaviour or the circumstance of injury; also that 'pain' is not used now for this feeling, now for another quite different one. These platitudes W. does *not* deny; but he repudiates the associative picture that here accompanies them.

(iv) RPP I §§304ff. emphasizes that what is called 'expression of pain' is *spontaneous* behaviour in certain circumstances. One is not taught to use 'I have a pain' by guessing which of the inner processes connected with falling and scraping one's knees is called 'pain'. Rather, one learns to use it as a manifestation of pain, i.e. as a piece of expressive pain-behaviour. Otherwise it would make sense to wonder on account of *which* sensation one cries out when one falls and hurts oneself (*this* one or *that* one). The question of how one knows whether the sensation one has is one called 'pain' does not arise; but it would if (*per absurdum*) there were no natural spontaneous expression of pain. We are inclined to think that mastering the use of 'pain' in the first person is a matter of attaching the word to the sensation, and *hence* that the child's pain-behaviour is just an occasion for the adult to get the child to attach the name to its sensation. But is there any such thing as attaching a name to a sensation *within oneself*? What are the consequences of this hypothesized act? W. draws an ironic analogy: if one shuts a door in one's mind, is it then shut? What are the consequences? That in one's mind no one can get in?

The argument intimated is that to shut a door in one's mind, if it means anything, is to imagine shutting a door, not to shut an imaginary door (*that* is what Marcel Marceau does on the stage, not in his mind!). The consequences of shutting a door in one's mind are not causal. One can imagine attaching a name-plate to a door, but what follows? That it does not fall off, fade, disappear? Well, one might say, it's your story! But can one attach a name to a sensation *in one's mind*? It is altogether opaque what this means. What is it to attach a name to a sensation *without* the mind? One cannot hang a name-plate on a sensation, hence one cannot imagine doing so either. The grammar of 'attaching a word to a sensation', W. argues, is not that of 'attaching a word to a physical object'. What is it then? 'Pain' is attached to the sensation of pain to the extent that exclaiming 'I have a pain' is an expression (*Äusserung*) of the sensation, and hence too a criterion for someone else to assert 'He has a pain'. If so, then there is indeed no such thing as attaching a name to a sensation *in the mind*. For to say to oneself (in one's imagination) 'I have a pain' is precisely *not* to manifest or give expression to one's pain.

PI §244 emphasizes the primitiveness of the sufferer's pain-behaviour. In other contexts it is no less important to remember the elemental character of our *reactions* to the pain of *others* (Z §545).

2.1   (i) 'How do words refer to sensations?': this seems but a special case of 'How do words refer?', and one is inclined to think that there is a global answer (e.g. by having a sense which determines a referent; or by standing to their referent in the name-relation; or by calling up an idea of their referent in one's mind). This is precisely what W. combats: Z §434 compares the shift from the language-game with physical objects (i.e. with expressions that name or refer to physical objects) to the language-game with sensations with the shift from talking of transferring possessions to talking of transferring joy or pride in possessions. There is something new here in each case, and it requires fresh investigations.

(ii) 'don't we talk about sensations every day': MS. 124, 222 adds 'for example, all kinds of pain, sadness, joy, etc.' As W. later pointed out (Z §§483ff.), it is incorrect to call sadness or joy 'sensations' or 'sense-impressions' (although 'Empfindung' has a wider range than its English counterpart); but it is clear already in §243 that W.'s target is larger than the domain of sensations.

(iii) 'und benennen sie': W. does not deny that 'pain' is the name of a sensation, but rather denies that the grammar of '"pain" is the name of a sensation' is akin to '"chair" is the name of an article of furniture' or '"Red" is the name of a colour'. So different are they that 'The word "pain" is the name of a sensation' is equivalent to '"I've got a pain" is a manifestation of sensation (*Empfindungsäusserung*)' (RPP I §313). To that extent it is potentially misleading to talk of *naming* sensations, and MS. 179, 25 remarks: 'Frage nicht so sehr, "Wie kann man Empfindungen benennen?" als "Wie kann man die Namen der Empfindungen anwenden?"' ('Do not ask so much "How can we name sensations?" as "How can one apply the names of sensations?"')

(iv) 'primitive': Z §541 (RPP I §916), the behaviour is *pre-linguistic*; it is the prototype of a way of thinking, not the result of thought. The language-game is based *on it*.

(v) 'adults talk to him and teach him exclamations': MS. 124, 223 adds 'first, perhaps, baby-language, then the language of adults'. Even the most elementary *verbal* expressions of pain are learnt (in England children say 'Ow', elsewhere 'Owa' or 'Aya'), and onto this adults graft further stages of the modes of verbal expression of pain, e.g. 'Has Johnny got an Ow in his knee?' ('Hast Du ein Weh-weh?') and only later 'Have you hurt yourself?' (cf. Vol. XVI, 220).

(vi) 'Here is one possibility': (a) MS. 124, 224 adds at the end of a draft of PI §244(b), 'Und so sind alle sprachlichen Äusserungen der Empfindungen mit den ursprünglichen Empfindungsäusserungen verknüpft worden'. ('And all linguistic manifestations of sensations have been bound up in this way with the primitive manifestations of sensation.') This obviously does not imply that all linguistic expressions of sensation are learnt as substitutes for natural behaviour (for throbbing or tingling sensations have no natural expression), but only that they are linked, directly or indirectly, via the concept of sensation, with primitive expressive behaviour, and are used, in the first-person present tense, as forms of expressive behaviour. Of course, they also have other uses, e.g. as reports.

(b) LPP 238–40 argues that one can give an ostensive definition of rage by pointing at a man in a fury and saying 'There, that is rage'. This then is a further possibility of teaching the name of a feeling (emotion), which could be extrapolated to teaching an adult what the English word 'pain' means. To be sure, it does not introduce a private sample, or indeed a public one, by reference to which one can justify one's avowals of pain (or rage). It can be called 'ostensive definition', since, as W. emphasizes, ostensive definitions are ostensive to a degree (LPP 239). Neither pain nor rage are kinds of behaviour, and whether the distinctive uses of 'pain' or 'rage' are successfully conveyed by such an ostensive explanation will be seen in what the learner does with these words. It is obviously wrong to say that one cannot acquire the concept of rage unless one has been enraged and learnt the use of 'I'm furious' as a substitute for a roar of fury. But the learner must realize that the utterance 'I'm furious' is an expression of rage and a criterion for saying of a person that he is enraged.

SECTION 245

1   How can one even want to use language to get between pain and its behavioural expression? What is it, or rather, what does it seem to be, to insert language between experience and its manifestation? And why is it that one is tempted to do this?

§244 argued that avowals of pain replace natural pain-expressions. To the blinkered eye, this seems unjustly to assimilate the avowal 'I have a pain' to *mere* pain-behaviour;[3] but pain-behaviour can occur without pain. And, it seems, when another manifests pain-behaviour, I can never be sure, but only believe, that he is in pain (cf. PI §§246, 303). But in my

---

[3] But note W.'s remark: 'Of course "toothache" is not *only* a substitute for moaning — but it is *also* a substitute for moaning: and to say this shows how utterly different it is from a word like "Watson"' (LSD 11).

own case, one is inclined to think, I *know* I am. So my saying 'I am in pain', unlike emitting a groan, is a *true description* of how things are with me, and not mere behaviour, let alone a description of my behaviour (§244(b)). In my case I can apprehend directly, virtually perceive 'clearly and distinctly', the difference between pain plus pain-behaviour and mere pain-behaviour unaccompanied by pain. And 'I am in pain', at any rate *for me*, describes the inner experience.

That is how one wants to insert language between pain and its expression, i.e. that is how one is tempted into this position. But why is this called 'inserting language between pain and its expression'? On this conception, 'I have a pain' is thought to be closer to the pain (i.e. to what it depicts) than is expressive pain-behaviour (which is conceived to a *mere consequence* of what 'I have a pain' depicts). For surely it is as close to it as a proposition is to the fact that makes it true (and what could be closer than that — they are even closer than a picture and what it is a picture of! (cf. Exg. §194)). But if so, then the meaning of 'pain' must be independent of the expression of pain (and so, indeed, it seems to be — for do I not know that I am in pain without waiting to see whether I groan?!) It is in this sense that we are tempted to insert language between pain and its expression, and we do not see that 'I have a pain' *is* an expression of pain (*Schmerzäusserung*) and not a picture (*Bild*) of pain.

It is, of course, true that when I groan, I can, if I wish, tell someone whether I am in pain or just groaning. It is also true that when I am in pain, I can say to myself 'I am in pain'. But these truisms do not force upon us the fallacious picture sketched above. In that picture a number of ramifying confusions reinforce each other, giving it a compelling force: (a) I know that I am in pain whenever I am (cf. PI §246); hence 'I know I am in pain' must make sense as a claim to empirical knowledge; (b) I can only believe, not know, that others are in pain (cf. PI §§246, 303); (c) 'I am in pain' is a description (cf. PI §§290f.); (d) behaviour, the outward sign of the inner, can always lie (cf. PI §§249f.; LPE 293). All these confusions are later assailed in the indicated remarks, but, of course, without denying the above truisms.

What are the immediate consequences of thus inserting language between pain and its expression? It would make sense to ask, 'How do you know that what you have is called "pain"?' Since the word 'pain' would not be connected with pain in the manner described in §244, we would be driven to suppose that it is attached to the sensation by mental ostensive definition — a supposition that will be shown to be incoherent (PI §§258ff.) Since the concept of pain would not be essentially connected with the natural spontaneous expressions of pain, the question of what makes *this* behaviour an expression of *pain* would, absurdly, be opened. For one could then properly ask what connection between pain (defined independently of behaviour) and action makes such-and-such action an expression of pain rather than of something else.

1.1   'Wie kann ich . . . treten wollen': 'How can I even want to . . . '

2   MS. 124, 270 introduces this remark in the context of PI §303(b): 'Just
try — in a real case[4] — to doubt someone else's fear or pain'. It makes it
clear that the classical conception of first-person psychological utterances
as true descriptions, known for certain by the subject, is committed to
wanting, absurdly, to insert language between pain and its expression.
Pretence is possible, the MS. elaborates, but only in special contexts. A
dog cannot pretend to be joyful, but not because it is too honest (PI
§250). We are inclined to say (PI §303(a)) that one can only *believe* that
another is in pain, whereas one *knows* in one's own case. This seems the
more appropriate expression when philosophizing here; but what we are
inclined thus to say, what seems appropriate, is of importance only in so
far as it makes clearer the temptations that beset us. One might say to a
philosopher, 'I assure you I am not just behaving as if I had pain, I really
feel it; I know exactly what "pain" means.' But why should he not reply,
'This too is just pain-behaviour'? Then follows PI §245, succeeded by PI
§§314, 271.
   RPP I §§305ff. elaborates: if one could learn what pain means
independently of one's spontaneous expressions of pain, how could one
learn *what* is an expression of *pain*? (cf. Exg. §244, 2 (iv)).

Privacy
1. The traditional picture   2. Private ownership
3. Epistemic privacy   4. Only a first step

SECTION 246

1   The private language introduced in §243 consists of words which refer
to the speaker's 'immediate private sensations'. Having explored the
connection of the word 'pain' to the sensation, W. now examines one
sense in which sensations are said to be 'private', viz. *epistemic* privacy:
we are inclined to think (a) that only the subject of experience knows
whether he is really experiencing pain, seeing red, feeling joyful, etc.,
and (b) that others merely surmise it. Taken one way, both these
thoughts are false; taken another, both are nonsense. (Cf. 'Privacy', §3.)
   It is false that *only I* know whether I am in pain; for others can and
often do know whether I am in pain. And it is false that others always

---

[4] E.g. someone screaming in pain after severe burns.

merely *surmise* that I am in pain: if someone is hit by a motor car and lies writhing on the ground, could one say 'I surmise that he is in pain'? Does one need more evidence to go beyond a surmise? What would justify a knowledge-claim if not this? There are, of course, cases when one guesses that another is in pain, but a surmise is intelligible only where it makes *sense* for one to know that which one surmises. If it were (logically) impossible for another to know that I am in pain, it would be equally impossible (unintelligible) for another to surmise it.

A philosopher might concede that in the ordinary use of 'know' we do say that we know that others are in pain, but nevertheless not with the certainty that the subject has of his own pain. Hence, he might claim, there is a special sense of 'know' in which I know whether I am in pain and in which others cannot really know this. This move reveals the nonsense underlying the two limbs of this conception of epistemic privacy.

(i) It cannot be said of me at all that I *know* that I am in pain. For this form of words to fulfil the role the classical epistemologist (e.g. the Cartesian, empiricist, or Kantian) allocates it, it would have to make sense for me to guess or surmise that I am in pain and to find out, learn, and confirm that I am (or am not). It would have to be intelligible that I be in pain and not know it, but only wonder whether I am. But none of this makes any sense; we have no genuine use for these forms of words. *Pari passu* it makes no sense to say that I am certain that I am in pain (whereas others cannot have that kind of certainty). For it only makes sense to be certain where it makes sense not to be certain, to doubt, to think but not be sure. 'I *know* I am in pain' may be used as an emphatic way of saying that I *am* in pain. It may be used as a joke ('He wonders whether I am in pain', I might say with a wry grin, 'I know!') or as a grammatical remark drawing attention to the senselessness of doubt in one's own case.

(ii) It is similarly nonsense to say that others learn of my sensations *only* from my behaviour. For that implies that there is some better way of learning of my sensations, inaccessible to others but available to me. Here we are inclined to think that others know of my sensations only *indirectly*, whereas I know *directly*. But this is nonsense, since I cannot be said either to know or not to know. To know that a person is in pain by observing his behaviour is not a defective, derivative way of finding out; it is what is called 'seeing that another is in pain'. It could even be called 'knowing directly that another is in pain' — if, for example, we called finding out by hearsay that someone is in pain 'knowing indirectly' that he is. There is no 'more direct' way of coming to know that a person is in pain; in particular, *having the pain* is not a direct way of knowing that someone (namely oneself) is in pain, since to have a pain is not to ascertain or come to know that one has a pain.

§246(c) extracts the meagre grammatical truth from the misconception of epistemic privacy, which is given further emphasis in PI §247.

1.1   'in einer Weise falsch': 'In one way this is false'.

2   Various grammatical points are being invoked here that are made explicit elsewhere. (a) LSD 13 (and elsewhere) emphasizes that it makes no sense to say 'I know that I see' if it makes no sense to say 'I don't know that I see'. Such a proposition and its negation constitute a logical space: the sense of one stands or falls with the other.[5] (b) Contrasting concepts such as 'direct/indirect', 'concealed/revealed', 'immediate/mediate' only make literal sense when we are concerned with *signs of one category* (LPE 280). To say '*His* pains (the 'inner') are hidden from me' is like saying 'These sounds are hidden from my eyes' (LW §885), not like 'The view is hidden by the fog'. (c) Families of concepts *together* surround the same logical space. If it makes sense to know that *p*, it must also make sense to learn, find out, investigate whether, confirm that *p*; and if it makes sense to be certain that *p*, it must make sense to doubt, conjecture, wonder, think but be unsure that *p* and to be right or mistaken (MS. 159, 21; Z §549; LPE 278). Note that these three points are not compromised by conceding that 'I know I have a pain' does have a use, viz. as an emphatic way of saying 'I am in pain' or as a joke. For these emphatic or jocular uses are not *epistemic claims*.

Vol. XVI, 13ff. examines the retort 'Surely I *must* know whether I have a pain'. Does this mean that I must know that what I have is *called* 'pain'? One is inclined to deny that and say it means that I must know that it *is* pain. But compare this with 'I must know that this is a chair', where one may know various things: that one can sit on it, that this contraption opens out into a chair, etc. What one really means is 'I must surely know what I have' — but what then does one *have*? For one can answer only with words or gestures. The only correct point here is that it is senseless to ask 'Are you sure you have a pain?' — but not because the bearer is obviously certain. One does employ the form of words 'Surely I must know . . .' (and this is a source of the philosophical confusion); but reflect on the circumstances in which it is used, e.g. when the doctor says 'But it doesn't hurt that much!' One might also retort 'Now don't tell me what I feel' (LSD 13). These, one might say, are not epistemic responses but grammatical ones.

MS. 159, 21 examines the notion of 'immediate awareness': propositions of which philosophers say we have 'immediate knowledge' seem

---

[5] But there are exceptions to the (grammatical) principle of contrast, which reveal the non-uniformity of the concept of a proposition: viz, the whole domain of *a priori* propositions (itself non-uniform) and propositions that are the subject of *On Certainty* (which are equally diverse). Each case must be judged on its own merits.

certain and unquestionable. (They are 'clear and distinct', 'self-presenting', or 'evident'.) And we are prone to think that that is because they rest securely on something — viz. on the experience one has (and, some philosophers have argued, one *perceives* the experience infallibly). But this is like saying that the earth rests on something that is firm in itself. These propositions rest on nothing (cf. Exg. §289). The expression 'immediate awareness' here is misleading, for it suggests that one is *right* about something. But there is no right or wrong here at all. No one would say 'I'm sure I'm right that I have a pain'.

LPE 280, 293f. examine a natural objection. I can lie about my experience, see something red and say 'I see green'. But surely lying is *knowing*[6] such-and-such and saying something else which one knows to be false. So lying about my pain is knowing that the proposition 'I am in pain' is *true* and saying 'I am not in pain', which one knows to be false. The objection rests on an unwarranted assumption about the uniformity of the concept of lying. To lie about what colour one sees is, e.g., to see red and say 'I see green'; to lie about one's pain is to have a pain and say 'I have no pain'. In short, 'a lie about inner processes is of a different category from one about outer processes' (MS. 169, 104)

SECTION 247

1   One legitimate use for 'Only you can know . . .' is as a grammatical proposition, part of an explanation of the use of certain psychological expressions. Thus used, it signifies that the expression of doubt or uncertainty (as opposed to indecision) in one's own case is senseless, and that for another to doubt one's sincere avowal of intent is equally absurd.

1.1   'If you had that intention': the tense is puzzling, since obviously you may have had an intention, told me, and forgotten about it, in which case I know that you intended to φ, and may remind you. But maybe what W. had in mind is 'Only you can know if just *this* was what you meant to do', as one might say, 'Only you can know whether by ". . ." you meant such-and-such'. These are grammatical statements drawing attention to the special evidential status of an agent's avowal. (But note that the German uses neither emphasis nor a demonstrative pronoun.)

2   RPP I §§564ff. examines 'Only I know whether or what I am thinking, another cannot know it'. What do I know? That what I am doing is thinking? No; there is no comparing what I am doing with a paradigm to ensure that *this*, which I am doing, *is* thinking. But, of course, it is true

---

6 Believing would suffice here.

that typically another does not know what I am thinking unless I tell him. Does this make a thought *essentially* private? After all, if I utter my thought *aloud* and no one hears me speak, no one will know what I think; but is it 'private'? And if I *tell* another what I am thinking, is the thought still 'hidden'? 'My thoughts are known only to myself' means roughly 'I *can* express my thoughts, say what I am thinking, if I wish'. But it is an important feature of the concept of thinking that if I do *not* tell another what I am thinking, he must typically *guess* (whereas if I do not tell another that I am ill, he may *see* that I am). And whether his guess is right is determined *by my word* (and by such-and-such circumstances).[7] Whereas whether I am ill or not is not determined for the doctor by my word. 'I cannot say what he is thinking (unless he tells me)' is not like 'I cannot say whether he is ill (unless I run such-and-such tests)'. Our confusion here stems from crossing different language-games.

MS. 171, 4: 'Nur ich weiss, was ich denke, heisst eigentlich nichts andres als: nur ich *denke* meine eignen Gedanken.' ('Only I know what I think actually means nothing other than: only I *think* my own thoughts.')

2.1   'And here "know" means . . .': cf. BB 30: 'Of course I know what I wish', unlike 'Of course I know the ABC', does not imply that I surely know something as simple as that. Rather, it signifies that there is no doubt in this case, since it makes no *sense* to talk of doubt. 'In this way the answer "Of course I know what I wish" can be interpreted to be a grammatical statement.'

What of 'unconscious wishes'? Surely it is a cardinal claim of psychoanalytic theory that we are ignorant of our unconscious wishes? This is confused: an unconscious wish does not stand to a wish as an unheard sound stands to a heard one. (Cf. Volume 2, pp.18f.) So a special explanation is called for. My 'ignorance' of my unconscious wishes (beliefs, desires) is wholly unlike my ignorance of your unvoiced wishes (beliefs, desires).

SECTION 248

1   'One plays patience by oneself' is not an empirical proposition about all hitherto observed games of patience. It is a grammatical proposition which explains an aspect of the game: there is no such thing as playing patience against another, just as there is no such thing as fighting a duel without an opponent. So too, 'Sensations are private' is a grammatical proposition which gives, or perhaps intimates, a rule (or rules) for the

---

[7] But, of course, one sometimes can say 'I could see what you were thinking written all over your face'!

use of sensation-words. Here it is used to indicate the senselessness of doubt (and hence too of certainty) in the first-person present tense (cf. Exg. §§246f.); in other contexts it might be used to emphasize the possibility of concealment and dissimulation (Vol. XII, 179) or the privileged status of a person's avowal as a criterion for how things are with him.

2   This occurs in Vol. XII, 179, preceded by the remark:

> Do not say 'one cannot', but say instead: 'it doesn't exist in this game'. Not: 'one can't castle in draughts' but — 'there is no castling in draughts'; and instead of 'I can't exhibition my sensation' — 'in the use of the word "sensation", there is no such thing as exhibiting what one has got'; instead of 'one cannot enumerate all the cardinal numbers' — 'there is no such thing here as enumerating all the members'. (Z §134)

Two points are noteworthy. First, what looks like an inability is a logical impossibility, and a logical impossibility is not a possibility which one cannot actualize. It does not signify limitations upon what can be done, but rather earmarks the bounds of sense. Beyond these is not something one cannot do, but only the void of nonsense. Secondly, in this context (Vol. XII, 179) W. appears to take 'Sensations are private' to signify that there is no such thing as exhibiting to public view the sensation one has, *in the sense* in which I can exhibit what colour something I saw was by pointing at a sample. In PI §248 the remark alludes to epistemic privacy, which is an illusion the truth behind which is only the senselessness of doubt in one's own case. Noted that below (PI §§311ff.) W. argues that one *can* exhibit pain (only not *privately*), but to exhibit pain is to *behave* in such-and-such a way — it is not to exhibit to another what one has 'got' (and one cannot do that to oneself either).

LPE 283 remarks, 'Does the solipsist also say that only he can play chess?' The solipsist mistakes the bounds of sense for metaphysical, super-physical, constraints, which he then misconstrues. Applied to the game of patience, the solipsist would claim that only he can play patience!

RPP I §570 adds: '"Thoughts and feelings are private" means roughly the same as "There is pretending", or: "One can hide one's thoughts and feelings; can even lie and dissimulate". And the question is, what is the import of this "There is . . ." and "One can".' That I can hide my thoughts does *not* signify that *thinking* my thoughts is hiding them, and that I can pretend or lie about my thoughts does not imply that I *know* my thoughts. Conversely, what I think to myself silently can only be said to be 'hidden' from another in the sense that he cannot *guess* it; it does not mean that he cannot perceive my thought because it is in my soul! (LW §977).

SECTION 249

1   This can be linked with §246 and perhaps §244. The connection with
§246 is simple. There the interlocutor claimed that one cannot know, but
only surmise, that another person is in pain. But, W. replied, if we are
using the verb 'to know' as it is normally used, then one often does know
when someone is in pain. §249 can be seen as an ironic amplification on
the certainty of such knowledge in one kind of case. In the case of an
infant's manifestations of experience, there can be no room for doubts
based on pretence, for the concept of pretence has no grip here (see
below).

The link with §244 (if intended) is more complex. §244 argued that
'pain' and the sensation of which it is the 'name' are connected via the
primitive, natural expressions of sensation; for the child is taught to use
'pain' or 'I have a pain' instead of merely crying. §249 can be seen as
raising a difficulty: might we not be wrong in assuming that this
primitive expressive behaviour is not a pretence? On what is our
assumption based?

Why is this a difficulty? And what answer are we expected to give?
The difficulty is this: if the smile of the unweaned infant were not an
expression of contentment, but a dissimulation, if the cry of the infant
when he falls were not an expression of pain, but an instance of
shamming pain, then it seems that when adults try to teach the infant to
use the word 'pain' as a verbal extension of or replacement for this
behaviour, he might learn to use 'pain' as a replacement for shamming
pain-behaviour rather than for the spontaneous expression of pain.
Indeed, if pain and shamming pain were different states of mind which
have the same behavioural expression, we might inadvertently be
teaching the child to call 'pain' not what we call 'pain', but whatever state
of mind constitutes shamming pain (RPP I §§142ff.). But this drags
scepticism in its wake. For if 'pain' is directly connected to 'mere'
behaviour, which may be an expression of pain *or* of feigning pain, then
what precise inner experience it is thereby connected with *in another* is
wholly speculative. Worse still, how do *I* know that I've learned to use
the word to express what my teachers (parents) wanted me to express?
Should I say that I believe (and hope) I have (LPE 296)? The meaning of
'pain' wavers, and the evidence for others' experiences seems worthless.
(Just as illusion threatens to engulf our knowledge of the 'external
world', so pretence threatens to nullify our knowledge of the experiences
of others.)

But we are not over-hasty in taking the infant's smile to express
contentment. And this 'assumption' is not based upon an experience, for

in the first place we do not assume the infant's smile to express contentment because we have observed numerous infants and noted that usually when they smile thus they are contented. 'I have never seen a new-born child shamming contentment' is like 'I have never seen a new-born child who thought that π is greater than √7'. Secondly, it is not an assumption:[8] 'Assuming it is not pretending, the child is content' would be a joke! Why is this?

> When I say that moaning is the expression of toothache, then under certain circumstances the possibility of its being the expression without the feeling behind it mustn't enter my game.
>
> Es ist Unsinn zu sagen: der Ausdruck kann immer lügen. [It is senseless to say: the expression may always lie.]
>
> The language-games with expressions of feelings are based on games with expressions of which we don't say that they may lie. (LPE 293)

The natural, pre-linguistic behaviour in certain circumstances is the hard ground upon which these language-games are played. But might it not turn out to be sand? Could we not be wrong? No; the foundations of our language-games are not assumptions, but forms of response and action.

Pretending, like lying, is a language-game that must be learned, and there are many things one must already be able to do before one can pretend. Feigning, dissimulating, pretending are false moves within a game; but one cannot make a false move in a game before one knows what counts as a correct move. A new-born child cannot be insincere, but neither can he be sincere. To dissimulate, he must first learn to mimic and to intend to mimic. But to mimic is not to dissimulate; for to dissimulate, he must further intend to deceive, hence to bring it about that others believe that he is content, in pain, etc. even though he is not. To do so he must be able to *think* that. But that thought and that intention presuppose a multitude of skills, which he must first acquire.

How do we know that he does not already have them? Because what we call an exercise of such capacities requires a highly complex background pattern of behaviour, just as what we call 'making a mistake in calculating' does. We do not say of a child that he has miscalculated until we ascribe to him the capacity to calculate.

The picture underlying the objection sketched out in the third paragraph above is therefore misconceived. Shamming pain is not a state of mind (although one who shams pain is in a different *frame of mind* from one who cries out in pain). The behavioural expression of pain is not

---

[8] LPE 295 remarks, 'I must assume an expression which is *not* lying', but W. would surely have corrected this later. I no more assume this than I assume that objects do not cease to exist when I do not perceive them.

linked with pain and shamming pain in the same way (MS. 171, 1), any more than money and counterfeit money are linked in the same way with purchasing power. It is no more possible for all behaviour to be pretence (or all perceptual experiences to be illusions) than it is possible for all money to be counterfeit. It is profoundly mistaken to think that the *same* behaviour is just connected with two distinct 'inner' states or experiences, the one pain and the other shamming pain. The behaviour *may* be the same (as a perfectly forged banknote resembles the genuine prototype), but even then the surrounding circumstances differ. Pretence, like forgery, has a model, and there is a skill and artifice in matching the prototype. The behavioural criteria for pretence differ from the criteria for unfeigned behaviour. The connection of behaviour to the 'inner' is conceptual, not causal, and shamming pain is not an expression (*Äusserung*) of an inner experience of the same category as pain.

1.1   'needs to be learned': one does not learn to lie as one learns to ride a bicycle. One may, in certain circumstances, learn to lie *better*; but one does not *learn* to lie as one learns (is taught) skills. It is true, however, that one must already have learned much, be able to do many complex things, before one is able to lie.

2   This theme preoccupied W. from 1936 onwards, especially after 1945. The following is a selection of points bearing directly on the incoherence of neonate pretence and what must be learnt in order to be able to pretend:

(i) Pretending to be in pain is just *one* form of pain-behaviour without pain (PI pp. 229f.). There are many others, e.g. automatism, perhaps induced by drugs (RPP I §137), hypnosis, miming (RPP II §631) or playing charades, acting the role of someone in pain on the stage (LPE 296), acting the role of someone *pretending* to be in pain on the stage (LW §863). Hence it is a very *specific* psychological process, though not an 'inner' process (RPP II §612).

(ii) Pretending to be in pain is an activity informed by specific motives and intentions. One may pretend to be injured and incapacitated with pain in order to attack someone who comes to help. The same behaviour can occur without these motives and intentions, and it is this which inclines us, rightly, to insist that there is an 'inner' difference between the cases. But 'inner' is a misleading metaphor here. That there is such a difference is manifest in the fact that one can *confess* that one was dissimulating, i.e. confess such-and-such intentions. But an intention is not something 'inner' (RPP I §824).[9]

---

[9] Of course, in a trivial sense it is (LW §959); but the point is that we have a wrong picture of what we call 'the inner'.

(iii) Pretence can (logically) occur only within a highly complex tapestry of life, for it is a pattern with infinite variations within the fabric of life (LW §862; MS. 169, 137). And recognizing behaviour as pretence is akin to recognizing a pattern in a weave. Imagine a long strip of tapestry: here I see pattern S, there pattern V; sometimes I don't know which it is for a while, and sometimes I say at the end, 'It was neither of them.' One is taught to recognize these patterns by being shown simple examples and then more complicated ones of both types, rather as one learns to distinguish the musical styles of two composers (MS. 169, 137). So too with pretence; and were pretence *not* such a complicated pattern within life, then it *would* be conceivable that a new-born child might pretend (MS. 171, 1).

The complexity ramifies in various directions. Pretence presupposes sophisticated capacities, even where the behaviour in question appears not to be sophisticated. An adult can pretend (or manifest sincerity) without saying a word, but merely by facial expression or gesture or even inarticulate sounds (LW §944). But for these apparently simple pieces of behaviour to constitute pretence presupposes complex motives, intentions, and conceptual skills, as well as a complicated *play of expressions*. Can one imagine a languageless new-born child with the play of features and gestures of an adult (LW §§945f.)? Not obviously, for the smooth features of a baby lack the multiplicity and possibilities of articulation characteristic of the lined face of an adult. But to the extent that we can, it is as something dissonant, slightly repulsive, since it would be a meaningless play of expression. For a creature to have such complex intentions, motives, beliefs, etc. as are presupposed by pretence, its pretending behaviour must occur against a backcloth of its own complex behavioural repertoire manifesting the capacity for appropriately sophisticated motives, beliefs, and so forth. Finally, note the variety and complexity of the endless contexts in social life in which we pretend, contexts which provide motives and reasons for different *kinds* of pretence, dissimulation, hypocrisy, and charlatanry. These forms of simulation, whether good, evil, or morally indifferent, are only possible against complicated backgrounds of human life.

(iv) A child may find that when he is in pain and screams, he gets coddled. Then he may scream in order to get coddled. But this is not pretence, merely one of its roots (LW §867). We may teach him to say 'toothache' instead of screaming with toothache, and likewise he may then say 'toothache' in order to get treated kindly. But this is not yet lying (LPE 295). There is much more to be learnt before one can pretend,[10] lie, or be insincere. For a new-born child cannot be malicious, friendly, or thankful; these are possible only within the context of

---

[10] But note the qualification below, Exg. §250.

complicated patterns of behaviour which he has not yet mastered (LW §942). A new-born child not only cannot be insincere, he cannot be sincere either.

(v) What then must the child learn? What must he understand and be able to do before we can justly say that he is pretending to be in pain, dissimulating, being sincere or insincere? W. indicated various features. He must learn to imitate pain-behaviour and must be capable of *intending* to imitate (MS. 171, 5f.). (The execution of such intentions, unlike the natural pain-behaviour which is being imitated here, may be *skilful* or clumsy and inept!) There are grades of pretence, of which simple mimicry is a primitive form. To pretend to be in pain, one must know how one who is in pain behaves and target one's behaviour on that model, *intend to reproduce* it. Dissimulative pretence is complex, for it involves an intent to deceive, to behave like someone who is in pain with the intention that someone else should believe falsely that one is in pain. This is a far more sophisticated matter. For this the child must understand such propositions as 'He thinks I'm feeling pain but I'm not' (LW §866). Hence the child learns to dissimulate pain only in the course of learning the complicated use of 'having pain'. He must learn not just the use of 'He has a pain', but also of 'I think (believe) he has a pain' and hence 'He thinks I have a pain' (RPP I, §142).

(vi) One can say of a child 'Today he pretended for the first time', but not 'Today he was sincere for the first time' — yet not because children are naturally sincere (LW §§940–2). Indeed, one *cannot* say of the expressive behaviour of the baby that it is sincere. In order to be sincere, the child must, for example, realize that *insincerity* is bad. Mere unrestrained expressive behaviour is no more sincere than uninhibited verbal expression is candid. One *can* say 'The child is already definitely sincere' (but not 'for the first time'), for the realization of the wrongness of insincerity dawns gradually over a totality of behaviour, informing a multiplicity of actions and not, as it were, illuminating them one by one (cf. Z §469).

(vii) The wordless sincerity or insincerity we see in the face of an adult exists only in a complicated play of expressions (as false moves exist only in a game) (LW §946). This develops cheek by jowl with the child's acquisition of a multitude of patterns of behaviour, reaction, and interaction. As these evolve, one might say, the soul is developing — something 'inner'. But it is noteworthy that from this perspective the 'inner' no longer appears as the prime mover of the 'outer' expressions (LW §947). Rather they are fused, as form and matter.

2.1   'Lying is a language-game that needs to be learned': Vol. XV, 84 elaborates. There is said to be a tribe that is too primitive to lie. This seems paradoxical, for one now thinks of a lying-intent as a product of a language-game. So one may think of such people as being good and innocent, and that they are made evil through learning a technique of language. But to say that one learns the specific language-game of lying is not to say that one therewith learns *pretence* for the first time. For a people who are unacquainted with lying-speech can nevertheless *pretend*, be false and deceitful, just as a child can pretend before he can lie.

SECTION 250

1.1   'die richtige Umgebung': 'the right surroundings', i.e. for a creature's behaviour to constitute pretending, it must occur against a background of highly complex behaviour *of that creature*, e.g. behaviour manifesting complex intentions and capacities.

2   LW §§859–70 clarifies: for behaviour to be an expression of pain, fear, or joy, it must occur in a very specific context. But for behaviour to be the pretence of pain, it requires an even more far-reaching, particular context. Not every creature that can express fear, joy, or pain can feign them. 'A dog can't pretend to be in pain, because his life is too simple for that. It doesn't have the joints necessary for such movements' (LW §862). To be able to pretend *or* be sincere, a complicated pattern of behaviour must be mastered. 'A dog cannot be a hypocrite; but neither is it sincere' (LW §870: PI p. 229).

MS. 169, 134 allows the concept of pretence more elasticity, presumably because we find it altogether natural to say, for example, of a bird which flutters on the ground to draw a predator away from its nest, that it is pretending to have a broken wing. But, of course, this is akin to (although, being innate, even more primitive than) the infant's crying in order to be coddled (and not to the child's crying in order to induce his mother to believe that he has hurt himself). Hence here W. observes that there are many simple forms of pretence: 'Kann ein Idiot zu primitiv sein, um sich zu verstellen? Er könnte sich auf tierische Art verstellen. Und das zeigt, dass es von da an Stufen der Verstellung gibt.' ('Can an idiot be too primitive to pretend? He could pretend in the way an animal does. And that shows that from there on there are grades of pretence.')

The limited applicability of psychological predicates to animals preoccupied W. (cf. PI §650; Z §§114–20), for it illuminates the character of our concepts. MS. 179, 17 describes human expectant behaviour and observes that a dog can expect only in a much more primitive sense than we do. The next remark is striking and clarifies the idea that the surroundings of behaviour are crucial for the applicability of psychological concepts: I may sit quietly in my room hoping that someone will come, but if *one minute* of this hoping were, as it were, isolated, cut off from its antecedents and sequel, this would no longer be hoping. The hopeful look at the door, the rising pulse, the muttered exclamation, thus isolated, signify nothing (cf. RFM 336). Behaviour and psychological state are what they are only in the rich tapestry of life; a single thread alone cannot provide the modelling and the contours. And the texture of life of an animal is too loosely woven and too simple to make intelligible its expecting its master to come home tomorrow, sincerity or insincerity, honesty or dissimulation.

2.1   'Perhaps it is possible . . .': cf. RPP II §631 (= Z §389), 'A clever dog might perhaps be taught to give a kind of whine of pain but it would never get as far as conscious imitation.'

Section 251

1   'Sensations are private' was compared with 'One plays patience by oneself' (§248). These are grammatical propositions. But the former, especially when cast in the form 'Only I can know whether I am in pain', looks like a description of the necessary limits of human knowledge (for others *cannot* know). In this way metaphysics disguises grammar, and expressions of norms of representation are dressed in the garb of what is represented.

Such propositions as 'My images are private' or 'Only I can know whether I am feeling pain' look like empirical propositions of an especially firm kind, scientific truths that no one would gainsay (BB 55). We often defend ourselves against such claims by trying to highlight their non-empirical character. We might ask, '"Is what you affirm meant to be an empirical proposition? Can you conceive (imagine) its being otherwise?" — Do you mean that substance has never yet been destroyed, or that it is *inconceivable* that it should be destroyed? Do you mean that experience shows that human beings always prefer the pleasant to the unpleasant?' (PG 130). And in the same spirit, when one wants to show the senselessness of such metaphysical turns of phrase (viz. the absence of an intelligible negation; that these sentences do not divide a logical space), one says 'I can't imagine the opposite of this' or 'What would it be like, if it were otherwise?' (cf. PG 129).

However, this defence against the empirical appearance of metaphysical propositions is almost as fraught with potential confusion as what it is meant to guard against. 'I can't imagine the opposite', although it points to the *a priori*, non-empirical character of, e.g., 'My images are private', *looks* like an appeal to the limitations upon one's powers of imagination. If that were so, one might respond that more imaginative exercises are necessary: sensations are private — that is a brute fact about the human condition, and if you cannot imagine it otherwise, you must get into training! But this is *not* what was meant by 'I can't imagine the opposite'; rather, it is that one cannot even *try* to imagine the opposite (PG 129), one does not know *what* one is supposed to imagine (MS. 176, 9); indeed, there is nothing here *to* imagine — and *that* is what one means.

Why is this so? Because the negation of an *a priori* proposition is not a description of a possible state of affairs; nor is it a description of an impossible state of affairs. For it is not a description at all, but a senseless form of words. Hence too, the *a priori* proposition itself (e.g. 'Sensations are private') is not a description, but a misleading expression of a grammatical rule (cf. 'Grammar and necessity', Volume 2, pp. 263ff.).

'I can't imagine the opposite', properly understood, draws attention to the fact that the proposition in question is a norm of representation. But if I cannot imagine or even try to imagine the opposite, one might just as well say that I cannot imagine the thing itself (PG 129). And that would not be like 'I can't imagine that Oxford is in England' (because I already *know* it to be so, and one can only imagine that *p* if one does *not* know that *p*), for that restriction limits 'I can imagine' to possibilities one does not know to be actualized. But so-called necessary truths which one acknowledges as such are not actualizations of possibilities, but expressions of grammatical rules; and that one cannot imagine things to be so is not a consequence of one's knowing them to be so, but of the fact that such propositions do not describe how things are at all.

Nevertheless, we do *not* say 'I can't imagine the thing itself', but only 'I can't imagine the opposite'. Why? Because we regard the senseless grammatical proposition (e.g. 'Every rod has a length') as a tautology as opposed to a contradiction (PG 129). Tautologies and contradictions alike are senseless, they say nothing; but we are inclined to favour tautologies, to say that they are true, that we know that it is either raining or not raining, that we are certain that it is not both raining and not raining, etc. But this is misleading in so far as it fosters a disposition to construe degenerate propositions on the model of genuine ones. Similarly here, our inclination to say 'I can't imagine the opposite' and not 'I can't imagine the thing itself' reflects our partiality for, e.g., 'This rod has a length' as opposed to 'This rod has no length'. But this is a parallel misunderstanding. It is based on the thought that 'This rod has a length' is verified by the fact that the rod has a length of 4 metres — after all, 4 metres is a length! But '4 metres is a length' is a *grammatical proposition*, a rule for the use of words. 'This rod has a length' is no less senseless than 'This rod has no length' (PG 129).

Our partiality for 'I can't imagine the opposite', rather than 'I can't imagine the thing itself', is not absurd, for it expresses a dim apprehension of the role of grammatical propositions (and that the negation of a

grammatical proposition is not a grammatical proposition). 'Every rod
has a length' is a grammatical proposition signifying that the expression
'the length of a rod' (unlike 'the length of a sphere') is meaningful (cf. BB
30), that it always makes sense to ask of a rod 'How long is it?' Now
surely one can imagine, make a mental image of, every rod's having a
length; one simply conjures up an image of a rod! Does this not show
that while one cannot imagine a rod without a length, one *can* picture to
oneself every rod's having a length? In a sense it does; but this mental
image, and hence this imagining, has a quite different role from the
image one might conjure up in connection with 'This table has the same
length as that one'; for in the latter case there is such a thing as a picture of
this table's *not* having the same length as the other. A picture attached to
a grammatical proposition is not a picture of how things are (let alone of
how they *necessarily* are), but a pictorial *sample* that might perhaps show
what such-and-such (e.g. 'the length of a rod') is *called*. And there is no
such thing as an 'opposite picture'.

1.1   (i) 'Wir wehren uns mit diesen Worten': 'We defend ourselves with
these words against . . .'.

(ii) 'Aber warum sage ich': 'But why do I say'.

(iii) 'Ich kann mir, was du sagst, nicht vorstellen': 'I cannot imagine
what you say' when you say that my images are private, etc. This refers
back to paragraph (a).

(iv) 'I simply imagine a rod. Only this picture . . .': mental images are
not a necessary accompaniment of imagining. But when imagining what
is picturable, one may have a mental image (*Vorstellungsbild*). Elsewhere
(PI §301, cf. Exg.) W. argues that imagining is not having a *picture*,
although a picture corresponds to it; i.e. a mental picture or image is not
a kind of picture (as drawings and paintings are different kinds of
picture). This does not affect the point being made here.

(v) '((Remark about the negation of an *a priori* proposition))': it is
unclear to which remark this refers. The argument, however, is clear.
The negation of an *a priori* proposition is altogether unlike the negation
of an empirical proposition. The latter describes a possible state of affairs,
something that is imaginable. The negation of a true *a priori* proposition
does not — but then neither does a true *a priori* proposition. The
negation of a true arithmetical proposition, e.g. '~ (2 + 2 = 4)' is not a
proposition of arithmetic (although '2 + 2 ≠ 5' is). The negation of a
tautology is a contradiction, and contradictions are not propositions of
logic (which is not to say that they have no role in logic). But both
tautologies and contradictions are senseless. The negation of a grammatical proposition (e.g. of 'Nothing can be red and green all over
simultaneously') is not a grammatical proposition, for it does not have
the role of a norm of representation (cf. 'Grammar and necessity',
Volume 2, pp. 276–81).

2   The ancestors of this remark (e.g. Vol. X, 121f.; Vol. XII, 75ff.) associate it with the venerable idea of the imagination's providing a criterion of logical possibility (now relocated at PI §512). This is evident in PG 128–30 (derived from Vol. X): it looks as if word-language enables senseless combinations of words, whereas the language of imagining does not; for when one wants to show the senselessness of metaphysical turns of phrase, one often says 'I can't imagine the opposite of that'. But this is doubly mistaken. First, the language of images, and hence of drawings too, does allow of senseless representations (think of Escher's etchings). A mistaken blueprint can be exactly analogous to a nonsensical pseudo-proposition. Secondly, this misconstrues the significance of 'I can't imagine the opposite' (and here follows a version of PI §251). We say that such-and-such is unimaginable or *inconceivable*, but do not pause to reflect on how strange it is that one should be *able* to say (or think!) this. For *what is it* that we *cannot conceive*? If we (wrongly) regard thought as an accompaniment of words (or 'ideas' and images as the gold backing for linguistic paper currency), then the words specifying what is inconceivable must be unaccompanied. So what sense does such a statement have? It indicates that this form of words is senseless, excluded from our language like some arbitrary noise. But then the reason for thus explicitly excluding it can only be that we are tempted to confuse it with a genuine sentence.

    RFM 89 criticizes Frege's conception of laws of human thinking, e.g. that it is impossible for human beings to recognize an object as different from itself. Frege presented these as psychological, empirical laws about the workings of the human mind (GA, Introduction, pp. xvff.). But that is absurd, for there is no such thing as recognizing an object as different from itself. If there were, one could *try* to do it (as one can try to run a mile in 4 minutes). But if I look at a lamp and say with greatest intensity 'This lamp is different from itself', have I *tried* to think something I cannot manage to think? It is not that I see immediately that the words I utter are false — they are not false — but rather that I can do nothing with this form of words, for it is senseless. Note that Frege sharply distinguished laws of truth from laws of taking-to-be-true (laws of thinking) and did *not* take imaginability to be a criterion of logical possibility. His confusion was to think that there is something to be imagined as the negation of an *a priori* proposition, and also that creatures might *think* in accord with the negation of 'laws of truth' (cf. Volume 2, pp. 317f.). This confusion is a product of his mistaken idea that *a priori* propositions have *sense*.

    Z §442 remarks that the opposite of an *a priori* proposition, i.e. of an expression of a norm of representation in the guise of a proposition about objects, really will be 'unthinkable', since what corresponds to it is a form of expression which we have *excluded*.

2.1   'This table has the same length as the one over there': for the relation
between 'has the same length as' and 'has a length', see PG 351f. (cf. also
PLP 385f.).

3   William James nicely exemplifies confusion about the role of imaginability. Round squares and objects both black and white all over are
conceivable, he argued. 'It is a mere accident, as far as conception goes,
that [these expressions] happen to stand for things which nature never
lets us sensibly perceive.' To be sure, they are not imaginable, but 'How
do we know *which* things we cannot imagine unless by first conceiving
them, meaning *them* and not other things?'[11]
       W. read James carefully, finding in his work a stark illustration of the
deep need for philosophical investigation (MS. 165, 150f.). James
claimed that psychology is a science, yet discusses hardly any scientific
question. His moves are just so many attempts to free himself from the
metaphysical spider's web in which he is caught. 'He cannot yet walk, or
fly at all,' W. added in English, 'he only wriggles.'

SECTION 252

1   A coda to §251. Why are we so inclined? We think of 'This body has
extension' as being verified by 'This body has a surface area of 4 square
metres' and '4 square metres is an extension' (cf. PG 129). But the latter is
a grammatical proposition, and the product of an empirical proposition p
and a grammatical proposition q is p – for a grammatical proposition is
senseless (cf. '$p. (q \vee {\sim} q) = p$').

SECTION 253

1   The epistemic sense in which sensations are conceived to be private
having been exposed, W. now turns to what might be called 'privacy of
ownership', viz. 'Another person cannot have my pains.' This too
appears to be a statement of super-physical constraints; but it is in fact a
nonsense (MS. 129, 40). Failure to apprehend this leads one to think that
another person cannot have the same pain as I do. That this is confused
becomes evident if one examines what counts as a criterion of identity
here. (Cf. 'Privacy', §2).
       W. approaches the question by inviting us to consider what makes it
possible, in the case of physical objects, to distinguish between being
identical (*dasselbe*) and being exactly the same (*das gleiche*) but not

[11] William James, *The Principles of Psychology* (Dover, New York, 1950), Vol. I, p. 463
and n.

identical. Why? What bearing does this have on the question? We are strongly inclined to project upon pain (or indeed upon anything that is 'inner') the grammar of physical objects. Someone who is disposed to say that another person cannot have my pains will also typically insist that he really means that another cannot have the *identical* pain (*dasselbe, identische*) I have, though of course he can have the same (sort of) pain (cf. Exg. §254). In the case of a chair we can draw this distinction; two chairs of a Chippendale set are exactly alike but not identical. They are located in different places, exist whether observed or unobserved, may belong to the same person, to different people, or to no one. Hence it makes sense to affirm that this is the chair I saw last week, or to say that it is not the same chair but one exactly like it, the other having gone to be repaired. Two people may successively (or even simultaneously) sit on the same chair, or they may sit on distinct chairs that are exactly alike.

If the distinction between being identical and being exactly the same but not identical applies to pain, then one might indeed argue (as Frege, for example, did) that although your pain may be exactly the same as mine, it is nevertheless not identical. And one might go on to argue that it *cannot* be. But does the distinction apply? What is the criterion of identity for pains?

We distinguish with respect to pain: phenomenal characteristics, intensity, and bodily location, rather as we distinguish with respect to colour: hue, saturation, and brightness. Two objects painted in the same hue, saturation, and brightness are the same (not merely similar) colour. And so too, if my headache is a dull throbbing pain in the temples, and yours is also a dull, throbbing pain in the temples, do we not have the same pain?

One might respond by saying that since your headache is in your temples and my headache is in mine, i.e. in different places, they cannot be the same. This is wrong. What we *call* 'having a headache in the same place' *is* having a pain in the same part of the body, you in yours and I in mine. And as we, including doctors diagnosing illnesses, use the expression 'same pain', two people are said to have the same pain if the pain each has tallies in intensity, phenomenal characteristics, and location.

The interlocutor might reply by saying that 'same place' thus used just means 'corresponding place'. The corresponding location, he might insist, is after all not the same location. So two people *cannot* have the very same pain! Rather than challenging this confusion over sameness and difference of pain-location, W. seems willing to allow this distinction to be drawn and meets the interlocutor on his own ground. Even if we grant that a 'corresponding location' is not 'the same location', it does not follow that two people *cannot* have the same pain. For Siamese twins might feel pain at the point of juncture, not just in 'corresponding locations'. The interlocutor must now concede that as far as this point is concerned, it is logically possible for two people to have the same pain.

This argument works as an *ad hominem* strategy. But it is noteworthy that W.'s concession is misleading. If the head of one of the Siamese twins is conjoined with the back of the other, then one has a headache and the other a backache. And a headache is not the same pain as a backache even though the twins point at and assuage the point of juncture. 'Having a pain in the same place' and 'the location of a pain' are not used to refer to a spatial co-ordinate. If I have a splitting headache and so do you, then we both have the same pain in the same place.

One might be inclined to object that even in this case another person cannot have the same pain as I do, for after all, my pain is *mine* and his pain is *his* (BB 54). But this is to make the owner of the pain *a property of the pain* (PR 91), and that is as absurd as claiming that my chair cannot be the same colour as your chair, because the dark brown of my chair has the property of belonging to my chair and the dark brown of your chair has the property of belonging to your chair, so the two chairs cannot have the same colour (BB 55; LSD 4f.). This misrepresents the grammar of 'the same colour' (and of 'belonging'), and so too the claim that my pain is not the same as his because mine is mine and his is his (or, even more confusedly, I feel mine and he feels his) distorts the grammar of 'the same pain'/'different pain'. Of course, this is not to say that the grammar of 'pain' is isomorphic with the grammar of colour-words: we ask what colour something is, but not what pain it is; we ask where A's pain is, but not where the chair's colour is; and so on.

In so far as it makes sense to say that my pain is the same as his, two people can have the same pain (and often do, when they have the same disease). One might add that in so far as it makes sense to say that my pain *differs* from his, it also makes *sense* for my pain to be the same as his. But why the 'in so far as'? Two explanations might be ventured. First, no qualification is intended on its making sense. Rather, given the clarification of §251, W. is now drawing our attention to the fact that the metaphysician is either making a claim or merely issuing a grammatical recommendation. In so far as he is making a claim, however, then what he says makes sense, and so does its negation. Secondly, the qualification may be in place in order to emphasize that the insertion of the possessive pronoun 'my' or 'his' in 'I have [a] pain' is misleading. W. emphasized this point in PR 93: 'What in my experience justifies the "my" in "I feel *my* pain"? Where is the multiplicity in the feeling that justifies this word? And it can only be justified if we could also replace it by another word.' The truth of the matter, W. then argued, is that 'our language employs the phrases "my pain" and "his pain", and also the expressions "I have (or feel) a pain" and "He has (or feels) a pain". An expression "I feel my pain" is nonsense' (PR 94; cf. LWL 18f.). This argument does not occur after 1932/3, perhaps because by then W. realized that there are contexts in which one can intelligibly say, for example, 'I have your headache now'. Nevertheless, there is an important point here.

Having a pain, unlike having a pin, does not signify a form of ownership or possession. I can have a pin which does not belong to me, but there is no such thing as having a pain which does not belong to me. I can borrow a pin and have it in my possession for a while before returning it to its rightful owner. But in the case of sensations such a distinction makes no sense; the requisite multiplicity is missing. 'My pain' does not mean 'the pain that *belongs* to me', but just 'the pain I have'. Someone else can have the same pain, i.e. a pain with just those characteristics. What he cannot have is the pain that belongs to me, but then neither can I!

This may incline one to insist that '"I feel his pain" is nonsense', but that would be too hasty. We do say 'He has his father's build' or 'She has the Mona Lisa's smile', as well as 'I have caught your cold'. In such cases the sameness of build, smile, or cold is signified, together with a form of connection, genetic, paradigmatic, or causal. There is nothing misleading about such propositions, because the form of connection in the context indicates the known character of the build, smile, or cold. The proposition 'I have his pain', except in a context in which his pain has been described, is anomalous precisely because no characterization of the pain is thereby intimated, since 'being his' is not a feature of the pain. But if we have both been eating the same food, and you complain of severe stomach cramps, and a few minutes later I too feel severe stomach cramps, I might say 'I've got your pains now', i.e. 'I have the same pains as you.'

The metaphysician wants to insist upon the metaphysical unshareability of pain. But he must also insist that it *makes sense* that two people should have the same pain, for otherwise he could not say what it is that is metaphysically prevented from occurring. If he relinquishes the latter claim, the former one collapses into a recommendation that we change the grammar of 'pain' and no longer say of two sufferers from migraine that they have the same pain, but rather that they have different pains that are exactly alike. However, now we have been given no *reason* for this shift of grammar (viz. treating the 'owner' as a property of the pain or treating *feeling* pain as distinct from *having* pain). The 'metaphysical limitation' was a recommendation masquerading as a reason, but it could be stated only in so far as it did not lead to a shift in grammar.

§253(c) highlights the reaction of one who thinks that being *his* is a property of the pain he has. He might be inclined to strike himself on the breast and say 'Another person can't have *this* pain!' But, we should respond, *which* pain? It is no use replying 'The one I feel', for 'the pain I feel' = 'the pain I have', and we should ask again, '*Which* pain is that?'

Stressing 'this' while thumping oneself does not define a criterion of identity; it does not specify *what* it is that another allegedly cannot have, any more than *staring* at the colour of the chair and saying to oneself 'Surely another object can't have *that* colour' does. Worse still, the emphasis deludes us into thinking that we are being reminded of the criterion of identity with which we are conversant (as if being felt by me were a criterion of identity of the pain I feel), whereas by merely thumping one's chest and saying '*This* pain', nothing is indicated about the actual criteria of identity, viz. intensity, phenomenal characteristics, and bodily location.

1.1   (i) 'Another person can't have my pains': once the mistaken claim that two people cannot have the same pain is unmasked, the primary interest in this proposition lapses. Nevertheless, one may still wonder whether some grammatical truth does not lurk behind it. One is tempted to concede that another person can have the same pain as I have, but that nevertheless he cannot have my pain. This makes scant sense.[12] The only truths one can squeeze out of this misbegotten proposition are as follows: (a) 'My pain' does not mean 'the pain that *belongs* to me' as 'my penny' means 'the penny that belongs to me', since pains do not in that sense *belong* to sufferers (see above). 'My pain' = 'the pain I have'. This is a trivial tautology, but it makes clear one purpose that might be served by the misleading metaphysical proposition 'Another person can't have my pain'. If I am asked 'How is your pain now?', it would be a joke to reply 'Much worse, but fortunately I don't have it any longer, John does' or 'I don't know, ask John — he has it'. In this sense, if I do not have it, it is not mine. And if John has it, and the pain gets worse, one cannot say that my pain is getting worse. (b) My pain is manifest in my behaviour, for the person who manifests pain is said to be the person who has a pain. My pain-behaviour is a criterion for *my* being in pain, just as my smile is a criterion for *my* amusement, not yours. Another person's manifestation of pain cannot show *me* to be in pain, any more than his smile can be a criterion for my amusement. Of course, another person may have the same pain or be just as amused as I. (c) If I step on your foot and you yelp 'Ow! That hurt', I might, in a moment of philosophical jocularity, reply 'I did not feel a thing'. Why is that a joke? Because it equivocates between 'It did not hurt *me*', i.e. 'I did not feel a pain in my foot' and 'I did not feel a pain (or the pain) in your foot'. Is the latter merely an empirical proposition? (If so, why is it funny?) Or should one say that there is no such thing as feeling a pain in another's body? W. denied this (WWK 49; PR 92; BB 49ff.) on the grounds that if someone were asked to indicate

---

[12] Contrary to what was argued in Volume 2, pp. 270f. and 279. This error has been corrected in the 2nd impression of the paperback edition of *Wittgenstein: Rules, Grammar and Necessity* (Blackwell, Oxford and New York, 1989).

where it hurts, he might (with eyes closed) point at his neighbour's leg. This can be envisaged in the case of a phantom pain. But it is not sufficient to establish a coherent case for having a pain in another person's body. The moot point is where he points when his neighbour moves his leg, leaves the room, or goes to America. Does the victim point in the direction of America and say 'That is where it hurts'? Would we understand him? And would anyone know *where* it hurts him? Who limps when he has a pain in his friend's leg? Who assuages the pain? The example no more establishes the intelligibility of having a pain in someone else's body than the parallel tale in which he points (with eyes closed) at the table leg demonstrates the intelligibility of having a pain in the table. And the suggestion that I might have toothache in another person's tooth, i.e. wince when his tooth is touched, etc. (WWK 49), is equally problematic. For both the concept of pain-location and the concept of a person's body are being shaken to pieces. If so, then 'I can't feel a pain in another person's body' expresses a grammatical proposition, viz. that there is no such thing. In so far as it makes sense for me to have your headache, it will be in my head. (But no one would say 'I feel your headache in my head'; rather, 'I have your headache' or, better, 'I have the same headache as you'.) (d) There is a noteworthy asymmetry between being aware of one's own pains and being aware of another person's pains. 'I was aware of the pain in my leg' means much the same as 'I had a pain in my leg and it occupied me, held my attention, etc.' But 'I was aware of the pain in his leg' does not mean 'I had a pain in his leg, etc.', but rather 'I was cognizant of the pain in his leg' (for someone told me about it) or 'I perceived that he had a pain in his leg, and this caught my attention'. It is doubtless this that motivates the misguided metaphysical remark 'I can't be aware of another person's pain *in the same way* as I am aware of my own pain'. This is confused, for I am not aware of my own pain in *any way*, i.e. there are no ways or methods of becoming aware of my own pains. It is nonsense to say that I am directly aware of my own pains but only indirectly aware of his. What is true is that I do not perceive that I am in pain, whereas I do perceive that he is. I learn, come to know, that he is in pain by perceiving his behaviour, but there is no such thing as my learning or coming to know that I am in pain. In particular, being aware of my own pain is not coming to know that I am in pain; it is just having a pain (and, perhaps, having my attention caught by it).

(ii) 'Welches sind *meine* Schmerzen?': 'Welches', not 'Welche', so better: '*My* pains — what are they supposed to be?' There are not two distinct questions here, one concerning the criterion for being the subject of pain, which is not answered here at all, the other concerning the criterion of identity for pains. The former question is resolved in §302: the subject of pain is he who manifests it. Here W. is concerned only with confusions over the criterion of identity of pain which incline one to think that two people cannot have the same pain.

(iii) 'Die Emphase spiegelt uns vielmehr nur den Fall vor': 'Rather, what the emphasis does is only to mimic that case in which'.

2   BB 54f. elaborates another objection which the interlocutor might bring. Surely two people could not have the same pain, because we might anaesthetize or kill one of them, yet the other would still be in pain! But if it were the *same* pain, and one ceased to have it, the other would surely lose it too. This objection projects the grammar of physical objects onto pains. If A and B jointly own a pin, and A destroys it, B cannot still have it. But if A and B have hair of the same colour, and A's hair goes white, B's hair need not go white; rather they no longer have hair of the same colour. Similarly, if A and B have the same throbbing headache in the temples, and A takes an aspirin which cures his headache, the sameness of the headache does not imply that B's headache is also cured, but only that they no longer both have a headache.

Vol. XVI, 61f. compares 'ownership' of pain with 'seeing' mental images. One is inclined to say that when I conjure up a mental image, I see it in my mind's eye. But someone standing next to me cannot see it — it belongs to me alone! But this 'seeing' is a mere metaphor, involving a simile of mental vision. If another person imagines the very same thing, why should one not say that he has the same thing before him? If one now objects that surely another cannot have the very same pain that I have, one should query why. Is it that he cannot have the same pain at the same time? If so, then when I have finished with it, he *can* have it! Or is it that he can't have it, come what may?

2.1   'emphatic stressing of the word "this"': MS. 129, 40 added (and then deleted) '(oder durch den Gebrauch des Wortes "identisch" statt des Wortes "gleich")' — ('(or by the use of the word "identical" instead of the word "same")'). This makes clear the connection between PI §253 and §254. The latter follows in MS. 129, 40 (which explains the deletion of the parenthesis).

SECTION 254

1   The substitution of 'identical' for 'the same' is a parallel tactical move to that in §253(c). The interlocutor is inclined to explain that when he insists that another person cannot have his pains, he does not mean that another cannot have the *same* pains (exactly similar), but rather that another cannot have the *identical* pains. (Like 'You can't have the identical chair I have, since I promised never to part with it, but you can have the

same chair — I have ordered an exact reproduction.') This makes it appear as if he is drawing our attention to subtle shades of meaning of 'the same pain', but his manoeuvre presupposes that we are familiar with the distinction between 'identical' and 'the same' (exactly alike but not identical) and know how to draw it. But what we are familiar with is: how to draw such a distinction in a *different domain*. That illuminates nothing about the use of 'the same pain', but rather misguidedly projects the grammar of physical objects onto sensations. Philosophical confusions do not stem from failure to discriminate fine shades of meaning (as it were, olive green from Brunswick green), but rather from failure to discern categorial differences (the greenness of the lawn, of youth, and of envy).

This is exemplified by many cases hitherto discussed. We talk of discovering the construction of a pentagon and of discovering the South Pole, and are unaware of the differences in what can be called 'discovering' in the two cases (BB 29; cf. Volume 2, pp. 295ff.); we speak of believing that it will rain tomorrow, believing that $25^2 = 625$, believing that it is wrong to lie, and fail to notice that the one differs from the others not as hitting the table differs from hitting the chair (the same act with different objects) but as hitting the chair differs from hitting treble C when singing an aria. In these and a myriad other cases our philosophical confusions do not result from failure to pin down the right *nuance* of meaning, but rather from blindness to categorial differences in meaning.

Finding the precise words, the exact shade of meaning, is important in philosophy, but as part of the diagnosis of philosophical confusion, not as part of the therapy. For one must capture the exact physiognomy of error (BT 410), its manifold forms and sources, otherwise one will not be able to follow the path from error to truth (GB 61). The fact that we are tempted to say that, e.g., another person cannot have the identical pain I have is the raw material for philosophy, the culture from which the skilled philosopher can extract the bacteria that plague us. The mathematician is tempted to say that 'Mathematical theorems are true or false; their truth or falsity is absolutely independent of our knowledge of them. In *some* sense, mathematical truth is part of objective reality', and he is disposed to think that the mathematical reality lies outside us, and that our function is to discover or observe it, as the geographer observes new mountain ranges and the explorer discovers the routes to the unconquered peaks.[13] The inclination to say such things, to cleave to these pictures, is something for philosophical treatment. These pictures are not in themselves a philosophy of mathematics, although they have stimu-

---

[13] G. H. Hardy, 'Mathematical Proof', *Mind*, 38 (1929), pp. 4 and 18.

lated philosophers to construct philosophical *theories* that will apparently
vindicate them (e.g. Frege's or Hilbert's philosophy of mathematics).
Such remarks are not a mathematician's *testimony* as to how things are in
the mathematical domain (cf. PI §§386(b), 594(c)). Nor are they *assumptions* one is forced to adopt by the nature of things (cf. PI §299). But *that*
one is inclined to say such things is an important datum, and discerning
why one is so tempted is a crucial diagnostic insight.

1.1   'a psychological exact account': i.e. an account which will exactly
articulate the confused philosopher's temptation and win from him the
acknowledgement: 'Yes, that is what I meant, that is exactly what I
meant' (BT 410). (Cf. Exg. §255).

2.1   'What we "are tempted to say"': BT dwells at length on the character
of philosophical temptation. It can be as hard to refrain from using an
expression as it is to hold back tears (BT 406). We are enmeshed in
grammatical confusions, and the tendency to think in such-and-such
confused ways is deeply rooted in us — for we *want* to think thus.
      The confusion of what one is 'tempted to say' with testimony is
remarked on in Vol. XII, 177:

> Wir verwechseln immer wieder Aussagen der Art: 'Ich bin geneigt dies *so* — nicht
> *so* zu nennen — mit der Mitteilung, dass etwas sich hier *so*, und nicht *so* verhält!
> Alle metaphysichen (unzeitlichen) Aussagen könnte man in der Form machen '*Ich
> bin geneigt . . .*'. 'Ich bin geneigt, eine Aussage über das, was geschehen *wird*, nicht
> "Sätze" zu nennen', 'ich bin geneigt, Farbe und Grösse und Lage "Gegenstände" zu
> nennen', 'ich bin geneigt, die Zahl 3 einen objektiven, nicht wirklichen Gegenstand zu
> nennen'.

> (We constantly confound statements of the form 'I am inclined to call this *this* —
> not *that*' — with [a piece of] information that something here is *this* and not *that*!
> All metaphysical (atemporal) statements could be made in the form '*I am
> inclined . . .*'. 'I am inclined not to call a statement about what is *going* to happen "a
> proposition"', 'I am inclined to call colour, size and location "objects"'. 'I am inclined
> to call the number 3 an objective, non-actual object'.)

SECTION 255

1   Philosophical assertions are expressions of misunderstandings, of
pictures that hold us captive, but they appear in the guise of information
about the nature of things. They take the form of *theses* that are
apparently part of a theory. A false thesis, it seems, must be replaced by a
true one so that our theory about reality approximate more closely to the
truth. But this is an illusion. A conceptual misunderstanding articulated
in the form of a thesis cannot be combatted by a counter-thesis or denial,

for the expression of a grammatical misunderstanding, taken one way, violates the bounds of sense, and taken another way, is plainly false (cf. PI §246). And the negation of a nonsense is a nonsense (cf. Volume 2, pp. 279f.). A metaphysical proposition such as 'Only the present is real' makes no sense in our system of representation (AWL 27); 'Only I can know whether I am really in pain', as propounded by the metaphysician, is nonsense (PI §246); but one cannot show such metaphysical propositions to be nonsense by propounding or defending their negations. Metaphysical propositions are *at best* disguised expressions of grammatical rules, e.g. 'Nothing can be red and green all over', 'Sensations are private'. But even in these cases, the philosophical task is not to amass argument or evidence in favour of the 'truth' of such propositions; it is rather to remove their disguise.

We are held captive by false analogies, e.g. between the grammar of objects and the grammar of numbers, between the linguistic forms of perception and those of 'introspection', between the grammatical form of first-person psychological sentences and that of third-person ones. But one cannot be liberated from a misleading analogy by denying it. As W. remarked on mathematics: 'Your concept is wrong — However, I cannot illuminate the matter by fighting against your words, but only by trying to turn your attention away from certain expressions, illustrations, images and *towards* the employment of the words' (Z §463). Mesmerized by analogies in *forms* of expressions, we are oblivious to disanalogies in their uses, for these are difficult to survey. Our confusions, however, can only be resolved by examining the way we use words, the circumstances and presuppositions of their employment. Hence W. assembles *reminders* for a particular purpose (PI §127). No new discoveries are involved in resolving philosophical problems, only the arrangement of what we have always known (PI §109).

The analogy between W.'s techniques of eliminating philosophical confusions and treating an illness is important. Philosophical problems and the theses philosophers propound in answering them are misunderstandings, not supra-empirical questions and false answers that must be displaced by true ones. Achievement in philosophy is disentangling the threads that constitute the philosophical problem (a knot in our understanding). Success lies in making the problems disappear (PI §133), as achievement in treating an illness lies in making it disappear. What remains once illness is cured is good health, in which the patient can function optimally; what remains after philosophical therapy is an understanding of grammatical articulations which will prevent those problems from arising. For one will see what misguided analogies in the grammar of the language one has mastered led one astray.

The diseases of philosophy are sicknesses of the understanding (RFM 302), intellectual maladies. But these surround us in the midst of life no less ubiquitously than the dangers of mental disease surround us (cf. RFM, 1st edition, 157). Although these illnesses are intellectual rather than psychological, it is not surprising that the analogy between his own methods and psychoanalytic techniques struck W. forcefully in the 1930s. The only correct method in philosophy consists in abstaining from philosophical assertion and *treating* the philosophical pronouncements of others (WWK 183f.; cf. TLP 6.53) by tabulating the rules, the entanglement of which led to these assertions. As in psychotherapy, it is all-important that the therapist should find precisely the right nuance to articulate the philosophical confusion (PI §254). Only when the patient acknowledges what the therapist articulates *as* the right expression for what he himself is inclined irresistibly to say *is* it the right expression (BT 410). Jokes are psychoanalytically revealing, and similarly grammatical jokes are philosophically revealing, for they shed light on the bounds of sense.[14] Just as the psychotherapist helps the patient to articulate emotions, urges, and beliefs that have been repressed since childhood, so too the philosopher of mathematics, for example, should encourage the person baffled by philosophical problems in this domain to articulate repressed doubts and questions. The mathematician has been trained to suppress these, 'he has acquired a revulsion from them as infantile . . . I trot out all the problems that a child learning arithmetic, etc. finds difficult, the problems that education represses without solving. I say to those repressed doubts: you are quite correct, go on asking, demand clarification!' (PG 382). In a sense, each person is a special case for treatment, for the precise physiognomy of error varies subtly from one to another, and what holds one person in thrall may not enslave another. Similarly, what liberates one person may not free another, although the interest of specific errors and diagnoses lies in our general, shared susceptibility to similar confusion. One might even claim that dialogue is the proper form for philosophy, for the philosophical therapist, like the psychotherapist, must help each person to work *on himself* (cf. BT 407). As the neurotic patient is disposed to cleave to his neurotic beliefs and to resist attempts to reveal their true character, so too the philosopher *in us* (TS. 219, 11; cf. Exg. §309) sinks into a morass of metaphysics and intellectual myth-making and resists attempts at extrication. The philosophical therapist is up against the *will*, not (or not only) the intellect (MS. 158, 35; BT 407). For these illusions of reason are deeply attractive to us, often *because* they are also repulsive (and here is an analogy between certain philosophical errors and psychoanalytic *theory* (LA 43)).

There is no single philosophical method, although there are methods, just as there are different therapies (PI §133). For there are many different analogies of form (cf. Volume 1, pp. 487 f.; MU pp. 289f.). But rather as

---

[14] Indeed, W. remarked that one could imagine a book on philosophy which consisted of nothing but jokes (see N. Malcolm, *Ludwig Wittgenstein: a memoir*, 2nd edn (Oxford University Press, Oxford and New York, 1984), p. 28).

in psychoanalysis, so too 'In philosophizing we may not *terminate* a disease of thought. It must run its natural course, and *slow* cure is all important' (Z §382). W. does not explain why; but perhaps the reason is that deep philosophical error is rarely rooted in one analogy and can rarely be rectified by uprooting *one* confusion. Typically, numerous different features give joint support to an overarching thesis, which will therefore *not* collapse through destruction of one of its supporting struts. Again, it is rarely only *one* misguided analogy that bewitches us, but rather a whole range, and as we cast light upon one, long shadows distort others. So one must slowly and patiently survey the structures of intellectual illusion from all sides, for they cannot be taken in at a glance. But in all cases, one's therapeutic endeavour, like the psychotherapist's, is to make *latent* nonsense *patent* nonsense (PI §§464, 524).

Furthermore, as in psychoanalysis, there is no mechanical, easy cure. Philosophical slogans ('Not all words are names' or 'Inner states stand in need of outer criteria') are not like pills that can effect a cure, but only reminders which are of help in conducting careful surveys of grammatical articulations. Again, as in psychoanalysis, what counts as a successful cure is problematic. It is arguably not just the disappearance of this, that, or the other specific problem; for one may readily lapse, and confusion (neurosis) may break out afresh elsewhere. It is rather being *able to fend for oneself* when confronted with fresh problems (PI p. 206).

It should be noted that the therapeutic role thus allocated to philosophy is not in conflict with, but complementary to, the more positive-sounding surview-giving role. A surview provides us with overall guidelines and helps us find our way around.

Private ostensive definition
1. A 'private' language   2. Names, ostensive definitions, and
samples — a reminder   3. The vocabulary of a private language
4. Idle wheels

SECTION 256

1   Having clarified the putative privacy of sensation, W. now returns to the language envisaged in §243(b). Here the sensation-words are not connected with sensations *qua* substitutes for natural expressions of sensations, as are simple sensation-words in our ordinary languages (PI §244). For if they were, the language would not be 'private', i.e. it would not be impossible for anyone other than myself to understand it. It is a crucial feature of a 'private' language not just that no one else under-

stands it (the language of the last Mohican) or that no community consensus on what counts as following its rules obtains, but that it be *logically impossible* that another person should understand it, i.e. that there be no public criteria (or no communicable rule) for correct application. This negative condition is not satisfied by the language of a Robinson Crusoe or a solitary caveman, etc., but only by a putative language in which sensation-names (or, more generally, names of experiences) are severed from the natural expression of sensation (or experience). How are we to try to conceive of them? As endowed with meaning *by association* with sensations. In one's own language, therefore, sensation-names are associated with *one's own sensations*. But then, it seems, that with which a name is associated is 'inaccessible' to another person. So another person cannot in principle know what I mean by 'pain' (just as a blind man cannot know what we mean by 'eau-de-Nil').

1.1   '*associate* names with sensations and use these names in descriptions': (a) Note the adherence of this conception of a 'private' language to the Augustinian picture: words are names which are for use in describing how things are. (b) This conception is committed to the idea that first-person present-tense psychological sentences are *descriptions* of the inner, that what is called 'a description of the state of my mind' is precisely analogous to a description of the state of my room, save that the latter concerns the 'outer' and the former the 'inner' (see 'Avowals and descriptions'). To query this presupposition, shared by rationalists and empiricists alike, is one of W.'s fundamental innovations.

2   MS. 179, 12 notes:

> Private Sprache für Erlebnisse. Tagebuch über eine Empfindung. Zeichen mit dem natürlichen Ausdruck der Empfindung verkuppelt. Dann ist das Tagebuch für Alle gleich verständlich. Wie aber, wenn es keinen natürlichen Ausdr. der Empf. gibt? Wie weiss ich, dass ich dieselbe Empf. habe?

> (Private language for private experiences. Diary about a sensation. Sign bound up with the natural expression of sensation. Then the diary is equally intelligible to all. But what if there is no natural expression of the sensation? How do I know that I have the same sensation?)

2.1   'I simply associate names with . . .': it is noteworthy that in so far as the *Tractatus* had anything to say about the 'name-relation' that connects a name to an object, the connection seems to be associative. And the association was conceived as effected by a mental act of *meaning* by such-and-such a name THIS object (cf. NB 70).

SECTION 257

1   This explores the immediate consequences of the supposition of §256 and indicates the trajectory of the sequel. The first and obvious anxiety is raised by the interlocutor: sensation-names would not be teachable. W. brushes this aside, for this is the least of the troubles consequent upon the supposition. We may, for the sake of argument, assume that the child invents a name for the sensation, and so does not have to be taught (for the genesis of a capacity is irrelevant to the explanation of what the capacity is). The interlocutor still worries about the possibility of interpersonal communication: given that the clever child invents the words of this language that can be used to describe his inner experiences (PI §§243, 256), still he could not make himself understood by others. This was precisely the conclusion of §243, but it too is not the *punctum saliens*.

What is supposed by the interlocutor's movement of thought is that the child himself understands these sensation-names, and understands the descriptions of his experiences. The difficulties are supposed to emerge only when it comes to communicating his thoughts *to others*. It is this supposition that W. challenges with the question 'So does he understand the name, without being able to explain its meaning to anyone?' And it is this line of attack that is pursued in subsequent sections. Understanding, as has been argued, is akin to a capacity, and among the things which one who understands an expression (knows what it means) is able to do is: explain what it means. Hence giving a correct explanation is a *criterion* of understanding, and inability to give a correct explanation is a mark of lack of understanding. Is the 'private linguist' here supposed to know what the putative sensation-names mean, but *not* be able to say what they mean — to explain them to another? The answer must be 'Yes, that is precisely the supposition — but, of course, he can explain them to himself!' W. pursues that thread in the sequel, but for the moment he turns to a related issue.

The supposition of a 'private' language involves the idea that the speaker of such a language *names* his sensations (or, more generally, his 'inner experiences'). This is a pivotal component of the Augustinian picture of language: 'One thinks that learning language consists in giving names to objects, viz. to human beings, to shapes, to colours, to pains, to moods, to numbers, etc.' (PI §26). But this conceals the diversity in what is called 'naming' and the dependence, in each kind of case, of what counts as naming upon the language-game to which the specific naming is preparatory. Naming a person is preparatory to such activities as calling him, talking to him, announcing him, introducing him, attributing responsibility or liability to him, etc. Naming a colour is preparatory to a very different array of language-games; for we do not address a colour by its name, call it, modify its name into a pet-name or nickname. But we tell people to reproduce *this* ↗ colour by mixing paints, to bring some cloth which is the *same* colour as the carpet; and we describe objects as being red or green, darker or lighter than others, etc. In the grip of the Augustinian picture, we think that naming is merely a matter of *attaching* a name to a thing (be it an object, a shape, a colour, or a pain) and that the entire grammar of the name flows from the nature of the thing correlated with it. How is this 'attaching' done? In some cases we can hang a label on a thing, but doubtless the best glue is mental — we *associate* a name with what it names (PI §256)! And thinking thus, we forget that naming is preparatory to a host of *different* language-games, for to name something is to give a certain expression a *use* within a language-game. Something constitutes naming only when it is thus preparatory, just as one can only arrange the chess-pieces *in their positions* as preparatory to a game of chess — i.e. without the rules of the game and the technique of playing it, an alignment of carved pieces of wood on a chequered board is not positioning chess-pieces.

So what counts as naming a particular pain, e.g. a toothache? The conception involved in the supposed private language is explored in §§258ff. Here W. reminds us of the 'stage-setting' in the language that is presupposed if the mere act of naming a sensation is to make sense. That complex stage-setting is crystallized into the grammar of the expression. For if what is named is a *toothache* (and not something else), then we can both have the same one. Equally, to have a toothache is not to perceive what one has, and if I perceive that you have one, I don't thereby have one. So too, if I have what is named a 'toothache', I don't doubt that I have it (but not because I know it), whereas if you have a toothache, I may not know it or I may wonder whether you do, but be unsure. If it is toothache that is named, it must be in a person's tooth and not in his toe, let alone in the foot of his chair. And so on. If this and a multitude of further articulations did not hold true of what is named, then what is named is not toothache at all, for it will not be a kind of *pain, in a tooth*. In this sense the grammar of 'pain' shows the post where the new word is stationed. And if a certain word is not stationed there, then it is not the name of a *pain*!

1.1   (i) 'invents a name': if the child has not yet mastered a language, one might doubt the intelligibility of his *inventing* a name (cf. 'Private ostensive definition', §1).

(ii) 'dass Einer dem Schmerz einen Namen gibt': 'someone's giving a name to a pain', i.e. picking up 'seinen Schmerz benannt hat'.

(iii) 'shows the post where the new word is stationed': this echoes §29.

2   This early remark (BT 209v.; cf. Vol. XI, 91) occurs in the context of PI §§25–27(a), where the connection with the Augustinian picture is even more prominent than here. The emphasis upon the diversity of what is called 'naming' and its dependence upon what, in the language-game, follows the assignment of a name was a key preoccupation at this stage. PG 71 emphasizes that giving an ostensive definition of a colour-name is not a kind of consecration or mystical formula. Pointing and saying 'That's red' works only as part of a system containing other bits of linguistic behaviour. LPE 290f. applies this to sensation-names. Just as we are inclined to think that naming red requires only that one *see* red and say 'That's red' while pointing at it, so too we think that to name a sensation requires no more than

pronouncing the name while one has the sensation and possibly concentrating on the sensation, — but what of it? Does this name thereby get magic powers? And why on earth do I call these sounds the name of a sensation? I know what I do with the name of a man or a number, but have I by this act of 'definition' given the name a use?

'To give a sensation a name' means nothing unless I know already in what sort of game this name is to be used. (LPE 290f.)

When W. gave the lectures, he developed the idea further. In some cases we name an object by writing a name on it (although this too is very diverse; compare writing a name on a ship's bow, on the title-page of a book, on a medicine bottle, and on a sample). But there is no such thing as writing a name on a toothache. It seems as though each of us names the sensation *in foro interno*, so that no one else knows what is thus named. But this is a muddle. 'If we know what it is to give a name to a physical object, we don't yet know what it means to give a name to a pain. We can give a name to a pain — but we can only do this in cases where the pain is not private — where the word is to be used by all of us' (LSD 33). This point was further emphasized in the 'Notes for a Philosophical Lecture': in order to *establish* a 'name-relation' between a word and a sensation, we do not need a christening ceremony for private objects that lie before the mind's eye, but a *technique of use* for the name (MS. 166, 6).

SECTION 258

1   §256 established that in the 'private' language, words cannot signify sensations in virtue of being tied up with one's natural expressions of sensation, for then the language would not be 'private'. §257 argued that if sensations lacked behavioural expression, one could not teach the use of sensation-names. It might seem that each speaker might invent names for his own sensations, although, of course, no one else would be able to

understand them. This further explores whether one could then name one's own sensations and whether one would be able to understand these putative expressions in one's 'private' language. Imagine that one wants to keep a diary about the recurrence of a certain sensation. This is, after all, something one might well want to do, perhaps for the sake of recollection in tranquillity (Vol. XII, 136) or for medical purposes (Vol. XV, 256f.). And it is certainly something we can do. But now suppose that we conceive of doing so *in accordance with the model of the putative 'private' language*. So we think that to do so, one must *associate* the sensation with a sign, say 'S', and then simply write 'S' down in a calendar whenever one has a sensation. To show the incoherence of this conception is the purpose of §§258ff.

W.'s first move is that a definition, i.e. a *rule* for the correct use of 'S', cannot be formulated. Why not? Because 'S' is supposedly the name of one's own sensation, which another person can neither have nor know of. We naturally think that one can give *oneself* a kind of ostensive definition of 'S', and that this functions as a rule for the correct use of the sign. Admittedly, it is a peculiar ostensive definition in as much as there is no such thing as pointing privately to the sensation itself, any more than one can point at a visual image of red. But it seems as if concentrating one's attention on the sensation is a kind of mental pointing for oneself alone. So is *this* not a satisfactory private mental ostensive definition!

No, for the function of a definition is to establish the meaning of a sign, to provide a standard for the correctness of its subsequent use. Concentrating on one's sensation while saying or writing 'S' seems to effect just that, for we think of this as a matter of impressing upon oneself the connection between 'S' and the sensation. But this is an illusion; for while one can impress upon oneself, i.e. memorize, the connection between a sign and what it already signifies (e.g. that 'Tisch' means *that* and 'Sessel' *that* (cf. MS. 180(a), 27f.; MS. 179, 47), in such cases there is a criterion (i.e. a standard or norm) of correctness and hence too a criterion for remembering *correctly*. (If I look at a chair and say to myself 'That, in German, is called "Tisch"', then I have made a mistake.) But here we are not concerned with memorizing the connection between a sign and what, in accord with its explanation, it signifies in the practice of using the language. Rather we are trying to mimic, *in foro interno*, the procedure of giving it a use by an ostensive definition employing a sample. W. gradually builds up a case that here we have only the semblance of such a procedure. This remark contributes the single point that unlike legitimate cases of impressing upon oneself the connection between a sign and what it signifies, here there can be no criterion of correctness. Why is this?

The point becomes clear if we compare this putative mental ostensive definition with a typical ostensive definition of a colour-word. If I point at a patch of colour and say 'That ↗ (or that ↗ colour) is eau-de-Nil', I may subsequently say of a piece of material 'That ↗ material is eau-de-Nil'. If challenged (or if I am uncertain), I may refer to the sample, compare the colour of the material with the sample, and say 'This material is *that* ↗ colour, so it is eau-de-Nil'. Here the 'post at which "eau-de-Nil" is stationed' is already prepared; it is a colour-word, and bringing *this* material is a correct response to 'Bring something coloured eau-de-Nil', whereas bringing that Brunswick-green stuff is not. There is here a method of laying the sample alongside reality, hence a technique of using the defined expression in accord with this rule for its use. Whether I remember correctly the connection between 'eau-de-Nil' and the colour of which it is the name is precisely the question of whether I understand 'eau-de-Nil'. And the criteria for this understanding are whether I use 'eau-de-Nil' correctly, characterize things as eau-de-Nil only if they are the colour of the sample. (Of course, samples are not always *invoked* in applying colour-words, but these expressions make sense only within a language-game in which samples play an *essential* explanatory and justificatory role (LSD 121).)

However, the putative ostensive definition in the private language is crucially different. For here there is no criterion of remembering correctly the connection between 'S' and the sensation. In some sense, one might say, there *is* no connection between 'S' and a sensation save that one had a sensation and initially wrote 'S'. But what followed from that? Did one thereby give 'S' a use? Did one fix a rule for the correct use of 'S'? One is, of course, inclined to think that one did. For surely if one has it again, one should write down 'S' again! But, if one have *what* again? One wants to say: the *same sensation* again; but why *sensation*? For 'sensation' too is a word of our common language (cf. §261). And what counts as *the same*? What one had (and concentrated one's attention on) should, if it were really analogous to a sample in a public ostensive definition, give one a rule against which to measure subsequent uses of 'S'. ('The table is one metre long if it is *this* ↗ length' — and I point at a metre-rule.) But here one cannot compare what one now has with a sample (cf. Exg. §265). In this sense the normal criterion for remembering correctly the connection between 'S' and what it signifies (viz. correct application in accord with an appropriate explanation) is suspended.

Of course, it may seem to one that 'S' is connected with *this* (and one focuses one's inner eye on something). But is it? And what is *this*? And *what* connection does 'S' have with it? There is no answer. And in the absence of a distinction between seeming right and being right, there is no such thing as right. Hence there is no such thing as remembering correctly *or* remembering *incorrectly* the connection between 'S' and the postulated 'sample' sensation, not because memory is fallible (then one might remember incorrectly), but because there is no criterion of correctness, nothing that *counts* as right.

2   The manuscript material underlying this remark runs to many tens of pages. Some salient points from published and unpublished sources are:
    (i) PG 194 (Z §248) gives a machine analogy for something that superficially appears like a proposition but is not one. Imagine a design for a steamroller consisting of a motor inside a hollow roller. The crankshaft runs through the middle of the roller and is connected at both ends by spokes with the wall of the roller. The cylinder of the engine is fixed onto the inside of the roller. This looks like a machine, but it is a rigid system. Unwittingly we have deprived the piston of all possibility of movement.

    RPP I §397 comments on the unobvious depth of the analogy. One sees immediately that the machine cannot function, since one could roll the cylinder from outside even when the 'motor' is not running. But one may not see straight off that it is a rigid construction and not a machine at all. This is analogous to a private ostensive definition. For here too there is, as it were, a direct and an indirect way of gaining insight into the impossibility. (Presumably what W. meant was this: it is immediately obvious that another person cannot understand my private ostensive definition, and hence that a mutually intelligible language cannot incorporate such linguistic (explanatory, normative) devices. It is less obvious, but is the salient point of the arguments against the possibility of a private language, that such devices are, as it were, 'perfectly rigid', that I have unwittingly deprived ostensive definition of any possibility of functioning even in my own case.)
    (ii) One can concentrate one's attention upon one's pains or on a colour, etc. And there is such a thing as impressing upon oneself the meaning of a word. In the case of private ostensive definition we delude ourselves into thinking that by concentrating one's attention on one's

sensation, as it were pointing at it inwardly and repeating a sign 'S', one can impress upon oneself the meaning of 'S'.

Gazing at, concentrating one's visual attention on, an object is not pointing at something *for oneself* (Vol. XII, 189; LSD 38), although looking intently at something may well serve to indicate to someone *else* what one is speaking about. *A fortiori*, concentrating one's attention upon one's toothache is not a kind of pointing at it. Similarly, one can impress on one's mind what a word means, as one does when learning a foreign tongue. One can check whether one has done so successfully by running through the list of words in one's mind. But, of course, it is an open question whether one remembers *correctly* — which can be resolved by looking the words up in a dictionary. For here there is a distinction between being right and seeming to oneself to be right (MS. 179, 47). In the case of a private ostensive definition one is not actually impressing upon oneself the meaning of a word (but merely concentrating one's attention on one's pain and saying 'S'), and there is no distinction in one's later use of 'S' between being right and seeming right, hence no such thing as right.

(iii) The private, pseudo-ostensive definition is meant to establish the meaning of 'S', in order that the name be used for the sensation on later occasions. The definition should therefore provide a standard for correct use in the future. But on what occasions should 'S' be used? When one has 'a certain sensation'! But that does not describe an (unspecified) occasion for its use, for the 'certain sensation' is *unspecifiable!* 'What seems to be a definition didn't play the role of a definition at all. It didn't justify one subsequent use of the word' (LPE 291). We fail here to see the disanalogy between genuine ostensive definition and this pseudo-ostensive definition. If one gives a name to an object, one can revert to the original in order to justify subsequent uses of the name. 'Aber wenn ich nun dem Erlebnis einen Namen gebe, wie greife ich dann vom Namen auf seinen Träger zurück, auf das *das*, was ich benannt habe? Die Definition sollte mich ja *zurückführen*, aber hier ist ja nur eine Hälfte der Definition, sozusagen, erhalten geblieben' (Vol. XV, 243). ('But when I give [an] experience a name, how do I then reach back from the name to its bearer, to the *this* which I named? For the definition was supposed to *guide me back*, but here there remains, so to speak, only half of the definition.') Of course, it seems otherwise. For we are inclined to think that our memory supplies the other half.

(iv) We are, in these reflections, prone to allocate to the faculty of memory tasks which it makes no sense for it to fulfil.

Was mich zurückführt, ist also mein Gedächtnis; aber nun nicht in dem Sinne, in welchem es noch durch andere Tatsachen kontrolliert werden kann und man von richtiger oder falscher Erinnerung reden kann, sondern sein Ausspruch ist hier *allein* massgebend. Wir müssen also hier sagen: Die Definition, die ich jetzt gebe, *ist* die gleiche die ich damals gegeben habe, *wenn* mein Gedächtnis es mir sagt. (Vol. XV, 243f.)

(So what leads me back is my memory; but not in the sense in which it can be checked against other facts and in which one can speak of correct or false memory, but rather its pronouncement *alone* sets the standard here. So here we must say: The definition that I now give *is* the same as I gave before, if my memory says so.)

W.'s point does not concern the *fallibility* of memory, and the argument is not a form of scepticism concerning memory. 'I cannot remind myself in my private language that this was the sensation I called red. There is no question of my memory's playing me a trick — because (in such a case) there can be no criterion for its playing me a trick. If we lay down rules for the use of colour-words in ordinary language, then we can admit that memory plays tricks regarding these rules' (LSD 8). Scepticism about memory requires that it *makes sense* to talk of remembering *incorrectly*. But here there is no correctness or incorrectness; only that we sometimes write 'S' and sometimes do not (cf. Exg. §265). In fact we mislead ourselves here in talking of *memory* at all, for what reason do we have in the private language story for saying that, *as he remembers*, this is what he called 'S'? Is it because of the peculiar character of the mnemonic *experience* (the *feeling* or flash of recognition)? That leads to an infinite regress, for how does the imagined user of the private language know that *this* feeling is what he previously called the experience of remembering (Vol. XV, 244f.)?

(v) One is inclined to object that surely if I had a certain sensation and named it 'S', I can *recognize* when it occurs again! But, first, how is one supposed to discern the experience of recognizing *as* recognizing. 'Recognize' is a word in our public language, and there are characteristic expressions (*Äusserungen*) of recognition and criteria for whether someone recognizes something, none of which apply in the envisaged case (MS. 180(a), 29; cf. MS. 124, 227). Secondly, 'recognize' is a success-verb. 'We use "recognize" where we can say "it *is* the same and he *recognized* it".' But we cannot say this in the case of a person's avowals of sensation, since the criterion of its being the same is his saying that it is the same. Here there is no distinction between appearance and reality, and we cannot say 'He has toothache but does not recognize it' or 'He has no toothache, but it seems to him that he has' (LSD 111f.). One can say 'I have the same toothache as before', but not 'This is the same toothache and therefore I recognize it'. 'This really means that it is impossible to recognize it wrongly — in fact that there is not any such thing as recognition here' (LSD 111). Elsewhere W. calls into question the very idea of 'recognizing' one's sensation even in a public language.

(vi) Vol. XV, 258ff. discusses the unintelligibility of a private memory sample of a sensation. Surely 'S' in the diary tells *me* something, precisely because I remember what is called 'S'. But why 'remember'? How do I know that what I am doing is called 'remembering'? The answer cannot be that I have the experience of remembering that I previously used the word thus. The justification can only be an *outer* one, for it is either an explanation by means of words or by means of a sample. One could also put it thus,

> Man kann die Vorstellung nicht als Muster nehmen, denn sie wäre dann wie ein Muster, das zerstört würde, also keinen Nutzen hat. Die Erinnerung aber, kann mir nur insofern helfen, als sie als 'Erinnerung' beglaubigt ist//wird//.

(One cannot take the image as a sample for it would be like a sample that will be destroyed and so is of no use. But a memory can only help me in so far as it is ratified as 'memory'.)

2.1   'concentrate my attention on the sensation': LPE 315 queries what it is like to concentrate on an experience — 'If *I* try to do this I, e.g., open my eyes particularly wide and stare.' Cf. Exg. §275, 2.

SECTION 259

1   A coda on §258: 'whatever is going to seem right to me is right'. The private ostensive definition purports to be a rule of the putative private language. But what the rule for the use of 'S' is turns out to be whatever *seems* to me to be the rule. But this makes no sense. The rules for the use of names of sense-impressions are the 'balance on which impressions are weighed'; but one cannot weigh impressions on the *impression* of a balance (cf. §267 and Exg.), any more than an image of the result of an imagined experiment is the result of an experiment (§265).

1.1   'on which impressions are weighed': the text here is opaque. Are these impressions the impressions *of rules* referred to in the previous sentence? Or is this a reference to impressing on oneself the connection between a sign and what it signifies, discussed in §258? The latter possibility can be dismissed, since *Eindrücke* does not etymologically echo *sich einprägen*. The former can be ruled out by reference to MS. 129. Page 51 of the MS. begins the following sequence of remarks: PI §§272, 274, 275, 277 (from page 1 of the MS., indicated by W.), 278 and 280 (from pages 23–4, indicated by W.), followed by a draft of the present section (also relocated from page 24). In this context it is obvious that the 'impression' in question is a *visual impression* ('visuellen Eindruck' (PI §277)), a private impression of a picture ('Sein privater Eindruck des Bildes' (PI §280)) or colour-impression ('Farbeindruck' (PI §§275, 277)), which is also referred to as a *sensation* (PI §§272, 274). Hence this remark becomes clear if this sentence is read thus: 'The balance on which sense-impressions are weighed is not the *impression* of a balance.'

2.1   'is not the *impression* of a balance': MS, 129, 24 adds 'Wollte man nun fortsetzen: "sondern eine wirkliche Waage", so wäre dies zwar wahr; aber irreführend, weil der Ton nicht auf dem Unterschied zwischen wirklich und unwirklich ruht'. ('If one now wanted to continue: "but a real balance", this, to be sure, would be true; but misleading, for the matter does not rest on the difference between real and unreal.') This remark was crossed out. Perhaps W. here is alluding to the fact that in saying 'I have a pain' or 'I have a visual impression of red', I do not 'weigh' my sense-impression 'on a balance' at all. I just *say* these words — although 'This is not the *end* of the language-game: it is the beginning' (PI §290). It is *others* who assess my sense-impression on the balance that weighs the public criteria for being in pain or having a red visual impression.

Section 260

1   Reverting to the diary record of a 'private' sensation, how should we describe what the diarist is doing in §258? Should we conceive of him writing 'S' when he believes that he is having the same sensation as he previously named 'S'? This is how he conceives of the matter. W. replies ironically: is it not rather that he believes that he believes it? Why so? Because if, as argued, it is merely an illusion that 'S' is a meaningful sign, then there is no such thing as *believing* that one has S again (any more than there is such a thing as believing that la-di-da). By the same token, of course, there is no such thing as believing that one believes a nonsense. But one may say 'You just think (imagine, believe) that you believe something here, but you don't really have any belief at all'.

    This is confirmed by the opening question of §260(b), for it does indeed follow from the argument that the diarist made a note of nothing whatever. But this should not be surprising; making a mark or marks on a calendar is not *per se* making a note of something. That requires that the marks have a function in the practice of speaking a language (PI §51), but 'S' in the private language has no such function.

    (c) offers an analogy: there is such a thing as talking to oneself (as indeed there is such a thing as keeping a diary about one's headaches), but not every case of speaking when one is alone is a case of talking to oneself. The analogy suggests that babbling when alone is not talking to oneself. But the point may be more general: not all solitary coherent speech is talking to oneself (see Exg. §243, 2); complex criteria differentiate, for example, thinking one is talking to someone (although no one else is present) from reciting poetry in practice for tonight's performance, from prayer, exclamation, or talking in one's sleep or in delirium, and all of these from talking to oneself, as well as from babbling. Similarly, writing marks on a calendar (or in a diary) may be doing a multitude of different things, such as registering an appointment for next week or recording an appointment, making a note of a birthday or a wedding, keeping a record of one's pains, etc. Or it may be none of these, but just doodling. Whether it is one or another depends on the context, and the variegated criteria that fix the different concepts of making appointments, keeping records, etc., and the use of the marks in other speech-activities.

2   MS. 129, 44 contains PI §260(a)–(b), but instead of (c) continues:

> Frage Dich, was der Sinn, der Zweck, einer Notiz ist. Denke *so*: Ist es nicht merkwürdig, dass wir manchmal Zeichen in einen Kalender einschreiben — wozu tun wir das eigentlich?

> (Ask yourself, what is the sense, the purpose, of a note. Consider: Is it not curious that we sometimes write signs in a calendar — why do we actually do this?)

W. does not answer (but goes straight on to PI §261). Vol. XII, 136 explores one possibility in the imagined case of the diarist. Perhaps, when he reads his diary later, it will enable him to recollect his experiences. Can we then say that the diary tells him something? But what does this consist in? Surely in the experiences of recollection which he has when he reads it! But, W. concludes, not everything that makes us recollect something can be said to communicate something to us. If looking at a row of trees makes him remember something, one would not say that the row of trees tells him something. The moral is that one should look closely at the language-game of communicating information, of telling someone something, and examine the analogue of this language-game when it is played by oneself. This is parallel to the examination of what counts as talking to oneself.

2.1   (i) 'Well, I *believe* that this is the sensation S again': Vol. XVII, 26ff.

explores the question differently. Does the following black spot

rest on these struts and this foundation (cf. RFM 378)? And does my use of the word 'black' rest on *recognizing* the colour, and my use of 'pain' on my *remembering* that I previously called *this* 'pain'? A *picture* is involved

here, and it clashes, not with the facts, but with *other pictures*. If we claim
that 'When he later has a certain feeling, he says "I have a pain"', this
makes it appear as if one could find out, by identifying the feeling (which
one, as it were, looks at), whether he uses the word correctly. Someone
who claims this lacks a clear picture of the use of this sentence. One form
of expression here clashes with another (one language-game is being
projected onto another). We are inclined to say 'If I later have this feeling,
then I say "I have a pain"' (as we might say 'If I later see this colour, then
I say "That object is eau-de-Nil"'). But should one not say 'If I later
believe that I have the same feeling . . .', or even 'If I believe that I believe
this'? (For in the language-game with colours, one *can* intelligibly say 'If I
later believe that I see this colour, then I say . . .'). But it obviously
makes no sense to say: 'I believe that what I have now is a pain, because it
is the same as what I had before, and what I had before I called "pain".' It
looks as if the sentence 'If I later have *this* feeling . . .' articulates a
criterion of identity for pain which determines the correctness of my
saying 'I have a pain' (as 'If I later see *this* ↗ colour, then I'll say . . .'
articulates a criterion of identity for such-and-such a colour, in as much
as it presents a defining sample). But this is a complete misrepresentation
of the language-game with 'pain', as well as a misinterpretation of 'If I
have the same feeling then I say . . .'. For this phrase does indeed say
something about our language-game, but not what we initially think it
does. It says something about the grammatical relationship between
'same feeling' and 'pain', viz, that we use 'pain' always for the same
feeling, not for a different one on every day of the week (which would be
possible too).

(ii) 'perhaps you believe that you believe it': a further strand could be
added to the argument, parallel to Exg. §258, 2(v). The diarist is not in
the position to insist that he *believes* that it is S again, for how does he
know that *this* is believing and not something else? For 'belief' too is a
word in our common language with public criteria for its (third-person)
application, not the name of a 'private experience' (cf. §261).

SECTION 261

1   In §260 the interlocutor retorted in astonishment, 'Did the man who
made the entry in the calendar make a note of *nothing whatever?*' The
story was that when the diarist has a certain sensation, he writes 'S',
which is a sign he has associated with the sensation (§258). So surely he is
making a note of a *sensation*! Not so, for 'S' so far has no function (§260).
But 'sensation' is a word of our common language for the (third-person)
use of which there are public criteria. We often know whether someone
else is feeling this or that sensation, and different people may have the

same sensation. *In as much as 'S' is meant to name what can be known only to the person speaking* (PI §243) *and cannot be had by anyone else* (cf. PI §253), 'S' cannot be the name of a *sensation* (cf. PI §257); 'S' cannot be stationed by this signpost any more than a sign pointing north can be placed at the North Pole.

One may remonstrate that when the diarist has what he wishes to designate by 'S' he surely *has something*, not *nothing* (cf. Exg. §§294, 296, 304). But this is of no avail, for 'has' and 'something' too are words of common language, with rules for their correct use. A person may *have* pains, but also emotions, thoughts, and love affairs, not to mention adventures and debts. In each case there are criteria for saying of him 'He has . . .' which are familiar to us all. But what criteria justify saying of the envisaged user of a private language that he *has* . . .? 'Something' too is a word of our public language, with rules for its common use. I may have something in my pocket (a penny), but not a pain; something may cross my mind (a thought), but not a penny. If I say 'I have something in my pocket' and am asked what it is, I must be able to produce it or provide a description, even if only of the form 'I don't know what it is; it is round, flat, and metallic, but it is not a coin'. If I look through a microscope and say 'I see something but I don't know what it is', I must be able to describe what it looks like, e.g. 'It is irregular in shape, covered with small dots, etc.' In short, 'something' is a place-holder for a sample or (provisional) description — it is not itself, as it were, a *minimal description*. The use of 'something' is complex and variegated, depending upon what it is a place-holder for (see Exg. §294, 1). But it is a mistake to think, as the interlocutor here intimates, that its role is to signify what is, as it were, so minimal that it cannot be gainsaid. What justifies saying of the diarist that at any rate he has something? Something about which nothing can be said provides no such justification (cf. PI §304).

We, as philosophers, are reduced to trying to characterize what role 'S' has in the private language by an inarticulate noise. We now want a sound *unconnected with grammar* to name what the diarist has, for 'something' was wrongly supposed to be the next best thing to such a noise in so far as it seemed to have a location independent of any signpost at all. But while an inarticulate sound can be given the role of an expression signifying something, this is possible (intelligible) only in a language-game. And what seems to be a language-game of keeping a diary of 'private' experiences is not one at all. §270 picks up the theme.

2.1 'So the use of this word stands in need of a justification which everybody understands': i.e. the use of the word 'sensation' in our common language. But when I say that I still have a pain in my shoulder, the same burning sensation I had yesterday, do *I* have a justification? No, of course not. But this is just what misleads us here. For now it seems

that if I say this and have no justification, then I am unjustified in saying
it, i.e. that I should not say it. Is it not the *pain* that justifies my saying 'I
have the same painful sensation as yesterday'? Here we misconstrue the
grammar of 'justify' and edge ourselves, quite naturally, into the position
under attack. MS. 124, 227f. clarifies this in the sequel to an early draft of
PI §260.

> Mit welchem Recht reden wir hier von 'gleich', von 'Empfindung', 'wiedererkenn-
> en', und 'glauben'? Denn das sind ja alles Wörter unsrer allgemeinen Sprache.
> Er hat ja eben kein Kriterium der Gleichheit! — Aber wenn er's nicht hat, dann
> haben wir's ja auch nicht, und doch reden wir von gleichen Empfindungen. — Ja,
> aber wir brauchen hier kein Kriterium; so wenig wie eines dafür, dass wir Schmerzen
> haben. Denn wir in unsrer Sprache benutzen die *Äusserung* des Schmerzes. Und wir
> *benutzen* sie zu verschiedenen Zwecken. Während wir vorgaben, dass jener Mensch in
> seiner privaten Sprache die Empfindungen wie *Dinge* benennt, die er in einem
> Guckkasten sieht, in den nur er allein schauen kann.

> (With what right do we talk here of 'the same', of 'sensation', 'recognizing', and
> 'believing'? For these are all words of our common language.
> He has no criterion of sameness! — But if he hasn't one, then neither do we, and
> nevertheless we talk of same sensations. — Yes, but we need no criterion here; as
> little as we need one for our having pains. For we, in our language, use the
> *avowal* of pains. And we *use* it for different purposes. Whereas we took it that the
> person names sensations in his private language like *things* which he sees in a
> peep-show which only he can look at.)

3   James nicely exemplifies these confusions:

> Any fact, be it thing, event, or quality, may be conceived sufficiently for purposes
> of identification, if only it be singled out and marked so as to separate it from other
> things. Simply calling it 'this' or 'that' will suffice . . . The essential point is that it
> should be re-identified by us as that which the talk is about . . . .
> In this sense, creatures extremely low in the intellectual scale may have conception.
> All that is required is that they should recognize the same experience again. A polyp
> would be a conceptual thinker if a feeling of 'Hollo! thing-umbob again!' ever flitted
> through its mind.[15]

SECTION 262

1   One can give an ostensive definition of, say, a new colour-word, but
that presupposes the grammar of colour, which provides 'the post where
the new word is stationed' (§257). A bare ostensive gesture, *a fortiori* a
mere concentration of one's attention on a sensation, does not give a sign
a *technique of application* (cf. PI §§30, 33–6). The proponent of the

---

[15] James, *Principles of Psychology*, Vol. I, pp. 462f.

possibility of a private language thinks that he can dispense with this, for it seems that he can supply the technique for the use of 'S' by inwardly undertaking to use 'S' in such-and-such a way. But how does he undertake this? His answer is given in §§263–4. It is clear that he cannot have found the technique ready-made, since then it would involve the grammar of 'sensation', which is a word of common language with public criteria for its application (in third-person cases). So he must invent it! Of course, he will deny this, insisting instead that he reads the technique of using the word off *the nature* of the private object.

Note that PI §34 has pointed out that 'to intend the definition in such-and-such a way' does not stand for a process which accompanies giving a definition, and §205 (cf. §337) that such intentions are *not* independent of pre-existing techniques.

SECTION 263

1   This clarifies what the wayward interlocutor thinks his invented technique of application for 'S' is, viz, to call *this* 'pain' (= 'S') in the future, and also how he thinks he undertakes to use 'S' thus, viz. by concentrating his attention on his feeling. But, as argued, the 'this' provides no criterion of identity for pain (PI §253), and concentrating one's attention on a feeling is not a criterion for intending to use a word in accord with a certain technique of application.

SECTION 264

1   This makes it clear that the interlocutor is firmly caught in the web of the Augustinian picture. The entire grammar of an expression seems to unfold from knowledge of what it stands for, i.e. acquaintance with the object named. This conception yields a distorted picture of understanding and of the criteria of understanding.

SECTION 265

1   It seems to us that by a private ostensive definition one can correlate a sign with a sensation, and that by concentrating one's attention one can impress upon oneself this connection, so that in future one will re-member it right (PI §258). W. has already argued that in this case there is no criterion, i.e. no standard, of correctness. Here the same point is made by means of a contrastive analogy.

We consult a dictionary to justify translating 'Tisch' as 'table'. We can imagine someone with a vivid visual memory trying to remember what 'Tisch' means by calling to mind the image of the relevant page of the dictionary. Whether he remembers what it means can be checked against the actual dictionary. But could he not have a purely private dictionary, i.e. one that exists *only* in the imagination? Could he not consult his mental dictionary to see what a certain word means? Of course, it would be a purely subjective justification for the use of the word in question!

Note that the 'private dictionary' is analogous to a private table of samples correlated with words, as might be envisaged by the defender of the possibility of a private language. If there can be public tables of samples (e.g. colour-charts), surely there can be private ones which exist only in the imagination? Hence one might think that the process envisaged in §258 might yield something akin to a mental table of samples.

But the idea of justification by reference to a private dictionary is incoherent. For justification consists in appealing to something independent. Otherwise 'whatever is going to seem right to me is right. And that only means that here we can't talk about "right"' (PI §258). The interlocutor objects, for we surely do appeal from one memory to another for confirmation; e.g. as I remember, the next train leaves at 12.35, but if unsure, I might call up an image of the timetable I was looking at yesterday, and if, as I thus imagine it, the time that follows 11.15 is 12.35, I shall rest satisfied. This is possible, for it parallels the above case of trying to remember what "Tisch" means. In both cases calling up a mnemonic image can have a confirmatory role only because it is an image of something objective, and hence can itself be tested for correctness. Here there is a manifest difference between remembering correctly and remembering incorrectly. But in the case of a dictionary that exists only in the imagination, *a fortiori* in the private diarist's case, there is no such distinction. He endeavours to remember what a word means *only* by reference to his memory of what it means. And *that* cannot be checked for correctness. There is here no *possibility* of an appeal to something independent, hence the manoeuvre he has in mind is like buying a second copy of *The Times* to check whether what is written in the first copy is correct. If the only thing *it makes sense* to appeal to in trying to remember what a word means is his memory of what it means, then 'whatever is going to seem right to me is right. And that only means that here we can't talk about "right"' (§258). §265(b) drives the point home.

1.1   (i) 'etwa ein Wörterbuch': 'a dictionary, for instance'.
    (ii) 'an eine unabhängige Stelle appelliert': 'consists in appealing to an independent authority'.

(iii) 'Nein; denn dieser Vorgang . . .': 'No, for this process must actually call forth the *right* memory.' The right memory here is the memory of what a certain word *means*, and the intelligibility of remembering correctly presupposes that something *counts* as correct. In the timetable case, misremembering involves an error which it *makes sense* to check against the actual timetable. Here, however, there is no further check; whatever is called forth is 'right'. But that means that there is no right or wrong — for the balance on which impressions are weighed cannot be the impression of a balance (§259). The issue is *logical*, not epistemological.

2   LSD 8f. confirms that scepticism about the reliability of memory is not at issue (cf. Exg. §258, 2(iv)).

Philosophers who conceive of ordinary language as discourse between speakers of private languages, i.e. who view public language as the congruence of private languages, imagine that each person possesses his own 'private dictionary'. W. discussed this aberration in Vol. XV, 87ff. (cf. 'Private ostensive definition', §4). It is a bogus explanation, which does no work at all (see Z §552).

Vol. XII, 249 has this preceded by the following discussion. One wants to say 'Surely I say that I have pains because that is how it really is'. But is that supposed to explain the use of the expression 'I have pains'? How can it do so when it presupposes it? One might, however, say this in contrast to saying '. . . because that is part of the role I am learning by heart'. What one would really like to say is 'Surely I say I am in pain because *this here* is the case'. Of course, if one says this and accompanies it with a demonstration which, after all, 'this here' demands, no one will want to contradict this explanation. The interlocutor now queries: 'Whence then the illusion that the words are a description of a feeling?' That is not an illusion, W. replies; the illusion is that the sentence 'Pains are *this* feeling' is an explanation even when it is unaccompanied by a *demonstration*. One would have to speak here of an explanation which can *only* be laid down in one's memory.

2.1   (i) 'No; for this process has got . . .': Vol. XII, 249f. was even more emphatic — 'Nein; denn es ist ~~(hier)~~ wesentlich, dass dieser Vorgang // Prozess // erfahrungsgemäss // wirklich // hilft, die *richtige* Erinnerung hervorzurufen' ('No; for it is essential ~~(here)~~ that this event // process // in fact // actually // helps to call forth the *right* memory'). There PI §265(b) is followed by a further analogy: it is as if, when playing dice, one were to determine the value of a throw by a further throw.

(ii) '(As if someone . . .)': Vol. XVI, 126 offers a different simile — isn't this as if I let my mouth confirm that what my hand writes is correct?

Section 266

1   The first of three remarks elaborating §265. The clock is the analogue
of one's memory. I can look at the clock to see what time it is, as I can
'consult my memory'. But I can also look at the clock face to guess what
time it is (e.g. if it loses time or perhaps has stopped) or move the hands
of a clock (that has stopped) till their position strikes me as right. In each
such case, however, there is an external, independent check on what time
it actually is — a way of determining whether the clock is *right*, whether
my guess is *correct*, whether its look's striking me as right is a true
intuition. But that is just what is *absent* in the case of looking up the table
(dictionary) in one's imagination.

1.1   '(Looking at the clock in the imagination)': cf. PI §607.

Section 267

1   A further variant on §265(b). Just as the image of the result of an
imagined experiment is not the result of an experiment, so too imagining
justifying the choice of dimensions for an imagined bridge is not
justifying an imagined choice of dimensions. Justification of dimensions
for an imagined construction takes the same form as for an actual
construction, viz. appeal to laws of mechanics, properties of materials,
etc. Hence one must cite genuine calculations and experiments to justify
an imagined construction being envisaged thus rather than otherwise.
Imagining calculations and experiments is to *imagine justifications*, not to
justify anything at all. Of course, an engineer might employ mental
images heuristically in elaborating his justification for his choice of
dimensions for a bridge (whether actual or only imagined in wishful
thinking). He might call to mind a page of an integral table in carrying
out a calculation or review an experiment in his mind's eye. But any such
justification is parasitic on ascertaining the reliability of his imagery in
relation to the objective standard of actual table and concrete experiment.
It is these that carry the real burden of justification.
   The idea of a private language is incoherent precisely because it fails to
distinguish imagining a justification for using a word and justifying the
use of a word in one's imagination (e.g. by recollecting a page in an
actual dictionary).

1.1   'Aber würden wir . . .': 'But would we . . .'.

SECTION 268

1   Giving oneself a 'private definition' in the manner described no more has the consequences of a genuine definition (viz. determining a standard for the correct use of an expression) than my right hand's putting money into my left has the consequences of a gift. The latter does not comply with the grammar of 'giving a gift', and similarly the former does not accord with the grammar of 'giving a definition'.

SECTION 269

1   A provisional summary linked to the last sentence of §268.

1.1   'Sounds . . . which I *"appear to understand"*': e.g. 'speaking with tongues'; this too might be called 'a private language'.

SECTION 270

1   In §258 we were asked to imagine wanting to keep a diary about the recurrence of a certain sensation (perhaps a pain or a feeling of nausea (Vol. XV, 256)). To do so on the private language model of associating the sensation with a sign 'S', giving oneself a private ostensive definition of 'S', inwardly undertaking to call THIS 'S', remembering what one previously inwardly called 'S', have all been shown to be incoherent. On those presuppositions no definition of the sign can be formulated; there can be no criterion of correctness for its use. A sensation, unlike a public sample, cannot (logically) provide one with, or be used as, a private standard for the correct use of a word.
    Now we are to envisage a genuine use for the entry of the sign 'S' in my diary. Suppose I discover that whenever I have a particular sensation, my blood-pressure, as measured by a manometer, has risen. So now I might keep a diary for medical purposes and enter 'S' whenever I think my blood-pressure has risen, i.e. whenever I have the sensation experientially correlated with rising blood-pressure. I might report to my doctor that my blood-pressure must have risen last Tuesday and Thursday, for I entered 'S' in my diary on those days (cf. Vol. XV, 257). This is perfectly intelligible.
    But might I not misidentify the sensation, think I recognize it, but be mistaken? The criticism of the private language theorist's conception, after all, turned on the unintelligibility of a private standard of correct-

ness for the use of 'S' as the name of a sensation and on his inability, within the constraints which he has set, to determine what he 'has' as the same again. Does the same difficulty not arise here? No! To be sure, if I recognized the sensation, then I might misrecognize it. If I had to *identify* my sensation, then it would make sense for me to identify it wrongly; and I would need a criterion of correctness against which to check my identification. If I had none (and a private object cannot provide one), then the inference about the rise in my blood-pressure would be unfounded. But 'S' here (in §270) is not assigned a meaning by private ostensive definition. I write 'S' in my diary whenever I believe my blood-pressure to have risen on the ground that I have had the particular sensation which I have found to be correlated with rising blood-pressure. It makes no sense to speak of my making a mistake about whether I have a certain sensation, for 'I think I have a certain sensation, but I may be wrong' is nonsense. The supposition of misidentification here (unlike the case in §258) is vacuous – but not because I happen to have an unbroken record of correct identifications, rather because no question of *identification* arises.

I can show that my inference about my blood-pressure is not unfounded because, *ex hypothesi*, I *am* able to say that my blood-pressure is rising, and I am able to say this *precisely because* of my sensation. (I don't infer it from *nothing*!) The supposition that I might regularly misidentify the sensation is wholly vacuous, an ornamental knob which does not connect with the mechanism. How do I *know* that I have the sensation? That too is a senseless question. Does this not mean that what I really discovered was that whenever I *believe* I have it, my blood-pressure rises – but my belief might be mistaken? No, it makes no sense to talk of *believing* one has a sensation (see 2 below).

The private language theorist will doubtless feel that W.'s story deprives him of the very thing — the private object that functions as a defining paradigm — which makes 'S' a sensation-word rather than an empty mark. §270(b) is a response to the interlocutor's puzzlement that we can speak of a *sensation*-word here *without* the collateral of a paradigm. What is *our* reason[16] for calling 'S' the name of a sensation here? W.'s reply is schematic: 'perhaps the kind of way this sign is employed in this language-game'. Evidently this stands in contrast to the pseudo-sensation-name in §§258, 260f. There the sign had no genuine use at all. Here it is used to register the occurrence of a particular sensation indicating (as I have discovered) that my blood-pressure has risen. And, presumably, I might explain this to the doctor. Further, I might say 'Look, I wrote "S" in my diary four times last week, so my blood-

---

[16] Not: what is *my* reason? The question is whether my use of 'S' satisfies the *public* criteria for sensation words.

pressure must be brought under control', or 'The pills you gave me are working, for that particular sensation is occurring less frequently — see, I wrote "S" only once last week'. Perhaps, too, the doctor might talk of my S-sensation.

Similarly, the private language theorist conceived of the private paradigm as providing a criterion of identity for the sensation. How else could one determine that what one has is the same again? Has W.'s story not eliminated the very thing that makes it intelligible to speak of the recurrence of the *same* sensation? No; I do not recurrently write 'S' in my diary because I observe that what I recurrently have matches a paradigm, anymore than I clutch my jaw when I have toothache because what I have is *this* ↗, and one clutches one's jaw when one has *this*. Rather, I just write 'S' or 'S again'. And in this language-game with blood-pressure-indicative sensations, *that* I recurrently write 'S' is a criterion for others to say in these circumstances: 'He has the same peculiar sensation, so his blood-pressure must be rising.'

1.1   (i) 'Nehmen wir an . . .': 'Let's suppose that I regularly make a mistake in identifying it.'

(ii) 'die Annahme dieses Irrtums . . .': 'The supposition of this mistake was mere show.'

(iii) 'Perhaps the kind of way . . .': It is unclear what qualifications, if any, is intended by the 'perhaps'. MS. 165, 229 has the rather more emphatic 'Nun vielleicht eben die Art und Weise . . .'.

2   The above interpretation is controversial. The source material is therefore given in some detail. The origin of the blood-pressure example is MS. 165, 145ff. Its introduction is in a context in which it is perspicuously genuine sensations that are at issue. We can, W. notes, on the basis of our sensations, make *immediate* inferences and predictions about processes in our brain, nerves, and organs. That is the point of the otherwise confused claim often made that one's states of consciousness are only another aspect of brain processes seen 'from the inside'. Then:

Wenn Du Schmerzen hast und daraus auf hohen Blutdruck schliesst, wirst Du doch nicht sagen wollen, Du habest aus *nichts* auf hohen Blutdruck geschlossen.

Und wie ist das Experiment zu beschreiben: Du beobachtest Deinen Blutdruck und siehst zu, wie er von Deinem Schmerzzustand abhängt. Dabei aber rufst Du nicht durch äussere Mittel die Schmerzen hervor, sondern vergleichst nur ihren Verlauf mit dem des Blutdrucks. Denk Dir nun, statt Kreuzchen in einen Kalender einzutragen wenn er Schmerzen hat, mache er dies Experiment! Ist das kein Experiment? Wird es nur dadurch zu einem, dass er einem Ausdruck der Schmerzen hat? Kann er nicht eben die Veränderung des Blutdrucks richtig, für jeden sichtbar, voraussagen?

Und hier spielt wieder das '*richtige*' Wiedererkennen seiner Empfindung gar keine Rolle, denn es genügt dass er sie wiederzuerkennen *glaubt*, da dass wichtige Resultat das *richtige* Voraussagen der körperlichen Erscheinung ist. Und daher muss es auch falsch sein, wenn ich sage, er *glaube* die Empfindung wiederzuerkennen.

(If you have pains and infer therefrom a high blood-pressure, you would not want to say that you inferred a high blood-pressure from *nothing*.

And how is this experiment to be described: You observe your blood-pressure and watch how it depends on the state of your pains. But you do not produce the pains by external means, rather you compare their course with that of the blood-pressure. Now imagine that instead of entering little crosses on a calendar when he has pains, he makes this experiment! Is it not an experiment? Does it only become one by his having an expression of the pains? For can't he just predict correctly every perceptible change in the blood-pressure?

And here again the '*correct*' recognition of his sensation plays no role at all, for it suffices that he *believes* that he recognizes it, since the important outcome is the *correct* prediction of the bodily phenomenon. And hence too it must be wrong when I say, he *believed* that he recognized the sensation again.)

The theme is resumed only on p. 227 of the notebook. There, preceded by a draft of PI §260(b), we find the first draft of PI §270(a). It is quite close to the final formulation. This is followed by:

Wie eher, wenn wir so sagen wollten: Er ist geneigt, immer wieder das selbe Zeichen ('E') zu gebrauchen // einzutragen //; darum sagen wir, er habe die gleichen Empfindungen. (Ähnlich etwa: Er ist geneigt, beim Beten nach oben zu schauen; darum sagen wir, Gott sei in der Höhe.) (MS. 165, 228f.)

(How if we wanted to put it like this: He is inclined always to use // enter // the same sign ('S') again; therefore we say he has the same sensation. (Perhaps like: He is inclined to look upwards when praying, therefore we say, God is on high.))

That is, the use of the same sign does not *rest on* an inner identification or recognition, but is a criterion for *others* to judge that the speaker (or diary-keeper) has the same sensation. (Cf. LPE 287: 'What is the criterion for his connecting the word always to the same experience [of having a red visual image]? Is it not often just that he calls it red?')

This remark is followed by a draft of PI §270(b), which opens, however, with a version of the first two sentences of PI §260:

'Empfindung' ist aber ein Wort der allgemeinen Sprache. Welchen Grund haben wir, 'E' die Bezeichnung für eine Empfindung zu nennen? Nun, vielleicht eben die Art und Weise, wie sie in diesem Sprachspiel (Steigen des Blutdrucks) verwendet wird. (MS. 165, 229f.)

(But 'sensation' is a word of common language. What reason have we for calling 'S' the name for a sensation? Well, perhaps just the kind of way in which it is used in this language-game (rising blood-pressure).)

This is evidently meant to contrast with the vacuous employment of 'S' in the private linguist's diary. For the next remark is a full draft of PI

§261 (this begins on the last page of the notebook (p. 230) and continues on p. 42, where W. had evidently left an empty page). This in turn is succeeded by another draft of §270(b).

It is noteworthy that the three paragraphs from MS. 165, 145ff. were transcribed with only minor modification into MS. 124, 282f. They do not, however, occur in MS. 129. MS. 129, 46 has PI §270 after PI §§258, 260, 261; it is followed by PI §§209(b) – (c): we hanker for a *deeper* explanation or a deeper understanding.

2.1   '*richtig* widererkannt habe, oder nicht': MS. 165, 227 adds 'oder ob Du den Glauben richtig als Glauben erkennst' (or whether you recognize the belief correctly as belief).

Section 271

1   One might monitor the fluctuations in one's blood-pressure (given the scenario of §270) by writing 'S' in one's diary whenever one has the sensation found to be correlated with rises in blood-pressure. The supposition that one might be mistaken in identifying one's sensation is vacuous (one does not *identify* one's sensation). A similarly vacuous supposition (free-wheeling cog) is examined here: can we imagine a person who cannot remember what 'pain' means, and so calls different things 'pain', but nevertheless uses the word whenever he hits himself, burns or cuts himself and screams, etc., etc.? No! If he uses 'pain' as we all do, then he does remember what it means (which is not to say that he remembers what inner thing is named 'pain').

Note that it would be a mistake to assimilate §271 into the argument of §270, as if what makes the hypothesis of error a mere show in §270 is that I might misidentify the sensation *and* misremember which sensation indicates rising blood-pressure. §271 is a *parallel* vacuous hypothesis, *not* part of the argument of §270.

2   LSD 9 supposes someone to have learnt what 'toothache' means ('Now I know what "toothache" means' sounds as if he has been given a sample, but that, W. emphasizes, is wrong). The next day he says 'Now I have a toothache, I know what it is like, etc.'. Would it make sense here to ask 'What if he has something entirely *different* today?' Only if one doubts whether he has learnt what 'toothache' means.

2.1   'whose memory could not retain . . .': the absurdity of the supposition can be invoked to dissolve the illusion of a 'private' object: 'Always get rid of the private object in this way: assume that it constantly changes, but that you do not notice the change because your memory constantly deceives you' (PI p. 207).

Section 272

1   Pain has occupied centre-stage hitherto; now W. switches to colours. Pain seemed to be defined by reference to a private sample; but that is an illusion, not because it is defined by reference to a public sample, but rather because it is not defined by reference to a sample at all. Colour-words are defined by reference to colour-samples, but because we typically apply colour-words such as 'red' without recourse to samples or colour-charts, we are inclined to misconstrue this and to project upon colour-concepts features of the grammar of 'pain' *as conceived on the private language model*. And we are further encouraged to do this by misconstruals of scientific investigations into light and visual perception. Bedazzled by such misunderstandings, it is easy to think that the real samples that define colour-concepts are private sense-impressions or 'sensations' (cf. 1.1 below), and that the last court of appeal for the application of colour-words is a private ostensive definition. §§272–8 dispel this illusion.

What is characteristic of a 'private language' is not that each person has his own exemplars by reference to which he explains and uses the words of his language. For that, after all, is perfectly intelligible; we might have our own tape-measures or colour-charts, which we could compare to ensure that we mean the same by '1 metre' or 'red'. Rather is it the supposition that each person's exemplar is essentially private, and hence that nobody knows whether others mean by 'red' *this* (and one concentrates one's attention upon one's own sense-impression) or something else. The immediate consequence of this would be that it is intelligible, though unverifiable, that what one section of mankind calls 'red' differs from what the rest call 'red'.

W. evidently holds this assumption to be unintelligible. But note that the objection to this assumption is not that it would be unverifiable and therefore meaningless. W. is not relying on the principle of verification as a premise in an argument. One should not argue: it is unverifiable, so it must lack meaning. Rather, one should ask: what is called 'having a red visual impression'? What are the criteria for saying of two people that 'they have the same colour-impression'? When is one licensed to say 'I have a different colour-impression of this than you?' We should examine the use of these phrases (for they do have a use) and the ways in which they are explained. The deep objection to the assumption of §272 is the one already spelt out, viz. that each person would not know what he *himself* means by 'red', for if the meaning of 'red' were 'determined' by a mental table of samples, then whatever seems right is right, and that means that there is no such thing as right (PI §§258, 265).

1.1   'eine Rotempfindung': the German 'Empfindung' is somewhat more flexible than the English 'sensation'. It is potentially misleading to speak of *sensations* of red (where? — in the eye or in the brain?), but W.'s point is clear enough. §§276–7 talk, with no sense of discontinuity, of *Farbeindruck*.

2   W. discussed the problem of 'spectrum inversion' in *extenso* in LPE, LSD, and Vol. XV, 87ff. (cf. 'Private ostensive definition', §4, for part of this discussion).

3   In MS. 124, 291 this occurs *after* §273 and is followed by §§274–5, then 'James ist eine Fundgrube für die Psychologie *des Philosophen*' ('James is a rich source for the psychology of *philosophers*'). On this topic, James, like von Helmholtz and numerous others before and since, argued:

> The real colour of the brick is the sensation it gives when the eye looks squarely at it from a near point, out of the sunshine and yet not in the gloom; under other circumstances it gives us other colour-sensations which are but signs of this — we then see it looks pinker or blacker than it really is . . . But all these essential characteristics, which together form for us the genuine objectivity of the thing and are contrasted with what we call the subjective sensations it may yield us at a given moment, are mere sensations like the latter.[17]

Section 273

1   We communicate to each other information about the colours of objects, obey orders to paint the wall blue or requests to bring something red. So does 'red', for example, signify something 'confronting us all'; but further, strictly speaking, each of us should have another word to name his own 'private' sense-impression of red? (If so, of course, the latter word could be understood only by the speaker himself.) Or is it rather that 'red' is actually ambiguous, signifying both something with which everyone is acquainted and, in addition (for each person), something epistemically private? Or is it that it signifies (*bezeichnen*) something known to us all, but *refers* (*sich beziehen*) to a 'private' sense-impression? These questions stem from a misconstrual of the use of defining samples and misunderstandings of meaning, explanation, and understanding.

[17] James, *Principles of Psychology*, Vol. I, p. 286.

1.1   (i) 'bezeichne': name, signify, or designate; it is important to co-ordinate this translation with §293.

(ii) 'etwas "uns allen Gegenüberstehendes"': this does not occur in early drafts (MS. 165, 178; MS. 124, 290f.) but only in MS. 129, 50. It seems to be a quotation from Frege's *The Basic Laws of Arithmetic*, Introduction, p. xviii, where there is an implied play on 'Gegenstand' and 'gegenüberstehen': 'Since the number one, being the same for everyone, confronts everyone in the same way, it can no more be investigated by making psychological observations than can the moon.' Frege thought that

no one has another's idea, only his own, and no one even knows how far his idea — e.g. of red — coincides with another's; for I cannot express what is peculiar to the idea I associate with the word 'red'. To be able to compare one person's idea with another's, one would have to unite them in the same consciousness, and one would have to be certain that they had not changed in being transferred.[18]

Hence he nicely exemplifies the confusions of §273 in this remark:

The word 'white' ordinarily makes us think of a certain sensation, which is, of course, entirely subjective; but even in ordinary speech, it often bears, I think, an objective sense. When we call snow white, we mean to refer to an objective quality (*so will man eine objektive Beschaffenheit ausdrücken*) which we recognize in ordinary daylight, by a certain sensation . . . Often . . . a colour-word does not signify (*bezeichnet nicht*) our subjective sensation, which we cannot know to agree with anyone else's (for obviously our calling things by the same name does not guarantee as much), but rather an objective quality. (FA §26).

Cf. BB 72f.

It is noteworthy that parallel to the temptation to conceive of 'red' as meaning both something known to oneself alone and something 'confronting us all' is the temptation to think that 'pain' means both something essentially private *and*, in a quite different sense, something confronting us all, viz. such-and-such behaviour. This strategy was essayed in *Philosophical Remarks*, Ch. VI.

3   The conception here alluded to is enshrined in the representational idealist tradition running from Descartes to Boyle, Locke and Newton, through Reid and von Helmholtz, to the present day.[19] On the one hand, what 'confronts us all', colour 'as it is in the object', is 'a certain disposition of the superficial parts of the object to trouble the light to reflect after such-and-such a determinate manner'.[20] On the other hand,

[18] G. Frege, 'Review of Husserl's *Philosophy of Arithmetic*', repr. in Frege, *Collected Papers on Mathematics, Logic and Philosophy*, ed. B. McGuinness (Blackwell, Oxford and New York, 1984), p. 198.

[19] See P.M. S. Hacker, *Appearance and Reality* (Blackwell, Oxford and New York, 1987), Ch. 1.

[20] R. Boyle, *The Experimental History of Colours, Works II* (London, 1744), p. 19.

'the more proper, though not the usual acceptation of the word colour',[21] is the private sensation which reflected light causes 'in us'.

SECTION 274

1   The switch in §273 from 'signify' (*bezeichnen*) to 'refer' (*sich beziehen*) is of no avail, but it is what one is inclined here to say (cf. §254). It is a hallmark of the misguided thought that I know what I mean by 'red' *because* I can call up a private sample of red in the imagination. Of course, I do know what I mean by 'red' (and can tell you); and equally, I can call up a visual image of red at will. But in telling you what I mean by 'red', I would use a public sample (or refer you to one); and a visual image of red is not a sample of red.

1.1   (i) 'more psychologically apt': why so? 'beziehe sich auf' here implies something one draws out from within oneself.
        (ii) 'auf die eigene Empfindung': 'at my own sensation'.

SECTION 275

1   W. elaborates upon the 'particular experience in doing philosophy' mentioned in §274. The thought that colour-words signify or refer to something 'private' does not cross one's mind when using colour-names in the bustle of life, but only in philosophical reflection as in §273, i.e. when language is idling (PI §132). Also, he might have added, when misconstruing scientific theory concerning the nature of physical objects and their light-reflective propensities and misunderstanding the causal explanations given in physiological psychology.

1.1   '(Consider what it means "to point to something with the attention")': cf. Exg. §258, 2(ii).

2   BB 66 remarks: 'To get clear about philosophical problems, it is useful to become conscious of the apparently unimportant details of the particular situation in which we are inclined to make a certain metaphysical assertion.' For example, (a) One is more tempted to say 'Only this is really seen' when staring at unchanging surroundings than when one looks around while walking (BB 66). (b) One is inclined to think that 'red' means one's own visual impression when one looks at a bright colour in which one can 'immerse oneself' (PI §277). (c) One is inclined to locate 'the self' in the head when one says 'self' to oneself and

[21] Ibid., p. 6.

concentrates one's attention while trying to analyse its meaning (PI §413). (d) 'The phenomenon of *staring* is closely bound up with the whole puzzle of solipsism' (LPE 309).

This preoccupation with the phenomenological context of the metaphysical urge evidently dates back to 1916, when W. succumbed to it:

> If I have been contemplating the stove, and then am told: but now all you know is the stove, my result does indeed seem trivial. For this represents the matter as if I had studied the stove as one among many things in the world. But if I was contemplating the stove *it* was my world, and everything else colourless by contrast with it. . . . For it is equally possible to take the bare present image as the worthless momentary picture in the whole temporal world, and as the true world among the shadows. (NB 83).

(See 'The world of consciousness', §1.)

Vol. XII, 224ff. reflects on different ways of seeing things: as we normally do; as 'the visual room' which is 'a world' which does not belong to a subject; as objects painted on a screen (cf. LPE 311), etc.

> Und worin besteht es denn: die Dinge so und so sehen? — Manchmal und teils darin, dass man den Blick ruhen oder wandern lässt und darin, wie er wandert; oder darin, dass man ganz *Auge* ist, und in dem, was wir dabei sagen und *nicht* sagen; in Gesten, die wir machen; und vielem andern.
>
> Mancher dieser Eindrücke erhalten wir nur, wenn man auf einen Fleck starrt; manchen nur, wenn alle Gegenstände um uns in Ruhe sind, nicht wenn sich etwas bewegt; manchen wohl nur im Zimmer, wenn alle Entfernungen klein sind; und wenn die Menschen immer im Freien philosophierten, würden sie auf manche Gedanken nicht kommen.
>
> Man kann sagen: wenn wir philosophieren, feiert nicht nur unsre Sprache, sondern auch unser Blick. Denn während ich den Ofen heize, sehe ich ihn anders, als wenn ich beim Philosophieren auf ihn starre — denke ich nicht an den 'visuellen Ofen', das Sinnesdatum, etc.

> (And what does seeing things thus-and-so consist in? — Sometimes, partly, in letting one's gaze rest or wander, and in how it wanders; or in that one is wholly *an eye*, and in what one then says and does *not* say; in gestures we make; and in much else.
>
> Some of these impressions we obtain only when we stare at a spot; some only when all objects around us are at rest, and not when something moves; some indeed only indoors when all distances are small; and if people always philosophized in the open, there would be some thoughts that would never occur to them.
>
> Certain of these impressions we obtain only when we stare at a spot; some only when all objects around us are at rest, and not when something moves; some indeed only indoors when all distances are small; and if people always philosophized in the open, there would be some thoughts that would never occur to them.

3   Schlick nicely exemplifies this sort of 'experience when doing philosophy':

when I look at the blue sky and lose myself in the contemplation of it without thinking that I am enjoying the blue, I am in a state of pure intuition, the blue fills my mind completely, they have become one, it is the kind of union of which the mystic dreams.[22]

Section 276

1   Here the interlocutor reverts to the initial questions in §273. Note that the first sentence (in the German) is in quotation marks.

1.1   (i) 'meinen': in contrast to 'bezeichnen' and 'sich beziehen' in §273.
(ii) 'and name our colour-impression': the characterization of how something sensibly impresses one is not a description of what one perceives (RPP I §1081), though it may subserve such a description. (If the impression is blurred, it does not follow that what one sees is blurred — though it may be if it is a poor photograph.)

Section 277

1   This connects the phenomenology of illusion with the misconceptions of colour-words under scrutiny. §274 noted the 'particular experience when doing philosophy' of, as it were, casting a sidelong glance at one's own sensation, etc. The experience is one of a philosophical illusion, and it is facilitated by the fact that one's gaze is idling. In these circumstances the misconstrual of grammar is smoother and easier. When one looks at a red object and says 'That's red' (meaning that the object is the colour known to us all), and when one looks at it, thinking 'red' to mean one's current sense-impression, one does not attend to the object in the same way. But, of course, the difference in attention is not like the difference between looking at the shape and looking at the colour of an object. There is a genuine difference in the mode of attention, but one is not attending to different things. Rather, when one 'immerses' oneself in the colour, it is easier to generate the illusion that there is one use of colour-words according to which they mean something wholly private, viz. one's own current visual impressions of colours.

1.1   'I immerse myself in the colour': cf. LSD 101.

[22] M. Schlick, 'Form and Content: an introduction to philosophical thinking', repr. in *Gesammelte Aufsätze* (Georg Olms Verlag, Hildesheim, 1969), p. 194.

SECTION 278

1   The interlocutor thinks that this proposition should be accompanied
by an 'inward glance' at the visual impression; and that makes no sense.
But this proposition does have a use, e.g. 'Ah! *I* know how the colour
green looks to me — it looks cool and fresh and sleek, whereas red looks
hot and angry', or, having put on colour-distorting spectacles, I might be
at a loss to specify how green looks to me and then exclaim 'I know how
green looks to me — it looks like the colour of the faded rug in the attic'.

SECTION 279

1   An analogy for the misconception discussed in §278. The sense-
impression is no more a confirming measure of 'how green looks to me'
than laying my hand on my head and saying 'I know how tall I am' is a
measure of my height, confirming what I say. 'How does green look to
you?' is answered by pointing at something 'outer' and saying 'Like *that*',
not by 'pointing' inwards.

2   Vol. XII, 339 adds in parentheses 'Ich bin hier' ('I am here'). One
might analogously claim 'But I know where I am, viz. *here*'. Hence the
joke 'Mummy, mummy, where is Daddy? We're lost!' — 'No, dear.
Daddy is lost — we're here!'

3   In Chapter 1 of *Alice in Wonderland*, Alice eats the cake but is not sure
whether she will grow larger or smaller. 'She ate a little bit, and said
anxiously to herself, "Which way? which way?" holding her hand on the
top of her head to feel which way it was growing, and she was quite
surprised to find that she remained the same size.'

SECTION 280

1   A final analogy to illuminate the illegitimacy of the supposition of
perceptual predicates' (e.g. 'red') having a double meaning (cf. §273). A
theatrical or cinema director may sketch on paper roughly (*etwa*) how he
imagines a scene. On the model of §273 it might seem that such a picture
has two distinct representative functions. For others it represents the
scene they are to create as the person envisages it. It tells them how he
imagines the scene. But for him it represents his mental image of the

scene which only he knows (since only he *has* it). Indeed, his visual impression of the picture he has painted *tells him* what he has imagined in a way in which, for others, it cannot. For in his case, his visual impression *of* what he has painted must surely *coincide* with the mental image he had when he imagined the scene!

This is a muddle. To paint what I imagine is not to *copy* a picture that is already 'painted' in my imagination (although I can, of course, imagine painting something, and then go on to paint what I imagined painting). The director's sketch does indeed represent how he imagines the scene; i.e. to the question 'How do you think it should look?' he might produce the sketch and say 'Like that'. This is what is *called* 'representing what I imagined it should look like'. But it is erroneous to think that the picture represents *to him* what he imagined in any different sense, for it does not represent it in virtue of *resembling* his mental image, any more than the verbal expression of what he thought *resembles* his thought. It informs others how he imagined things should look, but it does not inform him! What makes the picture a *good* representation of what he imagined? Not its likeness to his mental image, but rather his avowed acknowledgement that *that* was what he had in mind. But that acknowledgement does not rest on an 'inner glance' at his mental image. 'The image is not a picture, nor is the visual impression one. Neither "image" nor "impression" is the concept of a picture, although in both cases there is a tie-up with a picture, and a different one in either case' (Z §638). Hence it is a mistake to think that when I paint a picture to show you how I imagine a scene, the picture is a piece of information or a representation *for me*. It is an articulation or expression of how I imagine the scene, not an 'outer' picture of an 'inner' picture. Moreover, an impression of a picture is not a *representation* of a picture (cf. PI §366).

Similarly, although hearing the word 'red' may call forth a mental image of red (or of a field of poppies or a sunset), the answer to the question 'What do you mean by "red"?' is given by pointing to a sample. And if I ask myself 'What do I mean by "red"?', the answer is no different.

1.1   'Sein privater Eindruck des bildes sagt ihm . . .': 'His private impression of the picture tells him . . .'

2   In MS. 129, 23 this remark follows PI §§291, 278 and is followed by PI §259. It is thus linked with the important theme of the logical heterogeneity of *description*. Cf. Z §637: 'The descriptions of what is seen and what is imagined (*des Vorgestellten*) are indeed the same kind, and a description might be of the one just as much as of the other, but otherwise the concepts are thoroughly different.'

> Men, minds and machines
>   1. Human beings and their parts   2. The mind   3. Only in the
>   stream of life . . .   4. Homunculi and brains   5. Can machines
>   think?

SECTION 281

1   Sensation-words (or words for inner experiences) are tied up with
natural behavioural expression (PI §§244, 256). The categorial implications of this are now examined (§§281–6). Does it follow that there is
no pain without pain-behaviour and, *pari passu*, no perception without
perceptual response in behaviour, no thought without the expression of
thought (cf. PI §360)? This is a misunderstanding. Of course one can
have pains and not manifest them, see or hear things and not respond to
every passing sight or sound, think various thoughts and not voice them.
(Yet what is intelligible as happening some of the time may be senseless if
envisaged as happening all the time!) W.'s point is not reductionist.
     Only to a living human being (not a corpse) and what behaves like a
human being does it make sense to attribute psychological predicates *or
their negations*. Of a human being we may say that he sees or is blind, also
of a dog or a horse. But a tree or a table neither sees *nor is blind*; a robot
that responds to verbal instructions does not hear, and if it is malfunc-
tioning, it is not *deaf*; a computer, no matter how complex, is not
conscious, nor is it *unconscious* (or should we say 'One day it will
awake'?). One might add that the same applies to predicates of behavioural manifestations of the inner and their negations (e.g. 'smiles',
'laughs with amusement' (or 'ironically', 'cruelly', etc.)) and a wide
range of predicates of action.
     The theme of §281 is resumed in a different vein in PI §357–61.

1.1   (i) 'It comes to this . . .': note that a seemingly metaphysical question
is transformed into a grammatical one about what one can intelligibly
say.
     (ii) 'only of a living human being and what resembles it . . .': but also
pots in fairy-tales or dolls in play (cf. PI §283) and spirits (PI §360). But
these are essentially secondary uses *parasitic* on the primary application to
human beings (cf. Exg. §283, 1), and *different* from it (the gods hear our
prayers even if our words are drowned by noise, indeed even if
unspoken, and our deeds are not concealed from their sight even by
opaque solid doors).

(iii) 'and what resembles (behaves like)': how far must the resemblance reach? There is no clear answer, but not because of *ignorance*. Our concepts of possessing a perceptual faculty, of consciousness, of susceptibility to pain are essentially indeterminate at *this* boundary. It makes no sense to attribute pain to a table (save in fairy-tales) or a plant, but what of a wriggling fly (PI §284)? Here the concept gets a foothold — but no more; can a fly have aching joints?

(iv) 'It has sensations': why the asymmetry with 'sees; is blind; hears; is deaf'? 'Insensible' implies lack of consciousness, and numbness is itself a sensation. But one might say: has pain; is free of pain.

(v) 'it sees; is blind': whether it sees or fails to see this or that is not in question, but only whether it has or lacks a visual faculty.

2   MS. 165, 95f. introduces these reflections (and those of §282) in the context of the question of whether W. had not made things too easy for himself in the builder's language-game (PI §2) in as much as he had supposed circumstances (the construction of a building, building components, etc.) which are so similar to ours:

> Nein, die Sprache ist ein Teil des menschlichen Lebens und was diesem ähnlich ist. Und wenn im Märchen Töpfe und Pfannen mit einander reden, so gibt das Märchen ihnen auch noch andre menschliche Attribute. Ebenso wie ein Topf auch nicht lächeln kann, wenn er kein *Gesicht* hat.

> (No, language is a part of human life and of what resembles it. And if pots and pans talk to each other in a fairy-tale, still the tale gives them other human attributes too. Just as a pot can't smile, if it has no *face*.)

Later (MS. 165, 126f.) W. queries whether one who lacks a language can imagine things. But that amounts to the question of whether it makes sense to say of one who can give no expression to the imagination that he imagines something. Well, can a fountain-pen imagine things? And if not, why not? But in a fairy-tale one can talk of a fountain-pen's imagining things!

MS. 179, 56 picks up the theme of PI §281: the interlocutor concedes that W. is *not* arguing that there can be no sensation which is not expressed, but now further queries whether W. is not claiming that a creature that has no *capacity* to express sensations could have none.[23] W. replies: we couldn't // wouldn't // talk of sensations if there were no natural expression of sensations. 'Doesn't see' and 'is blind' mean the same (as do 'doesn't hear' and 'is deaf'); one does not say 'This man is

[23] That one may have sensations when paralysed is no objection. For neither the criteria for being in pain nor the criteria for *not* being in pain are satisfied. But after recovery from total paralysis, the criteria for *having been* in pain or not having been in pain are obvious enough.

blind, but perhaps he still sees'. (By implication, one cannot say 'The table does not see', for that is not like 'The table does not grow'; one does not know what it would be for a table to see! (cf. Z §129).) Does this mean that if there were no expression of sensation, there would be no sensations in the world? Can't one imagine them? — One then thinks of sensations floating around the world (as Hume did[24])!

Vol. XII, 338 observes that there can be a psychology only for beings whose behaviour resembles that of human beings.

SECTION 282

1   The interlocutor invokes ascription of psychological predicates to inanimate objects in fairy-tales as an objection to §281. W. concedes the point, but not as an objection. In fairy-tales pots are not inanimate; if they see and hear, they also talk, and to that extent resemble (behave like) human beings. If they see and hear, what do they see and hear *with*? And if they talk and smile (MS. 165, 96), do they not have mouths?

The interlocutor rightly objects that we surely *understand* fairy-tales. They relate what is not the case, but they are not *nonsense*! But, W. replies, this oversimplifies. Is it not a kind of nonsense to talk of pots seeing and hearing? Certainly we do not think that as a matter of empirical fact pots do not perceive or talk. We do not even have a clear picture of what it would be for a pot to talk. There are many different kinds of nonsense, and neither such a fairy-tale nor 'Jabberwocky' is nonsense as mere babbling is. (Just as Escher's 'impossible' etchings are not scribbles.)

Such uses of psychological predicates, like children's ascription of pain to dolls, are essentially secondary uses. A secondary use of an expression is parasitic on the primary one in as much as the secondary use would not have the significance it does if its prototype did not exist (it, as it were, echoes the primary use). Can one imagine ascribing pain to and pitying *only* dolls? The parenthetical analogy clarifies the parasitism: children who play trains but do not know what trains are or what they are for would not understand their game as our children do. It could not make the same *sense* to them as it does to us. (Similarly, imagine playing monopoly in a society lacking the institution of money and private property.)

---

[24] Hume thought that as a *matter of fact* there were no 'perceptions' that did not exist in 'bundles', i.e. in relations of causation and resemblance to others. James was agnostic, maintaining that we have no means of ascertaining whether in the room there is a mere thought that is no one's thought.

1.1   'is a secondary one': PI p. 216 elaborates — talking of days of the week as fat or lean or of vowels as coloured are secondary uses of terms. 'It is only if the word has the primary sense for you that you use it in the secondary one.' (Imagine colour-words being used *only* of vowels!) The meaning of the relevant word is *explained* by reference to paradigms involved in the primary, not the secondary, use.

2   MS. 124, 239 adds, after PI §282(a) – (b) and a remark about children playing, the observation that in magical and religious rites, inanimate things are treated as if they were animate. MS. 179, 67 notes that the child who says that his doll is ill does not believe that the doll is alive. *One* language-game can be played thus, *another* not. (If the parent rushed the doll to the hospital, the child would not understand what was going on, for *that* was not the language-game it was playing.)

2.1   (i) 'the fairy-tale only invents what is not the case: it doesn't talk *nonsense*': RFM 264 observes that in a fairy-tale the dwarves might pile up as many gold pieces as there are cardinal numbers. 'What can occur in this fairy-tale must surely make sense.' (As much, and as little, as the pot calling the kettle black!)
    (ii) It might appear that the example of playing trains is a poor illustration of the relation of a secondary to a primary use of an expression, precisely because the children of the alien culture *can* play trains, i.e. stand in a line holding on to each other and then shuffle along shouting 'chuff-chuff' and 'toot-toot', etc. But a secondary use of an expression is essentially parasitic on the primary use and without it has no sense. W. might defend his analogy by querying in what sense it is *trains* that they play. LW §800 observes, 'Only children who know about real trains are said to be playing trains. And the word "trains" in the expression "playing trains" is not used figuratively, nor in a metaphorical sense.'

SECTION 283

1   §283(a) reverts to §281, viz. that only to living human beings and what behaves like them can one attribute sensations, etc. What gives us the idea that beings (*Wesen*), which are objects (*Gegenstände*), can feel? W. explores this question in order to undermine the false dilemma upon one horn or the other of which Cartesians and anti-Cartesian materialists impale themselves. For it seems that sensations, perceptions, indeed consciousness itself, must be attributable either to physical things, viz. bodies (and if bodies, why not stones?), or to quite different things, indeed different substances, viz. minds or souls, which some bodies

have. But can a *body* have a pain? And if not, is it the soul which the body has that has the pain? But how can a body *have a soul*? And how does one get oneself into this pickle? *Inter alia*, by the natural thought that experience is 'private'.

It is tempting to think that we teach children sensation-words by getting them to associate such words with the sensations which they have (cf. Z §545). Then a child knows what 'pain' *means*; now he must learn to apply the word to objects outside himself, in conformity with the way we all use the word. So he must not ascribe pain to stones, plants, etc. But apart from the requirement of conforming to our use of 'pain', why should he not ascribe the idea of what he has to stones? (If he can imagine some other *person's* having what he has (cf. IP §302), why can't he imagine a stone's having it too? If he is to imagine a pain he does not feel on the model of a pain he does feel, why should he not imagine a stone's having one?)

§283(c) starts by strengthening the supposition. Can't I imagine that I turn into a stone while my pain continues, and would that not be a case of a stone's having a pain? If I can imagine it, surely it makes sense. In which case the grammatical remark of §281 is wrong. Consequently, W. places pressure on the supposition: in what sense will the stone have pains? Since stones cannot manifest pain (i.e. there *is no such thing* as a stone manifesting pain), how could the pain, which we suppose to continue after I turn to stone, be the stone's? Indeed, why, in this case, should it be *anyone's* pain?

One might reply that *ex hypothesi I* (*a bearer of pain*) *continue* to feel pain, and I can surely have a pain without manifesting it. This is correct, but (a) I do not *identify* myself as the bearer of pain when I have a pain or say to myself that I am in pain. (Nor, indeed, does *what* I say when I say to another 'I am in pain' identify the bearer. Rather it is my saying it, which is typically an *expression* of pain, that identifies who is in pain.) (b) That there is *sometimes* pain which is not manifest (a point conceded by implication in §281) does *not* imply that it is intelligible that there be bearers of pain who logically cannot manifest it (e.g. statues and stones). (c) If it is further argued that there is no such thing as *unowned* pains (suffering without sufferers), hence that in the imagined petrification *I* am the bearer of the pain, then it is partly conceded that the stone is not, or not directly, the bearer of the pain.

§283(d) takes up this point: one thinks here that *I* continue to have pain after *my body* has turned to stone. So the bearer of pain is the soul (self, mind, *res cogitans*, 'that which in us perceives and thinks'[25] (cf. BB 69, 73f.)) and the stone has pains 'indirectly' in as much as its soul has a pain.

---

[25] I. Newton, *Optics: or a Treatise of the Reflections, Refractions, Inflections and Colours of Light*, 4th edn (William Innys, London, 1730), p. 345.

But this is nonsense. For stones do not *have* souls (or pains): it is people, living beings, who laugh and weep, act and react, i.e. *behave* in an infinite variety of ways in the circumstances of life, who *have* souls. The representational form of ownership misleads us here, for we think that 'having' signifies a relationship between two substances (as indeed it does in 'A has (owns) a house'). But '*my* body' does not signify a relation of ownership between me and my body,[26] although it may be said that he who sells himself into slavery, sells his body but not his soul. (Yet note that he who sells his soul to the Devil does not cease to *have* a soul when he dies!) 'I have a body' is at best a grammatical proposition or a rhetorical exclamation, as is 'I have a soul (or mind)'. But 'My body has a soul' is nonsense. So too, it is absurd to suppose that a stone, e.g. my petrified body, might *have* a soul.

§283(e) reiterates the grammatical observation of §281: only of what can manifest pain in behaviour can one say (truly or falsely) that it *has* pain. And what thus manifests pain in behaviour is *a living human being* (and animals that behave like one). Mere bodies do not exhibit pain, indeed do not *behave* — for it is not the body that weeps and cries out, clenches its teeth and resolves not to complain, etc. Living human beings *have* bodies, but they are not identical with their bodies (cf. 'Behaviour and behaviourism', §4).

§283(f) is ironic (a supposition confirmed by §286 and BB 73f.), indeed a *reductio ad absurdum*. One must surely attribute pain *either* to a body *or* to a soul which some body has! (Either I or my materialist adversary must be in the right!) What *else*, the Cartesian will ask, is there to attribute pain to? Well, nothing *else*, no *third thing* over and above body and soul, but *not these either*.

1.1   (i) 'drawing my attention to feelings in myself': the supposition is that adults get the child to name his sensations by private ostensive definition. Cf. PI §258: 'I concentrate my attention on the sensation, and so, as it were, point inwardly.'

(ii) 'Seele': in this context, 'soul' or 'mind' indifferently.

(iii) 'Only of what behaves': frequentative, not occurrent.

2   MS. 165, 150ff. discusses this theme in the context of the general observation that the absurdity against which W. battles is that semi-solipsism which says that I am intimately acquainted with sensations in as much as *I* have them, and that I then generalize my own case. But the *concept* of pain is acquired in learning a language, and from this concept how can one arrive at the idea that there can be sensations without a bearer? That must rest upon a misconstrual of the concept. But 'to smell a rat is ever so much easier than to trap it'.

[26] Much of the early debate about natural rights turned on this misconception.

Then follows the supposition that one might turn to stone (or that one's body might disappear — the one supposition is just as good as the other) yet one's experience continue. But *which* experience? It is no good saying 'The one I am having now', for in order that that should make sense, I must have a criterion for the persistence of the same sensation. (For 'sensation' and 'same sensation' must have the same meaning for me as for others.) Why must I have such a criterion (after all, as things are, I don't employ a criterion in my own case)? Because on this supposition the sensation is severed from its expression and left hanging in the air[27] (cf. PI §288(c)). Then follows (after a detour through PI §421) a draft of PI §290: in the actual language-game with 'sensation' I do *not* identify my sensations but simply use the same word; but with us this is the beginning of the language-game, not its terminus (see Exg. §290).

MS. 124, 240f. explores the same issue in the context of a variant of PI §282. Couldn't my pains persist though I changed to stone? Would they cease to be *pains* just because I had lost the ability to express them? To be sure, the *stone* does not *have* pains! One would have to say that it is just a matter of fact that hitherto my pains were had by a human being, or indeed by *something*. But what this 'having' really means is that their actual expression is a cry (for he who cries out, flinches, etc. is he who is said to *have* the pain). And (by implication) is that supposed to be just a matter of fact?

W. adds that someone might take what he has said as a proof that it does make sense to say that a stone has pains or that one can never know whether a stone has pains or not, or even that disembodied or indeed unowned pains can exist. If one is stupid enough, he concludes, one can draw all manner of inferences here. In the sequel he explores how one slides down this slippery slope. It *is* curious that one is inclined to say that one's pains could persist though one had changed to stone. One supposes this because one can imagine opening one's eyes and finding that one's body is insensible, that one might see one's leg being cut off but feel nothing at all, that it might feel as if one were moving one's limbs, but they were motionless, etc. Indeed, one could imagine seeing one's body carted away, although one's visual field did not change save for no longer containing part of one's body. But now, *does* it make sense to suppose that there is before me in space a disembodied being who sees without eyes, indeed sees from a particular vantage-point in space, hears without ears, etc?

MS. 129, 19 has PI §283 *after* PI §302.

---

[27] MS. 124, 285 adds here 'and needs a new underpinning'.

Section 284

1   Living beings are said to feel; stones and other inanimate things are not. One cannot even get the idea of ascribing pains to stones (except in fairy-tales), save by the philosophical *cul-de-sac* of §283, for the concept of pain can get no grip in the absence of (the possibility of) behaviour that expresses pain. We *react* differently to what is alive, *respond* differently in countless ways. These natural reactions are not the product of a theory or hypothesis, nor are they the foundations for one, but rather the bedrock of our language-games. Furthermore, we do not merely see living people *move* in certain ways, we see them smile amicably, scowl in anger, grimace in pain as well as *acting* intentionally, deliberately, etc.

1.1   (i) 'pain seems able': The 'seems' is noteworthy. The category boundaries are *not* clear, and this indeterminacy is an important feature of such concepts (see Exg. §281, 1.1(iii)).

(ii) 'das Lebendige'/'das Tote': 'the living'/'the dead': There is no suggestion in §284(b) that the living are 'things'.

(iii) '"from quantity to quality"': a Hegelian, and later a Marxist, term of art signifying an abrupt qualitative change resulting from a marginal quantitative change. Here W. responds to the interlocutor's query as to whether the 'mere movement' of a creature can make a difference between the unintelligibility and the intelligibility of predicating pain by pointing out that here there is a *categorial* difference. CV 74 invokes the same phrase apropos the change in the *character* of a musical theme when played at different tempi. (Cf. also MS 165, 120 and RPP II §145.)

Section 285

1   This illustrates the 'transition from quantity to quality' of §284. The difference between a friendly smile, a wry, sarcastic, ironic, or cruel smile may be no more than a *minute* difference (a thousandth of an inch) in the orientation of the lips, but we recognize it — and not by *measuring* the difference. And we describe facial expressions thus, and would not explain our different descriptions by reference to measurement. For we *react* differently to such different facial expressions (cf. LA 30f.). And we can *reproduce* such expressions without looking in the mirror, i.e. without checking on the precise disposition of our features. It is an important fact of human nature that we are immensely sensitive to the play of features on a human fact. We *see* friendliness in a face; we do not

infer it from such-and-such a facial configuration which we know (by looking in the mirror?) accompanies our own friendly feelings.

2.1   'Think, too, how one can imitate . . .': cf. Z §220.

Section 286

1   This is a direct continuation of §283(f).[28] *Does* one have to say of a body that it has pains? Isn't it, rather, absurd — the Cartesian may urge — to say that? And in acknowledging that it is absurd, are we not recognizing the truth of a metaphysical thesis? '. . . it is as though we looked into the nature of pain and saw that it lies in its nature that a material object can't have it. And it is as though we saw that what has pain must be of a different nature from that of a material object; that, in fact, it must be of a mental nature' (BB 73). This is doubly confused. For, in the first place, it is not the soul that feels pain, but the human being. And, secondly, the absurdity of attributing pain to the body is not because of gross factual (or even 'metaphysical') error. That it is not my hand that feels pain, but I in my hand is a *grammatical* truth.

'Is it the body that feels pain?' looks like an empirical question, but as soon as one reflects upon how it might be decided, what experiments might determine it, it becomes evident that it is not. We do not say 'This body feels pain' any more than we say 'This body must take an aspirin' or 'This body must keep a stiff upper lip'. Of course, we *could*; but that would involve a shift in grammar and an alteration of concepts (cf. BB 73f.). How does our existing grammar (our attribution of pain to a *person* and our ruling out such attributions to a body as senseless) show itself? With what features of our life does it smoothly mesh? If someone has hurt his hand, his hand does not avow pain; *he* does. He may nurse his hand, but we comfort *him*.

1.1   'Wie macht es sich geltend': 'plausible' smacks of *belief*, which can be true or false; so better, 'validate itself', 'show itself', or 'claim recognition'.

2   Vol. XVI, 243ff. has the interlocutor query whether one can say 'My *body* loves, meditates, intends, etc.' Why not?, W. replies. This way of speaking is, after all, not yet 'occupied', i.e. this logical space has not yet been made (it is neither true nor false that my body loves). The interlocutor misunderstands: would it be *true* to say such a thing? It

---

[28] In MS. 129, 20 and MS. 179, 69f. it follows directly after PI §283.

would be true, W. responds, if the corresponding proposition in our current notation were true.

SECTION 287

1   A coda to §286: one comforts the *sufferer*, not his hand. *What* one pities (the object of one's pity) is not the hand, but the person whose hand it is. That comes out in the fact that one looks into his face, talks to him, puts one's arm around his shoulder. And this constitutes the natural background of the *grammatical* fact that it makes no sense to pity a hand.

SECTION 288

1   Having clarified the concept of the subject of sensations (§281–7), W. now reverts to first-person sensation-sentences, building on the example in §283. The supposition of turning to stone yet one's pain continuing is one which severs the concept of pain from the criteria of its application to others, in as much as pain, in this case, could not intelligibly have any behavioural expression. Given this supposition, how do I (who have turned to stone) know that what persists is *pain*? The interlocutor balks: I *can't* be in error here; 'I have a pain' is a Cartesian thought, and *cogitationes* are transparent. If I have a *cogitatio*, I *know* that I have it; it means nothing to doubt whether I am in pain!

It is true that it means nothing, but not because I *know* that I am in pain. Doubt is excluded not by certainty, but by grammar! An expression of doubt about whether one has a pain or something else (barring borderline cases, e.g. 'It's unpleasant but it doesn't really *hurt*') can only signify that the speaker does not know what the word 'pain' *means*. For since there is no such thing as doubting whether one is in pain, an expression of doubt here is a criterion for not knowing what the word means.

One can explain what 'pain' means to a person who does not know this English word, perhaps by enacting injury and showing how someone behaves when he hurts himself, viz. by crying out 'Ow! That hurts!' Or one might prick the learner with a pin, and when he starts and cries 'Ow!', one would say 'See, that's what pain is'. This explanation (see 1.1 below) might be understood, misunderstood, or not understood, like any other. How the person goes on to use the word after having been given the explanation will show (is the criterion of) whether he now understands what 'pain' means. What if he insists that he *does* know what 'pain' means (and perhaps, indeed, does generally use it correctly), but nevertheless does *not* know whether what he now has is pain? We should not know what to do with him, any more than we should know what to do with someone who claims to remember believing things before he was born. Here is an abnormality for which our concept of understanding is ill-tailored (and that is no coincidence, for were it tailored for these cases, it would not fit normal ones — and, moreover, it would not *be* our concept of understanding). Criteria for understanding are here satisfied cheek by jowl with a criterion for not understanding.

The expression of doubt (and the claim to knowledge) have no room in the language-game *we* play with avowals of sensation. So how can W. query whether, on the supposition that one has turned to stone, one might not be mistaken in thinking one's pain continues? Precisely because that supposition abrogates the normal language-game: it severs pain from the possibility of its behavioural expression, and hence the concept of pain from the criteria for its application (to others). In our language-game there are criteria in behaviour for whether a person is in pain, and for whether what he has is the same pain as he had previously. The sufferer who avows his pain and its continuity does not employ these (or any other) criteria in his avowals, but others do; and it is these criteria that *give sense* to 'pain' and 'same pain' both in my utterance 'I still have the same headache' *and* in the judgement that another person's pain is still as severe as before. But in the envisaged case there is no longer *any such thing* as the behavioural expression of pain (stones do not *behave*, and though the Laocoön wonderfully expresses suffering, it does not do so *behaviourally*, but by the *depiction* of behaviour). So a criterion of identity for the sensation *is* required here, i.e. something must be determined as *counting* as having pain, and having the same or different pain. But if the (petrified) bearer of the (imagined) sensation needs a criterion of identity for it (unlike the bearer of pain in our language-game), then the possibility of error exists (as it does in third-person ascriptions of pain based on criteria in the normal language-game). Hence it *looks* as if I might legitimately doubt whether what goes on, when I turn to stone, is pain or something else. But, to be sure, it only *looks* thus, for the argument is a *reductio ad absurdum*. The envisaged 'sensation' is no sensation at all; there is no such thing as a *non-behavioural* criterion of pain, for the *concept* of pain is determined by its behavioural criteria.

1.1   'by pricking him with a pin and saying "See, that's what pain is"': this is a perfectly licit explanation of what 'pain' means, but one which is liable to be misconstrued by philosophers. For one is immediately tempted to think that this explanation will be understood if the learner *has* what we *have* when we are pricked, and associates the word 'pain' with what he has. Thinking along these lines, it will seem that the explanatory device of pricking the learner is a means of producing in him a private sample of pain which will be 'qualitatively' identical with the private samples we use to give the word 'pain' its meaning. These are precisely the misconceptions which the private language arguments strive to eradicate.

Since the pain produced by pricking the learner is not a sample of pain (for reasons elaborated in PI §§243ff.), how can the envisaged explanation *be* an explanation? Clearly we are demonstrating (explaining) to the pupil when to use the expression 'I have a pain' or 'It hurts'. If, as normal, he flinches and cries 'Ow!', we can teach him to replace his cry with an avowal of pain and also to say of others who display pain-behaviour in similar circumstances that they are in pain. But if his limb is anaesthetized and he does not react to the pinprick, or if he is abnormal and merely giggles, our explanation will misfire.

Such an explanation of a sensation-word is not an explanation by means of a sample, even though it may look like one, save that the sample is 'private'. But there is no such thing as a 'private' sample.

2.1   (i) LSD 110f. examines the explanation of 'pain' by pinching someone. Here W. declared that in so doing one gives a sample of pain. But, he queried, is the *sensation* the sample or the *pinching*? In so far, as one is inclined to say that only the person pinched knows what the sensation was and that the sensation was that which was *present*, then the sensation could not have been the sample. The reason W. gave was that samples are akin to words in that (a) they must endure: 'a sample is, just as a word is, something which lasts', (b) they must be publicly accessible: 'I show you the sample, you see it, I see it, we look at it for five minutes.' A fleeting sense-impression therefore cannot be a sample. On the other hand, one can say that the sensation is the sample if (a) one means that it's that sensation which is called 'pain', not just the pinch, so that if the learner were anaesthetized, he would not understand, or (b) if, when one pinches him, one says 'It's this sensation' (presumably parallel to 'Red is this *colour*').

This reasoning is unhappy (and is not repeated elsewhere). First, while the relative permanence of the written word resembles that of, e.g., colour-samples, this is not mirrored by the spoken word. Yet if one says 'Repeat after me "Abracadabra"!' the quoted word is a sample to be reproduced by the hearer. Many samples are no more permanent than this, e.g. explanations of verbs that employ samples ('*This* [and I thump the table] is what is called thumping') or explanations of names of sounds or notes ('This [striking the keyboard] is middle-C'). Secondly, the reason why a sensation cannot be a sample used in defining a sensation-word is not because it is fleeting, for a persistent pain would be no better than a momentary one. Rather it is because sensations, though they can be exhibited (i.e. manifested) in behaviour (PI §313), cannot be exhibited *as samples*, as objects for comparison. There is (and can logically be) no *technique* of employing them (laying them alongside reality like measures) as standards for the correct use of a word in a *practice* (see 'Private ostensive definition', §3).

It is this point that makes it unintelligible that sensations should function as samples in a genuine (public) language. And although it *seems* as if they might function as private samples in a 'private' language, this, as has been argued, is an illusion. MS. 130, 209f. (≃ Z §§546–8) demonstrates this nicely in a pertinent context. Suppose someone always pricks himself with a pin when he says 'I'm not certain whether he is in pain', supposing thereby to have the meaning of 'pain' vividly before his mind to ensure that he knows *what* he is to doubt about the other man. But would his pain tell him what he is to doubt about the other? How would the pain *he* feels engage with his doubt about someone *else*'s pain? Is he in a better position to doubt whether another person has a pain because *he* has one? In order to doubt whether someone else has a cow, must I have a cow? Can he doubt whether someone else has *this* (and he pricks himself)? It is as if one were told 'Here is a chair. Can you see it clearly? — Good — now translate it into French!' In order to doubt whether someone else is in pain, one needs, not pain, but the concept of pain.

In short, it is the *use* that makes something a sample for this or that, and there is no such thing as using a sensation as a paradigm for the correct application of a word.

(ii) 'I might *legitimately* begin to doubt afresh': MS. 124, 246f. (derived from MS. 165, 143f.) interpolates here

Der Satz 'Wenn ich mich nun irrte und es gar nicht Schmerzen wären' ist Unsinn, weil ein Kriterium der Identität der Empfindung vorgespielt wird, das es gar nicht gibt. (Ähnlich wie im Satz; 'Ein Anderer kann nicht *diese identischen* Schmerzen haben, die ich jetzt habe.'

(The sentence 'Suppose I were in error and it wasn't pain at all' is nonsense, for it gives the illusion of a criterion of identity for the sensation which does not obtain. (Just as in the sentence: 'Another cannot have *these identical* pains which I now have.'))

Then follows the rest of (c). The back-reference to PI §253(c) is noteworthy: in both cases an 'inner' criterion of identity is misguidedly intimated.

SECTION 289

1   The expression of doubt has no place in the language-game with avowals of pain. It is, however, tempting to think that the reason for this

is Cartesian certainty, indubitability, about 'inner experience'. Am I not 'immediately acquainted' with the sensation which *makes it true* that I am in pain, and is it not the occurrence of this sensation that is *described* in saying 'I have a pain'? Of course I cannot justify this certainty to others, but surely I am justified *before myself* — by the immediate private experience!

This is precisely the misconception against which W. wars. That which seems here to be founded on the bedrock of experience (the foundation of all empiricist architecture) is actually free-floating. This seems absurd. If it were so, what would stop it slipping from beneath our feet? That which is most certain would become unreliable, subject to the eroding waters of sceptical doubt! But these fears stem from misunderstandings. The earth too is free-floating, but does it slip from beneath our feet? Does the fact that it is unsupported in space make our buildings less well-founded? It is true that I cannot doubt whether I am in pain, but not because that is the most certain kind of empirical knowledge I have.

What does it mean to claim that in avowing pain I am justified before myself? It seems that I fit the word 'pain' to what I experience. If another could experience what I have, he would agree that my description 'I have a pain' fits this experience, i.e. that I am using the word correctly on this occasion to describe my experience. But, of course, this experience is 'private', and another cannot know what I am calling 'pain'! This incorporates all the confusions hitherto raked over. First, in what sense am I *calling* something 'pain' when I say 'I have a pain'? Certainly not in the sense in which I call something 'a magnolia' when I point at a tree and say 'That's a magnolia'. Secondly, in the thin sense in which I can be said to be calling something 'pain' when I say 'I am in pain', another *can* know what I am calling 'pain'. Does the dentist *not* know what I am talking about when I say 'I have toothache'? Thirdly, would someone else (the dentist, for example) *not* admit that I am using the word 'pain' correctly when my cheek is swollen, I flinch if my tooth is touched, I chew on the other side only, etc. It is mistaken to think that *I* have a justification for using the word 'pain', and equally fallacious to suppose that another can have no justification for judging me to be using it correctly.

It is a mistake to think that to use a word without evidential grounds or without a defining paradigm is to use it wrongfully. It is easy to see why one is tempted to think thus, for one is inclined to suppose that W. is suggesting that when one sincerely says 'I am in pain', there are just the words and nothing else, viz. no *pain* (Vol. XVII, 10f.). And surely, when one says 'I am in pain', one has a *reason*, viz. that one *is in pain* (cf. MS. 162(b), 92)! This is confused. Of course when one sincerely avows pain, one *is* in pain. But *that one is in pain* is not a reason (a grammatical justification) for saying that one is in pain! To think otherwise is like thinking that the reason it is right to say that $\frac{\delta x^2}{\delta x} = 2x$ is *because it is so*

(MS. 158, 83). But, of course, there is all the difference in the world between being in pain and saying 'I am in pain', and saying 'I am in pain' without being in pain — the difference, in fact, between sincerity and a lie (cf. PI §304). Nevertheless, there *is* such a thing as a reason for saying 'I am in pain', e.g. to elicit sympathy, or, differently, because these words belong to the role I am acting in a play. But that a sincere avowal of pain does not rest on a grammatical justification does not derogate from its role in the language-game: 'You have to regard the utterance (without a reason) with the same respect as a statement that rests on a reason, not as something that *lacks support*' (MS. 158, 83f. (in English)). For this utterance is the beginning of the language-game (cf. Exg. PI §290).

1.1 'es zu Unrecht gebrauchen': 'to use it wrongfully' (as in RFM 406).

2 Vol. XVII, 10f. queries how one knows that in saying 'I have pains' one is using the word 'pain' correctly? One does not *know*, W. retorts, i.e. there is here no criterion, rather the word forces itself upon one. And that is why it seems that one *must* have a justification for using it, an inner justification. But even if one had what one imagines, i.e. an inner image of pain, it would not be a justification, for the existence of an inner object cannot justify the use of a word. But this gives the false impression, W. adds, that he is arguing that there are just the words of the utterance and nothing else.

Later (Vol. XVII, 42f.) W. contrasts 'He has the same pain as I' with 'I now have the same pain as I had earlier'. In the first case there is a criterion of identity, but what of the second? Should one say 'I *know immediately* that it is the same'? Do I then know immediately that the word 'same' fits here, or that such and such a picture (an inner image) fits? And in what way does it 'fit' (i.e. is there here a technique of comparison determining what *counts* as 'fitting')? The interlocutor queries: does this mean that one just *says* the word 'same' without its being somehow justified? 'The word "just" is wrongly applied here', W. responds. The suggestion that 'same' is here used without justification discomforts one much as the claim that the earth floats free in space without support disturbs some people.

MS. 162(b), 71ff. examines the temptation to say that we can never really know whether someone else is justified in saying that he has a certain experience, since it depends precisely on *his* experience. This is wrong: we can know it perfectly well. For the 'experience' is not the justification of the use — not, that is, in the grammatical sense.

How do I know that I can imagine purple, but not the (unsurveyable) figure ||||||||||||||? How do I know that what I imagine is purple, or that what I sometimes imagine is not the figure ||||||||||||||||? The image is no justification, but the material picture (at which one may point, saying 'That's what I imagined') is.

But there is indeed a justification for the use of the words 'I can imagine that.' Suppose someone said 'I can imagine what Pavlova experienced during that dance'. One might query 'How can you imagine that; what have you experienced that is similar to that?' And he might reply, 'The most similar experience that I have had was to imagine what Mozart felt while composing.'

2.1   'To use a word without a justification . . .': RFM 406 (= MS. 124, 132) has PI §289(b) in the context of a discussion of sameness (see Exg. §292, 1).

Avowals and descriptions
  1. Descriptions of subjective experience   2. Descriptions
  3. Natural expression   4. A spectrum of cases

Section 290

1   §290(a) smoothly continues the argument. One says 'I am in pain' without justification. Whereas I identify the pain of another by reference to behavioural criteria (including his verbal behaviour), I do not identify my sensation by criteria, nor does a 'private' sample justify my utterance. Indeed I do not *identify* my sensation (for there is here no possibility of any misidentification). Rather, I repeat an expression the use of which is a manifestation or expression of pain, a learnt extension of natural behavioural manifestations of pain (cf. PI §244). My utterance no more rests on justifying grounds than do my groans of pain. But this is not the end of the language-game; it is the beginning. In this respect the language-games with avowals are altogether different from the language-games with descriptions of physical objects. *There* the language-game terminates with a description[29] (e.g. of my room) which may be true or false, ill-informed or well-informed, more or less accurate, perceptive and skilful, or crude. And *that* language-game begins with observation, perhaps with careful scrutiny. Its terminus is subject to correction, improvement, and refinement.

§290(b) indicates one source of confusion. We are inclined, when philosophizing, to project the features of one language-game onto

---

[29] Of course, the language-game may continue, e.g. with an argument about the correctness of the description, in which case the description is the terminus of the first phase of the game.

another. We think that the concept of *description* is uniform across language-games. (And at root, we think, all words are names, all sentences descriptions!) We take 'I have a pain' to be a description of the speaker's state of mind, and so conceive this language-game to begin with the sensation, which is observed, identified, ascribed to a subject (I) to whom one refers in the description which is the terminus of the language-game. For when I describe my room, e.g. 'The sofa-table has a K'ang-Hsi vase on it', I observe the items in the room, identify them, satisfy myself that I know how things are, and refer to them in the description I give. But these language-games are altogether different. I do not observe my sensations, nor do I identify them. There is no question of my knowing or not knowing how things are with me here. The first-person pronoun thus used is not a referring expression (see 'I and my self', §4), and in an avowal such as 'I have a pain' I do not ascribe an experience to a person to whom I refer (cf. Exg. §§404–10). An avowal of pain is not a description of one's state of mind, nor is it a description of one's pain (see 'Avowals and descriptions', §2).

2   This theme preoccupied W. throughout the late thirties and early forties, and becomes even more prominent in the *Remarks on the Philosophy of Psychology* and *Last Writings*. The following is a selection of only a few remarks leading up to the *Investigations*.
    LPE 302 observes:

There seems to be a *description* of my behaviour, and also, in the same sense, a description of my pain! The one, so to speak, the description of an external, the other of an internal fact. This corresponds to the idea that in the sense in which I can give a part of my body a name, I can give a name to a private experience (only indirectly).
    And I am drawing your attention to this: that the language-games are very much more different than you think.
    You couldn't call moaning a description! But this shows you how far the proposition 'I have toothache' is from a description . . .
    In 'I have toothache' the expression of pain is brought to the same form as a description 'I have 5 shillings'.

    And in the lectures (LSD 11) W. nicely crystallized this thought: 'What we call the description of feeling is as different from the description of an object as "the name of a feeling" is different from "the name of an object"' (cf. LSD 44).
    Vol. XVI, 114 gives a striking analogy: I explain draughts to a fool. I show him the initial positions and the black and white pieces. He says, 'I understand: and whoever gets the white has won'. I reply, 'No, this has as yet nothing to do with winning and losing'. This is similar to: with someone's utterance 'I have pains', the language-game only begins.

Subsequently (Vol. XVI, 133) W. elaborates: Another person can no more *check* that what he has is really what we call 'pain' than I can,[30] for there is no such thing in this language-game. The language-game begins with his *saying* that he has pains, not with his *knowing*. The great difficulty here is not to present matters as if there were something one cannot do, i.e. as if there were an inner object from which one derives a description, but which one cannot show anyone else; as if the language-game really began not with the expression (*Äusserung*) of pain but with the 'private object'. On p. 137 W. queries whether his remark that the language-game begins with the expression of pain is a grammatical truism (as it should be). He compares it with 'The game begins with *telling one's dream*', for this of course does not mean that one does not believe someone who says, 'Last night I dreamt . . . !' One can apparently say both: the game begins with the dream, and the game begins with telling it.

This hesitation disappears in the longer discussion in Vol. XII, 242ff. in which the material is reworked. One is tempted to say that I can never really *know* whether another has said the ABC to himself in his imagination. But can he know that? What if one said 'He too cannot know this, he can only say it'? So does he *not* know? No, that would be wrong too! (He *cannot* know, not: he does not know — and the *cannot* here is logical, not epistemological; it signifies senselessness, not ineradicable ignorance.) To say that he does not know would mean that he doubts, is uncertain. Rather, there is here no question of either knowing or doubting. The language-game begins with someone saying that he imagines . . . The language-game begins as it were with a description which does not correspond to something described (cf. Vol. XVI, 133); but this grammatical remark could also be wholly misleading. The conception of remembering as an inner process makes it possible for us to make an assumption about this process, apparently without concerning ourselves about how and whether this inner process is expressed. But now this assumption is *empty* as long as it is not coupled with an assumption about the outer process. Then follows a re-draft of Vol. XVI, 137 (see above), with the comparison of expressions of pain with telling a dream, but without the qualifying clause. For presumably W. came to think that although it may appear that one *can* say that the game begins with a dream, this is *far more* misleading than to block that route. 'The language-game only begins with the expression (*Äusserung*)', W. concludes, *is* the difference between a description of an inner experience or process and a description of a physical fact or fact of the 'outer world'.

Earlier in the volume W. remarked:

---

[30] Of course, I can check — but not in the way envisaged. And in *that* way, he cannot check either.

Eine Äusserung der Empfindung kann man vergleichen mit dem Blatt das ein Kartenspieler erhält. Es ist eine Ausgangsstellung des Spieles, aber noch kein Ergebnis desselben. (Vol. XIII, 170)

(A manifestation of a sensation is comparable to the hand which a card-player holds. It is a starting-point of the game, but not the outcome of one.)

MS. 165, 160f. contains the first final draft of PI §290, followed by a remark contrasting a description of a room, which, as a matter of fact, only I have seen, with a description of something which only I *can* (logically) 'see'.

Section 291

1   This highlights the conclusion of §290. The form of the sentence 'I have a pain' does not show that it is a description (although in certain circumstances, such a sentence might be used as a *report*, e.g. the doctor asks 'How are you this morning?', and I reply 'I have a pain in my back'). But that is not to say that there is no such thing as a description of one's own state of mind (see 'Avowals and descriptions', §4). In the grip of the Augustinian picture of language, philosophers are prone to conceive of the essential role of propositions as describing. The *Tractatus* did so in claiming that the essential function of propositions is to describe states of affairs and that the general propositional form is 'This is how things are'. More recently, it has been extensively argued that the sense of a sentence, no matter whether it is declarative, interrogative, or imperative, is given by its *truth-condition*, which specifies how things must be for it (or, with more refinement, for its sentence-radical) to be true. Hence we think of propositions as word-pictures (descriptions) of the facts (and may, as in the *Tractatus*, make this idea into the pivot of a general account of the essential nature of any possible language).

This is misleading. First, it disregards the *diversity* of pictures: still-lives, portraits, landscapes, mythological or fictional representations, historical paintings, ornamental designs, maps, diagrams (Vol. XII, 233), not to mention *trompe l'oeil* pictures, abstract paintings, collages, etc. Secondly, the idea abstracts from the diverse *functions* of pictures: we think primarily of pictures that hang on the wall, that are there to be looked at. (Although *even here* one should distinguish the different function of a picture of the Pantocrator in a Byzantine church from that of a picture of the crucified Christ or of the Madonna of Mercy, and these from a picture of Charles I by van Dyck glorifying the monarch, and that too from Bosch's moralistic fantasies, and these from genre-paintings, from *mementi mori*, etc.) So we tend to forget such pictures as machine drawings, cross-sections of mouldings, architectural blueprints with elevations and measurements, which are *used* in making or building things or in checking whether they are properly constructed.

By analogy, we should examine the different *uses* of propositions, for although they may all appear as if they are descriptions of how things are, they are not. '25 > 24' sounds like 'John is taller than Mary', but it is not a description of how things are in the realm of numbers, since there is no such thing as a realm of numbers, and propositions of arithmetic are not descriptions of anything. 'Nothing can run faster than a cheetah' and 'Nothing can be red and green all over' look alike; yet the latter is not a description of an impossibility, but the expression of a grammatical rule. So too 'I have a pin' and 'I have a pain' look alike, but while the former describes a state of affairs, the latter is typically in *Äusserung*.

Furthermore, within the domain of what *can* legitimately be called 'descriptions' there is much greater logical diversity than comes to the blinkered philosophical eye. A description of my room, a fictional description of a house, a description of my state of mind, and a description of a project are very different. They are subject to different kinds of fault, are correctable or improvable in altogether different ways, and involve different skills. A Proust may excel at describing his state of mind, but not because his inner vision is so superior to normal mental eyesight. A Tolstoy may wonderfully describe the lives, thoughts, and feelings of his characters, but not because he can see possible worlds in the realm of fiction. A Marlborough may describe his campaign plans in meticulous detail, and things may happen just as he planned; but the excellence of his description is not a matter of the foresight of the gypsy crone reading off the future from a crystal ball — although it is, in another sense, a matter of meticulous foresight.

2   Vol. XII, 219f., in the course of a long discussion of descriptions, observes that we do not note, e.g., the fact that the description of a landscape, coupled with an ostension that it is in such-and-such a place, lends itself to a further possibility of application; viz. it enables one to find one's way. Contrast this with a description of one's visual impression (i.e. of how things visually strike one). We forget that what we call 'description' can occupy different positions in the language-game.

Section 292

1   The conception of a proposition as essentially a description, *a fortiori* the conception of a proposition as a word-picture of the facts, is often associated with the thought that we 'read it off from the facts'. For it seems that we observe that things are thus-and-so, and that we then make use of names correlated with the observed things to frame a

proposition describing the fact observed. In this way it appears as if a fact is portrayed mechanically according to the rules of correlation that give words their meanings and that the description can be straightforwardly compared with reality to check on its truth.

This, however, is doubly misleading. First, in the case of first-person psychological utterances, 'there is no comparing of proposition and reality. (Collating.)' (LPE 294). In one's expressions of sensation or perception, of memory or intention, there is no such thing as observing *in foro interno* an array of psychological facts accessible only to the eye of the mind, which one then *describes* for the benefit of others. Secondly, given that the first point is accepted, the comparison of 'I have pains' with 'The rose is red' becomes misleading in a different way. It encourages the misconception that whereas the latter is well-founded, resting firmly upon a rule (viz. an ostensive definition of 'red' by reference to a sample) which can be invoked to justify the proposition and employed in comparing the proposition with reality, the psychological utterance is free-floating and hence vulnerable, for it is unjustified. Though this conception is in one sense quite correct, it misrepresents matters. For the avowal, though unjustified in the sense elaborated (cf. Exg. §289), is as firm as the earth beneath our feet, as reliable (barring insincerity, etc.) as the natural cry of pain, exclamation of joy, or snarl of anger. And on the other hand, we forget that even in cases where we can characterize propositions as having a grammatical justification, e.g. by reference to a sample which is a constituent of a rule, the rule does not contain its own application. The sample does not guide us in its use. Rather, *we* have to apply the rule (and employ the sample) in a general practice. W. insists that when one says 'I am in pain', one says so without justification and this seems to deprive one of any right to say it. But that thought rests on a misconceived comparison. For one has here a confused picture of normative compulsion. One has as much right (though no justification) to say 'I have a pain' in appropriate circumstances as one has to say 'That thing is red' (even though in this latter case one can adduce a grammatical justification or rule).

Note that W.'s point is not to show that expressions (*Äusserungen*) of the 'inner' and judgements of the 'outer' are equally shaky and vulnerable, that a kind of naturalistic scepticism is something we must live with, a part of the human condition. On the contrary, it is to remind us that though the earth is unsupported in space, it is as firm as firm can be, and we need not fear falling!

Section 293

1   W. reverts to the issue of privacy. One is inclined to think that one knows what 'pain' means only from one's own case, for it seems that it is

the sensation one *has* that gives the word its meaning (cf. §283). One is 'intimately acquainted' with one's own sensations (for, one argues, '*I* have them', and no one else can have *my* sensations). And what one *has* is conceived as a private sample that defines 'pain'. This is the *semi-solipsism* against which W. wars (MS. 165, 150) — 'semi-solipsism' since the proponent of this philosophical mythology does *not* argue that he is the only person who has pain (indeed, the only person who *can* intelligibly be said to have pain). Rather does he claim that others likewise know what 'pain' means from their sensation; i.e. he generalizes his own case. But can one generalize this one case so irresponsibly, particularly when one has not the slightest guidance as to *how* one should generalize it (MS. 124, 255)?

Note that the problem of 'generalizing one's own case' here does not address the question of how I know that others are in pain, but rather how I know how others assign meaning to 'pain'. For 'the essential thing about private experience is really not that each person possesses his own exemplar, but that no one knows whether other people also have *this* or something else' (PI §272). The solipsist, of course, argues that it is unintelligible that anyone but he should have *this*. But the 'semi-solipsist' pretends that each person, in his private language, names his sensations, as if they were objects in a peep-show into which only he can peer (MS. 124, 228).

§293(b) explores an analogy: 'beetle' is the name given to whatever is in each person's box, into which no one else can look; and everyone says he knows what a beetle is (what 'beetle' means) by looking into his own box. But here (a) every person might have something different in his box, and (b) what is in each person's box might change constantly. If (a) were the case, no one could know it (PI §272). If (b) were the case, it would make no difference to the meaning of 'beetle', which simply signifies whatever is in the box. Now suppose that 'beetle' had a use in the *common* language of these people. One point is clear: it would not be used as the name of a thing; it would not be used as we use names of ordinary objects. (One might say here that the phrase 'Whatever is in my box' is not the name of an object. But, of course 'beetle' in each person's envisaged 'private' language is not used as the phrase 'Whatever is in my box' is used in ordinary language.) If 'beetle' were to have a use in their common language, then it would have no connection with what is in each person's private box – which might, as far as mutual communication by means of a common language is concerned, be empty. It would not even mean merely *something* (cf. PI §261). If what is in the box is relevant to the meaning of 'beetle', then no one else can understand what I mean by 'beetle'; and if 'beetle' is understood by others, it cannot signify what is in each person's private box.

§293(c) draws the conclusion: *if* we construe the grammar of the expression of sensation on the model of object and name, then the object drops out of consideration as irrelevant. If we think of 'pain' as the name of a sensation we have on the model of names of objects (in a generalized sense of 'object'), then solipsism is unavoidable. A public language cannot be construed as the confluence of private languages that happen to coincide. (A good angel is always necessary (RFM 378), but even a good angel could not engineer *this*!) And the incoherence of solipsism is a consequence of the logical impossibility of a private language.

1.1   (i) 'Nun, ein Jeder . . . ': 'Well, everyone . . .'.
         (ii) 'One might even imagine such a thing constantly changing': cf. §271 and the method of demonstrating that the hypothesis of a private object is an idle wheel in the mechanism.
         (ii) 'Gegenstand und Bezeichnung': 'Bezeichnung eines Dinges' was translated in the previous paragraph as 'name of a thing', so better 'object and name'.

2   LSD 124 clarifies how the 'private object' drops out of consideration as irrelevant. Suppose that each person has a private object which no one else can see. Everyone has mastered the colour-vocabulary, and now a game of describing the colour of one's private object is introduced. Suppose someone, quite sincerely, looks into his private box, sees a blue object, and says 'red'. Is he wrong? No, he is neither right nor wrong, for there is no technique of applying colour-words to private objects *on the model of applying them to public ones*. There is no *method* of comparing a sample with a private object. (Of course, we can say what colours our after-images are; but does it make sense to say 'He had a red after-image, knew what colour-words mean, but believed his after-image was 'blue'?) It makes no sense to say 'Play the same game with the private object', for nothing has been determined to *count as the same*. (Contrast 'Play the same game as tennis, only without the ball' with 'Play the same game as chess, only the winner is he who gets checkmated'). Of course, the premise of the argument is *absurd* (for this argument is a *reductio*), for does it really make sense to say 'It was blue but he said it was red'? One might respond by saying 'All right, let's lay down a rule for application of colour-words to what is "internal" — viz. that it shall make no difference (i.e. they shall be applied just as they are applied to what is "external")'; W. replies ironically, 'Yes, that's just it, it *doesn't* make any difference.

2.1   'not even as a something'; cf. MS. 158, 80; the 'something' is an idle wheel in the mechanism.

1　　This draws together the argument of §261 and §293, but here, unlike §293(a), W. is not concerned with the private object as a pseudo-sample which is purportedly used to give a meaning to a sensation-word, but with the private object as an object of description. To conceive of a sensation, sense-impression, or mental image conjured up when recollecting or imagining something as a *private picture* is to conceive of it as an object that can (logically) be *described* in the sense in which a public picture can be described. So to say of another that he has a private picture before him is already to make an *assumption* about what he has (e.g. we assume, in the analogy of §293, that he has a beetle in his box). In particular, this assumption implies that we too can or do describe more closely what he has. For the idea of a describable object which is *logically* describable by only one person is incoherent. It is the correlate of the equally incoherent idea of a rule that can *logically* be understood and followed by only one person. For the private object, which we envisage as being described by the person who has it, is also conceived as being used as a private sample in the mental ostensive definition of a word which only he can understand.

　　But we must admit that we have not the faintest idea of what kind of thing it might be that he has before him (cf. §§261, 272). That is to say, even the *category* of the thing is undetermined; for we cannot say that he has a *sensation* (or *mental image of a colour*) before him, since these expressions too are words of common language which need (and have) rules for their use. So with what right do we say that, despite our total ignorance, at any rate we know that he has *something*. For the word 'something' is not, as it were, a minimal description that cannot be faulted. In its significant use it is akin to a variable the value-range of which is determined in advance. 'Something happened in the street just now' determines an *event*; 'Something is at the back of the drawer' determines a physical *object*. 'Something crossed my mind' determines a thought or idea; 'He did something astonishing' determines an act; 'I felt something in my leg' determines a sensation (a twinge or pain) or bodily state (a swelling or a lump); 'He told me something interesting' determines a piece of information; 'I thought I heard something' determines a noise — in short, the use of 'something' commits one to something, not to nothing. And what it commits one to is a more or less determinate range of possibilities, *not* a minimal piece of knowledge that is indefeasible. But the misguided philosopher's use of 'something' here is cut free of these constraints, hence is comparable to 'He has something; but I don't know whether it is money or debts or an empty till', i.e. if that is all I know, then I know *nothing* about what he has, not even whether he has anything of whatever kind. For if nothing can count as something, then having a mere something before one counts for nothing!

2   This derives from Vol. XII, 205ff. We imagine that there is such a thing as a subjective regularity, which exists only for the subject and only he can know, etc. But this is incoherent, for we have no reason for calling whatever he purports to have 'a regularity', or for thinking that what he purports to be doing is rightly called 'a (language) game', or indeed that what we are dealing with is 'a language'. That is, we employ here a picture of a 'private object' which only he can see. But is this really a picture? It is of the nature of such a picture that we can make further suppositions about this object and about what he does with it; it is not enough to say that he has a private something and does something with it! Then follows a comparison of a description of a dream or of a sense-impression. Here too one cannot say that what the person describes is something (an inner picture) which only he can see. After a lengthy detour, a draft of PI §294 occurs on p. 209, followed by the remark 'Isn't it like this — you first imagine for yourself what it is that he has before him (viz. a private picture), which you then explain as being quite groundless (since we admit that, *ex hypothesi*, we cannot know what he has before him), and yet you still insist that he has something before him!'

Vol. XVI, 58 has the last sentence of PI §294 followed by the query 'How do you know he has a private picture before him?', to which the interlocutor replies 'Because I have one before me'. This W. denies; one *says* that, but there are neither more nor less grounds for using this figure of speech in one's own case than in the case of others. One wants to reply that one imagines something vividly, one sees it before one, but one's neighbours cannot see it, for it belongs to oneself alone. But, W. retorts, it is here just a metaphor to talk of seeing something 'before one' or 'in one's mind's eye'. If someone else imagines the same, does he not see the very same thing before him? One might reply, 'He surely can't have the same pains as I'. But why not? What is the criterion of identity? Then follows PI §398.

SECTION 295

1   A deflationary remark on §293(a). If the proposition that one knows what 'pain' means only from one's own case were empirical, then it might be otherwise — i.e. one might know what 'pain' means without reference to one's aches and pains. But that the private language theorist will not wish to concede, for, he will insist, one *cannot* know what 'pain'

means unless one has had pains (cf. §315). Yet if it is not an empirical proposition, is it a *grammatical* one? If it were, then it would be a rule of grammar that someone who had never suffered pain but who used the word 'pain' correctly did *not* know what the word 'pain' meant, even though he said of others that they were in pain only when they had hurt themselves and of himself that he had no pain. But we employ no such rule; on the contrary, such a rule would conflict with what we mean by 'understands or knows the meaning of "pain"'.

Suppose everyone *did* say (as so many philsophers have) that they know . . . only from their own case. This remark gives no information, either empirical or grammatical; but it might be viewed as a picture, an iconographic representation in words of a segment of our grammar. What fragment of our language might it illustrate? W. gives no clue here (nor do the MS. sources 124, 258f. and 129, 60). But whatever W. had in mind here, the moral is clear enough. When doing philosophy, we adduce such pictorial representations as if they were descriptions. But we misinterpret such a picture as a description of the facts, rather than as an emblem — as if we were to take the sand-glass of Father Time to be the master-clock of time-measurement. Other such illustrated turns of speech are manifest in our talking of the flow of time (the river of time), in our pictures of the mental as inner, and in our representation of the laws of logic as adamantine.

SECTION 296

1   The interlocutor reverts to §294, for it constantly strikes him as if W. is denying that when one emits a cry of pain, there is *any pain*! But no one would deny that when one stubs one's toe and cries out, one cries out *in pain*. Or that when one cries out thus, one cries out *because* one has hurt oneself. Or that the pain is sometimes frightful. Or that it is important. But this is news from nowhere. The almost irresistible temptation to object that 'there is *something* accompanying my cry of pain' is rooted in the ideas that an inner 'something' defines the concept of pain, that 'pain' means this inner accompaniment of a cry of pain, and that the verbal expression of pain is *justified* by reference to it. But these moves have been shown to be futile. They reflect multiple misconceptions of the grammar of 'pain' and, more generally, of the grammar of the expression of sensation (§293). Like 'I know . . . only from my own case' the interlocutor's remark here conveys no information. It is merely another pictorial representation of our grammar.

2   Vol. XVII, 7ff. has a twenty-page discussion of this.

SECTION 297

1   In §296 the interlocutor insists, quite rightly, that when he cries out in pain, he is *not just behaving*. But this truism is accompanied by a complete misconstrual of the grammar of sensation, manifest in his insistence that there is *something* accompanying his cry of pain (§296). Moreover, he conceives of the pain which he expresses in his utterance 'I have a pain' as akin to a private picture which he describes (§294), so that 'I have a pain' is read off these inner facts and portrayed in words according to rules (§292). He thinks that he knows what the word 'pain' means by reference to the private picture that is before him, viz. his pain or what he conjures up in his imagination when he imagines a pain (§§293(a), 300). That is, he thinks not merely that *pain* enters into the language-game with sensation-words, but that a private *picture of pain* does too. It gets described; and it also functions as a private sample or paradigm that defines what 'pain' means.

The analogy of §297 is meant to undermine this conception. In a picture of water boiling in a pot ('a kettle' would be more vivid here) picture-steam comes out of the pictured pot. But it would be absurd to claim that there must also be *something* boiling in the picture of the pot. Rather, the picture is a picture *of* water boiling in the pot; we do not need to add anything to the picture of a kettle with steam coming out of its spout to make it a picture of water boiling in the kettle. Indeed, we could not; that is already what it is a picture of.

Here the pot (or kettle) in the picture is the body, the steam is the behaviour (the cry of pain), and the water is the pain. 'There must be something boiling in the picture of the pot' resembles 'Somebody who expresses pain must have *something* that accompanies his cry of pain (something important and frightful)'. It is as misguided to treat pain as *something* which accompanies an avowal of pain as it is to say that *something* must be boiling in the picture of the pot if picture-steam comes out of a picture-pot. (How can picture-steam come from nothing, given that steam cannot come from nothing?!)

Elaborating further: in the language-game with pain (as in the picture of the boiling pot) no *picture* or *paradigm* of pain plays any role, just as no picture of bubbling water plays any role in the picture of water boiling in a (closed) pot. But it is a picture of water boiling in a pot for all that!

This analogy points both backwards and forwards in the text. Looking backwards to §294, it clarifies the absurdity of making an assumption about what he has before him (viz. a private picture). This is as absurd as *assuming* that there is something boiling in the picture of the pot. It also makes clear why the interlocutor's remark in §296 stems from misunderstanding. For the 'something' that 'accompanies' one's cry of pain is not important *because* it gives meaning to the word 'pain' as a picture or paradigm which one knows only from one's own case (§295). The metaphor points forward to §300, for in the language-game with pain, there is no such thing as a *picture* (paradigmatic sample) which plays a role in the grammar of 'pain'.

2   This derives from Vol. XII, 207 (Vol. XVI, 56f.) introduced above (Exg. §294, 2). In our conception of a subjective regularity we employ a picture (a simile) of a 'private object' which only its owner can see; but we must make it clear to ourselves that this is *only a simile*. W. examines the case of someone describing his dream. Here too, one is inclined to say that he saw a picture (or image) before him which he describes for us. But a picture that is described is something visible to all. That is evidently not in question here; so one might say that the 'picture' described when describing a dream is not a 'material' picture, but rather akin to one's *sense-impression* of a material picture. But then one cannot characterize it as 'a picture which only I can see' (for I don't *see* my sense-impression, and others do not *overlook* it). Rather, the *Vorstellungsbild* is the picture which is described when one describes *what* one imagines (cf. PI §367), i.e. to describe what one imagines is not to describe an *image* but a state of affairs, which one has imagined. To characterize one's sense-impressions, imaginings, or dreams as *pictures* (i.e. something from which one can read off a description) is to employ the *simile* of a 'material' picture. Then follows PI §297.

Section 298

1   'This *something* is the important thing' (PI §296) is the interlocutor's refrain; and he thinks that he can pick out the 'something' (without committing himself to what sort of thing it is) by pointing inwardly. Yet nothing but misunderstanding engenders this thought. Dozens of false pictures succeed each other here, false pictures of the 'inner' and 'outer', of meaning and understanding, of language and explanation, of experience and knowledge, of doubt and certainty, of naming and describing, of the use of 'having' and of 'something', all reinforcing one another. Hence the strength of the inclination to make such empty remarks as 'This is the important thing', 'I have *something*' (§294), or 'I know . . . only from my own case' (§295).

2   In MS. 124, 259f. this is followed by the remark that 'Yes, but there is something there all the same . . . ' (cf. PI §296) already incorporates the wrong picture. For one says 'something' in order to leave open the

possibility that it need not always be the *same*, but only something upon which the cry of pain can rest.

SECTION 299

1   That we are inclined, even irresistibly inclined, to make such philosophical observations as 'I surely have something (at least that's certain)' or 'I know . . . only from my case' does not mean that one is being forced (by the facts!) into making an *assumption* (for these are not meant as empirical observations which could be otherwise (§295(a)). Nor does it mean that one has here immediate or intuitive knowledge which inclines one irresistibly. On the contrary, what we, when doing philosophy, 'are tempted to say' in all these cases is the raw material of philosophy, something for philosophical treatment (PI §254).

2   BB 59f. emphasizes that the solipsist's 'Only I feel real pain' is not stating an opinion (parallel to 'an assumption' in §299). 'That's why he is so sure of what he says. He is irresistibly tempted to use a certain form of expression; but we must yet find *why* he is.'

SECTION 300

1   This examines one of the things which we are 'irresistibly inclined to say' (PI §299) when we surrender ourselves to philosophical reflection on the 'inner' and the 'outer'. Grasping W.'s remarks here is made difficult by the fact that while 'image' corresponds to 'Vorstellungsbild', it does not uniformly correspond to 'Vorstellung'. The English 'image' is much more closely associated with what can be pictured or sculpted (as in 'graven images') than is the German 'Vorstellung'. It is with some strain that we speak of 'auditory images', and 'image of a taste' or 'image of a smell' is surely going too far. But 'Die Vorstellung des Geschmacks von Zucker' is perfectly licit, as is 'Die Vorstellung des Schmerzes'. However, the latter is unhappily translated as 'image of pain'. Moreover, although we speak of the memory of an event still being fresh or of the memories that come flooding back to one, there is in English, unlike German, no corresponding expression for 'imagination' and its cognates. The divergences make the accurate translation of W.'s remark here and in related texts almost impossible. Consequently the verbal form 'imagining pain' has, with misgivings, been adopted as a rough rendering of 'Die Vorstellung des Schmerzes', and, at the cost of clumsiness, the German 'Vorstellung' has often been retained in what follows.

We are tempted to say that it is not just the picture of behaviour, or *paradigm* of behaviour, that plays a role in the language-game with 'He is in pain', but also the picture or paradigm of pain. Many reasons incline us to think thus: (a) It seems that I know what 'pain' means only from my own case, which furnishes me with a picture or paradigm of pain. (b) It appears that when I say 'I have a pain' I describe the inner facts (as I describe a picture) in words, just as when I say 'I have a penny' I describe 'outer' facts. (c) To say of another that he is in pain is not to describe his behaviour, but, it seems, it is to attribute to him what I have when I am in pain; and here one must be able to recollect what it is that one has when one has a pain (and is that not an 'inner picture'?). (d) We readily think that to understand a sentence, one must be able to imagine something for every word; in particular, to understand what 'I am in pain' means, one must know what it would be like to be in pain, i.e. to imagine it (PI §449(a)). So surely to understand the sentence 'He is in pain', one must be able to imagine pain. Does this not show that the picture or paradigm of pain plays a role in the language-game?

The point upon which W. focuses here is a confusion concerning the relationship between the concept of a mental image and that of a picture. Clearly, pictures are objects of comparison, and equally clearly, mental images can correspond to pictures. So we are inclined to think that mental images are likewise objects of comparison. Indeed, we are prone to conceive of mental images *as* pictures. They seem to be just like pictures, save for being mental! This is multiply confused. Imagining pain (*Die Vorstellung des Schmerzes*) is not having a picture of pain (*ist kein Bild*). One can imagine a toothache or remember a headache, but this does not furnish one with a picture; there is nothing here employable *as* a picture or a paradigm, not even as a picture which only oneself (as it happens) can see. The description of the imagined is not a description of an inner picture, but a description of what one imagines (e.g. the face that launched a thousand ships (cf. PI §367)). Similarly, the description of the recollected is a description of what I remember, perhaps only hazily, not a description of a hazy picture. There is no such thing as using a *Vorstellung* of pain (as one *can* use a picture of something) as a sample or paradigm. Even in those cases where one can intelligibly talk of (vivid) images (*Vorstellungsbilder*), one's mental image is not a sample or paradigm, for there is no such thing as a method of projection for a mental image. One cannot lay a mental image alongside reality for comparison. But it is important that if, e.g. I imagine a shade of red (and perhaps have a vivid image of it), I can paint what I imagine, and *that can* be used as a paradigm. 'That ↗ is how I imagined the backcloth to be', I might say to the scene-painter, while pointing at a patch of paint. Here the image of red is replaceable by a paradigm (picture) of red. But nothing corresponds to imagining a pain (*die Vorstellung des Schmerzes*) as a red sample corresponds to imagining, having an image of, red. Hence the *Vorstellung* of pain is not replaceable by anything that can function as an object of comparison.

It is obvious that when I imagine a toothache, I cannot compare the *Vorstellung* directly *with another's behaviour* to determine whether he has such a toothache. Nor can one lay it alongside another person's toothache for comparison, as one can lay a sample of red alongside an object to determine whether the object is to be said to be red (cf. BB 53). And one cannot paint a picture of the imagined toothache, as one can paint imagined toothache-behaviour or the colour one imagined. Indeed, the *Vorstellung des Schmerzes* is not replaceable by *anything* that could be called a picture or paradigm of pain, for there is no such thing. There is such a thing as a picture of someone's being in pain. Also such a thing as imagining a pain, and such a thing as imagining someone to be in pain without showing it (cf. PI §393 and Exg. §302) — and here one does *not* imagine pain-behaviour.

How does the *Vorstellung* of pain enter the language-game? *Not* where we would expect it (cf. Z §636), but in all sorts of ways: for we tell each other to imagine how awful this or that pain must be, we empathize with each other, saying 'I can well imagine it, it must have been dreadful', and so on (see 2.1 below).

1.1　　'*this* image': viz. of pain; other images (*Vorstellungsbilder*), of course, are replaceable by pictures.

2　　Much material underlies this remark. Some of the salient points are as follows: (a) An image is not a kind of picture and cannot be used as one (WWK 97; cf. Exg. §301). (b) One can imagine another person's pain no less than his pain-behaviour. If one imagines another person's pain-behaviour or his black eye, one can replace the imagining by a painted image. This picture can be compared with what it is a picture of to see whether it is correct. 'The sense in which an image is an image is determined by the way in which it is compared with reality. This we might call the method of projection' (BB 53). But now, if we vividly imagine that someone suffers pain (and perhaps imagine that, by a great effort of will, he does not show it), is there any such thing as comparing the imagined pain with his actual pain? 'If you say, you compare them "indirectly" via his bodily behaviour, I answer that this means you *don't* compare them as you compare the picture of his behaviour with his behaviour' (ibid.). (c) An 'image of pain' contrasts with an 'image of pain-behaviour'. In the latter case, one can show another person what one's image is like. In the former, one might ask 'How did you learn the expression "imagining pain"?', but one cannot *point* at an image (LSD 39). (d) The idea that a picture of pain plays a role in the language-game stems from thinking of imagining pain as having a private picture of pain. W. draws an analogy with his example of a private table of colours which is apparently consulted (privately) by each player, but which actually plays no role in the game. The impression that there is a (genuine) private table in the game (and a *picture* of pain in the language-game) stems from the *absence* of a table (and a picture) coupled with the similarity of the game to one played with a table (picture) (Z §552). Here, one might say, the language-game with 'pain' is deceptively similar to the language-game with *colours*. (e) Imagining or remembering pain cannot serve to *define* 'pain' (Vol. XVII, 10). (f) One is misled by the fact that descriptions of what is seen and what is imagined are of the same kind (indeed, the same description may, in different contexts, serve both roles). But the concepts are otherwise utterly dissimilar. Imagining is more a doing than a receiving, a creative act (RPP II §111 = Z §637). Yet the similarity inclines one to compare a description of one's imaginings to a description of a picture, which, one adds, is an 'inner' one!

2.1   'Wohl tritt die Vorstellung des Schmerzes in einem Sinn ins Sprach-spiel ein': Vol. XII, 84, after a draft of PI §449, has:

> Damit meine ich natürlich nicht, dass es in manchen Sprachspielen nicht wesentlich ist, dass man an gewissen Punkten den Übergang von den Worten zur Vorstellung mache — wenn wir dem Arzt mitteilen, wir hätten Schmerzen — in welchen Fällen ist es nützlich, dass er sich einen Schmerz vorstellt? — Und wie ist es übrigens: sich einen Schmerz vorstellen? Geschieht dies nicht auf sehr mannigfache Weise. (So mannigfach, wie: sich an einen Schmerz erinnern.)

> (Naturally I do not mean that it is not essential in some language-games that the transition at certain points from the words to imagining be made — when we tell a doctor that we have been having pains — in what cases is it useful for him to imagine a pain? — And doesn't this happen in a variety of ways? (As great a variety as: remembering a pain.))

SECTION 301

1   An image, which one may have when one imagines or remembers something, is not an 'inner picture'. But a picture may correspond to such an image, for one can often paint a picture of what one imagines and say 'This is how I imagined it' (cf. §280). Is this always possible, i.e. does it always *make sense*? No; for it is clear from §300 that though I can imagine a severe toothache, no picture corresponds here as a picture of someone clutching his swollen jaw corresponds to imagining someone manifesting a bad toothache.

2   This remark derives from MS. 130, 33, where it occurs in a list of chapters or section-headings for a book. W. never did collect together the huge mass of remarks on mental images and their relation to pictures. In the *Investigations* the subject is taken up in §§363ff.

It is noteworthy that already in 1930 W. categorially differentiated mental images from pictures, thus taking a stand against the pervasive tradition in philosophy and psychology:

> An image of 'yellow' is not a picture of yellow that I have seen in the sense in which I carry a picture of my friend, for instance, in my wallet. An image is a picture in an entirely different, formal sense . . . *an image of colour has the same multiplicity as the colour.* That is what its connection with reality consists in. (WWK 97)

This is partly right and partly wrong. That an image must have in one sense the same multiplicity as that of which it is an image is clear enough — that I cannot even imagine something that is both red and green all over is not due to the poverty of my imagination. But, in a different sense, the multiplicity of the image differs from that of which it is an image. One might say that the yellow imagined must have the same multiplicity as the yellow seen, but the image of yellow does not have the multiplicity of the patch of yellow. For I can *look* at the latter, but not at the former, examine it more closely, be deceived in respect of its shade, show it to someone else, fail to notice features of it (e.g. that it has an orange tinge at the corner), etc.

In *Philosophical Remarks* W. noted that:

> speaking of images as 'pictures of objects in our minds' (or some such phrase) is a metaphor. We know what a picture is, but images are surely no kind of picture at all. For, in the first case I can see the picture and the object of which it is a picture. But in the other, things are obviously quite different. We have just used a metaphor and now the metaphor tyrannizes us. (PR 82)

In Vol. VI, 241 he wrote:

> Sagt aber der Realismus die Vorstellungen seien doch 'nur die subjektiven Bilder der Dinge', so ist zu sagen, dass dem ein falscher Vergleich zwischen der Vorstellung von einem Ding und dem Bild des Dinges zu Grunde liegt. Und zwar einfach, weil es wohl möglich ist, ein Ding zu sehen *und* sein Bild (etwa nebeneinander), aber nicht ein Ding und die Vorstellung davon.
>
> Es handelt sich um die Grammatik des Wortes 'Vorstellung' im Gegensatz zur Grammatik der 'Dinge'.

(If realism says that images are 'just subjective copies of things', it must be pointed out that this rests on a false comparison between the image and the picture of a thing. And simply because it is quite possible to see a thing *and* its picture (perhaps side by side) but not a thing and the [mental] image of it.

This has to do with the grammar of the word 'image' in contrast to the grammar of 'things'.)

Despite this warning, in PG 102, 147 he made just this comparison, but later (LPE 285) noted that 'In part of their uses the expression "visual image" and "picture" run parallel; but where they don't, the analogy which does exist tends to delude us.' In MS. 164, 164f. things finally crystallize:

> Ein Spiel kann Einer wohl mit sich selbst spielen. Und kann er es nicht doch in der *Vorstellung* mit sich selbst (oder mit andern) spielen?
> Wann aber würden wir sagen, er habe z.B. Schach mit einem Andern in der Phantasie gespielt? Wie weiss er, dass es Schach war? Hatte er Schach-in-der-Vorstellung gelernt? Nun, wir könnten ihm ja ein wirkliches Schachspiel zeigen und ihm fragen 'War *dass* was Du Dir vorgestellt hast?' Wenn er ja sagt, so hatte er also ein Vorstellungsbild einer Schachpartie. Aber welcher Art war das Bild? Was für eine Projektion des Schachspiels war es? Darauf gibt es keine Antwort, und es ist keine Frage, denn die Vorstellung ist eben kein Bild. Vergleiche ich sie einem Bild, so wäre es eines, von dem niemand, auch ich nicht, wüsste, wie es ausschaut. Denn auf die Frage, *was* ich mir vorstelle, kann auch ich nur *für* mich auf die für Andere sichtbaren Gegenstände zeigen. Die Antwort für mich besteht z.B. nicht darin, dass ich mir auch noch einen zeigenden Finger vorstelle. Denn der wäre ja nur eine unnötige Farce. Aber das Konzentrieren meiner Aufmerksamkeit ist für mich kein Zeigen.

> (Someone can, of course, play a game by himself. And can he not do so by himself (or with others) in his imagination?
> But when would we say, e.g., that he had played chess with someone else in his imagination? How does he know that it was chess? Did he learn chess-in-the-imagination? Well, we could show him a real chess game and ask him 'Was *this* what you imagined?' If he says 'Yes', then he did indeed have a mental image of a chess game. But what sort of picture was it? What sort of projection of a chess game was it? There is no answer to this, and it is no question, for the image is not a picture. If I compare it with a picture, it would be a picture which no one, not even I, knows what it looks like. For in response to the question *what* I imagine, even I, for myself, can only point at objects perceptible to others. The answer, for me, does not consist, e.g., in my further imagining a pointing finger. For that would just be a redundant farce. But concentrating my attention is, for me, not a kind of pointing.)

In *Investigations* §370 the guiding principle is specified: 'One ought to ask, not what images are or what happens when one imagines anything, but how the word "imagination" is used.' The subsequent extensive writings on this theme (RPP I, II and LW) explore the connections between the concepts of image, picture, and visual impression. The general conclusion is epitomized in RPP II §112 (Z §638): 'The image is not a picture, nor is the visual impression one. Neither "image" nor "impression" is the concept of a picture, although in both cases there is a tie-up with a picture, and a different one in either case.' (See 'Images and the imagination', §§4–5.)

Section 302

1   W. further explores the incoherence of the supposition that the picture
of pain (i.e. imagining pain, wrongly conceived as involving a private
picture or paradigm) enters the language-game with 'He has a pain'.
    Of course, I can imagine someone else being in pain, even someone
being in severe pain and not showing it. Here I would imagine what
effort he must make not to wince, how he must be saying to himself
'This is ghastly, but keep smiling', etc. (cf. PI §391). But it is incoherent
to suppose that I imagine another person's pain *on the model* of my pain.
For in imagining *his* pain, I do not imagine that my pain is in his
head — that would be to imagine that *I* feel a headache in his head
(which, W. argues, is possible (see 1.1 below)). Rather, I must imagine
that *he* has a headache. But now, how am I to imagine a headache I do *not*
feel on the model of one which I *do* feel? For, after all, this is *not* like
imagining a house I do not see on the model of a house which I do see;
rather it is like imagining a negative integer on the model of a natural
number. (And it would not make sense to give myself a headache and say
'Now, imagine that he has *this*' (Z §§546f.).)
    The nexus between §302(a) and (b) is not immediately obvious, but
can be clarified. To imagine someone else's pain on the model of one's
own *seems* simply to involve making a transition in the imagination from
pain in my body to pain in his. But §302(a) has shown that that confuses
imagining *my* having a pain in his head with *his* having a pain in his head;
i.e. the *location* of a pain does not determine a subject. (Phantom pains,
which are not 'in' anyone's body, are not therefore 'unowned', and pain
at the juncture point of Siamese twins may be suffered by one of the
twins or the other or both.) I have to imagine not *my* having a pain in his
body, but *his* having a pain in his body. The location of a pain can be
determined by pain-behaviour (pointing at the painful spot and/or
assuaging the injured limb), the pain-behaviour *of the subject*. And the
subject of the pain is *he who manifests it*. To imagine someone else's being
in pain is not to imagine that someone else 'has' *this*, or that *this* is located
in his foot; that would suit imagining someone else having my pin in his
foot. Rather is it to imagine *someone's* suffering (though not necessarily to
imagine him *expressing* his suffering). But I cannot imagine *someone's*
suffering 'on the model of my pain', since my pain — for me, as it
were — has no owner (see 2 below).

1.1   (i) 'which would also be possible': W. seems to have found intelligible,
at least in certain circumstances, the idea of my feeling a pain in another
person's body (cf. WWK 49; PR 92; BB 49f.). It is the act of pointing that
determines the place of a pain one suffers (BB 50). If I am groaning with

pain and am asked where it hurts, I might (perhaps with my eyes closed) point to the locus of my pain and find that I have pointed to my neighbour's limb. This, W. suggests, would be a case of feeling pain in another's body. The supposition, however, seems more problematic than this (see Exg. §253, 1.1(i)).

(ii) 'die leidende Person ist die, welche Schmerz äussert': 'the suffering person is he who manifests pain'.

2   LSD 7 remarks on the inclination to say 'I can imagine him to have a toothache, for I can imagine that he has what I have'. But, W. observes, 'When I have a shilling, I can imagine him to have what I have. So also if I have a black eye. But is it the same sort of transition when we take "*seeing*" or "*toothache*"? "Having" is used in an entirely different sense when we speak of "having a toothache" and "having a blackeye".' Vol. XVI, 24ff. reflects on the asymmetry between 'I have . . .' and 'He has . . .'. To say 'If I can have an image of such-and-such, so surely can someone else' makes it appear as if my having an image shows me what it is for someone to have an image, just as a clock in a drawer shows me how I must imagine a clock's being in a drawer. But 'I have . . .' *for me* signifies nothing (one might say that my having . . . does not have the multiplicity of 'X has . . .'). Do I experience *my having* a pain or just a pain? I *say* 'I have a pain' to another; for myself, I just groan. And the groan corresponds perhaps to the word 'pain', but not to 'I'! Of course, my grown may show someone *else* that I am in pain, viz. in virtue of the fact that *I* groan. But if, when I am in pain, a groan escapes from me rather than from someone else, that is not because I chose to groan with *my* mouth. That is, I do not *thereby* express the fact that *I* and *not someone else* groans.

Vol. XII, 161 elaborates the distinction between imagining another to be in pain and imagining my having a pain in another's body. If I am told 'You know what it is like when *you* feel pain; now just make the transition to someone else!' then there are different transitions I can make; and that shows that one cannot say '*This* is what "pain" signifies, and you know what "I have", "You have" mean, etc. so you know what "He has pains" means.' These are *two* misleading pictures, W. claims. Presumably one misleading picture is the compositionalist conception of sentence-meaning (viz. that the meaning of a sentence is composed of the meaning of its constituents), the other the conception of the meaning of 'having pain' (viz. as given by private ostensive definition). One must learn to see the expression '*I have* pains' as just as derivative (*übertragenen*) as 'The straight line cuts the circle at two imaginary points' (p. 162). The latter does not indicate an intersection of line and arc, and the former does not signify a kind of ownership, nor does it specify a possessor. Then follows PI §426: the misconception we have of attributing pain to others is comparable to our misconceptions in set-theory of infinite series as unsurveyable totalities which only a god can survey.

Does not the whole matter turn on the fact that the words 'I have pains' correspond to a groan and that it is the groaning of the sufferer that leads us to him, whereas *I* could moan with pain and in a certain sense not know *who* is in pain (cf. PI §§404ff.). The person who moans is he of whom one says '*He has* the pains'; and that is why one cannot say that the moan (indeed, the wail 'I have the pain') *states* who has the pains (pp. 163f.).

We are misled by the superficial similarity of 'I have' and 'he has'. But it is not as if 'I' and 'he' are, as it were, pointers in '. . . has pains', the former pointing at my body, the latter at another person. One is tempted to say that I know that another person has a pain because I observe his behaviour, but I know that I have a pain because I feel it. But this is senseless, since 'I feel pain' means the same as 'I have pain'. It looks as if one employs two different senses (seeing and feeling) to determine the subject of pain (as one *looks* for an object or *listens* for it). One can say that in the one case my visual impressions lead me to the location of (his) pains, and in the other my feeling of pain. But my feeling of pain does not lead me to the *owner* of the pain (pp. 164f.).

MS. 179, 66 has the first sentence of §302. In parentheses W. adds that it is misleading to say that the emphasis here (viz. 'pain which I *do not feel*' and 'pain which I *do feel*) is wrong, that I just have to imagine pains which *I do not* feel on the model of pains *I* do feel. The primitive pain-behaviour can point to the location of the pain, but not to a person. This person who suffers is he who moans.

See also BB 68f.

Section 303

1   In the grip of a misguided picture which seems to fix the sense of 'pain' unambiguously (PI §426), we are driven to say 'I can only *believe* that someone else is in pain, but I *know* it if I am' (cf. §246). For it seems as if in order really to *know* whether another is in pain, one would have to 'see clearly into the breast of another, and observe that succession of perceptions, which constitutes his mind',[31] but, we think, only a god can see thus into human consciousness (just as only a god can survey an infinite totality). So it appears as if the form of expression we use were designed for a god, who knows what we cannot know (§426).

This is a muddle. In truth, the insistence upon substituting 'I believe he is in pain' for the confident assertion 'He is in pain' (or, indeed, for 'I

[31] Hume, *A Treatise of Human Nature*, Bk. I, Pt. iv, Sect. 6.

know he is in pain') is not an expression of justifiable epistemic caution based on experience. Rather it is the replacement of one way of talking (*Redeweise*), one form of expression, by another. For evidently *there is no such thing*, on this conception, as *knowing* that someone else is in pain (cf. BB 54).

Of course, it *looks* otherwise. For one is inclined to say '*He* knows whether he is in pain, I can only believe it', and this looks like an explanation of an epistemic limitation. But it is not, for (a) he neither knows nor is ignorant (PI §246), and therefore (b) the appearance that there *is* such a thing (on this conception) as *knowing* that he is in pain (but *I* fall short of achieving it) is doubly mistaken. In so far as he can be said to know that he is in pain, he does not know that *he*, as opposed to *someone else*, is in pain (and that means that he need not know *who* is, i.e. having a pain identifies no bearer). So what he is alleged to know merely by feeling pain is not what I allegedly can only believe but not know. For what I believe (and may indeed know) is that A (someone else) is in pain, but what A (allegedly) knows is not that A is in pain, but rather that *he* is in pain.

The proposed exclusion of 'I know that' as a prefix to 'He is in pain' does not rest on *doubt* about the suffering of others, for then one would not say that I *can* only believe . . . , i.e. it would make sense for me to know, and one could specify the circumstances under which one knows that another is in pain, e.g. when doubt is put at rest. But the global exclusion of knowledge (which is a mere grammatical move) does not differentiate circumstances wherein one *merely* believes *because* there is some doubt from cases where there is no doubt at all. Hence §303(b): just try, in a case when someone is writhing in pain or a baby is screaming with colic, to say 'There is some doubt here; I only *believe* he is in pain'. Here it is perspicuous that the interlocutor's demand is no more than a demand to employ a different *form* of words, not (as it is presented as being) an expression of strict epistemic standards.

2 LPE 302 remarks:

> One could from the beginning teach the child the expression 'I think he has toothache' instead of 'he has toothache', with the corresponding uncertain tone of voice. This mode of expression could be described by saying that we can only believe that the other has toothache.
>
> But why not in the child's own case? Because there the tone of voice is simply *determined* by nature.

In this way of speaking, one might say, the difference between an *expression* of toothache and a *statement* of toothache is marked by the different forms of words 'I have . . .' and 'I think he has . . .'. So here the proposition 'We can only believe that the other has toothache' would be a grammatical proposition to the effect that *others* cannot *express* A's toothache, but can only *state* that he has one. But, of course, provision of a distinction between certainty and doubt regarding another's toothaches has yet to be made.

Vol. XVI, 119f. pursues matters further:

> Und warum soll man nicht sagen: 'Man kann nie *wissen*, dass einer blind ist, nicht sieht, die Tatsachen können es nur höchst wahrscheinlich machen'? Warum soll man nicht auch diese Ausdrucksform// *diese* Ausdrucksweise// gebrauchen, so kompliziert// sehr verwickelt // und irreführend wie sie ist?
>
> Wenn ich annehme, dass er die und die Erscheinung vor sich sieht — auch gegen alle äussere Evidenz, so nehme ich eigentlich ein Bild an.
>
> Wie geht die Annahme eines Sachverhaltes in die Annahme einer Ausdrucksform über? Wie geht das arbeitende Rad in ein leerlaufendes über? Die Annahme leistet keine Arbeit mehr.

> (And why shouldn't one say 'One can never *know* that someone is blind, cannot see, the facts can only make it highly probable'? Why shouldn't this form of expression // *this* mode of expression // be used too, complicated // thoroughly entangled // and misleading as it is?
>
> If I suppose that even contrary to all external evidence he sees such and such an appearance before him, then I am really accepting a picture.
>
> How does the supposition of a state of affairs go over into the acceptance of a form of expression? How does a working cog go over into a free-wheeling one? The supposition ceases to do any work.)

Behaviour and behaviourism
1. Behaviourism in psychology and philosophy   2. Wittgenstein: first reactions   3. Crypto-behaviourism?   4. Body and behviour

---

SECTION 304

1   So strong is the inner/outer picture under which we labour, the model of object and name, the idea that the 'image' of pain (*die Vorstellung des Schmerzes*) enters the language-game as a paradigm, the supposition that having a pain is knowing something which others cannot know, that when W. repudiates these misconceptions, it will appear as if he is a behaviourist (cf. §307), denying that there is any difference between pain-behaviour accompanied by pain and pain-behaviour without pain. We do not see that these pictures are merely *emblematic* representations of our grammar, not pictures of the facts. Hence W.'s description of the grammar of sensation-words looks to our astigmatic vision as if it were a denial of something we all wish to affirm.

Why, in particular, does he appear to be denying the difference between pain-behaviour with and without pain? Because he denies that pain is an inner object, a *something*, which its owner may scrutinize and describe for the benefit of those who cannot perceive it. And is that not tantamount to saying that pain is *a nothing*? (If it isn't a something, it must be a nothing!) No; this is to misunderstand him altogether. What he is doing is rejecting the grammar of name and object (§293) which tries to force itself upon us here. To deny that a pain is a mental object (a kind of substance, only in an ethereal realm), to deny that having a pain is akin to having a penny, to deny that one can have a pain now which is just like one's pain yesterday, only not the same, is not to say that pain is a nothing. It is rather to insist that the grammar of pain is not the grammar of objects — indeed, not even the grammar of items that can be said to be *something*, let alone of what can be said to be *nothing*. For 'I have something in my mouth' — 'What is it?' — 'A toothache' is surely appropriate only in the Looking Glass world. And *nothing* is, as it were, the *absence* of something (e.g. there is nothing, no money, in the purse; nothing, no noteworthy event, happened in the street; nothing, no sound, could be heard). But it is, of course, no part of W.'s argument that *pain* is the absence of something.

The argument that repudiated the name/object model for 'pain' reached the conclusion that a nothing would fulfil the *apparently* requisite roles of private sample, of justification for saying 'I am in pain', or of a private picture before the mind's eye *no less well* than a something about which nothing can be said. Why 'a something about which nothing can be said'? This ground has been raked over. (a) The something, unconnected with any behavioural manifestation, has no criteria of identity; one cannot even say that one *believes* that it is the same as before (§260). (b) It does not belong to any superior category such as 'sensation' or even 'something' (§261). (c) If the word for it has any use, it does not matter at all if one recognizes the 'something' correctly or not (§270). (d) It would not matter for the imagined language-game with a name for such a something whether each person had something different answering to the name, or even nothing at all (§293). (e) The something, thus conceived, is like the water in the picture of the boiling kettle; it is not 'boiling in the picture' — indeed, it is not picturable. In short, *nothing at all* will fulfil the role of such a something, about which nothing can be said.

This seems paradoxical, but is not. It is merely to repudiate the idea that the grammar of pain can be coherently represented on the model of correlating a word with an object. But the appearance of paradox will disappear only when one frees oneself from the trammels of the Augustinian picture of language, according to which language always functions in the same way (the function of words is to name, sentences are combinations of names that describe a state of affairs). According to that pervasive *Urbild*, the purpose of communication by means of language is equally uniform, viz. to convey thoughts (PI §363). Ridding oneself of this picture will enable one to see the role of verbal manifestations of pain, and so too of expressions of intention, emotion, or mood, the grammatical character of telling one's dream or recounting one's recollections. It will also bring home to one how *specialized* is the activity of conveying one's thoughts to another (see 'Thinking: the soul of language', §4). The bulk of our discourse, contrary to philosophical tradition, is not to communicate our thoughts, reflections, or ruminations. Everything will appear different when seen from the correct logical point of view! One will distinguish between *expressions* (*Äusserungen*) of the inner and *reports* of the inner (which are not descriptions); and one will be led to examine in detail just what *are* descriptions of mental states.

2   MS. 124, 19ff. elaborates: not only do 'He has pains' and 'He behaves thus-and-so' mean something quite different, but their uses are far *more* different than philosophers who attack behaviourism imagine! For when they emphasize and try to show us this difference, they represent the uses of the two kinds of sentences on the model of the same schema. W.'s observation here is penetrating: both behaviourism *and* dualism labour under related confusions. (See 'Behaviour and behaviourism', §§3–4.)

The theme of a something or a nothing is given a forty-page investigation in Vol. XVII, 7ff. Cf. also MS. 166, 24ff.

3   'to convey thoughts': this venerable misconception was a pivotal point in Frege's conception of communication by means of language.

Section 305

1   This involves a parallel movement of thought to §304. The question 'Surely remembering involves an inner process?', like 'Surely pain is not a nothing?', is what is misleading. If one affirms the interlocutor's proposition, one subscribes to a mythology of mind; if one denies it, one seems to be denying what is most obvious.

What needs to be denied here is not a fact, but a picture that informs a description. It is the picture that is misguided; it leads to the morass of 'inner perception' that dogs empiricism (and much empirical psychology). For then we think that the 'inner process of remembering' is *seen* by the recollecting person, and that he who remembers must *know* that it is *memory* that he is invoking. And how should he know that save by reference to (privately) observable features of the inner process, such as vivacity (Hume) or familiarity (Russell)? The phrase 'inner process' is immensely misleading; we think that there are two broad genera of processes, outer ones and inner ones. So an inner process is a *process*, just like fermentation in a vat, only it happens to be 'inner'! (See 'Thinking: methodological muddles and categorial confusions', §§3–4.) To insist that the form of words 'inner process of remembering' incorporates a misguided picture is not to deny that people remember things, nor is it to insist that remembering is behaving.

2   PG 85 connects the objections to the picture of psychological processes with parallel objections to the picture of numbers as objects. What does remembering *consist of*? (*That* surely is a misguided question!) W. notes that remembering is not at all the mental process one imagines at first sight. The most varied things may happen when I say 'I remember that *p*'; and also nothing at all, save just rightly saying it! 'The psychological process of . . . is in the same case as the arithmetical object three. The word "process" in the one case, and the word "object" in the other produce a false grammatical *attitude* to the word.'

Vol. XII, 252, contains PI §305 followed by the remark that when someone says 'You surely know that when you remember a certain thing you experience something inner', one is inclined to answer 'Yes'; i.e. one is inclined to use this picture. But what next? What happens with it now? (It is noteworthy that in Vol. XVII, 7ff., having discussed the something/nothing schema at length and observed that he is searching for the magic words that will break the spell here (p. 22), W. notes that 'Yes — and now what?' or 'What are these words good for?' are the *entzaubernde Wort* (p. 39), the spell-breaking word. For in the grip of philosophical illusion, one constantly describes a picture here, not the application of a picture; one describes an imaginary, free-wheeling (*leerlaufende*) language-game behind the real one. Asking what the consequences are, what the function in the language-game of the inner 'something' is, will therefore break the spell; for reflection will show that it has *none*.) Vol. XII, 253 continues: if we are, in certain circumstances, inclined to repeat to ourselves idle sentences (*leerlaufende Sätze*), why should there not also be idle dialogues, such as the above exchange. The interlocutor queries: 'You surely don't want to say that nothing went on within you!' — Well, W. replies, I said: I remembered . . . Should there have been something *else* going on? After all, you didn't mean a process in the sense of 'eating' or 'knitting'. Nothing is being denied here, W. concludes, save the wrong picture that is imposed by the expression 'inner process', just as calling the number three 'an object' imposes the wrong picture.

Vol. XVI, 134f. explores a different route: 'Remembering is surely an inner process' is a grammatical remark which actually says that the language-game begins with the *expression* of the memory. The grammatical remark gives the *appearance* of justifying us in making assumptions about a person's inner processes of remembering; but one could say that just because remembering is an inner process, an assumption about the inner processes of remembering is quite senseless if it is not an assumption about the expression of these processes. The theme is resumed on pp. 249–70.

Section 306

2   Vol. XII, 246 contains this, preceded by a remark on the vacuity of assumptions about an inner process that are not coupled with assumptions about its outer expression (parallel to remarks just quoted from Vol. XVI, 134f.). W. then gives an analogy for the *picture* of remembering as an inner process. It is as if we had inherited a form of language that represented all things as the product of casting a material (a 'stuff') in a form, so that in this language one could not talk plainly of a table, but always of the matter of the table having been introduced into the form of the table. Then one would be led to believe that simply to talk about the table is a kind of linguistic crudity, in that one should distinguish first the matter and then the form into which it enters. The result of philosophy here would be that one *did* talk plainly of the table and viewed this as a perfectly good form of expression. PI §306 follows; clearly 'mental process of remembering' is analogous to 'matter and form of a table' in the imagined form of representation. For here too it seems that if we talk about remembering without mentioning a mental process, it appears as if we are being crude and imprecise.

Section 307

1   W.'s riposte here epitomizes the argument of §§304–6. (See 'Behaviour and behaviourism', §3.)

2   In MS. 124, 5f. a draft of this occurs, preceded by a variant of PI §217(c), quoted in Exg. §217, 2.1(iii). Then:

> Aber bist Du nicht doch nur ein verkappter Behaviourist? Denn Du sagst, dass *nichts* hinter der Äusserung der Empfindung steht?
> Sagst Du nicht doch im Grunde, dass alles Fiktion ist, ausser dem <u>Benehmen</u>? – Fiktion? So glaube ich also, dass wir nicht wirklich etwas empfinden, sondern nur Gesichter machen/schneiden/?!// So glaube ich also, dass wir nicht eigentlich empfinden; sondern bloss so tun?// Aber Fiktion *ist* der Gegenstand hinter der Äusserung.// Fiktion aber ist *wirklich* die Erklärung der Äusserung mit dem/mittels

d̲e̲s̲/privaten Gegenstand/Gegenstands./ vor unserm innern Sinne.// Fiktion ist es, dass unsre Worte, um Bedeutung zu haben// etwas zu bedeuten//, auf ein Etwas anspielen müssen, das ich, wenn nicht einem Andern, doch mir selbst zeigen kann. (*Grammatische* Fiktion.)

(But aren't you just a behaviourist in disguise? For you say that *nothing* stands behind the expression of the sensation?

Aren't you at bottom saying that everything except b̲e̲h̲a̲v̲i̲o̲u̲r̲ is a fiction? — Fiction? So I believe that we don't really have sensations of anything, but only make/pull/faces?!// So I believe that we don't really have sensations but only pretend to?// But the object behind the expression *is* a fiction?// What is *really* a fiction is the explanation of the expression by the / by means of the/ private object before our inner sense. It is a fiction that in order for our words to have a meaning // to mean something // they must allude to something, which I, if not another, can show myself. (A *grammatical* fiction.))

The proposition that nothing stands behind the expression of a sensation, W. continues, is a *grammatical* one; it does not say that we do not have sensations. The interlocutor protests: 'Aren't you saying that "The soul is just something bodily"?, that when you have described people's behaviour, you have described everything?' But, W. retorts, he who *gives expression* to his pain does not describe his own behaviour! Yet, the interlocutor queries, if nothing stands behind the expression (*Äusserung*), does that not mean that it is not the expression of something (*nicht der Ausdruck von etwas ist*)? No, W. replies, for what it expresses, is not what we have agreed to call *thus*.

3   J. B. Watson argued in *Behaviourism* that belief in the existence of mental states, of consciousness, is mere supposition; that there is no objective evidence for the existence of minds (see 'Behaviour and behaviourism', §1).

SECTION 308

1   This describes, and prescribes the antidote to, the natural dialectic of reflection in the philosophy of psychology. Dualism insists that there are mental states and processes; after all, we experience them, are intimately acquainted with them, know them by introspection. Behaviourism insists that this is a pre-scientific mythology, that there are no mental states and processes, that these are fictions; and logical behaviourism argues that mental states are just logical constructions out of behaviour and dispositions to behave. Torn between these poles, materialism attempts a synthesis: there are indeed mental states and processes, only they are identical with brain-states, which cause behaviour. But this too is unsatisfactory for a multitude of reasons, and we replace it by

something more up to date, viz. functionalism: mental states and processes are functional states of an organism that cause behaviour and are 'realized' in the nervous system. And so on. Far from this 'Hegelian' development being Reason successively approximating to the Real, it is a picture of Reason caught in the Hall of Mirrors: one illusion after another captures our attention for a while before we move on to the next.

The initial error escaped our attention, for it seemed altogether innocent. We talk of states and processes and very carefully avoid committing ourselves to characterizing their nature. *That*, we think, will become clear in the course of subsequent investigations. What could be more careful than such a procedure? But it is precisely here that the error lies: for the expressions 'state' and 'process', although vague, have specific grammars. Their unreflective adoption in psychology commits us to a definite (and misleading) way of looking at things. In one use of the expression, a state is an array of objects, with various properties, standing in certain relations to each other; that is how we talk of the state of the room (as tidy, the books being in the bookcase, the furniture in place) or of the garden (as untidy, with untrimmed bushes, weeds, and an unmown lawn), the state of the economy or the nation. Rather differently, we talk of being solid, liquid, or gaseous as three states of matter. A physical process is a more or less regular sequence of causally related events, themselves constituted by the transformation of substances; it goes on in time, has successive phases, can be slowed down or speeded up, interrupted, reversed, etc. We have a definite concept of what it is to know such a process better, but that concept does not apply in the same way in the domain of the mental! If we apply our 'definite concept of what it means to learn to know a process better' to the psychical sphere, we shall, *inter alia*, think that the subject of psychical states and processes can 'see' them, observe their obtaining, going on, and changing, and then report back to the psychologist what he has found out about these inner processes accessible directly only to him.[32] (James exemplifies this (see Volume 1, p. 602; MU p. 328). So if we say that 'reading is a quite particular process' (PI §165), we might try to find out more about this peculiar mental process by reading and attending to what happens. Is it too quick? Try reading Cyrillic! (MS. 152, 5; cf. Exg. §165).

Is it still obvious that talking of mental states and processes, *and leaving their nature undecided*, is innocuous? We do indeed talk of mental states (e.g. of intense concentration, nervous agitation, deep depression) and of processes (e.g. of adjusting to new situations, coming to terms with the loss of a loved one, of the growth of self-knowledge). But instead of examining the rather special uses of 'mental state' and 'mental process',

[32] It is noteworthy that in Vol. XII, 333 a version of PI §571 occurs between two different drafts of PI §308.

which vary from case to case, philosophers (and psychologists) transpose the expressions 'state' and 'process' from the physical to the mental domain, leaving their nature undecided, as if *the facts*, if we are lucky, will reveal it to us. But *their nature is their grammar* (PI §373), and if we do not determine it, i.e. determine the *grammatical* differences between *mental* process and *physical* process, we shall unavoidably project the grammar of the latter onto the former. This will force upon us whole ranges of questions which, in the domain of the mental, make scant sense; or, at least, not the sense one expects, for one will be using the wrong paradigm. (See 'Thinking: methodological muddles and categorial confusions', §§3–4.)

1.1   'And now the analogy . . .': presumably the analogy between physical states and processes and, e.g., remembering, understanding, thinking. For there is indeed an analogy. But if we project upon these concepts our quite definite idea of what it is to come to know a *physical* process better, we fall into nonsense, and the analogy crumbles.

2   In many places W. issued warnings about the promiscuous and misleading application of the concepts of state and process to the mental. Thus:

> We say that understanding is a 'psychological process', and this label is misleading, in this as in countless other cases. It compares understanding to a particular *process* like translation from one language to another, and it suggests the same conception of thinking, knowing, wishing, intending, etc. That is to say, in all these cases, we see that what we would perhaps naively suggest as the hallmark of such a process is not present in every case or even in the majority of cases. And our next step is to conclude that the essence of the process is something difficult to grasp that still awaits discovery. (PG 74f.)

In this context in the *Grammar* W. suggested that understanding signifies a whole family of interrelated processes in specific contexts. But in *Zettel* he insisted, 'But don't think of understanding as a "mental process" at all. — For *that* is the way of speaking that is confusing you' (Z §446; cf. PI §196; see also Volume 1, 'Understanding and ability', §§6 – 8). Similarly, we are puzzled as to how our thought is connected with what or whom we are thinking about, and so 'we think of meaning or thinking as a peculiar *mental activity*; the word "mental" indicating that we mustn't expect to understand how these things work' (BB 39). We wonder what the nature of imagination is and expect the answer to be given by a *description of a process*; but 'One ought to ask, not what images are or what happens when one imagines anything, but how the word "imagination" is used' (PI §370). The present tense of expressions of ability, e.g. 'He is capable of . . .', 'He is able to multiply', 'He can play chess', etc., wrongly suggest that 'the phrases are descriptions of states which exist at the moment when we speak' (BB 117), and this gets in the way of seeing that potentialities are not shadowy actualities, and that earlier and later performances are *criteria* for having abilities at a particular time.

Despite these remarks, W. himself sometimes apparently indulges an inclination to the promiscuous use of 'mental state', albeit with qualifications. Thus in *Investigations* §§572f. he observed that expecting, opining, hoping, knowing, being able to do something are states. The crucial qualifications are (a) that these are *grammatically* states, implying that surface grammar (the mere forms of expression that can be taken in at a glance) here misleads us (for 'sleeping' is *grammatically* an activity, 'refraining' is *grammatically* an act, etc.); (b) that only examination of the criteria for, e.g., reaching an opinion, having an opinion, changing an opinion, will show *what* gets treated *grammatically* (formally) as a *state* here. More carelessly, in *Remarks of the Philosophy of Psychology* he characterized seeing (RPP I §1; RPP II §43), believing (RPP I §704), hearing, and having a sensation (RPP II §45) as *mental states*. On the other hand, in the same work he explicitly denied that believing, knowing, intending, etc. are states of consciousness, stressing their lack of 'genuine duration' (RPP II §45). There seems to be an unclarity in his thoughts in this text, which he surely would have remedied had he lived to prepare these notes for publication. His most important remarks on this subject are two late, methodological observations. The first warns against taking these very general concepts as ultimate logical categories, sharply defined and providing pre-prepared pigeon-holes for everything:

The concept of experience: Like that of happening, of process, of state, of something, of fact, of description and of report. Here we think we are standing on the hard bedrock, deeper than any special methods and language-games. But these extremely general terms have an extremely blurred meaning. They relate in practice to innumerable special cases, but that does not make them any the more *solid*; no, rather it makes them more fluid. (RPP I §648)

The second manifests a sharpened awareness of the misleading character of such questions as 'Is X (where 'X' holds a place for a psychological expression) a mental state (process, activity, act, disposition, etc.)?' Apropos expecting someone, knowing since this morning that he is coming, W. wrote:

Wenn man fragt: ist dies ein Zustand der Seele — so sieht man, das weder die Antwort 'Ja' noch die Antwort 'Nein' etwas nützt. Es gibt zu viele (psychologische) Kategorien, die man alle 'Zustände der Seele' nennen könnte. Die Einteilung // Klassifizierung // hilft hier nichts mehr. Man muss die Begriffe einzeln von einander unterscheiden. (MS. 167, 6).

(If one asks: is this a state of mind — one sees that neither the answer 'Yes' nor the answer 'No' helps. There are too many (psychological) categories all of which could be called 'states of mind'. The division // classification // no longer helps here. One must di̲s̲t̲i̲n̲g̲u̲i̲s̲h̲ the concepts from one another individually.)

2.1   'the first step': Vol. XII, 332 elaborates:

Der erste Schritt ist die unschuldige pneumatische Auffassung, wobei man (aber) die 'Art' der Vorgänge oder Zustände offen lässt. Der nächste aber ist, dass man sieht: welcher *Art* immer dieses Etwas ist, wovon man reden will — es erkläre nichts und sei eine unnütze Fiktion. Gibt man nun aber diese Fiktion auf, so scheint man alles Geistige zu leugnen und dadurch zu sagen, es gäbe nur Körperliches.

(The first step is the innocent ethereal conception in which one (nevertheless) leaves open the 'kind' of processes or states. But the next is that one sees that no matter what *kind* of thing this something is of which one wants to talk, it explains nothing and is a useless fiction. But now if one gives up this fiction, it seems as if one is denying everything mental and thereby saying that there is only the bodily.)

3   The disease of thought here diagnosed was, and still is, pervasive. W. himself succumbed to it, as is strikingly evident in his 1919 letter to Russell (R 37). Frege was similarly infected (PW 145). So was James, who (apparently innocuously) assumed 'a direct awareness of the process of our thinking as such, simply insisting on the fact that it is an even more inward and subtle phenomenon than most of us suppose'.[33] Similar cautious confessions of ignorance about the *nature* of mental states, activities, processes, or acts are to be found in Moore, Russell, Ramsey, etc., coupled of course with complete confidence that *there are such*; and so a *picture* is prepared into which subsequent reflections will be made to fit!

SECTION 309

1   Ryle asked 'But what has the fly missed, that has never got into the bottle and therefore never looked for or found the way out of it?' This is misleading, and the tempting answer that 'It has missed philosophical insight' is equally so. The correct answer would be: nothing at all save the experience of being trapped — but has there ever been such a fly? Only a clod or a god could resist being drawn into the fly-bottle of philosophical bafflement, a clod because he barely flies (thinks), a god because he already sees both the way in and the way out, so is not tempted in.

[33] James, *Principles of Psychology*, Vol. I, p. 305.

He who always knows his way about the grammar of his language and never loses his bearings, who is not even inclined to conceive the grammar of number-words on the model of the grammar of names of objects or the grammar of mental states on the model of physical states or the grammar of moral discourse on the model of empirical discourse or the grammar of infinite sets on the model of finite sets, etc., has no need for philosophy. For he would see immediately that the verb 'to be' is not used like the verb 'to eat', that the predicate 'is true' has a quite different kind of use from 'is blue', that 'time flows' and 'time passes' signify in a different way from 'the river flows' or 'the storm passes', and so forth. Such a person already possesses philosophical insight and does not need to work his way through the quagmires of philosophical confusion in order to attain it.

But we are not like that. The grammars of our languages are immensely difficult for us to survey; philosophical questions masquerading as factual questions about the nature of things come naturally to us, and we are enmeshed in philosophical confusions that spring from the language we use, from the endlessly misleading forms of language which mask categorial differences from our eyes.

Die Menschen sind tief in den philosophischen, d.i. grammatischen Konfusionen eingebettet. Und, sie daraus zu befreien, setzt voraus, dass man sie aus den ungeheuer mannigfachen Verbindungen herausreisst, in denen sie gefangen sind. Man muss sozusagen ihre ganze Sprache umgruppieren. — Aber diese Sprache ist ja so entstanden // geworden //, weil Menschen die Neigung hatten — und haben —, so zu denken. (BT 423)

(Human beings are deeply embedded in philosophical, i.e. grammatical, confusion. And they cannot be freed without first being extricated from the extraordinary variety of associations which hold them captive. You have, as it were, to reconstitute their entire language. But this language grew up // became // as it did because human beings had — and have — the tendency to think in this way.)

Moreover, we *love* our chains:

Das was den Gegenstand schwer verständlich macht, ist — wenn er bedeutend, wichtig, ist — nicht, dass irgendeine besondere Instruktion über abstruse Dinge zu seinem Verständnis erforderlich wäre, sondern der Gegensatz zwischen dem Verstehen des Gegenstandes und dem, was die meisten Menschen sehen *wollen*. (BT 406f.)

(What makes it difficult to understand the matter — if it is significant, important — is not the lack of some special instruction in obstruse things necessary for its understanding, but the conflict between the right understanding of the matter and what most men *want* to see.)

For who among us would not prefer the glitter of gold encrusted with jewels brought into view by metaphysics to the heap of rusting iron and old stones revealed when the spell is lifted.

It is not just philosophers who are drawn into the fly-bottle, but scientists, psychologists, mathematicians — in fact all who reflect on the nature of the soul, the relation of mind to body, the character of thought, the scope of possible knowledge, the strangeness of mathematics, etc. 'Philosophy is a tool which is useful only against philosophers and against *the philosopher in us*' (TS. 219, 11; my emphasis).

To ask what the fly which has never got into the bottle has missed is rather like asking what the man who has never been ill has missed. Doctors are not likely to become redundant (or iatrogenic diseases to cease to multiply!).

2   LPE 300 has the first occurrence of the fly-bottle metaphor: 'The solipsist flutters and flutters in the flyglass, strikes against the walls, flutters further. How can he be brought to rest?' PI §309 occurs in Vol. XIV, 142f. and Vol. XIII, 92, with the addendum 'Diesen Weg zu finden, ist unter gewissen Verhältnissen un̲m̲ö̲g̲l̲i̲c̲h̲; unter andern ganz leicht; und unter wieder anderen ungemein schwer' ('To find this way is in certain circumstances i̲m̲p̲o̲s̲s̲i̲b̲l̲e̲; in others altogether easy; and in yet others extraordinarily difficult'). When is it impossible? Perhaps when the will to illusion cannot be broken!

SECTION 310

1   W. now reverts to §304: viz. the difference between pain-behaviour accompanied by pain and pain-behaviour without any pain. §310(a) sets the scene: I avow pain; the hearer may believe, disbelieve, be slightly suspicious, etc. §310(b) follows up the interlocutor's question in §304(a): does not the hearer's response 'It's not so bad' *prove* that he believes that there is *something* behind my pain-behaviour, something to which he *refers* in saying that *it* is not so bad? No; his attitude is what it is, commiseration or gentle reproach. It is an attitude towards a soul, towards a human being, a person (PI p. 178). That the hearer may take up this or that attitude manifests his belief that I am in pain or his suspicion that I am not suffering as much as I make out, but *that* is not proof of a philosophical thesis (mythology) that pain is *a something* behind pain-behaviour. His attitude, expressed by his utterance 'It's not so bad', could also be expressed by instinctive noises and gestures. Would they prove that he believes that pain is an inner object known only to its owner? — No more than an instinctive cry of pain proves that the sufferer believes that he has something no one else could have!

2   In MS. 165, 171 this is followed by a contrast with the role of the truth or falsity of a statement in other language-games. If I look out of the

window and say 'The wind has blown the tree over', you may rush to
the window and see whether I was pulling your leg or speaking the truth.
Clearly this is disanalogous to the way in which we establish whether in
saying 'I am in pain', you were only pulling my leg.

2.1   'His attitude to me . . .': cf. Z. §545.

SECTION 311

1   §304 agreed with the interlocutor that of course there is all the
difference in the world between pain-behaviour without pain and
pain-behaviour with pain. But this is readily misunderstood as a
concession to his *picture*; for the interlocutor eagerly explains the
difference on his preferred model. It seems that the difference is such as
can only be exhibited or displayed to oneself, privately. I can exhibit
publicly the difference between a broken and an unbroken tooth, but
pain-behaviour with pain differs from pain-behaviour without pain only
by the presence of *pain*; and *that*, the interlocutor insists, I can exhibit
only to myself.
       But, W. retorts, for the 'private exhibition' one does not have to prick
oneself with a pin (and, even if one did prick oneself, that would be
having a pain, not *exhibiting* a pain to oneself). It should suffice that one
imagines a pain. Then one can say to oneself that when pain-behaviour is
accompanied by *this*, it is pain-behaviour *with* pain, otherwise not! But
what does one *do* when one imagines pain? Perhaps one screws up one's
face a little! Does *that* tell one what it is that one is imagining? Although
one can imagine pain-behaviour with pain and pain-behaviour without
pain, to imagine anything presupposes a grasp of what is to be imagined.
Hence here it presupposes that the difference is crystal-clear to one *prior*
to one's imagining these two cases. Moreover, to imagine a pain is not to
exhibit pain to oneself. There is no such thing as a *private* exhibition of the
private.

1.1   (i) 'Den Unterschied aber . . .': 'I can, however, exhibit . . .'.
       (ii) 'You screw up your face a bit': to imagine pain is not to have a
picture of pain before one's mind, for there is no such thing. You can
imagine pain all right, but not by way of a mental image (*bildliche
Vorstellung*) of pain (cf. Exg. §§300f.). Of course, when you imagine
pain, a mental image may cross your mind too — perhaps an image of
something brown or violet-brown (MS. 161, 52)!

2   The illusion of a 'private exhibition' of experience, of displaying the
'content' of experience before one's mind, is discussed in various

passages in RPP I. One is sorely tempted to say that one knows what toothaches are like, that one is acquainted with them, and so too with the experiences of seeing different colours, feeling emotions, remembering, intending, etc. In all these cases one is inclined to say that one has a 'privileged access' to the phenomena, and surely one can 'parade these experiences before one's mind', exhibit them to oneself! W. responds acidly, 'So I know, do I, what it means to parade these experiences before one's mind? And what *does* it mean? How can I explain it to anyone else, or to myself?' (RPP I §91). The very concept of the content of experience thus invoked in philosophy 'is the private object, the sense-datum, the "object" that I grasp immediately with the mental eye, ear, etc. The inner picture' (RPP I §109; cf. RPP I §896).

Section 312

1   §311 argued that there is such a thing as a public exhibition or display of the public (e.g. the difference between a broken and an unbroken tooth), but no such thing as the *private* exhibition of the private. Yet it may seem that the cases of the tooth and of the pain are similar, for do I not note the difference between a broken and an unbroken tooth by *seeing* it; and does not the visual sensation (or sense-impression) in this case correspond to the sensation of pain in the other?

W.'s answer comes in two stages. First, I can exhibit (display) the visual impression *privately* as little as I can exhibit (display) pain to myself privately; i.e. there is no such thing as a *private exhibition*. For neither *having* (or imagining) a pain, nor having (or imagining) a visual sense-impression, count as exhibiting a pain or as exhibiting a visual sense-impression even to oneself. Does it follow that one *cannot* exhibit pain or exhibit having a visual sense-impression? No, one *can* exhibit pain and one *can* exhibit having a visual sense-impression — only not *privately* (cf. §313). To exhibit these to myself does not differ from exhibiting them to someone else. Of course, a sensation of pain does not correspond to a visual sensation or sense-impression; for having a pain is not involved in perceiving an object. But that does not affect the argument.

§312(b) gives the (opaque) second stage of W.'s reply. The absence of an object perceived does not hinder a public exhibition of pain. One can indeed imagine a closer association between pain and perception. If surfaces of plants had areas on them which produced pain on touch, and if it were useful to notice these patches and their shapes (e.g. if they correlated well with the nature, medicinal or nutritious character, of the plants), then the sensation of pain had on touching these plants would be akin to perceiving. What one perceived by touching and having a sharp pain would be conceived as a pain-patch, and these pain-patches thus apprehended would be important in identifying or characterizing the plant. Sensitivity to pain on touching plants would then be a faculty for apprehending features of the world around us (some people might be better than others at discerning whether a plant was such-and-such).

How does this bear on §312(a)? Perhaps as follows: one would display the difference between a broken and an unbroken tooth by pointing at them; one would display having a visual sense-impression of a broken tooth by looking at one and maybe saying 'Aha! This looks like a broken tooth!' or otherwise giving expression to how it strikes one visually. How then does one, in a parallel manner, exhibit feeling pain? We do not, as it happens, talk (much[34]) of pain-patches. But that does not matter. In the envisaged story one could exhibit pain-patches to touch as one exhibits red patches to sight. One would, further, exhibit feeling pain, e.g. by touching a pain-patch on a plant and drawing one's hand back and exclaiming 'Ow!' One can, in this sense, exhibit the sensation of pain for oneself no less well than one can exhibit the visual sense-impression of a broken tooth. The fact that we do not speak of pain-patches as we speak of colour-patches is irrelevant to the nature of exhibiting seeing or pain. But there is nothing private about such exhibiting. Pain is not an object of perception, and sensitivity to pain is not a sense-faculty; but there is no impediment to the *public* exhibition of (feeling) pain.

The argument here is puzzling. A visual sense-impression or sensation (*Gesichtsempfindung*) corresponds to the sensation of pain only in the sense that neither can be exhibited 'privately' (see 2(ii) below). That one can exhibit the sensation of pain publicly, i.e. *manifest* pain, is a point which gets no significant support from the story of pain-patches; nor does it need it. Whether or not there are pain-patches on objects which are perceptible by touch, the concept of a sensation of pain is fundamentally different from the concept of a 'visual sensation' or a visual sense-impression. The concept of a visual impression of X is parasitic on the concept of X. So, for example, the concept of a visual impression of red is parasitic on the concept of red, and the latter can be defined ostensively by reference to a red patch, used as a sample. But the concept of pain is not parasitic on the concept of its cause. It is determined by the criteria for pain. Even if we talked of pain-patches, the concept of a pain-patch would be parasitic on the concept of pain, not vice versa. A pain-patch

---

[34] We do a little, as in '*stinging* nettles', '*burning* sand', '*painful* shoes'; but it is easy to see why we do not extend this. Almost anything can cause pain, hence its capacity to do so is a poor guide to its nature. Most things that can cause pain do not always do so when touched. And pain so caused typically persists *after* contact is broken.

would *cause* pain on touch, but it would be mistaken to suppose that a red patch *causes* a visual impression of red (though this cannot be argued here). §312(b) does not really seem to advance the argument at all.

1.1   (i) 'visual sensation': arguably a stretched use of 'sensation'. Are there such things as *visual* sensations as opposed to visual impressions? The best candidate for the title would be the sensation of being dazzled; but that is not what W. has in mind.

(ii) 'that we can infer important properties from them': as things are, of course, we cannot infer important properties of objects from the fact that they can cause us pain, but only 'accidents' of objects (e.g. that they are, at the moment, hot). Indeed, that is one reason why we do not talk of pain-patches.

2   (i) MS. 165, 176f. imagines getting an electric shock from certain areas on the surface of things. Sensitivity to pain could be employed (in these circumstances) in discerning features of the external world in a similar way to tactile sensation (cf. RPP I §697).

(ii) Z §§665ff. argues that I can exhibit something to myself only in the way I exhibit it to others. I can exhibit my good memory by interrogating myself and answering (the dates of the English monarchs, for example); and this serves both for others and for myself.

SECTION 313

1   This draws the conclusion from §312. One *can* exhibit pain, but not as the interlocutor envisaged. We need to bring to mind what is *called* exhibiting (or displaying) pain. W. does not here note the manifold *differences* between exhibiting pain and exhibiting red, but concentrates on the reminder that the former is no less public than the latter. That much is true. But it is surely misleading to suggest that one can exhibit pain *as* (in *the same way* as) one can exhibit red).

2   In MS. 165, 178 and MS. 124, 290 this is followed by PI §§273ff., which clarifies that exhibiting red is not a private exhibition either.

SECTION 314

1   A concluding remark: the philosophical problem(s) about sensation are not to be resolved by studying (concentrating on) one's sensations. For it is nonsense to suppose that the 'nature' of pain, for example, can be read off the sensation. And it is misguided to construe the grammar of 'pain'

on the model of name and object. Rather, one should proceed by analysing the concept of sensation (cf. PI §§383f.), which is done by studying the *use of the word* 'sensation' (cf. Z §§546–8).

This remark is the hook upon which §§316ff. hang.

Section 315

1   The ideas that understanding the word 'pain' turns on the possibility of my giving myself a *private* exhibition of pain (or, more generally, of the 'inner') and that it is only from my own case that I know what 'pain' means (PI §§311, 293(a)) go hand in hand with the thought that a necessary condition for understanding the word 'pain' is to have felt pain. But is this meant to be an empirical truth? Have we discovered that people who have never suffered pains do *not* understand the word? Clearly not. (Have we ever come across such a person? Is our immediate inclination to assent to this claim based on our experience with such people?)

Confronted by the fact that the apparent obviousness of the claim is not based on social surveys, we are inclined to insist that one could not *imagine* pain without having previously felt pain. (For are 'ideas of the imagination' not faint copies of antecedent impressions?) And surely, it seems that 'using a sentence involves imagining something for every word' (PI §449). Is it not obvious that 'I must know what it would be like if I were in pain' (ibid.)?

This common line of thought is confused. First, it is, for many reasons, misguided to think that in using a sentence with understanding one must imagine something corresponding to it. For example, in the case of the order 'Imagine a red circle here', must I already obey it in order merely to understand it (PI §451)? Secondly, the phrase 'knowing what it would be like' equivocates precisely over the matter at issue. Does it mean 'knowing what ". . ." means'? Or does it mean 'having experienced . . .'? And in the case of pain, if I *have* felt pain, *do* I therefore know *what it is like*? The experience of pain is surely not a sufficient condition for knowing what it is like! (Does an injured cat know what it is like to have a pain?) Indeed, what is it like? That is, what *kind* of answer does this question invite? It obviously steers us in the direction of answering 'Like *this*' — and thumping ourselves on the chest; but then, what is *this* like? The answer is modelled on 'I know what magenta looks like, viz. like *this*' — and pointing at a sample. But this model, as has been shown, has no application here. Thirdly, if one knows what 'pain' means, does one *not* know what it is like to have a pain?

To this question, one might be inclined to reply 'Yes, one does, but one cannot know what "pain" means unless one has had pain!' This is where we started. How can one get off the merry-go-round? Only by asking a different question: viz. 'What are the criteria for knowing what "pain" means?' If a person uses the word 'pain' correctly, says of others that they are in pain when they exhibit pain, says that they are no longer in pain when they exhibit relief from pain, etc., would we deny that he understands what 'pain' means? Would we investigate his medical history before pronouncing on his linguistic competence? Since it is evidently not an empirical claim that one must have felt pain if one knows what 'pain' means, is it a grammatical truth? No; we do not have a rule that prohibits saying of a person that he knows what 'pain' means if, although he uses it correctly, he has never suffered pain. (No more need a person have debts in order to know what a negative number is!)

2 LSD 35f. pinpoints *one* source of the confusion here in the misguided projection of the grammar of colour-words on to the grammar of sensation-words:

> Suppose someone who has never had a toothache, but has heard the word. Then one day he has a toothache, and says 'Now I know what "toothache" means'.
>
> But then suppose I ask him, 'Well, what *does* it mean?' Or: 'Does it mean what I had?'
>
> When I have a sample of red, then if you ask me 'Well, what *does* "red" mean?', I çan answer 'It means *this*'. In the case of toothache, the temptation is to say 'Well, I know, although I can't express it'. There is a suggestion that you have a private ostensive definition. And I say you have not got one.
>
> Just as there is an inclination to say that the ostensive definition of 'red' might be secret — recorded in my diary (which no one else sees); but further, that it is *essentially* secret.

2 'Is experience to teach me . . .': Z §267 elaborates: 'Is it supposed to be an empirical fact that someone who has had an experience can imagine it, and that someone else can *not*? (How do I know that a blind man cannot[35] imagine colours?) But: he cannot play a certain language-game (cannot learn it). But is this empirical, or is it the case *eo ipso*? The latter.' That the blind cannot play (or can only partially master) the language-game with colour-words *is* a grammatical proposition. So too is the remark that, synaesthesia apart, the blind cannot imagine colours. For they do not know what colour-words mean: they can neither use them nor explain them as we do (as they are to be used and explained). So they do not know *what* they are to imagine when told to imagine a red expanse, for example.

[35] The German transcription and translation alike have omitted the negation (see MS. 162(b), 33).

The inner and the outer
  1. Semi-solipsism   2. Inside and outside   3. The indeterminacy of
  the mental

CHAPTER 2

Thought

(§§316–62)

INTRODUCTION

§§316–62 examine the nature of thinking. The grand-strategic role of this 'chapter' is to undermine the idea that it is *thinking* that breathes life into otherwise dead signs. Having demolished the conception of private ostensive definition as fixing the foundations of language, W. now turns to the equally tempting picture of an inner process of thought as constituting the soul of language. This too is a mythology. The strategy perspicuously builds on previous clarifications. Part A (§§316–26) is a preliminary investigation of the 'dual-process' conception of thought. §316 applies the principle of §314 (viz. one cannot clarify philosophical problems about sensations by studying one's headache) to thinking. §317 emphasizes the difference between the relation of pain to a cry (its expression) and of a thought to a proposition (which expresses that thought). The appearance of a parallelism encourages the false notion that the use of a proposition is to communicate an inner process going on in one's thinking apparatus to which one has privileged access. But 'expression' means something quite different in each case. §318 provides a further reason for our conceiving of thinking as an introspective inner process, viz. our idioms of a thought crossing one's mind in a flash and of the lightning speed of thought. §§319–20 clarify these idioms, and §321–3 harken back to the discussion of sudden understanding in §§179–84, bringing those earlier clarifications to bear on the current issue. What 'a thought's going through one's mind like lightning' or 'seeing the solution in a flash' mean is no more to be answered by describing an inner process than sudden understanding is to be clarified by answering the question of what *happens* when one suddenly understands. §§324–6 repudiate the suggestion that one's conviction that one understands (has grasped a thought, seen the solution to a problem) when one has a flash of insight or understanding rests on induction from similar experiences in the past. This conviction requires no reasons and is typically justified.

The structure of Part A:

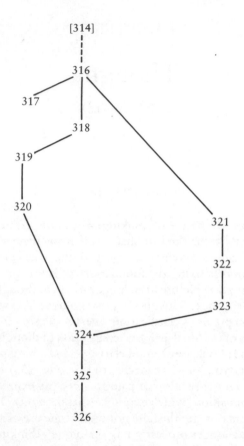

Part B (§§327–41) investigates the relation between thought and speech, misunderstandings of which lie at the heart of the dual-process conception introduced in the preceding remarks. §327 raises the question of whether one can think without speaking, a question which sounds as if it is about the interdependence of two processes. To answer it, the concept of thinking must be clarified, but, of course, not by observing what goes on in oneself when one thinks (cf. §316). First steps are taken in §328, which reminds us of the senselessness of error in saying that one is thinking (but that is not because the inner process is so well lit that one cannot but see it) and of the dissimilarity between the flow of thought and the flow of speech. §329 elaborates the opening sentence of §318: speech with thought (i.e. which is not parrot-like) is not a *pair* of activities. §§330(a) poses the central problem perspicuously: is thinking a kind of speaking? It seems to be a concurrent process the occurrence of which distinguishes speech with thought from parrot-like speech. §330(b) and §§331–7 attempt a variety of antidotes to this insidious poison. In an appropriate context, the only thing that may *happen* outwardly *or* inwardly when one thinks such-and-such is that one makes a gesture, pulls a face, etc. (§330(b)). §331 invites us to imagine people who can think only aloud. §332 concedes, as a behaviourist would not, that speech with thought often involves mental processes concurrent with speech. Nevertheless, that accompaniment is not what is meant by 'a thought'. §333 offers an analogical case in which the pressure is lower. We say 'only someone convinced would say that', but we do not think of the conviction as an inner accompaniment of the speaking, and no more so is the thought when someone speaks with thought. §334 brings to light another phrase which incorporates the misleading dual-process picture, viz. 'You really wanted to say . . .' — as if what one wanted to say coexisted in thought with whatever one ill-advisedly said. But when we look at the actual use of this phrase, it is obvious that that is not how things are. §335 deals with a parallel case: we often, as we say, try to find the right phrase to express our thought; and that looks like trying to find the right phrase to *translate* such-and-such an expression from another language. So this picture makes it appear as if the thought 'is already there' in our mind, and we are just looking for its correct outward expression. But here too, scrutiny of the application of this picture dissolves the illusion. §336 adduces a similar, very natural idea (to a non-German speaker), viz. that one *could not* think a sentence with the word order of German. So one has the picture of thinking the thought and then translating it into word-language. §§337–8 embroider the equally tempting converse thought: viz. that surely one must have *intended* the whole construction of the sentence in advance of uttering it, i.e. one must have constructed it in *thought*? But this idea misconstrues the concept of intention. To intend to do something does not mean that one does it in thought in advance of doing it. §§339–41 bring this part of the discussion to a head. Thinking is not an 'incorporeal process'. One must examine the use of the word, not guess it. Speech with and without thought is comparable to playing a piece of music with and without thought, and playing a sonata with thought does not mean accompanying it with an inaudible process!

The structure of Part B:

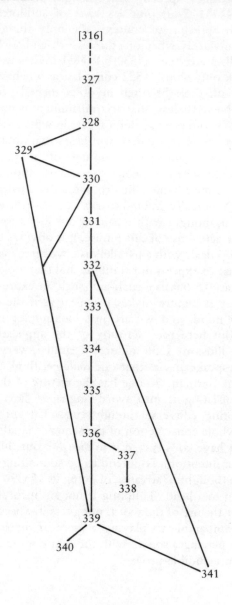

Part C (§§342–52) reverts to the question of §327: can one think without speech? James presented the Ballard case as an empirical proof that one can think sophisticated thoughts even though one cannot speak at all. W. queries not the truth of Ballard's claim, but its intelligibility. 'I remember that I thought . . .' is not a report of an inner event (§343) that one apprehended in the past, and it is unclear what, in Ballard's case, could possibly *count* as his having had thoughts which he could not have expressed or articulated in any way at all. §344 raises much the same question again, not on the grounds of apparent empirical confirmation, but on logical grounds. For we all often think without voicing our thoughts; so the supposition that people who cannot speak an audible language might nevertheless speak to themselves in the imagination (i.e. think) is just a form of the supposition that what sometimes happens can (logically) always happen. §§344–5 challenge the cogency of the latter inference. The criteria for someone's saying something to himself in the imagination lie in his *behaviour*, and we say it only of someone who is able to speak (hence not of a parrot, which can mimic what it hears but cannot speak, has not mastered these techniques). §346 challenges this, for can we not imagine that God gives understanding to a parrot, who now speaks to itself? But to invoke God is precisely to lift the constraints of the language-game! §347 attempts another route to establishing the independence of thought from the possibility of speech, viz. that I know what talking to oneself in the imagination means *from my own case*, and if I lost the power of speech I could still talk to myself. W. challenges the premise. §348 is reduced to defending only the letter of the proposal of §344, while abandoning its spirit. It queries whether deaf mutes who have learned only gesture-language might not nevertheless talk to themselves in their imagination in vocal language. The idea is fishy, W. retorts, for we are applying a picture in a context where it has no grip (§349). §§350–1 investigate analogous illegitimate cases of attempted extrapolation. §352 examines a misuse of the law of excluded middle which we commonly indulge in when we insist that there must be an objective fact of the matter, viz. either they talk to themselves or they do not, etc.! But the law of excluded middle *presupposes* the sense of its constituent propositions and cannot be used to establish it!

The structure of Part C:

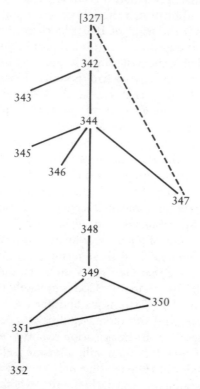

Part D (§§353–6) interpolates a brief set of remarks on verification. The link with the foregoing is twofold. First, §352, like §350, showed that appeals to identity or the law of excluded middle, far from clarifying the meaning of propositions about thinking, actually presuppose the meaning to be given. But by what is it given? Second, §340, concluding the prior discussion, stressed the need to examine the use of problematic expressions. The examination of whether and how a proposition is verified *is* an examination of an aspect of its use, and hence can clarify its meaning and contribute to a description of its grammar (§353). And this is what needs to be done with words such as 'thinking', 'saying something to oneself in the imagination', etc. §354 emphasizes the fluctuation between criteria (fixed by grammar) and symptoms (inductive correlations) and identifies this fluctuation as a source of the misguided thought that nothing exists but symptoms. §§355–6 embroider on an example given in §354. The structure of these four remarks is linear.

Part E (§§357–62) reverts to the theme of talking to oneself in the imagination, which was broken off at §349. We do not say that maybe a dog talks to himself. Why not? Because the verifying grounds for such a proposition, the criteria for saying of a creature that it talks to itself in its imagination, lie in its behaviour, in what it does and *says*. But, of course, I don't say that *I* am thinking on any such grounds. §358 is a digression: my avowal that I am saying something to myself does *not* make sense because of an underlying 'act of meaning' I might perform. §359 switches from the dog to a machine and to the question of whether a machine can think or be in pain. A single thrust resolves the question: a human body comes as close as can be to such a machine, but we do *not* say 'My body thinks' or 'My body has toothache!' §360 echoes §281: a machine cannot think; but that is no empirical statement, for we say only of a living human being and what is like one that it thinks! §§361–2 clarify the point of §360 by examining the idea of attributing thought to something that is both inanimate (unlike the dog) and does not execute intelligent tasks (unlike a computer), viz. a chair. §362 concludes this 'chapter' by emphasizing that the expression 'to speak to oneself' is not taught indirectly by inducing the learner to give himself a private ostensive definition.

The structure of Part E:

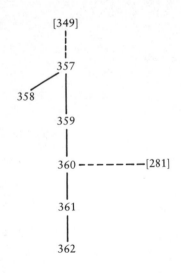

Correlations

PI§	PPI(I)§	MS. 129	MS. 124	MS. 165	Vol. XII	Others
316	255	68–9	274–5			MS. 179, 48
317						Vol. XIII, 134; BT 222[1]
318	256	70–1	215–16			MS. 180(a), 15–17
319	257	71	218			
320	258	71–2				MS. 180(a), 17–18
321		185f.[2]				
322		186				
323	259	72–3	217–19			MS. 180(a), 18–19
324	260	73–4	220–1	137		MS. 180(a), 19–20
325	261					MS. 130, 8–9
326		11				
327	262	10		206–7		
328	263	10		207–8		
329						Vol. X, 151
330	264	90–1		59–61;2		
331						MS. 130, 23
332					103–4	
333						Vol. X, 225
334						Vol. XI, 53
335						Vol. XI, 48
336		102–3				Vol. XIII, 135
337		103				
338					302	
339	265	91–3		61–2; 3–4		
340		106		20–1		
341	266	115	282	135		
342	267	4–5		195–6		
343		152			181	
344	268	3, 69		133–4[3] 192[4]; 209[5]		
345	269	5–6,69–70	279[6]	197–8[7]		
346	270	3–4		209–10		
347	271	4		194		
348	272	6–7		198–200		
349					140	
350					141	
351					142–3	
352					148–50	
353						Vol. VIII, 99; Vol. XI, 72
354						Vol. XI, 73
355						Vol. XI, 74
356						Vol. XI, 74
357	273	7		200–1		
358	273.1[8]	93		5		
359						Vol. XIII, 129
360		177–8		61		
361	275–6	9–11		204–6, 208 211–12		
362	277	11		212–13		

[1] PI §317(a) only.
[2] PI §321(a) only.
[3] PI §344(a) only.
[4] PI §344(b), but without the last sentence.
[5] PI §344(b), last sentence only.
[6] PI §345(c) only.
[7] PI §345(a) and (b) only.
[8] On p. 183 of the typescript.

Thinking: methodological muddles and categorial confusions
   1. Thinking: a muddle elevated to a mystery   2. Methodological
   clarifications   3. Activities of the mind   4. Processes in the mind

Thinking: the soul of language
   1. The strategic role of the argument   2. The dual-process
   conception   3. Thought, language, and the mastery of linguistic
   skills   4. Making a radical break

SECTION 316

1   This opens the investigation into the concept of thinking. The point of departure is parallel to one of the exploded fallacies with respect to the concept of sensation. Just as we are prone to study our aches and pains in order to get clear about philosophical problems regarding sensations (PI §314), so too we are inclined to suppose that by watching ourselves while we think, we will observe what the word 'thinking' means, i.e. the stream of thought, the inner phenomenon of thinking.[1]

W.s riposte is terse and supported only by an analogy. The concept of thinking is not used like that. But like what? The point arguably cannot be that the *meaning* of the word 'think' is not an object, event, or process which one might observe; for it has been established that the meaning of an expression is never an object, event, or process of any kind, but is rather what is given by an explanation of meaning, a rule for the *use* of the expression in question. But of course there are many expressions which *are* explained by pointing at an object which one may observe and saying '*That* ↗ is X' or '*That* ↗ is what is called "X"' or even '"X" means *that* ↗ F' (e.g. 'That is red', 'That is what is called "red"', or '"Red" means that colour'). To be sure, what is pointed at is not a meaning; rather, by pointing at a sample, one gives an explanation of meaning.

It is surely correct that just as 'pain' is not explained by private ostensive definition, so too 'thinking' is not thus explained. But it is not W.'s purpose here merely to distinguish the 'inner' from what is ostensively defined by reference to samples. More is intended, as is made clear by the parenthetical analogy. The categorial differences between thinking and having sensations, neither of which are ostensively defined, are no less than those between sensations and material objects or colours.

Whereas I can observe (attend to) the course of my pains (their waxing and waning, etc.) and report what I note to the doctor, to observe what goes on 'in me' while I am thinking (pondering, reflecting) is *not* to observe the course of my thoughts. Although there are phenomena of thinking, thinking is not itself a phenomenon (Z §471; RPP II §§31ff.). And 'it is very noteworthy that *what goes on* in thinking practically never

---

[1] James, *Principles of Psychology*, Vol. I, Ch. IX, provides a vivid illustration of this perennial temptation.

interests us' (Z §88), for, of course, these inner goings-on are not my thoughts, and only rarely would one be able to derive what I was thinking from my report of what went on when I thought whatever I thought (cf. BB 147). Telling someone what I think is not giving them a report on inner goings-on. Thinking is not an *experience*; and to tell you my thoughts is not to describe the character of an experience I have suffered or enjoyed. Reporting my pains is categorially altogether unlike reporting my thoughts, and were I to describe what went on in my mind when I thought up such-and-such, what I had to say (if anything) would typically be irrelevant to the question of *what* I thought. It is *this* feature to which the parenthetical analogy draws attention. Observing the last move of a game of chess will not clarify for one what 'mate' means; similarly, observing what goes on in one when one thinks will not clarify for one what 'thinking' means. *That* is not how one learns to use the verb 'to think'. How far does the analogy stretch? In the case of chess one can say that *in these circumstances* of the game, moving this piece thus *is* to mate one's opponent. But in typical cases of thinking one *cannot* say 'In *these* circumstances, such-and-such's going on in me (such-and-such pictures crossing my mind, such-and-such fragmentary sentences occurring to me, etc.) constitutes thinking that so-and-so'. (It is noteworthy that BB 147f. drifts towards this erroneous view.) What then did thinking such-and-such *consist in*? Why should it *consist in* anything? (Cf. Exg. §335, 2.1.)

2.1   'It would be as if . . .': MS. 179, 48 uses a different simile. It would be like observing a piece of cheese in order to see how the cheese increases in price (cf. PI §693).

Section 317

1   If we suppose that thinking is an inner process the observation of which will clarify what 'thinking' means (§316), we may be tempted into further error. We may take pain (something 'inner') and its outer expression as a paradigm on which to construe thinking and its verbal expression. Just as a cry is an expression of pain, so too, we will then argue, a proposition (the utterance of a sentence expressing a proposition) is an expression of thought. ('In a proposition a thought finds an expression that can be perceived by the senses' (TLP 3.1).) It will then seem that the utterance of a proposition is an outward expression of something inner. This misconception is firmly associated with the Augustinian picture of language. Hobbes, for example, imagined that 'the general use of speech is to transfer our mental discourse into verbal,

or the train of thoughts into a train of words. . .'.[2] The proposition uttered is then conceived as an outward mirror of the inner processes going on 'in the thinking mechanism'.

(b) clarifies why the parallel is misleading. When the doctor probes our abdomen, we cry out when it hurts, and the purpose of the cry (in such a case) is to let him know how it is with us in our abdomen. But if we construe the relation between thought and the expression of thought on that model, it will seem that the purpose of the proposition is to let the hearer know how things are 'in the thinking mechanism'. But to utter a sentence which expresses what one thinks does not have as its purpose to let another know what images crossed one's mind or what words one said to oneself. The answer to the question 'What do you think about . . .?' is not a description of an inner process.

1.1   (i) 'Der Schrei, ein Ausdruck . . .': 'a cry, an expression of pain; a proposition, an expression of thought'.

(ii) 'Denkapparat': thinking device or mechanism.

2   BT 222 has §317(a) (*without the words* 'Misleading parallel') as a hand-written addition to the section entitled 'Gedanke und Ausdruck des Gedankens' ('Thought and expression of thinking'). Underneath is a further addition indicating the target aimed at: 'Das Denken ein Vorgang in einem ätherischen Mechanismus' ('Thinking a process in an ethereal mechanism'). These two inscriptions could even be alternative titles for the section. The drift of the argument is evident from the following excerpts:

Der Gedanke ist wesentlich das, was durch den Satz ausgedrückt ist, wobei 'ausgedrückt' nicht heisst 'hervorgerufen'. Ein Schnupfen wird durch ein kaltes Bad hervorgerufen, aber nicht ausgedrückt.

Man hat nicht den Gedanken und *daneben* die Sprache. — Es ist also nicht so, dass man für den Andern die Zeichen, für sich selbst aber einen stummen Gedanken hat. Gleichsam einen gasförmigen oder ätherischen Gedanken, im Gegensatz zu sichtbaren, hörbaren Symbolen.

Man hat nicht den Zeichenausdruck und daneben, für sich selbst, den (gleichsam dunklen) Gedanken. Dann wäre es doch auch zu merkwürdig, dass man den Gedanken durch die Worte sollte wiedergeben können.

D.h.: wenn der Gedanke nicht schon artikuliert wäre, wie könnte der Ausdruck durch die Sprache ihn artikulieren? Der artikulierte Gedanke aber ist in allem Wesentlichen ein Satz. . . .

Der Gedanke ist kein geheimer — und verschwommener — Prozess, von dem wir nur Andeutungen in der Sprache sehen . . . . (BT 222ff.)

---

[2] Hobbes, *Leviathan*, Ch. IV.

(Thought is essentially what is expressed by a proposition, where 'expressed' does not mean 'produced'. A cold is produced by a cold bath, but not expressed by it.

One has not got thought and *side by side* with it language. — For it is not as if one has signs for others, but for oneself only dumb thoughts. As it were, a gaseous or ethereal thought as opposed to perceptible or audible symbols. . . .

One does not have the symbolic expression and side by side with it, for oneself, the (as it were, shadowy) thought. For then it really would be too remarkable that one should be able to reproduce thoughts in words.

I.e.: were the thought not already articulate, how could its expression by means of language articulate it? Rather the articulate thought is in all essentials a proposition. . . .

Thought is no secret — and blurred — process of which we see mere indications in language . . .)

W. here linked the concept of thought with the concept of its expression, and was inclined at this stage to advocate, as an *Übersicht* of the concept of thinking, an identification of thinking with operating with symbols (as he linked understanding with mastery of a system of symbolism (cf. BT 93, 143; PG 106, 131)). The *contrast* between the expression of thought (viz. essentially articulate) and the expression of pain (viz. an inarticulate cry) was not emphasized in this text.

Some unpublished dictations to Waismann, roughly contemporaneous with the 'Big Typescript', made W.'s reflections at this stage even clearer. He characterized his position as 'die Gleichung von Gedanken und Ausdruck des Gedankens' ('the equating of thinking with the expression of thinking' ('Denken', p. 2)), a remark comparable to 'Der Ausdruck der Erwartung ist die Erwartung' ('The expression of expectation is the expectation' (BT 355)). This, he noted, runs contrary to the traditional conception ('die traditionelle Auffassung'), which construed the expression of thought as a *translation*. Equating thinking with its expression, he argued, gives a valuable *surview* of the grammar of the words 'denken' and 'Gedanke'. (Similarly, the notion that believing is an inner experience is an obstacle to clarifying the use of the word 'believe'.) By contrast, 'Die Ersetzung des Glaubens durch seinen Ausdruck liefert uns mindestens einen konzisen Auszug aus der Grammatik des Worte(s) "Glaube"/"glauben"' ('Glaube', p. 3). ('Replacing believing by its expression gives us at least a concise epitome of the grammar of the word "belief"/"believe".')

It is noteworthy that this elaboration of the intentionality of thought (including expectation, understanding, belief, and desire) turns on contrasting thoughts with pains.

Der Glaube [das artikulierte Glauben, dass wir einem neuen Weltkrieg entgegen gehen] ist kein gleichbleibender Zustand, der den Satz begleitet, also nicht von der Art eines Gefühles. ('Glaube', p. 1)

(The belief [the articulate believing that we are approaching a new world war] is not a constant state which accompanies the sentence, hence not akin to a feeling.)

Acknowledging that a belief is articulate is incompatible with taking belief to be a mental state like a feeling or a sensation. For toothache, for example, is amorphous or inarticulate ('Intention', p.1). Hence too, W. summed up his treatment of understanding in this way:

Die Ansicht, gegen die ich mich in diesem Zusammenhang kehren möchte, ist die, dass es sich bei dem Verstehen um einen *Zustand* handelt, der in mir vorhanden ist, wie z.B. die Zahnschmerzen. ('Intention', p.1)

(The view against which I should like to turn in this connection is that according to which understanding is a state, which is present in me, like toothache, for example.)

PG 107 emphasizes that though we speak of thought and its expression, the expression of thought by a sentence uttered is not a causal mechanism, like a drug, designed to induce in the hearer the same thought which.I have and express in my utterance. This misconception informed classical empiricism; thus Locke argued that each man will 'use these sounds as signs of internal conceptions; and . . . make them stand as marks for the ideas within his own mind, whereby they might be made known to others, and the thoughts of men's minds be conveyed from one to another'.[3] This picture was duly enshrined as the foundation-stone of modern theoretical linguistics in the writings of de Saussure. This conception of communication by means of language views discourse as a form of *thought-transference*. But, W. queries, what sort of process might actually be called 'thought-transference' or 'thought-reading'?[4] Clearly, if I learn what you think from hearing you express your views on a certain matter, I should not be said to read your thoughts off your words. But I might read your thoughts *on your face*. Reading your letter is not a case of thought-reading, but reading *between the lines* of your restrained prose might be so called. Similarly, telling me what you think is not a case of thought-transference; but if you put your hand on my brow, and we both concentrate, and I say such-and-such,

---

[3] Locke, *An Essay Concerning Human Understanding*, Bk. III, Ch. I, Sect. 2.
[4] LWL 25f. (1930) emphasizes that thought is a symbolic process:

Language is not an indirect method of communication, to be contrasted with 'direct' thought-reading. Thought-reading could only take place through the interpretation of symbols and so would be on the same level as language. It would not get rid of the symbolic process. The idea of reading a thought more directly is derived from the idea that thought is a hidden process which it is the aim of the philosopher to penetrate. But there is no more direct way of reading thought than through language.

This is partly right and partly wrong. W. would subsequently certainly not have claimed that thought is 'a symbolic process' or, indeed, a non-symbolic process (see PG 106 for the beginning of the shift in his position); and one would expect greater subtlety in handling the notions of thought-reading or thought-transference. The following account is not W.'s, though it is intended to be in the spirit of his later reflections.

and that *was* what you were thinking, then this might, in certain circumstances, be called 'thought-transference'.

Vol. XIII, 134 has a draft of PI §317 followed by:

> Frag nicht: 'Was ist der Gedanke?' — denn diese Frage stellt // zeigt // ihn Dir schon als ätherisches Wesen hin // dar //.

> (Do not ask: 'What is the thought?' — for this very question already presents // shows // it to you as an ethereal entity.)

2.1   Ausdruck': In a dictation to Waismann ('Ausdruck und Beschreibung'), W. distinguished two different senses of 'expression'. The sense in which a groan is an expression of a pain differs from that in which an utterance is an expression of a wish (expectation, thought).

SECTION 318

1   This introduces *one* factor which induces the idea that thinking is an inner process which accompanies overt activities. When we speak or write thoughtfully, that idea would *not* strike us as apt. Here thought does not seem separate from its verbal expression; it does not seem to accompany its expression, only half a pace ahead as it were. We are not inclined for the most part, in such cases, to suppose that we think faster than we speak. But we do talk of the speed of thought, of a thought flashing through our head, of solutions to problems becoming clear in a flash. These pictures suggest that thinking is an inner, high-speed process. For it seems as if in lightning-like thought we think, just as we ordinarily do in speech that is not thoughtless, only very much quicker. Then it *will* seem as if in ordinary speech, the thought *accompanies* the words, keeping in step with them, hence proceeding relatively slowly. It is as if speech were the escapement that prevented the clockwork from running down all at once, and hence as if lightning-like thought was the same, only without the escapement!

1.1   (i) 'Wenn wir denkend sprechen': 'think while we talk' carries precisely the connotations W. is trying to *avoid*: viz. the suggestion of a dual process. So better, though still not quite right, 'when we speak thoughtfully', or 'when we speak with thought'.

(ii) 'wie beim nicht gedankenlosen Sprechen': 'as is the case with speech that is not thoughtless'.

2   MS. 124, 216f. (= MS. 180(a), 15ff.) has this in a quite different, but revealing, context. Pages 212f. have PI §241 (viz. agreement in form of life is not a kind of subjectivism about truth) followed by the objection that one can imagine each person having a unique language of his own

which is used *only* for reflexive speech-acts (see Exg. §243). Then follows
a draft of §243(a): an explorer might learn how to translate the
monologuists' languages. A fresh issue is then raised (pp. 214f.): if a
monologuist orders himself to climb this tree, and if, on the other hand, *I*
order myself to climb this tree, then in the latter case (but not the former)
the utterance could be used to order another person! So is the *thought* of
the order the same in both cases? This, W. responds, can be answered as
one pleases, as long as one does not imagine the thought to be an
accompaniment of speech. Thinking does not accompany speaking like the
text which the tune of a song accompanies, but is more akin to the
expressiveness with which the song is sung (cf. BB 148; PI §341). The
verb 'to think', one might say, is not an activity word. Then follows a
draft of PI §318. Instead of the last sentence, W. replies to the question:
'Ich glaube, das wird man nicht sagen wollen' ('I think that one would
not want to say that'). Then follows an allusion to Mozart's letter (see
Exg. §148) about hearing a whole composition in a flash: with what right
does Mozart claim to have heard a piece of music in his head? How did
he know that a piece of music corresponded to what he heard? We say 'I
saw the solution in a flash', but if we see it in abbreviated form, how do
we know that *this* is what the abbreviation is an abbreviation of? Then
follows the first sentence of P§323 and PI §319.

MS. 130, 236 queries whether the 'lightning speed' of thought is a
psychological property of many people's thinking? Is it comparable to
the speed of talking or writing? Can one *measure* the speed of thought (as
one can measure a secretary's shorthand rate)? And why can't one? We
are left to answer that ourselves (cf. Exg. §§319f.); it is evident that the
speed of thought is not the speed of an *activity* (and is hence unlike the
speed of writing), but the time taken to achieve something (hence more
akin to how long it takes to hit the bull's-eye). Of course, we can
measure how long it took a person to think of the answer to a problem.

BB 148 cites other phrases which induce the picture of thinking as an
inner process that accompanies outer activities, e.g. 'Think before you
speak', 'He speaks without thinking', 'What I said didn't quite express
my thought', 'He says one thing and thinks just the opposite', 'I didn't
mean a word of what I said'.

SECTION 319

1   This, and the next remark, divert us from the misleading picture of
high-speed inner processes towards the more fruitful analogies that will
reduce the pressure that forces us into myth-making. One can indeed
sometimes 'see a whole thought before one in a flash' or understand a
thought in a flash, but this is not comparable to being able to enunciate a

long sentence incredibly fast. Rather, it is comparable to making a note of a complex thought in a few words or a fragmentary diagram.

What makes such an opaque note, typically unintelligible to others, an epitome of a given thought? MS. 124, 218 answers: the use which I make of it. My terse lecture notes suffice for me to give the lecture, are adequate reminders of what I had in mind, and provide the basis for writing up these ideas in an article, etc. Note that although an epitome of a thought may be a reminder, not every reminder is an epitome of a thought (e.g. a knot in a handkerchief is not). For a note or diagram to be an epitome of a thought, there must be an internal relation between the sign *thus used* and the articulate expression of the thought.

1.1   'Ich kann . . . einen Gedanken ganz vor mir sehen': 'I can see a thought completely in my mind's eye in a flash'. A curious turn of phrase, seemingly equivalent here to completely understanding or grasping a thought in a flash. Grasping a thought, seeing the solution to a problem, does not involve articulating the thought in one's imagination, but the dawning of a capacity (hence 'in a flash') to say what the solution is or otherwise to act on it.

2   Ms. 124, 218 has this preceded by the example of the Mozart letter and that of seeing the solution to a problem in a flash. Then follows the first sentence of PI §323. The lightning-like thought is more akin to suddenly being able to do something than to doing something suddenly, and the thought or solution one sees in a flash is more of a pointer than a product.

MS. 130, 236f. imagines people who think only aloud and who draw pictures where we imagine things. This provides a clue, for what would lightning-like thought look like here? Presumably a few muttered words, a scrawl on the drawing pad!

SECTION 320

1   A further, related analogy to clarify understanding a whole thought in a flash. What crosses my mind when I suddenly grasp it, see the solution, etc. can be related to what I say in elaborating what I think as the formula of a series is to the sequence of numbers I write down. The analogy is not, of course, that what crosses my mind in a flash is a rule in accord with which the spoken thought is expressed. It is twofold. First, what actually happens, the picture that comes to mind or the key word that occurs to me, etc. (the analogues of a note or a few pencilled dashes (§319)) do not *contain* or *constitute* an inner, private expression of the thought any more than the algebraic formula *contains* the sequence that is developed in accord with it. Secondly, my conviction that I have

understood such-and-such an idea in a flash, seen the solution to a certain problem at an instant, etc. is akin to my conviction, on seeing an algebraic function, that I can work out its values for a sequence of arguments. In the case of certain formulae, my conviction will be said to be well grounded, in as much as I have learnt how to compute such functions. In other instances my certainty is justified by success.

1.1   (i) 'blitzartige Gedanke': an explicit reference to the first sentence of §319: 'blitzartig einen Gedanken ganz vor mir sehen'.
     (ii) 'kann sich . . . verhalten': 'can stand to the spoken thought as the algebraic formula to the sequence of numbers'.
     (iii) '"wohlbegründet"'/'nicht begründet': '"well grounded"'/ 'without any grounds' would make clearer the connection that is explicit in the German.

SECTION 321

1   We misguidedly suppose that we can clarify what 'thinking' means by watching ourselves while we think (§316), and we similarly suppose that the concept of sudden understanding can be clarified by observing what happens when one suddenly understands. W. here sheds light on the former confusion by elucidating the latter. As argued in §§151–5, 179 – 84, whatever happens when one suddenly understands something (and all sorts of things may happen (§151)), it is not the process or experience of understanding; for understanding is neither a process nor an experience. It is in this sense that the question 'What happens . . . ?' is misleading; for in as much as the answer is meant to clarify the meaning of 'sudden understanding', the question, as it were, faces the wrong direction.

Taken at face value, the question might be understood as a query about the psychical accompaniments, the (inner) tokens, of sudden understanding. These may be very variegated; but they are merely inessential inner accompaniments of understanding. For (a) one may understand, and be justified in saying so, even though *no* inner event occurred (§151(d), Z §136); (b) any inner event is compatible with one's not understanding (including saying the answer to oneself, for one may simply have learnt it by heart without understanding it!); (c) one's avowal of understanding is not justified by such a token's occurring (cf. §§151, 179(c)).

Of course, there is a different sense in which there are tokens of understanding: e.g. a sudden intake of breath, a gleam in one's eye, a change of expression. But these are tokens of understanding *for another*. There is no reason to suppose that the person who suddenly sees the solution to a problem or understands a complex thought feels these physical changes at all, even if he does once his attention is drawn to them. He does not say 'Now I know!' on the grounds that he felt his facial muscles relax and his breathing-rate change!

1.1　'((Posture))': an allusion to a parallel point concerning our capacity to say how our limbs are disposed. Here too one is tempted to say that one knows that one's arm is bent because one has such-and-such sensations. After all, if one's arm were anaesthetized and lacking any sensation, one would *not* be able to say whether it was bent or not! Nevertheless, it does *not* follow that when it is not anaesthetized and I say rightly that it is bent, I do so on the grounds of any sensation, *even if*, when my attention is drawn to the matter, I do have such-and-such sensations! (See RPP I §786 and N. Malcolm, *Ludwig Wittgenstein, A Memoir* (Oxford University Press, Oxford, 1984), p. 42).

2　PI p.218 briefly explores the case where *nothing went on*, and yet I exclaimed 'Now I know!' Why am I so sure that I knew? Does it follow that I did *not* really know? Of course not. One is looking at this language-game wrongly, for one is viewing it from the perspective of games with evidential grounds, games in which it makes sense to ask 'What grounds do you have?', 'How do you know?' But this is not like that. We need to remind ourselves what the *signal* (cf. PI §180) 'Now I know!' is for. It is, one might say, an announcement; but whether it was correctly used is to be seen by its *sequel*, not by its antecedents or grounds. The 'knowing' is not an accompaniment of the exclamation, *a fortiori* not its grounds.

SECTION 322

1　The question of what 'sudden understanding' means is not answered by describing what happens 'within one' when one suddenly understands. But this in turn may mislead one; for if one finds that when one 'peers into one's mind' one cannot find any describable event or process which *constitutes* understanding, one may jump to the conclusion that understanding is a 'specific indefinable experience' that lies behind such events as one *can* describe. But this says nothing unless we have laid down criteria which determine what counts as the occurrence of this alleged 'specific indefinable experience' (cf. LPE 287, 291; LSD 42; RPP I §200).

1.1　'was *legen wir fest* . . . ': 'what *do we fix* as a criterion of identity for its occurrence?'

1   This complements §§180–2. 'Now I know how to go on!' is not a
description of a state of understanding, justified by reference to evidence
accessible only to the speaker. It is rather an exclamation (comparable to
'Of course!'), and corresponds to an instinctive (natural) sound or
gesture. But my feeling that I can go on or my feeling of certainty does
not *guarantee* that I can go on. Sometimes I will *not* be able to do so. In
some cases I may then say 'I thought I understood, but I didn't' (cf.
PI p. 53n.); in others I should say, 'When I said I knew how to go on, I
did know' (just as I might insist that when I said 'I can pick up that
weight' I *could* pick it up, even though when I tried to do so, I slipped a
disk and was unable to (cf. §182)). This would be legitimate if my chain
of thought were disrupted, my attention distracted, or my concentration
interrupted by some intervening event.

   (b) adds that a persistent illusion of understanding might afflict
someone, in the sense that he is always exclaiming that he has understood, but can *never* actually go on. This would be a strange form of
aberration. It is noteworthy that it is *not* intelligible that we all suffer such
persistent illusions of comprehension. For 'Now I understand' and 'Now
I have it' would not retain their meanings in such circumstances.

2   MS. 124, 218f. has, after the first sentence, the sentence 'Wie das
Lachen einem Witz, so folgt dieser Ausdruck und etwa Worte wie "jetzt
hab ich's!"' ('This expression, and perhaps such words as "Now I have
it!", follow, as laughter does a joke!') This is apt, for the laughter is a
reaction of understanding, not a consequence of an inner event that assures
one that one has understood. On p. 219, after §323(b), W. compares the
feeling of certainty that we can elaborate a thought with the feeling of
certainty that we can continue a tune if given a few bars. It is of great
interest that this feeling is usually not deceptive.

1   The feeling of certainty is, on the whole, reliable. Would it be correct
to say that my certainty that I can continue the series rests on induction,
viz. that whenever in the past I have had the feeling that I can go on, I
have always been able to go on successfully, and since I now feel that I
can go on, I am certain that I shall be able to? §179 has already repudiated
this suggestion. I should indeed be surprised if I could not continue the
series 2, 4, 6, 8, . . . , as I should be surprised if I dropped a book and it

remained hanging in the air. But my certainty that the book will fall is not 'based on' induction (cf. §326), and likewise my certainty that I can continue the series of even integers beyond 8 does not rest on any *grounds*. That I *am* justified in being certain is evident in my unhesitatingly continuing 10, 12, 14, 16, . . .

SECTION 325

1   This explores the first sentence of §324. What exactly is meant by saying that my certainty that I can continue the series (when I have seen how to go on, had the experience of sudden understanding) is based on induction? W.'s reply is analogical: a philosopher might say that my certainty that fire will burn me is based on induction. But if that is supposed to mean that I *reason* myself into this certainty by arguing that in the past fire has always burned me, so it will burn me now, that is obviously wrong. First, I do not do so. On the contrary, 'The belief that fire will burn me is of the same kind as the fear that it will burn me' (PI §473); and no one would say that my fear is based on induction, any more than one would say that the dog's fear of fire is so based. Secondly, if it were based on induction, would it justify this rock-solid certainty? After all, 'it is *only in the past* that I have burnt myself' (PI §472). But *nothing* could induce me to put my hand into a flame; it is here that we see the meaning of certainty, what it amounts to (PI §474). I neither have nor need reasons for a belief as deeply rooted, as animal, one might say, as that (PI §477).

Should one then say that the previous experience of burning myself (and bear in mind that *one* experience suffices!) is the *cause* of my certainty? That is an empirical matter, to be determined within the framework of the system of hypotheses or natural laws of the empirical theory which we invoke. Hence it is not a matter upon which philosophy need pronounce.

Note that W. is not 'repudiating inductive reasoning'. One *can* produce reasons for opinions, beliefs, and assumptions about the future, and such-and-such statements about the past are 'simply what we call a ground for assuming that this will happen in the future' (PI §480). And if someone challenged this language-game, insisting that information about the past could not convince him that something would happen in the future, we would not understand him (PI §481). All this may be admitted while denying that our certainty that fire will burn us *rests* on any reasons at all. Far from our patterns of inductive reasoning justifying such reactive beliefs and expectations, it is the fact that we respond to experience in this way that constitutes the framework within which the activity of inductive reasoning and justification takes place (cf. PG 109f.).

So too, one's certainty that one can continue an algebraic series after having seen the formula and exclaiming 'Ah, I have it!' does not rest on reasoning, even though it may be true that typically, when one has this experience (sudden illumination), one can go on. But is this confidence *justified*? Granted that I am not confident on the ground that . . . , is my confidence justified, as it were, in the eyes of others? The answer was given in §320. In some cases it will be said to be well grounded, in as much as I have learned to compute such functions, etc. In other cases no grounds will be given, but my *success* will justify my certainty *ex post actu*. This is what we *accept* as justification.

2.1   'the *cause* of my certainty, not its ground': cf. C §429; I believe I have five toes on each foot (although being shod, I cannot see them) but:

> Is it right to say that my reason is that previous experience has always taught me so? Am I more certain of previous experience than that I have ten toes?
>   That previous experience may very well be the *cause* of my present certitude, but is it its ground?

Section 326

1   A coda to this series of remarks. That chains of reasons terminate is a recurrently emphasized point in W.'s reflections (cf. Exg. §217), particularly in clarifying the notion of the *boundary* of a language-game. The point is made, as here, in association with inductive reasoning (PG 111), following a rule (BB 14f., 143; PG 97; Z §301), and in emphasizing the danger in philosophy of looking for explanations and justifications beyond the point at which it ceases to be intelligible to give further reasons (RFM 199; Z §§314f.). We expect fire to burn us; this is how we *respond* to being burnt. We are surprised if we find that we get stuck in running through the series of even integers; this is something we *can* do. These *regularities* set the framework within which our reasonings take place.

Section 327

1   This opens the investigation into the relation between thought and speech. 'Can one think without speaking?' has the appearance of a question about the interdependence of a pair of processes or activities (like 'Can one talk without breathing?'), the one 'inner', the other

'outer'. To answer, one must clarify the concept of thinking. W. replies ironically, taking us back to §316. 'Thinking' is not the name of an introspectively observable inner process that typically accompanies speaking, but may also go on (perhaps very much faster) without it.

SECTION 328

1   This begins the answer to the question raised in §327. What does one call 'thinking'? To answer this we must examine the use of the word, not observe what goes on in us when it is correct to say 'I am thinking'. What is the word used *for*? W. does not answer here (but see 'Thinking: the soul of language', §§2, 4); rather, he examines one feature of the use of 'to think' which is pertinent to the picture of thought as an inward, introspectively observable process. Is there room for *error* or *misidentification*? Someone may sincerely exclaim 'Now I understand!' or 'I've got it!' yet *not* have understood. Does it make sense for a person to make a parallel mistake in the case of thinking?

The first question, 'Are these circumstances . . . ?', seems rhetorical and invites the answer 'No'. The second question, 'Has he interrupted the thought . . . ?', seems likewise to invite a negative answer (as is made clear in §330) and also in some way to confirm the response to the first question. This requires clarification.

Suppose someone is thinking about how to rearrange his room. The portrait would look excellent in *that* niche, he thinks, and it might be a good idea to put the chest below it, *if* it fits. And he takes out a tape-measure and measures the chest and the niche. Does he *stop* thinking if he says nothing to himself while measuring? If someone enters and asks 'What are you up to?', could he not correctly reply 'I was thinking about moving the chest into the niche'? And before he started measuring, *must* he have *said* anything to himself? And if he did, need it be more than 'Hm, that will look good'? But saying 'Hm, that will look good' is not, *per se*, thinking that the portrait will look excellent in the niche, and even better if we can fit the chest in beneath it! In short, a train of thought is *not* like a train of words. A train of words is interrupted by a hiatus of silence. But a train of thought need not (though it may) be broken off by an activity during which nothing is said to oneself. For whether or not I say something to myself while measuring is *irrelevant* to whether I am (still) thinking about how to rearrange the room and what it would look like. What *is* relevant is whether, having measured, I pause bemused and ask myself 'Now, what was I doing?' or 'What *was* I thinking about?'

How does this bear on the previous question, viz. whether there is room for error in saying 'I am thinking?' The picture we have of error here is of a process of thinking going on, but my not noticing or recognizing it, or, conversely, of my misidentifying a certain mental going-on as thinking when it is really something else. We may, like Descartes, think it impossible to err; but then we would be hard put to explain *why* it is impossible. But, of course, this is the *wrong* picture; nothing at all need be going through my mind as I measure the chest of drawers, but I am nevertheless thinking about the rearrangement of the room. And conversely, I may be frantically saying things to myself (e.g. reciting the alphabet) in order to *avoid* thinking about something (perhaps while being subjected to a lie-detector test).

PI pp. 222f. resumes the discussion and confirms the above interpretations. Three important points are made. (a) Assume that someone can always successfully guess my thoughts. What is the criterion for his guessing right? Obviously, my truthful confession. But might *I* not be mistaken. Can my memory not deceive me? Might it not *always* do so when I truthfully say what I thought? This is now perspicuously a wheel that does not engage with the mechanism. For 'now it does appear that "what went on in me" is not the point at all. (Here I am drawing a construction line.)' Why so? Because (b) 'The criteria for the truth of a *confession* that I thought such-and-such are not the criteria for a true *description* of a process. And the importance of the true confession does not reside in its being a correct and certain report of a process. It resides rather in the special consequences which can be drawn from a confession whose truth is guaranteed by the special criteria of truthfulness.' Here, as in the case of a dream-report, we have *laid down* no criterion to distinguish truth from truthfulness. A truthful report *is* a true report. (c) Imagine a game of *guessing* thoughts. Suppose I am putting a jigsaw together; the other person cannot see me, but guesses my thoughts. He says 'Now, where is this bit?', '*Now* I know how it fits!', 'I have no idea what goes in here', etc. He may well be guessing right, but *I need not be talking to myself either out loud or silently at the time.*

1   (i) 'Nun, was nennt man . . . ?': 'Well, what does one call "thinking"?'
       (ii) 'hat er das Denken unterbrochen . . . ': 'has he interrupted the thinking . . . '.
       (iii) 'says . . . to himself': saying things to oneself in one's imagination, talking to oneself inwardly, is more problematic than springs to the eye. It is scrutinized later (cf. Exg. §§344, 347–9, 357, 361).

2.1   (i) 'Are the circumstances in which . . . ?': MS. 165, 207f. has here 'Hat man das Wort "denken" so zu benutzen gelernt, das man sich fragt: "War, was ich getan habe, wirklich ein Denken?"?' ('Did one learn to use the word "thinking" in such a way that one asks oneself "Was what I was doing really thinking?"?') This even more obviously invites a negative answer.

(ii) 'says . . . to himself': MS. 165, 203f., prior to its draft of PI §327 (on p. 206), makes explicit the problematic character of this concept. If saying something, or talking, means producing appropriate *sounds*, then saying something to oneself *without producing sounds* is none too perspicuous a notion. If I tell someone to use the word 'sugar' for something which is just like sugar, only neither sweet nor edible, it is by no means obvious what he should call 'sugar'. This is followed by 'The chair talks to itself . . . ' (cf. PI §361) and then PI §§327–8.

Section 329

1   A further argument against the misconception of thinking as an inner process. When I speak with thought, or indeed when I 'think aloud' (ruminate), there are not two simultaneous processes going on: speech and a parade of meanings, or senses, before my mind (cf. §318). The language itself is the vehicle of the thinking. What I have said *is* what I think, not a description of something else, which is my true thought (seen from afar, as it were); nor is the sentence I utter a *translation* of my thought, as if the thought *an sich* were in 'Mentalese' and my overt utterance translates it into English. The thinking is not a process *behind* the utterance.

1.1   (i) 'When I think in language': this is an unhappy expression, for while I can speak in English, German, or French and say things to myself in English, German, or French, when I speak, and do not speak thoughtlessly but reflectively, I am not 'thinking in language'. It is possible, however, that 'in der Sprache denken' is intended to be equivalent to 'denkend Sprechen' (§318) and accordingly could be translated 'When I think in speaking', i.e. when I speak with thought.

(ii) 'the vehicle of thinking': surely an unhappy metaphor since vehicles carry passengers, and thinking does not need transportation. But when I speak with thought, the thinking is not distinct from the use of language. Moreover, whereas I may communicate my thoughts in speech, the words are not vehicles and communicating is not transporting thoughts.

2   Z §100 describes someone engaged in a practical activity requiring thought. Nothing needs to be said *sotto voce* or *in foro interno*. Z §101 concludes: 'Of course we cannot separate this "thinking" from his activity. For the thinking is not an accompaniment of the work, any more than of thoughtful speech.'

SECTION 330

1   *One* conception of thought is as an inner process running parallel to
overt speech (when it is not thoughtless). Many considerations induce
this false picture. One is cited here: we do distinguish speech with
thought from talking without thinking, and these very phrases intimate
that thinking is a process that may accompany speech or may go on by
itself.

(b) endeavours to break the hold of this picture of parallel tracks by
reminding us what it is to utter a sentence without thinking the thought
that it expresses and what it is to think that very thought without
expressing it.

(i) To say 'Yes, this pen is blunt. Oh well, it'll do' and to *think it* is not
to say it and simultaneously do something else in the confines of one's
mind, e.g. observe 'meanings' going through one's mind (§329) or go
through the *mental process of grasping (Erfassen) a thought*, conceived as an
abstract entity (cf. Frege, PW 145). It is rather to say it and mean it, i.e.
to say it seriously, not as a joke, a white lie, or an example of an English
sentence, etc. If this is correct, then, of course, I cannot while reading
W.'s text say 'Yes, this pen is blunt . . . ' and think it; at the very least I
need a blunt pen. Alternatively, W. might simply mean: say the sentence
with understanding (this interpretation is supported by BB 43(b)).

(ii) To say 'Yes, this pen is blunt. Oh well, it'll do' *without* thinking it
can likewise be given various interpretations. I can *read* the sentence;
then, of course, I do not mean or think that my pen is blunt, etc. Or I
might hold a pen in my hand and utter the sentence, but *not* think that the
pen is blunt or not think that it will do. Or I might utter the sentence
parrot-wise, concentrating 'my attention on something else while I was
speaking the sentence, e.g., by pinching my skin hard while I was
speaking' (BB 43).

(iii) To think that the pen is blunt, but that it will do nevertheless,
without saying anything even to oneself might, in appropriate contexts,
amount to no more than testing the point of the pen, making a face, and
then shrugging one's shoulders and continuing one's writing. The moral
of (iii) is that what here constitutes thinking that the pen is blunt but that
it will do is *not* something that needs to accompany the utterance 'The
pen is blunt. Oh well, it'll do' in order that the utterance not be
thoughtless.

A parallel argument is applied to meaning what one says in
PI §§507–11 (cf. MS. 165, 9ff.).

1.1   (i) 'While taking various measurements': an answer to the final
question of §328.

(ii) 'Aber was hier das Denken ausmacht': 'But what constitutes thinking here'.

2   MS. 165, 3 has this, followed by a draft of PI §339(b), which adds a further reason for the misconception of thinking as an inner process that accompanies speech. One might, as a grammatical remark, say that thinking *is* a process, only an incorporeal one. This has a point, for it draws attention to the grammatical differences between 'thinking' and 'eating'. It is nevertheless ill-advised, for it makes the differences look *too slight* (see Exg. §339). And it is misleading in generating the picture of parallel activities, vocal and mental.

BB 41ff. has an earlier discussion of this theme. The following points bear on the matter: (a) The aim of the investigation is to rid us of the supposition that there *must* be a mental process of thinking independent of the process of expressing a thought. (b) A parallel experiment to PI §330 is suggested, viz. to say and mean 'It will probably rain tomorrow' and then to think it, but without saying anything either aloud or to oneself.

If thinking that it will rain tomorrow accompanied saying that it will rain tomorrow, then just do the first activity and leave out the second. — If thinking and speaking stood in the relation of the words and the melody of a song, we could leave out the speaking and do the thinking just as we can sing the tune without the words. (BB 42; cf. PG 155)

This, though correct, is a less refined position than that in PI §330(c). Speaking and meaning what one says is distinguished from speaking without thought, but not necessarily by what happens *at the time one speaks*. The distinction may lie in what happens before or after one's utterance.

Z §§93–6 supplements this. The distinction between 'thinking' and 'not thinking' applies to an utterance only in rather special circumstances. One would not know how to apply it to a normal conversation, for example; i.e. if asked what that very conversation would look like if one of the participants was speaking without thought, one would not know how to reply. Certainly any such distinction would have nothing to do with concurrent inner processes. If we *must* speak of thinking as an experience, then it is exemplified in the experience of speaking as well as anywhere. But thinking is not an experience, for we do not compare thoughts as we compare experiences. We compare thoughts by comparing what is thought, viz. *that* such-and-such. We compare experiences by comparing what was done or undergone and what it was like, e.g. how one responded to it hedonically, etc.

SECTION 331

1   A further blow at the conception of thought under attack. We can (up
to a point)[5] imagine people who can think only aloud. Are we then to
imagine that with them speech with thought consists in saying everything twice?! This move exemplifies W.'s strategy: 'If you are puzzled
about the nature of thought, belief, knowledge, and the like, substitute
for the thought the expression of the thought, etc.' (BB 42).

2   BB 42 objects to the strategy on the grounds that the expression of
thoughts may always lie, for we may say one thing and mean another.
W. responds that we could imagine beings who do their private thinking
by means of 'asides', and so lie by saying one thing aloud, followed by an
aside asserting the opposite.

SECTION 332

1   A thought is not the accompaniment of an utterance, even if the
utterance has an accompanying mental process. Saying *in foro interno*
'Oh, it would be so nice!' and conjuring up images of snow falling,
snow-covered fields, roaring log fires in the hearth, etc. might well
constitute all that happens when thinking that a white Christmas would
be welcome. And if asked 'What are you doing?', one might well reply,
'Thinking of a white Christmas'. But the sequence of images that cross
one's mind is not the thought that a white Christmas would be welcome.
   Similarly, saying something with understanding is not to accompany
the saying with anything, any more than listening to *Tosca* with
enjoyment is accompanying the listening with a sensation (for then one
might obtain the very same enjoyment from a gin and tonic!). An
analogy illuminates the point further: to sing a tune with expression is
not to *accompany* the song with its expression, even though there are
various repeatable, autonomous things one does while singing express-
ively. The 'with' of 'with thought or understanding' is the 'with' of
'with expression, humour, seriousness', not of accompaniment. Similarly, to do something with thought is akin to (and, indeed instantiated
by) doing it with care, attention, or concentration; hence that notion is,
to use Rylean terminology, *adverbial*.

[5] But only for certain uses of 'think'. For it is not clear what the thoughtful tennis-player is
meant to be saying to himself as he lobs, smashes, drives, etc., or whether someone who
only thinks aloud would have time to articulate an ordinary tennis-player's thoughtful
tactics in the thick of the game.

Note that the criticism of the dual-process conception of thinking is *not behaviourist*. W. does not deny the occurrence of mental events and processes. The criticism is *grammatical* (not theoretical or 'ontological'): these goings-on are not what we *call* 'thinking' or 'a thought'.

1.1   (i) 'While we sometimes call it "thinking" to accompany a sentence by a mental process': it is unclear what W. has in mind here, unless it is a phenomenon such as that described above. In general, 'In philosophy, the comparison of thinking to a process that goes on in secret is a misleading one' (RPP I §580).

(ii) 'Say a sentence and think it; say it with understanding': this suggests that what W. has in mind by 'denkendes Sprechen' just is saying it with understanding and perhaps, in certain cases, also meaning what one says.

(iii) 'aber "Gedanke" nennen wir nicht jene Begleitung': 'is not what we call . . . '

SECTION 333

1   Yet another move against the conception of thinking as an accompaniment of speech (§330). 'There's been no happiness in your life, but wait, Uncle Vanya, wait. We shall find peace. We shall find peace,' Sonya exclaims in the closing lines of *Uncle Vanya*. Reflecting on this, we might indeed say that in such circumstances only someone convinced can say these words, that conviction (in this particular case, faith) burns bright in them. And similarly we say of many a remark that one *cannot* say such a thing without thought (if *that* is talking mechanically, then my name is Jack Robinson!), i.e. that particular remark, said in these circumstances, uttered in that way, cannot be called 'mechanical' or 'without thought'! But we would not wish to say that the conviction with which a passionate declaration is made is something that exists side by side with the utterance, as breathing with walking. True enough, one can be convinced that such-and-such without saying anything, and one can say that things are thus-and-so without being convinced (which is not the same as saying it without conviction). But it does not follow that when one says something with conviction, one's conviction accompanies one's utterance; rather, it informs or infuses it, so that one's words are charged with faith. And speech with thought is not an overt activity masking an accompanying covert one, any more than meaning what one says consists of a pair of activities.

1.1   'What if someone were to say . . . ?': a second analogical argument. To sing a tune *from* memory is not to reproduce publicly what one is hearing 'privately', but to reproduce publicly what one previously heard publicly. To sing from memory, one does not have to 'hear it in one's mind', but to have heard it in the past. Similarly, to speak with thought, one does not first have to recite what one is about to say in one's mind and then say it out loud.

Section 334

1   A further phrase that misleadingly intimates the dual-process picture is 'So you really wanted to say . . .'. For it suggests that the thought which we articulate for him was actually present in his mind. (Normally, when *he* says what he thinks, he, as it were, pulls a string of beads out of a box through a hole in the lid, revealing what was present in the box; in this case, *we* pull the beads out of his box, bringing them to light. But they are present in the box all the same; otherwise they wouldn't be 'what he really wanted to say'! (cf. BB 40).)

But this is to misconstrue the use of this phrase. We see the picture, as it were, but do not advert to its application. The function of 'You really wanted to say . . . ' is to lead someone from one form of expression to another, which does not have such-and-such unwarranted or misleading implications or which highlights more perspicuously such-and-such a point.

To clarify this, W. gives a mathematical example. For more than 2,000 years mathematicians tried to find a general method for trisecting an angle with a compass and rule, until it was shown that such a construction is impossible, that there is no such thing. But this is problematic; for what is it that mathematicians were trying to do? (If there is no such thing as checkmate in draughts, then there is no such thing as trying to checkmate in draughts.) What has the impossibility proof effected? No one would want to say that it has shown that mathematicians were not trying to do anything! But one could say that the proof gives them a clearer idea of what they were trying to do (LFM 87). How so?

Suppose we have a method of constructing polygons with a rule and a fixed pair of compasses, so that we can construct an octagon, a 16-sided polygon, etc. Now we are asked to construct a 100-sided polygon in this way. We repeatedly fail; then someone proves that it cannot be done. The proof shows that if we want to construct an n-sided polygon in this way, then n must be a power of 2. The last power of 2 before 100 is 64; after that is 128, so 100 does not occur in this series. The proof changes our idea of constructing an n-sided polygon by bisections. Before the proof one would explain what one was trying to do in one way, viz. by drawing circles and lines; after the proof one would give a different explanation of what one was trying to do, viz. to see whether 100 is a power of 2. To be sure, one may say that our idea of what we were trying to do is changed by the proof; but one could also say that this is a different way of expressing the *same* problem, that *this is what we had in mind* (LFM 87f.)! So too, in the case of trisecting an angle with compass and rule, the proof transforms the question into the question of whether one can solve a general cubic equation with square roots: 'the proof gives us a new idea of trisection, one which we didn't have before the proof constructed it. The proof led us [by] a road *which we were inclined to go*; but it led us away from where we were, and didn't just show us clearly the place where we had been all the time' (BB 41). Of course, we say: that is what I meant (had in mind), since the proof led me along a road I was *inclined* to go. 'The process was one that led from one symbolism to another, and led with my consent' (PLP 400).

These examples cast light on what kinds of things may persuade us to give up one expression and replace it by another, and also what is *meant* by 'So you really wanted to say . . . ', 'So what you really had in mind was . . . ', or 'What, in effect, you were trying to do (aiming at) was . . . '. In particular, it shows that although what you really wanted to say was . . . , that does not mean that the thought was already present somewhere in your mind.

2   Vol. XI, 47f., preceding the draft of §334 (on p. 53), reflects on those cases where someone says something equivocal. On being asked what he meant, he may be none too clear, and may ask us for a clarification of a word or for a formulation that will capture his point perspicuously. And here we will often reply: 'What you really wanted to say was . . . '. But this can easily be misunderstood, for it *need* not be a description of a process in which one says one thing while wanting to say another (viz. a slip of the tongue); nor is it as if what one really wanted to say had already been said inwardly.

2.1   'The concept "trisection of the angle with ruler and compass"': this is discussed at length in PG 387–92, the primary purpose of which is clarification of the nature of an impossibility proof, and hence of a 'search' for the construction. LFM 86–90 examines a parallel case and brings it to bear on the description or re-description of what one meant or what one was trying to do. See also PLP 398–400.

SECTION 335

1   This introduces yet another phrase, and experience, which induces the idea that thought is an inner process which underlies thoughtful speech. 'To make an effort to find the right expression for our thoughts' is misleadingly akin to the phrase 'to make an effort to find the right

English expression for Goethe's sublime thoughts'; i.e. it suggests that in expressing our thoughts we *translate* from the thoughts, which are already *there* ('in' images or 'Mentalese'), into English! Equally, it is deceptively similar to the phrase 'to make an effort to find the right expression to describe such-and-such (a view, a picture, an artefact)'; i.e. it suggests searching for the right words to describe something in view.

The picture is not wholly inappropriate, though it is misleading. There are all sorts of *different* cases in which this turn of phrase is legitimately used. In many cases there is a co-ordination of words (the expression of thought) and something else. But the something else is not itself the thought that then gets expressed in words. Sometimes it may be a mood, a frame of mind, which crystallizes into a word, and I write to my friend 'I am feeling despondent'. Or a picture may cross my mind, and I try to describe it (but to describe a picture before my mind is as different from describing a picture before my eyes as describing how I intend to act is from describing my intentional action). Or as I write in German and get stuck, searching for the right expression of my thoughts, an English word occurs to me and I try to hit on the German one, for this will express what I wanted to say. And so on.

§335(b), in two brief questions, highlights the gulf that can open between the picture and its application, in particular in cases where one is not merely looking for a translation or paraphrase. Does one have the thought before finding the expression? — Does the farmer have the fruit before the seed has grown? If one fails to find the 'right expression', can one deliver the thought in some other way? Not always; and does one not then say, after a pause, 'No, it's gone' or 'I thought I had the answer, but it's gone'? (And, of course, this figure of speech perpetuates the picture!) And in such cases what did the thought *consist in*, before one found the right words to express it? It did not *consist in* anything. For although all sorts of things may have occurred, none of them constitutes thinking such-and-such a thought.

2.1   'consists in': the question 'What does X consist in?' makes sense only for very particular kinds of things. Applied to thinking or thoughts, it makes none. PI §678 emphasizes a parallel point explicitly: 'What does the act of meaning (the pain or the piano tuning[6]) consist in? No answer comes — for the answers which at first sight suggest themselves are of no use. — "And yet at the time I *meant* the one thing and not the other." Yes — now you have only repeated with emphasis something which no one has contradicted anyway.' And Z §16 embroiders further: 'The

---

[6] I have a toothache and can hear a piano being tuned. I say 'It'll soon stop'. Which did I mean, the pain or the tuning? (PI §666).

mistake is to say that there is anything that meaning something consists in.' Cf. BB 86 on 'comparing from memory'.

SECTION 336

1   A further context in which the dual-process conception of the relation of thought to the expression of thought seems irresistible is when one imagines that one could not straightforwardly think a thought in the expression of which the main verb comes only at the end of the sentence (as the main verb comes at the end of a Latin sentence). For how would one know what one was thinking if one had to wait until the completion of the thought? So one supposes that one first has to think the thought and then to express it in a sequence of words in the curious order of Latin or German. Only altogether superior languages strictly mirror the sequential ordering of thought-constituents!

1.1   'einen Satz . . . denken': better perhaps 'think a proposition', although that too is strained. Nevertheless, W.'s point is clear.

2.1   'A French politician': Vol. V, 177 suggests that it was Briand. The observation, W. points out, is most significant even though sheer nonsense, for it earmarks a particular conception of thought and its expression.

SECTION 337

1   This introduces the diametrically opposite thought, which nevertheless still induces the dual-process conception. I surely know what I am going to say before I say it. The sentence I am about to utter is surely already complete in thought before I begin to speak; otherwise how would I know how to complete the sentence? And if it was in my mind in the form of the intention to say such-and-such, then, contrary to the thought of §336, must it not have been there in the ordinary word-order?

   This is a confusion exacerbated by a misleading conception of intention as *containing* a picture of its own satisfaction. But that conception was undermined by §§197 and 205. It is the *expression* of an intention that can be said to depict what will satisfy it. I can, of course, intend to play chess now; but that does not mean that my intention *contains* all the rules of chess (§197). It is *not* true of an intention to play chess or, for that matter, of uttering a certain sentence, that 'the existence of a custom, of a technique, is not necessary to it' (§205). Chess is defined by its rules, but these are not 'contained in' the intention to play chess. They are present in the mind of the intending player only in the sense that he has mastered them and can say what they are. Far from an intention being independent of any custom or technique, 'an intention is embedded in its situation, in human customs and institutions'. If the technique of chess did not exist, I could not even intend to play a game of chess. Hence it is *not* imaginable that two people should intend to play chess in a world in which no games exist (cf. §205 and Exg.). Hence too, in so far as I intend the construction of a certain sentence in advance, that is possible just because I speak the language, have mastered its techniques. To intend to say such-and-such does not mean that what one intends must already 'exist in one's mind' in advance of saying it.

The argument is left incomplete here, and W. does not return to it until §§633–7. There, the following points round the matter off: (a) If I was interrupted, but still knew what I was going to say, that does *not* mean that I had already thought it before, only not said it, unless one takes the certainty with which I continue as a *criterion* of the thought's having been completed before. (In that case the confident continuation will be an aspect of the *grammar* of 'He had completed the thought, but not the sentence, when he was interrupted', not a symptom of antecedent psychological processes.) (b) Nevertheless, the situation and the things which did cross my mind will typically contain all sorts of things to help me continue the sentence (like reminders or cryptic notes). (c) However, these 'hints' are not *interpreted*, for I do not choose between alternatives; I remember what I was going to say!

1.1   (i) 'of the sentence (for example) . . . ': similarly, I intend to sing the whole sequence of notes when I begin to sing a tune (cf. §333), but that does not mean that I must first sing it or hear it in my mind (see Z §2).

(ii) 'embedded in its situation': (cf. PI §581, where the argument is applied to the parallel case of expectation). One cannot intend to play chess unless there is a practice of playing games; one cannot intend a deed of knight-errantry in the twentieth century or a violation of copyright in the twelfth.

2   MS. 130, 239f. returned to this theme, comparing James's idea that the thought is already complete at the beginning of the sentence with the idea of the lightning speed of thought and with the concept of the intention to say such-and-such. To say that the thought is already finished by the beginning of the sentence[7] means the same as: if someone is interrupted after the first word and is then asked 'What did you want to say?' he can often answer the question. But here too James's remark *sounds* like a psychological one, but isn't. For if it were, then whether thoughts are

---

[7] And why not, W. adds in parenthesis, by the beginning of the *previous* sentence?

complete at the beginning of the sentence would be something to be discovered by asking individual people. But although we sometimes cannot answer the question of what we were about to say, in this case we say that we have *forgotten*. After all, is it conceivable that in such cases people would say 'I only said that word; how should I know what was going to follow it'?

3   The passage in James to which W. was alluding in the above remark (and Z §1) is in *The Principles of Psychology*, Vol. I, Ch. IX, e.g. 'Whatever things are thought in relation are thought from the outset in a unity, in a single pulse of subjectivity . . . ' (p. 278), and again, 'Even before we have opened our mouths to speak, the entire thought is present to our mind in the form of an intention to utter that sentence.' A dim inkling that there is no more any such thing as thinking half a thought than there is such a thing as half a proposition is here confused with a piece of putative psychological phenomenology! W. seems to have James in mind in PG 107f., and his diagnosis fits perfectly James's curious diagrams of the stream of thought: '. . . we are comparing the thought with a thing that we manufacture and possess as a whole; but in fact as soon as one part comes into being another disappears. This leaves us in some way dissatisfied, since we are misled by a plausible simile into expecting something different' (PG 108). LW §§843f. compares James's claim with the idea of a 'germinal experience', e.g. having a mental image which one 'knew' to be of N. without interpretation or recognition. One knew it from the beginning; but, of course, knowing is not an experience! Similarly James's claim that the thought is complete when the sentence begins, wrongly treats *intention* like an experience. Of course, 'It has *not* been there from the beginning' would be wrong, for 'The thought is *not* complete from the very beginning' means: I didn't find out or decide until later what I wanted to say. And one obviously does not want to say that.

SECTION 338

1   §337 concluded that I can intend the construction of a sentence in advance only in so far as I can speak the language in question. In this sense, the intention is 'embedded in its situation, in human customs and institutions'. §338 expands the point, but this time gives the diagnosis before identifying the error into which we are typically tempted.

One can say something only if one has learned to talk, so to *want* (and to intend) to say something, one must have mastered a language. But one can obviously want to speak (or dance or exercise any other skill) without doing so. And when we reflect on this, our mind reaches for the *image* of speaking, dancing, etc., and we misguidedly think that intending to ϕ must contain a 'representation' of ϕing; for otherwise what would make it an intention to ϕ (rather than to ψ)? And how would we know that *that* was what we intended?

2   Vol. XII, 300ff. incorporates this in a long discussion of 'I wanted to say'. It opens by dwelling on the oddity of remembering that I wanted to say something on some previous occasion. It appears odd in as much as there seems no event *to* remember! (hence akin to 'I meant . . .'). So could one substitute 'It seems to me that yesterday I wanted to say . . .' for 'Yesterday I wanted to say . . .'? But one can also say 'I *know* that yesterday I wanted to say', and one says this with conviction. It is the expression of one kind of remembering; has it then no use? And sometimes one believes someone who avows this ('Yes, I could see on your face that you were about to say that'), and sometimes one does not.

The grammar of 'wanting to say something' is related to 'being able to say something', and the grammar of 'I then wanted to say . . . ' to 'I could then have continued . . .'. The one is a case of remembering an intention, the other of a recollection of understanding. One does not learn what is called 'wanting to say something' by having a state or process pointed out to one!

Then follows PI §338, followed by 'Als wäre nämlich das Tanzenwollen einen *Plan* für den Tanz machen. Aber man kann doch auch einen Plan machen *wollen*.' ('As if wanting to dance were making a *plan* for the dance. But one can also *want* to make a plan.') Clearly that route generates a senseless regress.

In MS. 124, 228f. the interlocutor objects to W.'s suggestion that hoping, believing, fearing, expecting, etc. that such-and-such is the case essentially involve a technique of thinking (hence customs and practices) without which there can be no thinking. For, he argues, it is obvious that one knows immediately that one can hope, whether or not one has hoped or thought before. It is evident that a single act of hoping can exist irrespective of what is earlier or later! If you had said, W. replies, that you are *inclined to say* this, rather than that it is obvious to you, then there would be no disagreement, for I too am often inclined to say this!

2.1   'grasp at the *image* of . . .': LA 30 remarks that we conceive of imagery as the international mental language. BB 5 explores the suggestion that what gives life to a sign is a mental image we correlate with it.

SECTION 339

1   This is the leading member of a triad of concluding remarks to this phase of the argument. The picture of thinking that is embodied in the

many expressions examined in the preceding remarks is of a process that runs parallel to, and is essentially detachable from, i.e. logically independent of, speaking. Closer scrutiny of each such phrase and of each experience picked out by one phrase or another has shown the picture to be wholly misleading. When we examine how these expressions are used, it becomes clear that we have been taken in by a picture.

Thinking is not an incorporeal process which gives life and sense to speech. What makes dead signs live is not something immaterial. (And what makes a body a corpse is not the loss of an immaterial substance.) We do indeed use signs with understanding and thought; we mean something by them. But what gives them life is not the accompanying processes of understanding, thinking, and meaning, but the *use* we make of them in the stream of human life. And understanding, thinking, and meaning are not processes. Though we speak with thought, thought is not detachable from speaking as Schlemiehl's shadow is detachable from Schlemiehl. Rather, as was intimated in §332, thought infuses speech as expression informs the singing of a tune (but whether the singing was expressive can be heard immediately, whereas whether the utterance was made with thought can often be discerned only by reference to antecedent and subsequent events).

Even this negative point is misleading, however, not because a categorial point is being made (which looks like a *truth*, but is in fact the expression of a *rule*), but rather because the expression 'an incorporeal process' has not had any clear sense assigned to it. We know about biological processes and are acquainted with industrial processes of manufacturing materials or artefacts; we speak of *psychological* processes, e.g. of maturation or adaptation to the loss of a loved one or of preparing oneself mentally for an ordeal. But the notion of an *immaterial* process is unclear: is inflation an immaterial process? What of the rise and fall in the morale of the nation? And that of an *incorporeal* process is even more obscure. We introduce the suspect expression 'incorporeal process' when floundering around for an explanation of what 'thinking' means. Thinking, we say, is not a physical or corporeal process, as digestion is. Rather, thinking is a process that takes place in the mind. And one then thinks of the mind as a gaseous medium that is little understood and in which extraordinary things mysteriously occur (cf. PG 100; BB 3ff.; and 'Thinking: methodological muddles and categorial confusions', §4).

§339(b) explains how one might, less crudely, introduce the term 'incorporeal process' in this context. One might do so in the course of distinguishing between different grammatical categories.[8] 'To eat' falls in

---

[8] See R. Quirk, S. Greenbaum. G. Leech, and J. Svartvik, *A Grammar of Contemporary English* (Longman, London, 1972), pp. 94ff. Grammarians distinguish between *dynamic* verbs and *stative* verbs, and within the category of dynamic verbs they distinguish *activity*- and *process*-verbs from other subcategories. We might think to follow them, only refine matters further. Just as they distinguish *concrete* from *abstract* nouns, we might distinguish physical or concrete activity- and process-verbs from incorporeal activity- and process-verbs.

one category, we would then explain, whereas 'to think' falls in another. But this is still too crude. There is some point to the distinction, but it is still misleading (just as it is misleading to call 'to sleep' an activity-verb!). It makes the differences between *concepts* look too slight, as if 'to eat' signified an activity performed with the mouth and 'to think' signified an activity in just the same way, only not performed with a corporeal organ! This is visibly similar to Frege's distinction between actual and non-actual (but real) objects (GA, p. xviii; cf. PG 108f.), numerals being actual and numbers non-actual. (And he too was prone to explain what a non-actual object is by claiming that it is just like an actual object only not in space or time (PW 148)!) The expression 'incorporeal process' is unsuitable, for it adverts only to the similarity of surface grammar (e.g. to those rather obvious features, alluded to above, which 'to think' shares with 'to eat') and seems to save us the trouble of a careful examination of differences in *use* by offering us an apparently acceptable category, viz. 'incorporeal process', to capture the difference. (As does 'abstract object', when invoked to explain what numerals name!) In this sense, the jargon actually bars the way out of confusion.

1.1   (i) 'The Devil takes the shadow of Schlemiehl': see Adelbert von Chamisso's tales entitled *Peter Schlemiehl*.
       (ii) 'da ich die Bedeutung . . .': 'because I was trying to explain . . .'.

2.1   'look *too slight*': perhaps like the difference between -1 and $+1$, whereas what we are dealing with is comparable to the difference between -1 and $\sqrt{-1}$ (cf. RPP I §108).

SECTION 340

1   The grammar of an expression, particularly of an expression which is so deeply woven into our lives as 'to think', cannot be *guessed* on the basis of mere unreflective familiarity with the word. Yet that is precisely what is being done when one too easily pigeon-holes *thinking* as an 'incorporeal process' or erects philosophical theories on the assumption that thinking is an activity of the mind. The correct method is to *look* at the use of 'to think' and it cognates in widely varying sentential contexts and diverse circumstances. Then it becomes evident that thinking is not an inner process that accompanies speaking, that it is not an activity of the mind in the way that writing is an activity of the hand, that it is not logically independent of speech, etc.

A powerful prejudice, however, stands in the way of investigating philosophical problems thus. It is not obvious to what W. is alluding —

or indeed why he suggests only *one* prejudice. Perhaps what he had in mind is the impression of trivialization which this method produces. We are asking deep questions about the essence of things; and not just any old things, but the most fundamental things in our experience — time, matter, mind, thought, experience, etc. — and we are told to examine how mere *words* are used! But words are merely arbitrary names, and what we are interested in are the immutable natures of things (cf. §§370–3)! And to investigate those, surely we must examine the entities named, not their alterable, arbitrary, dispensable *labels*! This interpretation is rendered plausible by RPP I §§548–50. Alternatively, the prejudice to which W. is alluding may be 'our craving for generality'. We are, after all, seeking the *essence* of things, what is common to *all* cases of, e.g., thinking, meaning, and understanding. This craving for generality fosters contempt for the particular case; for if someone suggests, on the basis of a particular example and context, that *here* and in these circumstances *this* is what is called '. . .', we will dismiss this as irrelevant, because it is *insufficiently general*. And this prejudice prevents us from examining the multitudinous interwoven, overlapping, particular cases that together make up the use of the expression in question and constitute the 'essence' that we are seeking. This interpretation rests upon BB 16–20.

Either way, the prejudice is not *stupid*. (a) Our interest in words is very different from that of the grammarian. We are not especially concerned with the *English* verb 'to think', as opposed to the German 'denken' or the French 'penser'. We may concede immediately that we do *not* want to talk only about words. But, as W. clarifies with respect to philosophical investigations into the faculty of imagination (PI §370), the question as to the nature of thinking is as much about the word 'thinking' as is the question how the word 'thinking' is used. And this question is not to be decided — either for the person who does the thinking or for anyone else — by pointing; nor yet by a description of any process. The first question also asks for a word to be explained; but it makes us expect a wrong kind of answer. (b) Similarly our craving for generality is not stupid. We are indeed concerned with clarifying the essences of things (PI §92), but we have a wrong conception of what constitutes the essence of something. In the kinds of cases that are of philosophical concern, essence is expressed by *grammar* (PI §371), for what define number, proposition, proof, thought, sensation, etc. are grammatical structures (BB 19). Moreover, the essence of a thing need not be determined by common properties at all, but by a multitude of overlapping family-resemblances.

2   In both MS. 165, 20 and MS. 129, 106 this follows a draft of PI §§440–1, hence was stimulated by the peculiarities of the concepts of desire and wish and their internal relation to their fulfilment.

Z §§110–14 emphasizes the diversity, unruliness, and indeterminate boundaries of the use of 'to think'. Its use does not conform with what we unreflectively expect, and its description is difficult; one cannot guess how it functions from a couple of examples.

SECTION 341

1　A coda to §§327ff. Far from thought being an inner accompaniment of speech with thought, speaking with thought ('nicht gedankenloses Sprechen') is comparable to playing a piece of music with thought. And no one would think that the difference between playing a sonata with thought and without thought consists in an inner (and hence inaudible) accompaniment of the music. On the contrary, it consists in the expressiveness with which the piece is played (cf. Z §§163f.), in the pattern of variation of loudness and tempo that manifest the player's understanding of the piece (PI §527).

2　W. frequently compared language with music, understanding a language with understanding music, experiencing the meaning of a phrase in language and in music (see esp. Z §§156–77). He emphasized the 'strongly musical element in verbal language. (A sign, the intonation of voice in a question, in an announcement, in longing; all the innumerable *gestures* made with the voice.)' It is these, *inter alia*, that distinguish speech with and without thought.

SECTION 342

1　After the careful examination and repudiation of the dual-process conception of thinking, W. returns to the question posed in §327: Can one think without speech? James argued that one must think *in a material*; with most of us, mental images are the 'mind-stuff' of thought (as was ascertained, James observes, by Galton's experiments[9]). However, can a deaf and dumb man weave his tactile and visual images into a system of thought? '*The question whether thought is possible without language* has been a favourite topic of discussion among philosophers. Some interesting reminiscences of his childhood by Mr Ballard . . . show it to be perfectly possible.'[10] The idea that this question can be settled empirically, by asking the deaf and dumb, is what W. challenges.

The challenge is powerful. The first move opens the question of whether Ballard has correctly *translated* his wordless thoughts about God

[9] James, *Principles of Psychology*, Vol. II, pp. 50ff.

and the world into words. But, forewarned by what W. has already clarified, it should be obvious that this question is odd. For no amount of play of images constitutes thinking that such-and-such is the case. (It is, at most, the 'logical germ' of a thought (cf. LW §843).) There is no such thing as *translating* a play of images into the verbal expression of thought; rather, one *expresses* the thought that occurs to one *when* such-and-such images, as it happens, cross one's mind. To express this thought is not to *translate* it. But Ballard, before he had mastered sign-language, had no means of expressing thoughts about God and the world; i.e. nothing in his behavioural repertoire could *count* as the expression of the thought that God had created the world. But if so, what constituted thinking this thought? (Could he also play mental chess before he learnt how to play chess?)

The second move is subtle: the question of whether one is sure that one has correctly translated one's wordless thought into words is not a question which normally exists, so why does it raise its head *here*? The normal non-existence of the question is not because the answer is usually too obvious, viz. that ordinarily all human beings do translate their thoughts correctly into language. Rather, the question is *senseless*. It is senseless not only because we do not *translate* our thoughts into words, but also because it makes no sense for a person to be mistaken about what he thinks. This is not because he knows what he thinks in the sense in which he might know what someone else thinks; rather, both knowledge and ignorance are grammatically excluded (cf. PI p. 222). Equally, error about one's own thoughts is ruled out; it makes no sense (save in special cases) to suppose that a person might think that *p*, but mistakenly think that he thinks that *q*! In these respects one's sensations and one's thoughts are on the same level. So why does this otherwise meaningless question arise here! The answer was given in PI §288(c):

That expression of doubt has no place in the language-game; but if we cut out human behaviour, which is the expression of sensation, it looks as if I might *legitimately* begin to doubt afresh. My temptation to say that one might take a sensation for something other than what it is arises from this: if I assume the abrogation of the normal language-game with the expression of a sensation, I need a criterion of identity for the sensation; and then the possibility of error also exists.

Mutatis mutandis, the same applies here. What happens to a person when he thinks something, i.e. what images cross his mind and so forth, does not constitute a thought; nor does it furnish a criterion of identity for the thought. And, of course, it makes no sense for *him* to doubt whether he thinks what he says he thinks. (It is absurd to suppose that he might *mistake* the thought that it is cold today for the thought that Shakespeare wrote *Hamlet*!). But if, as in the Ballard case, we cut out the verbal or

---

[10] Ibid., Vol. I, p. 266.

symbolic behaviour which articulates the expression of thought, then it *looks* as if one might legitimately doubt. For if one assumes the abrogation of the normal language-game with the expression of thoughts, then one needs a criterion of identity for the thought — and then the possibility of error exists!

The third move follows from the second. We should not say that Ballard *mis*remembers, any more than we should say 'He misremembers' if we heard someone say 'I distinctly remember that some time before I was born I believed . . .' (cf. PI §288). For what would it be for him to remember *correctly* what he thought before he could talk (or what he believed before he was born)? Rather, we should just treat these 'recollections' as a queer memory-phenomenon, an aberration, a 'queer reaction which we have no idea what to do with' (PI §288).

2   Vol. XII, 202f. observes that if someone were to say of something that today he sees it as red, but that yesterday he saw it as green, then in certain circumstances we should accept this, e.g. if we had an appropriate physiological explanation. But if someone recurrently made such claims, for which nothing else spoke, we would say not that he remembers yesterday seeing it thus, but that he *says* that he remembers, and we might add 'But what that actually means, I don't know'. And if someone now said that this person has what we call 'the experience of remembering', we would be inclined to brush this aside as irrelevant to whether he remembers or not, i.e. to view any 'inner experience' in these circumstances as idle. In parenthesis W. adds 'James's quotation from Ballard'; i.e. something counts as a mnemonic experience only within a context in which something counts as remembering, not vice versa.

Section 343

1   This confirms the interpretation of §342, for 'memory-reaction' here stands in contrast to the supposition entertained *faute de mieux* in §342 that Ballard's words are a *translation* of his memory.

2   PG 181f. elaborates the point that to avow or report a memory is not to translate an experience into words. Rather, one is, for example, asked a question about what one did, and one answers with certainty. And isn't *that* the 'experience' of remembering? One is inclined to ask what *makes* one certain, and that very question invites the answer: a mental picture, off which one reads what happened (a stored photograph in the medium of the mind!). But the correct answer is: nothing *made* me certain; I *was*

certain. It is a mistake to suppose that memories expressed in language are, as it were, mere threadbare representatives of the real memory-experiences (cf. PI §649). Vol. XII, 181 remarks that one does not normally read off what one remembers from any inner picture. Rather, one says, 'I remember doing . . .', and one's words are the manifestation (*Äusserung*) of memory; expressing them is itself the memory-phenomenon (experience), not the description of an inner picture.

SECTION 344

1   Another probe at the supposition that thought is independent of the capacity to speak. Is it not imaginable that people should never speak any language aloud, yet still speak a language to themselves *in foro interno*, in the imagination? The interlocutor observes innocently that this supposition merely suggests that it is imaginable that people should always do what they sometimes do. And it is true that we often say something to ourselves in the imagination, without expressing our thought aloud in any way. But this generalization is not licit. The fact that 'Some things have property F' makes sense does *not* ensure that 'All things have property F' makes sense; it is a fallacy that 'some' and 'all' are topic-neutral. In particular, the transition from 'It is possible that people should sometimes speak to themselves in the imagination' to 'It is possible that people should always speak to themselves in the imagination' is not licit. For our criterion for someone's saying something to himself in the imagination is what he tells us (and related behaviour). And a pre-condition for that is that he *can speak* in the ordinary sense of the term, i.e. *not* in the sense in which a parrot or gramophone can. (We do not say that maybe the parrot speaks to itself in its imagination!)

1.1   'nur in ihrem Innern zu sich selbst sprächen': 'If people only spoke inwardly to themselves'. It is important to bear in mind that it is speaking to oneself *in the imagination*, or *inwardly*, that is at issue, not talking only to oneself (which has been countenanced in PI §243). Evidently in this context (and in the succeeding remarks up to §362) W. is treating speaking to oneself in the imagination as a kind of thinking, as is made quite explicit in §361. It is noteworthy that PI p. 211 cuts finer here: '"Denken" und "in der Vorstellung sprechen" — ich sage nicht "zu sich selbst sprechen" — sind verschiedene Begriffe.' ('"Thinking" and "speaking in the imagination" — I do not say "speaking to oneself" — are different concepts.') One can think without speaking in the imagination, as when one talks with thought or works intelligently or hits on a solution to a problem, etc. And one can speak in the imagination without thinking, as in a daydream or in reciting a poem in the imagination or doing a mechanical calculation 'in one's head'. And speaking to oneself need not be in the imagination, but can be aloud; while, conversely, not all one's internal speakings are addressed to oneself.

2.1   (i) 'Like: "An infinitely long row of trees . . . "'": the absurdities that result from attempted extrapolation from the finite to the infinite are examined in PR 165 ff. and 306ff. It is no explanation of what is *meant* by 'infinitely long row of trees' to say 'You know what "a row of trees" means, you know what "the row comes to an end after the *n*th tree" means, well — an infinite row of trees is one that *never* comes to an end!' For no criterion for the row's being infinite has been given, since 'never' here does not refer to a time *interval* (as it does in 'He never coughed during the whole hour'). So it incorporates the very problem it appears to resolve!

(ii) '. . . if, in the ordinary sense of the words, he *can speak*': MS. 165, 192 embroiders. We do not say that maybe a dog speaks to itself in a European language. And if someone agrees that this is *highly improbable*, this is a misuse of the word 'improbable'. Of someone who has not learnt to speak, we do not say that he speaks to himself.

SECTION 345

1   This amplifies the general critical point of §344. The supposition that if F(*a*) makes sense, then so too does (*x*)F(*x*) is indefensible. Although the topic-neutrality of the quantifiers is a postulate of the formation-rules of the predicate-calculus, that alone suffices to show that it does not capture the 'logical form' of generality and of inferences involving generality in natural languages. W. here gives a pair of examples where an inference of this kind is patently invalid.

2   PG 265ff. dwells on the inadequacy of the Frege–Russell notation for generality, and criticizes the conception of generality in TLP. There are many different *kinds* of generality, as many different 'logical forms' of generality as there are different logical forms concealed by the subject–predicate grammatical form.

In many other writings W. pointed out, in particular cases, the illegitimacy of parallel transitions from the intelligibility of a singular proposition to the intelligibility of its generalization. Thus, for example, it makes sense to order someone to write down any cardinal number, but not to write down all cardinal numbers (PG 266). 'There is a circle in the square [($\exists x$). fx]' makes sense, but not 'all circles are in the square [$\sim \exists x. \sim$ fx]' (ibid.). LPE makes parallel points about deception (293), lying (295), and someone's always seeing as red what we see as green

(316). Z §571 argues for the unintelligibility of the supposition that all behaviour might be pretence. More generally, a condition for the existence of our mathematical practices is that mistakes be the exception, not the rule; and even more generally, a condition for the existence of shared language-games and for the possibility of communication is that there be agreement in judgements. Note that the *reasons* for faulting the transition are not uniform.

Section 346

1   A further objection to the claim that thought (speaking to oneself in the imagination) is possible only for those who *can* speak. Why is it an important fact that I imagined a deity in order to imagine a parrot's saying things to itself? Because this abrogates the rules of our ordinary language-games (God sees, even *in the dark*; He hears my *inaudible* prayers). By the same token, the expressions must be given a new role in this different language-game, or else they are senseless. So 'Couldn't we imagine God giving a parrot understanding . . . ' amounts to 'Let's forget about sense, and let our imagination roam beyond the bounds of sense' — which is excellent advice for a would-be Lewis Carroll.

Section 347

1   The interlocutor plays the private-language card: surely I know *from my own case* what it means 'to speak to oneself in the imagination'. And if so, then the concept of thus speaking to oneself (which one often does when thinking) *is* detached from any public, behavioural criteria. For would anyone deny that if I were deprived of the organs of speech I could still talk to myself thus?

W. does not deny the latter claim. What is awry is the former one: viz. that I know what speaking to oneself in the imagination is from my own case. A putative 'private' paradigm can have no role in explaining the common (shared) concept of speaking to oneself. So *if* I know only from my own case, then I do *not* know what is called 'speaking to oneself in the imagination', but only what *I* call this — which I cannot explain to anyone! (And hence, not to myself either!)

Section 348

1   The interlocutor's objections weaken, but also grow more subtle. Granted that the intelligibility of the occurrence of inner speech depends

on being able to speak publicly, hence on something's *counting* as an expression of thought, is it not intelligible that a Ballard, having learnt a gesture-language, should then talk to himself in his imagination in a *vocal* language? If so, then in this *thin* sense, the question of §344 would get an affirmative answer (but not that of §327, save trivially).

W.'s riposte is delicate: it is not obvious that one *does* understand the supposition. Certainly one cannot argue: 'You know what "being able to communicate only by means of a gesture-language" means; and you know what "talking to yourself in vocal language" means; so you must know what it means to say that someone who communicates only by means of a gesture-language talks to himself in a vocal language!' (The bankruptcy-order on compositionalism should not be lifted here!) What can one *do* with this claim? Have we been told *when* to say that a deaf mute is talking to himself *vocally* in his imagination? And when he allegedly does so, does he *pronounce* the words he says to himself correctly? in an English or Welsh accent? Or is it not rather that these questions get no grip here? (The supposition is analogous to the idea that the blind have vivid visual images of shapes they feel.)

SECTION 349

1.1   'this supposition': not the supposition that these deaf mutes who have mastered a gesture-language nevertheless talk to themselves in a vocal language, but rather the supposition that someone (a normal speaker) engages in internal monologues. Hence 'these words', which have a familiar application in ordinary circumstances, are 'speaking to oneself inwardly in a vocal language'.

2   This originates in Vol. XII, 139f. in a different context. After an early draft of PI §243(a) (see Exg. §243, 2) W. examines the sentence 'I assume that a picture crosses his mind' (Z §531). One cannot assume that such a picture occurs to a stove. But why not? Is it because a stove lacks human form? W. leaves the question hanging, and turns to examine the supposition. After all, it amounts to no more than words and a picture, and a pretty crude picture at that, viz. of a human head with an image nebulously in it.

Then follows PI §349, in which, in this context, the 'supposition' is that 'a picture crosses his mind'. The 'falling away of its application' is exemplified by the attempted application of the phrase to the stove. In such cases, bereft of the normal human context, the phrase and crude picture stand naked. The (genuine) application, W. concludes, is a timely wrapping for the sign.

What gives expressions such as 'talking to oneself vocally in the imagination' or 'a picture crossing one's mind' their sense is a very specific context of application. When this does not obtain, the expressions lack any genuine use, and all that remain are words, a primitive picture, and philosophical bewilderment.

SECTION 350

1   The target of this remark was identified in §349, viz. that if a supposition makes sense in one circumstance, then it makes sense in any circumstance; hence too, if one understands what an expression means in one context, then one must understand it in any context.

The interlocutor's opening remark insists that the intelligibility of the supposition that another has pain is guaranteed by extrapolation from one's own case, viz. what is supposed is that *he* has the same as I have when I am in pain. This runs parallel to the claim that the supposition that a deaf mute talks to himself vocally in the imagination just is the supposition that he does what I do when I talk to myself vocally in the imagination.

W.'s objection is that the explanation by means of *sameness* does not work here, and he explains why not by an analogical case. One cannot explain what 'It is 5 o'clock on the sun' means by saying that it is the same time as here when it is 5 o'clock here. For obviously enough, if it is 5 o'clock on the sun and 5 o'clock here, *then* it is the same time there as here. But that presupposes, and does not explain, the intelligibility of 'It is 5 o'clock on the sun'. Given our methods of measuring terrestrial time (by reference to the sun's zenith) and our conventions of time-zones relative to Greenwich, we can readily explain what it is for it to be 5 o'clock (GMT) here (in Oxford). But nothing has been stipulated as to how to measure time on the sun; nothing has been laid down as the appropriate ground for saying 'It is *n* o'clock on the sun'. The method of determining time by reference to the sun's zenith has no application to the sun itself; hence the expression 'It is 5 o'clock on the sun' has no sense. This is not to say that we could not *give* it a sense by stipulation; we could. But it is to say that we cannot explain what sense it *has* by saying that it is the *same* time as here.

Pari passu, one cannot explain what it is for another to have a pain by saying that it is for him to have the same as I have when I am in pain. To be sure, if he has a throbbing pain in his leg and I have a throbbing pain in my leg, then we both have the same pain. But equally, if the stove has a throbbing pain in its leg, it too has the same pain! The question is, when should one say 'He has a pain'? The explanation by sameness does not work, because in my own case I neither have nor need a criterion for determining whether I am in pain. Hence my own case furnishes me with no criterion for judging another to be in pain, just as our method of measuring terrestrial time provides us with no method for measuring time on the sun.

1.1   'the stove has the same experience': the reference to the stove is somewhat surprising here; for what has the stove got to do with this discussion? In Vol. XII, 141 this perspicuously picks up the reference in the draft of PI §349 (see Exg.) to the questionable intelligibility of the supposition that a picture might occur to the stove.

2   Vol. XII, 141 has the first draft of this. After the second sentence, it has 'Die Frage ist ja eben: wie *appliziere* ich diese meine Erfahrung auf den Fall des Andern?' ('The question is just: how do I *apply* this experience of mine to the other's case?') This, though deleted in PI, is answered by 'If one has to imagine someone else's pain on the model of one's own, this is none too easy a thing to do: for I have to imagine pain which I *do not feel* on the model of the pain which I *do feel* (Vol. XII, 160; PI §302; see Exg. §302, 2).

   Vol. XV, 224 invokes the analogy with time-measurement in a related context. If one concedes, as one must, that one can have a certain experience without expressing it, then surely another can have the same experience? I'll concede everything, W. responds, as long as I know what I am conceding! The question is, what counts here as *the same experience*? How do we 'measure' the two experiences to determine that they are the same? For, *ex hypothesi*, the ordinary scales on which we weigh experiences, viz. behavioural expression, have been excluded here. Might the person (e.g. a deaf mute) not subsequently say: 'I once had such-and-such an experience'? To be sure, under normal cir-cumstances that is a criterion for what he experienced. But not always: e.g. 'I remember that before I was born I dreamt . . . '. These moves are akin to insisting that since you concede that it may be 5 o'clock here, even though you haven't looked at your watch, you must concede that it may be 5 o'clock on Mars. But one must not forget what Einstein taught the world: that the method of measuring time belongs to the grammar of the time-expression.

   RPP II §§93f. invokes the analogy again: could we not imagine a creature that lacked sense-impressions but had mental images? Surely a 'higher being' could know what mental images such a creature had? But this is by no means obvious; one can talk about this, but that doesn't show that one has thought it through. In parenthesis W. added ('5 o'clock on the sun').

SECTION 351

1   Despite the clarifications there is still a temptation to reply 'Pain is pain
— whether *he* has it or *I* have it; and however I come to know whether
he has pain or not'. Why so? And what does this objection seem to
achieve?

At a very general level one is tempted to cut the cackle and insist that
there is an objective 'fact of the matter' as to whether someone is in pain,
irrespective of how and whether we find out that he is. For has not W.'s
preoccupation with how we *know* that another is in pain or talking to
himself in the imagination, etc. allowed epistemological concerns to
distort our grasp of 'ontological realities'? More locally, if the objection
is correct in insisting on the objectivity of pain and on the independence
of the *truth* of propositions about another's pain from how we know
whether he is in pain, then we should equally insist that whether deaf
mutes talk to themselves vocally, whether people who cannot speak can
nevertheless say things to themselves in the imagination, is equally an
objective matter independent of whether we know that they do or not.
(And something similar applies to the question of whether the blind can
have 'ideas of colour' without any preceding 'impressions'.) Tactically,
the objection seems to rebut the time–measurement analogy of §350. For
while a case has been made out for denying that 'It is 5 o'clock on the sun'
has any use (is meaningful), no such case has or could be made out for
'He is in pain'. One could not, therefore, say '5 o'clock is 5 o'clock,
whether it is in Oxford or on the sun!', as one surely can say 'Pain is pain,
whether *he* has it or *I* have it!'

W., however, immediately concedes that pain is pain, whether *I* have
it or *he* has it. Who would wish to deny *that*? This parallels the move in
§350: viz. if he has a throbbing headache in the temples and I have a
throbbing headache in the temples, then we have the *same* pain. But just
as the latter concession still precludes an explanation by sameness of what
it means for him to have a pain (viz. he has the same as I have when I
have a pain), so too this apparent concession gives nothing away; for the
question still remains: what is it for him to have a pain?

Similarly, W. concedes that if another has a pain, then he has a pain
however I might happen to find that out. For, to be sure, the *truth* of
propositions about others' inner states is independent of how, and indeed
whether, we establish it in a particular case. It is the *meaning* of such
propositions that is at issue, in particular that their meaning cannot
intelligibly be explained by extrapolation from one's own case. And the
clarification of meaning is a matter of reminding ourselves how certain
expressions are *to be used*; hence it is a grammatical investigation, not an

epistemological one. (Although that is not to say that the question of how such propositions are verified is irrelevant (PI §353); it is rather to insist that whether we know is a matter of the truth of our judgements; how we can know, i.e. what method is to be followed, may well be part of the grammar of an expression.)

The concession, it is evident, grants the interlocutor little. He would like it to license such sentences as 'The stove is in pain' — pain is pain, whether *I* have it, *he* has it, or the *stove* has it! He would then argue that, as a *matter of fact*, the stove is never in pain! The proposition is meaningful, but false. But this he cannot do (for what would it be for the proposition to be true? — It would be for the stove to have what I have when I am in pain! But *this* roundabout was brought to a halt in §350). W.'s move recapitulates the argument of §349; we have the words and certain images or pictures; but they have no application here.

The second half of the remark adds a further example to clarify the illegitimacy of the compositionalist extrapolation that W. is criticizing. The interlocutor might argue that 'Above is above, whether it is above the wardrobe or above the earth'. But that is precisely wrong. For 'above' and 'below' applied to objects and structures on the earth do not have the same meaning when applied to the earth (globe) itself.

1.1   (i) 'Damit könnte ich mich einverstanden erklären': 'I might go along with that.'

(ii) 'cannot be used in the ordinary way': the subsequent parenthetical example explains one deviation. If A lives on the fifth floor and B on the fourth floor, A may rightly say that he lives above B, but B cannot say that he lives above A; whereas if we say that the Antipodeans are 'below' us, they *can* say that we are 'below' them.

2.1   'We are indeed all taught at school . . .': PG 381f. contrasts W.'s concern with mathematics with a mathematician's. The latter has been trained to *repress* these kinds of question, and finds them repulsive. 'That is to say, I trot out all the problems that a child learning arithmetic, etc. finds difficult, the problems that education represses without solving. I say to those repressed doubts: you are quite correct, go on asking, demand clarification!'

SECTION 352

1   Just as we are inclined to insist that 'pain is pain, whether *he* has it or I have it' (§351), so too we are tempted to invoke the law of excluded middle in this context and to insist that either X is in pain (talks to himself vocally in his imagination, has an image in his mind) or X is not

in pain (etc.), no matter whether X is a normal person, a deaf mute, or a stove!'

But this is deceptive. The law of excluded middle, if presented in the form '$p \vee \sim p$' is a *tautology which says nothing at all*. Or, more accurately, on the assumption that 'p' and '$\sim p$' are indeed expressions of propositions, then '$p \vee \sim p$' is an empty tautology. Why then does it seem to say something, indeed something quite definitive? If we take 'p' to be a proposition the sense of which is perspicuous, it would not even occur to us that '$p \vee \sim p$' says anything. It conveys no information whatever, not even the grammatical truth that if 'p' is a proposition then either it is true that p or it is false that p. But if the sentence 'p' is, in one way or another, problematic, if its sense flickers, as it were, then we can derive from the tautology '$p \vee \sim p$' the illusion of a picture of how things are, viz. either like *this*: p or like *this*: $\sim p$! And now, it seems, all we have to do is to find out which of these is true. This gives us the illusion that there is no problem about sense or meaning at all, but only a problem about how to establish truth (and, in that sense, an epistemological problem which takes meaning to be given!).

It is indeed remarkable that we can be taken in by the form of a tautology. For the question with which we are concerned is not whether it is true that p or it is true that $\sim p$, but rather, what is it for p to be true. Or, more accurately, what does 'p' mean? 'When someone sets up the law of excluded middle, he is as it were putting two pictures before us to choose from, and saying that one must correspond to the fact. But what if it is questionable whether the pictures can be applied here?' (RFM 268). But these are precisely the cases we are concerned with: viz. whether it makes any sense to talk of a stove having a pain or of a picture's occurring to it, or whether 'these deaf mutes talk to themselves inwardly in a vocal language' expresses a proposition at all. And if, in our contortions, we have rendered the proposition 'He is in pain' problematic (e.g. by arguing that it is to be understood by analogy with 'I am in pain'), then insisting that 'Either he is in pain or he is not in pain, there is no third possibility' achieves nothing. For we owe an explanation of what it is for him to be in pain. This law of excluded middle gives us a picture, a picture of a pair of pictures one of which corresponds with reality and the other of which does not. And this seems to fix the sense of 'He has this experience' and 'He does not have this experience' absolutely unequivocally. But that is exactly what it does *not* do.

The argument is parallel to that of §350, but with a further irony. In §350 the interlocutor attempts to invoke sameness in order to explain attributing pain to another; whereas only if one has laid down what it is for another to be in pain and has found out that someone is in pain is one in a position to say that he has the same as one has oneself if one is in pain. Here we try to invoke a tautology in order likewise to by pass the difficulty of clarifying the sense of 'He is in pain', whereas 'Either he is in pain or he is not in pain' only *has* a sense if 'He is in pain' has a sense — which we still need to explain. And the irony is that if 'He is in pain' has a sense, then, of course, the sense of 'Either he is in pain or he is not in pain' is, like that of all tautologies, zero sense!

1.1   (i) 'unendlichen Entwicklung von π': 'infinite (decimal) expansion of π'.

(ii) 'either the group "7777" occurs or it does not': a famous and much discussed matter. Though invoked here merely as an example, W. examined it at length elsewhere (WWK 71 – 3; PR 146ff., 206ff.; AWL 140, 189 – 201; PG 451ff.; RFM 266ff.). A number of points are noteworthy to avoid misinterpretation here:

(a) W. is not arguing that, contrary to classical logic, there are propositions, such as 'There are four consecutive 7s in the infinite expansion of π', to which the law of excluded middle does not apply — i.e. of which one cannot say: either this or its negation is true. This was what Brouwer thought, and it was for this that W. criticized him:

> Brouwer talks of a range of propositions for which the law of excluded middle does not hold; in this branch of mathematics this law does not *apply* . . . Brouwer has actually discovered something which it is misleading to call a proposition. He has not discovered a proposition, but something having the appearance of a proposition . . . To say the law of excluded middle does not hold for propositions about infinite classes is like saying 'In this stratum of atmosphere Boyle's law does not hold'. (AWL 140)

But it is absurd to conceive of laws of logic on the model of laws of science! If the law of excluded middle does not 'apply', then (*ceteris paribus*) we are not dealing with a proposition.

(b) W. was not therefore impugning the validity of the law of excluded middle or the principle of bivalence. On the contrary, the principle that every proposition is either true or false (which might be expressed, not by a particular tautology '$p \vee \sim p$', but rather by the statement *that* '$p \vee \sim p$' *is a tautology*) partially *defines* what a proposition is (AWL 140). Hence one might say in the spirit of PI §136 that, contrary to Brouwer's view, the law of excluded middle does not 'fit' propositions (so that one could intelligibly ask whether it *applies* to *this* proposition), it 'belongs' to propositions! (But for later qualms about the excluded middle in relation to certain conditionals, see RPP I §§269–74.)

(c) W.'s agreement with Brouwer that the law of excluded middle does not apply to 'There are four consecutive 7s in the infinite expansion of π' does not rest on an awareness of limitations on human recognitional capacities. If it did, it would make sense to suggest that God sees the whole of the infinite expansion of π, but that we, with our 'medical limitations' (as Russell put it) cannot see so far. But that is precisely what

W. repudiated: "'Can God know all the places of the expansion of π?" would have been a good question for the schoolmen to ask. In all such cases the answer runs, "The question is senseless"' (PR 149). It is senseless in so far as it treats infinity as a quantity and an infinite decimal as a series. But the concept of an infinite decimal is a concept of the unlimited technique of expansion of a series (RFM 278f.)

(d) It would be a complete misunderstanding to suggest that W. was trying to restrict mathematics to finitistic statements, let alone that he was doing so *on the grounds* that the law of excluded middle does not apply to infinitary statements. What he was doing in his discussion of this issue was drawing attention to grammatical differences between statements dealing with finite totalities and those dealing with infinite processes. It makes sense to talk of an infinite series containing a certain pattern only in certain circumstances, e.g. if the law of the series determines a recurring decimal. For then the criterion for the occurrence or non-occurrence of the pattern is its occurrence or non-occurrence *in the period* (AWL 190). But no such criterion obtains in the case of a lawless (irregular) infinite decimal. Here the question 'Do four consecutive 7s occur in the expansion?' *makes no sense*. One can only intelligibly ask 'Do four consecutive 7s occur in the first n places of the expansion?', for this question is a finite (extensional) one, and in the absence of periodicity we cannot take the former question about the infinite decimal extensionally.

It is important not to fall into a further fallacy here. In recent years the value of π has been calculated (by a computer) to 100,265 places.[11] There are four consecutive 7s beginning at the 1589th place. It is tempting to see this as a proof that there are four consecutive 7s in the expansion of π, and hence as a refutation of W.'s claim that the question makes no sense. It is, one might argue, a proposition which is not *falsifiable*, hence it is unlike finitistic mathematical propositions; but it is verifiable, and has now been verified! But this is a confusion. What has been determined is that there are four consecutive 7s after the 1589th place, i.e. in *an* expansion of π, not that there are four consecutive 7s in *the* expansion of π. For 'there isn't any series that is called *the* expansion of π. There are expansions of π, namely those that have been worked out . . .' (PG 480). The confusion becomes perspicuous when we reflect on whether we should say that before the calculation had been carried through until the 1589th place, we did not know whether the proposition made sense? Were we then trying to answer a question which we did not know made sense? But is there any such thing as trying to answer such a question?

---

[11] D. Shanks and J. W. Wrench, Jr, 'Calculations of π to 100,000 decimals', *Mathematics of Computation*, 16 (1962), pp. 79 – 99 (see S. G. Shanker, *Wittgenstein and the Turning-Point in the Philosophy of Mathematics* (Croom Helm, London, 1987), p. 102).

Here we are perspicuously in the grip of a *picture* of an infinite series; it is there, we think, and all we have to do is to walk down this road and we will find what we will find (either that there are four consecutive sevens or that there are not)! But 'there are . . .' in mathematics is not a prediction about what we will find. The further expansion of π is a further expansion of mathematics.

2.1   'Entweder es schwebt ihm ein solches Bild vor': 'either such a picture crosses his mind'. In Vol. XII, 148 this occurs after a discussion of what it is to understand the sentence 'He imagines a red circle'.

.

SECTION 353

1   Having examined a variety of false pictures and temptations that should be resisted, we are left at an impasse. Neither extrapolating from one's own case nor appealing to the law of excluded middle is of any avail in trying to make clear whether the suppositions that concern us (e.g. that deaf mutes speak to themselves vocally in their imagination) make sense. For both moves presuppose the meaning of third-person ascriptions of thought to be given. But *how* is it given? §340 noted that one must *look at* the use of a word ('thinking') and learn from that. Now a concrete suggestion, implicit in the foregoing, is made: whether and how a proposition is verified is part of its grammar, and a description of it is a clarification of the meaning of an expression. And that is indeed *one* task that needs to be done in elucidating the nature of thought, of talking to oneself in the imagination, etc.

2   Though derived immediately from Vol. XI, 72, this remark can be traced back to 1930/31, i.e. when W. had only just returned to philosophical work (Vol. VI, 238; Vol. VIII, 99; ETB 270, 449, 590). It was at this stage that he introduced the principle that inspired the Vienna Circle,[12] viz. that the meaning of a proposition is determined by its method of verification. The atomism of the *Tractatus* was repudiated in 1929, and replaced (briefly) by the conception of a language as an interconnected system of proportional systems (*Satzsysteme*) and a

---

[12] This is confirmed by Carnap, 'Intellectual Authobiography', in R. A. Schilpp (ed.), *The Philosophy of Rudolf Carnap* (Open Court, Illinois, 1963), p. 45; B. Juhos, 'The Methodological Symmetry of Verification and Falsification', in his *Selected Papers on Epistemology and Physics*, ed. G. Frey (Reidel, Dordrecht, 1976), pp. 134ff.; V. Kraft, *The Vienne Circle, the origins of neo-positivism* (Greenwood Press, New York, 1969), pp. 31, 197; and F. Waismann, 'A Logical Analysis of the Concept of Probability', first published in *Erkenntnis*, 1 (1930 – 1), repr. in translation in his *Philosophical Papers*, ed. B. McGuinness (Reidel, Dordrecht, 1977); see esp. p. 5. Cf. also Waismann's 'Theses', in WWK 243ff.

tripartite distinction between types of proposition or 'propositions' in different senses of the term. 'Genuine' propositions concerning immediate experience were distinguished from 'hypotheses', and both were sharply differentiated from mathematical propositions. It is important to note that W.'s verification dictum was employed for a very specific purpose, viz. as a determinant of what kind of *propositional system* a given proposition belongs to and of what kind of proposition it is. Thus 'This is red' is compared with reality in a similar way to 'This is blue'; hence they both belong to the same propositional system, which differs from the propositional system of 'This is hot' and 'This is B-flat'.

> You can only search in *a space*.[13] For only in a space do you stand in relation to where you are not.
>
> To understand the sense of a proposition means to know how the issue of its truth or falsity is to be decided.
>
> . . . You cannot search wrongly: you *cannot* look for a visual impression with your sense of touch.
>
> You cannot compare a picture with reality unless you can set it against it as a yardstick.
> (PR 77)

Furthermore, if a proposition can be conclusively verified, then it is a different kind of logical structure from one which cannot be verified, viz. a hypothesis (WWK 210; PR 285). Vol. IV, 108 (a precursor of PI §353) argues that if one wants to know what a proposition means, one can always ask how one knows it. Does one know that there are so-and-so many permutations of three elements in the same way as one knows that there are six people in the room? No, and that is why they are propositions of different *kinds*! (Cf. PR 200; PG 458f.) In these senses, clarification of how a proposition is verified is obviously a contribution to its grammar. W., of course, abandoned his distinction between genuine propositions and hypotheses, and replaced his conception of propositional systems by the much more flexible and richer conception of language-games. But this did *not* mean that he had to abandon the simple point that how a proposition is verified is an aspect of its grammar, as long as this point is not taken as a dogmatic *thesis*:[14] 'How far is giving the verification of a proposition a grammatical statement about it? So far as it is, it can explain the meaning of its terms. In so far as

---

[13] E.g. in visual space for colours in auditory space for sounds.
[14] Hence his reported remark many years later:

I used at one time to say that, in order to get clear how a certain sentence is used, it was a good idea to ask oneself the question: How would one try to verify such an assertion? But that's just one way of getting clear about the use of a word or sentence . . . Some people have turned this suggestion about asking for verification into a dogma — as if I'd been advancing a *theory* about meaning.

See D. A. T. Gasking and A. C. Jackson, 'Wittgenstein as Teacher', repr. in K. T. Fann (ed.), *Ludwig Wittgenstein: the man and his philosophy* (Dell Publishing Co., New York, 1967), p. 54.

it is a matter of experience, as when one names a symptom, the meaning is not explained' (AWL 31). Of course, there are many sorts of propositions for which it makes no sense to ask how they are verified; but that very fact is an important feature of their grammar and is a mark that distinguishes them from other kinds of propositions.

SECTION 354

1   The preceding remark has suggested that clarifying how and whether a proposition can be verified is a contribution to characterizing its grammar. But if it is a proposition of the kind for which it makes sense to ask how it is verified, not any sort of verification belongs to its grammar (AWL 31, quoted in Exg. §353). One can verify whether Cambridge won the boat race by reading *The Times*, but that *The Times* reports that it did is not part of the grammar of the proposition; it is merely a 'symptom' (cf. M 266).

But though there is in one sense a sharp distinction between criteria (fixed by convention) and symptoms (discovered inductively), in another sense there is not. For there is often a widespread fluctuation, especially in science, between symptoms and criteria. As long as certain phenomena are virtually always concomitant, there is no need to decide whether $e_1 \ldots e_3$ define h as its criteria, whereas $e_4 \ldots e_7$ are merely inductive evidence, or vice versa. And for certain purposes in one context, one may take $e_1 \ldots e_3$ as criteria, and for other purposes in another context one may treat $e_4 \ldots e_7$ as criteria. Hence it is very often the case that one cannot ask globally whether a certain theory (e.g. Newtonian mechanics) treats such-and-such as a criterion for so-and-so. Rather, one must ask whether *this* specific argument does so, or whether this person, in this argument, is doing so (see 'Criteria', §2).

This fluctuation between criteria and symptoms can make it appear as if there were nothing at all but symptoms. And, by implication, the troubles besetting us in this investigation into thinking stem from failure to distinguish criteria from symptoms and from overlooking their fluctuation (but this has not been shown). Hence we are inclined to think that all we *ever* have to go on when it comes to judgements about another's thoughts, mental images, or interior monologues are symptoms. But avowals (*Äusserungen*) of the 'inner' are *not* symptoms; they are *criteria*.

W. applies pressure to the supposition that there are nothing but symptoms by invoking an example from a different area. We say, quite correctly, that experience teaches us that when the barometer falls, it rains. This is an inductive correlation, the fall of the barometer being a symptom of rain. But we are wrongly inclined to say likewise that experience teaches us that when we have certain sense-impressions, it rains. We even defend the claim that this is a matter of experience by citing the indisputable fact that sense-impressions may deceive us, i.e. having a visual impression of rain does not *entail* that it is raining, so the relation must be inductive or experiential!

The conclusion does *not* follow. It may indeed look to me as if it is raining, yet *not* be raining. But that possibility does not imply that the proposition that normally when it looks to one as if it is raining, then it is raining is an empirical proposition, discovered to be true by inductive correlation. For the *concept* of 'looking to a person as if it is raining' is not independent of the concept of its raining. That this (false) visual impression is one of *rain* is founded on a *grammatical* nexus; we explain what 'It looks to me as if it is raining' means by pointing to the *rain* and saying 'When it looks like *that* ↗, then it looks as if it is raining!'

So far, so (tolerably) good! But in order to illustrate the point at stake, W. would have to claim that its looking to me as if it is raining (my having a visual impression of rain) is a *criterion* (not a symptom) of its raining. Yet that, surely, he would not want to do! We do not say that it is raining *on the grounds* that it looks to us as if it is raining, as we say that A is in pain on the grounds that he fell and is groaning. 'It looks to me as if it is raining' is not my *evidence* for the fact that it is raining; indeed, I *need* no evidence, I can *see the rain*! It is true that if asked 'How do you know that it is raining?' I would have an answer: viz. 'I can see it.' But that answer does not supply the questioner with my *evidence* for the rain. We learn to say 'It's raining' in circumstances in which we have certain visual and tactile impressions, but *not on the grounds* of having those impressions. On the contrary, we learn to characterize the impressions only after having mastered the concept of what the impressions are impressions of — viz. *rain*!

2   Like §353, this derives from Vol. XI, 72ff., written in 1933/4. It is noteworthy that prior to this draft there occurs the following:

> Wie weiss man, wenn es regnet? Wir sehen, fühlen, den Regen. Die Bedeutung des Wortes "Regen" wurde uns mit diesen Erfahrungen erklärt. / Ich sage, sie sind 'Kriterien' dafür, dass es regnet / 'Was ist Regen?' und 'Wie sieht Regen aus?' sind logisch verwandte Fragen. — Die Erfahrung habe nun gelehrt, dass ein plötzliches Fallen des Barometers und ein Regenguss immer zusammengehen, dann werde ich ein solches Fallen des Barometers als ein *Symptom* für das Niedergehen eines Regengusses ansehen. Ob ein Phänomen ein Symptom des Regens ist, lehrt die Erfahrung, was als Kriterium des Regens gilt, ist Sache der Abmachung (Definition)/unsere Bestimmung. (Vol. XI, 72)

> (How does one know whether it is raining? We see, feel, the rain. The meaning of the word 'rain' is explained to us with those experiences. / I say, they are 'criteria' for

its raining. / 'What is rain?' and 'What does rain look like?' are logically related questions. — If experience has taught that a sudden fall of the barometer always goes together with rainfall, then I shall consider such a barometric fall as a *symptom* of rainfall. Whether a phenomenon is a symptom of rain is taught by experience, what counts as a criterion of rain is a matter of stipulation (definition)/our determination.)

This is followed by a version of Z §438: nothing is commoner, especially in science, than for the meaning of an expression to oscillate, due to a fluctuation between criteria and symptoms. This long remark is followed by a draft of PI §§354–6.

It is noteworthy that this sequence of remarks was *not* tailored for the purpose of clarifying an aspect of the grammar of psychological expressions in general, let alone 'thinking' or 'speaking to oneself in the imagination' in particular. Furthermore, it is a relatively early remark which antedates W.'s exploitation of the concept of a criterion in philosophy of mind. Arguably it fulfils its current role poorly. First, though we can distinguish symptoms from criteria in the case of psychological features, it is less than obvious that the difficulties encountered thus far are due to any *fluctuation* between the two. Rather, the appearance of there being nothing but symptoms in the case of ascribing psychological predicates to other people arises through the inner/outer picture of the mind and through failure to grasp the grammatical nature of the first-/third-person asymmetry in the case of psychological terms. Secondly, though its seeming to me as if it is raining is not a symptom of rain, it is not a criterion either — at least, not if W. conceives of a criterion as a *justifying ground* that is fixed by convention. For the concept of its looking to X just as if it is raining *presupposes*, and does not determine, the meaning of 'It is raining' (cf. Z §§422ff.), and that it looks to me as if it is raining is not my reason or ground for judging it to be raining, although I might, in certain circumstances, use this form of words to *draw back* from the judgement that it is raining.

The general point at issue in connection with psychological predicates is perhaps better made by RPP I §292. One is inclined to think that psychologists, who study the workings of the mind, are handicapped relative to other scientists. For unless they engage in introspective psychology, are they not condemned to study the phenomenon of the human mind from afar, indirectly as it were? For what they observe are the words spoken by their subjects and their behaviour, but these are surely only *signs* of the mental processes the psychologist is interested in! This is confused. It is true that words and behaviour that are *learnt by heart* are of no interest here to the psychologist. But the expression 'signs of mental processes' is misleading, for we speak of the colour of the face as a sign of fever, i.e. as inductive evidence. But the utterances (*Äusserungen*) and behaviour of a subject are not uniformly symptoms, but *criteria* of the mental.

SECTION 355

1   This repeats the conclusion of §354. Because sense-impressions can be
deceptive (it may look to me as if it is raining, yet not be) one is inclined
to think of sense-impressions as mere symptoms of what they are
sense-impressions of. But that they are not symptoms (inductive evidence, i.e. externally related to what they are impressions of) is shown
by the fact that we understand what our sense-impressions are impressions of. We 'understand their language', for we are not at a loss as to
whether the sense-impression we are having is one of rain or of a pink
elephant.

1.1 'is founded on convention': characterizing how things strike one
visually by 'It looks to me as if it is raining' requires mastery of the rules
for the use of these expressions. And it is correct to use these words only
if it looks to me like *that* ↗ — and here one points to rain! (cf. Z
§§418ff.)

SECTION 356

1   The opening move provides a link with §352 which is perhaps the
primary rationale for the occurrence of §§354 – 6 in the argument. For
here too one vacuously invokes the law of excluded middle while
brushing aside the question of verification, of the circumstances justifying the use of the proposition, as irrelevant to its meaning.
   How the information that it is raining has reached one, one is inclined
to insist, is irrelevant to the truth or falsity of the proposition in question.
And so, indeed, it is, if that simply means that truth is independent of
whether or how it happens to be known. But *meaning* is not so
independent. One learns to use the expression 'It is raining' when one has
certain visual, auditory, or tactile sense-impressions, i.e. when it looks
like *that* ↗, sounds *thus*, or feels like *this*. One knows (verifies) that it is
raining by perceiving the rain (or someone tells one that it is, or one
infers that it is from one's visitor's wet umbrella). But it is misleading to
characterize perceiving the rain as a matter of information being *transmitted* to one; in perception one often acquires information, but not by
information *reaching* one, rather by perceiving how things are. What
gives this 'information' the character of information about something is
that one is now in a position to give someone else that information, e.g.
to *say* 'It is raining'. It is not that one was *given* information oneself (e.g.
in the form of ambient light), for light hitting the retina does not give the
retina or anyone else information, and though one's optic nerve trans-

mits electrical impulses to one's 'visual' striate cortex, this too is not a case of one's eyes giving one information or even giving one's 'visual' striate cortex information. Hence the opening claim here is muddled. How I know is *not* 'another matter', but the heart of the matter in this case, for I did not acquire the information that it is raining by acquiring some other information (viz. that it looks to me as if it is raining) from which it follows.

SECTION 357

1   After the two pertinent digressions, §§349–52 (on the apparent sense of a supposition involving illegitimate extrapolation and the failure of the law of excluded middle to support its sense) and §§353–6 (on the relevance of verification to meaning), W. now returns explicitly to the theme of the antecedent remarks and picks up the thread of §348, viz. the investigation of the concept of talking to oneself in one's imagination. §348 expressed doubt over the intelligibility of supposing deaf mutes to speak to themselves vocally in the imagination. The issue turns upon the limits of intelligible applications of this expression and, as has now been argued, on what verifies the judgement that someone says something to himself in the imagination.

We do not say that perhaps a dog talks to itself. Is that because we are so well acquainted with its soul (or mind)? If one is caught in the net of the inner/outer picture one will, of course, deny that one is 'acquainted with its soul' at all. And one will also be prone to agnosticism in respect of the question of whether possibly the dog talks to itself. But one should jettison the philosophical ideas that accompany that picture anyway. (I am not *better* acquainted with my soul than those who know me well; indeed, I am not *acquainted* with my soul at all.) One sees the soul of a living being in its behaviour, and in this sense one might (perhaps ironically) *agree* that we do not say that possibly a dog talks to itself because we *are* well acquainted with its soul. For nothing in the behavioural repertoire of a dog could count as a criterion for its talking to itself in its imagination.

The interlocutor questions this; for after all, I do not say that *I* am saying something to myself in the imagination on the grounds of *my* behaviour. W. agrees immediately. I do not say that I am thinking, in pain, or that I intend such-and-such on the grounds of observing my behaviour either. But the first-person avowal or report *makes sense* only in as much as I generally do, in my behaviour, give others grounds for saying of me 'He is talking to himself in his imagination' ('He is thinking, in pain, intends to . . .'). The concluding sentence provides the transition to §358.

1.1   (i) 'Well, one might say this': it is not clear what it is that one might say
— that we are so well acquainted with the soul of the dog and hence do
not say that perhaps it speaks to itself, or that if one sees the behaviour of
a living thing, one sees its soul. In MS. 165, 200f. the 'this' is perspicuously anaphoric (see below).

(ii) 'One sees its soul': after all, one might say, a dog is wholly
transparent to us, one sees its delight, its fear, its anger — there is neither
simulation nor repression.

2   MS. 165, 200f. and the later MS. 129, 7 have the draft of this remark
following directly after PI §348.

MS. 165, 200f. has, in place of the third sentence

Nun, man *könnte* so sagen. Nur vom Menschen sagen wir, er spreche zu sich
selbst — und nur vom sprechenden Menschen. Nur von dem, was/der/sich so und so
benimmt.

(Well, one *could* say this. Only of a human being do we say, he speaks to
himself — and only of a human being who can speak. Only of/that which/one
who/behaves thus-and-so.)

This links the remark far more clearly with §348, to which it offers an
answer, and also with §281 and §283 ('only of a living human being and
what resembles (behaves like) a living human being can one say . . .'),
which is appropriate given that it is succeeded in draft by §361 ('The
chair is thinking to itself . . .') and §327, rather than §§359–60. But
prior to §361, MS. 165 interpolates two further remarks.

The first picks up an earlier remark (MS. 165, 7): 'Denk Dir, statt in
einen Stein würdest Du in ein Grammophon verwandelt' ('Imagine that
instead of being turned into a stone [see PI §283] you were turned into a
gramophone'), and observes that a gramophone 'speaks', so could one
not suppose that it has a soul and *means* with it what it says? This might
be difficult to imagine, W. says ironically, but is it impossible? The
second stresses the problematic character of the concept of speaking to
oneself. If speaking means to emit sounds, then the transition from the
concept of speaking to the concept of speaking to oneself in the
imagination (i.e. when no sounds are emitted) is none too perspicuous. It
is comparable to telling someone to use the word 'sugar' for something
that is just like sugar, only neither sweet nor edible.

2.1   'If one sees the behaviour of a living thing [being] one sees its soul': cf.
PI p. 178: 'The human body is the best picture of the human soul,' and
RPP I §280: 'What better picture of believing could there be, than the
human being who, with the expression of belief, says "I believe . . ."?'

Section 358

1   §357 argued, in conformity with the thrust of the private language
arguments, that though my avowal that I am saying something to myself
in the imagination rests on no grounds, in particular not on my own
behaviour, nevertheless it only makes sense because I do (sometimes)
manifest such-and-such behaviour. Hence, of course, 'I am in pain' or 'I
was saying to myself that . . .' do not make sense simply because I mean
something by them. Indeed, quite generally, it is not mythical 'inner acts
of meaning' which give sentences their sense, endow them with life.

1.1   (i) 'And here, of course, belongs the fact that one cannot mean a
senseless series of words': a thought that had played an important role in
W.'s reflections when working on TLP. One is tempted to argue that
word-language allows senseless combinations of words (cf. PI §512), but
that the language of thought (cf. R 37) does not allow senseless
combinations of thought-elements. Hence one cannot *think* a nonsense
(PI §511). So one cannot *mean* a nonsensical combination of words; hence
'Green ideas sleep furiously' is nonsense *because* one cannot mean it! An
alternative route to the same thought, and one equally prominent in W.'s
first philosophy, is that *meaning* the words one utters is what connects the
words with reality (cf. 'Thinking: the soul of language', §1). But, one
might then think, one cannot connect a senseless combination of words
with reality precisely because they will not mirror the logical multiplicity
of the facts (of representable states of affairs).
       (ii) 'a dream of our language': a nightmare of reason.

2   MS. 165, 5ff. has this at the beginning of a long discussion of meaning
something. Immediately following the first draft is a remark, which
surely echoes TLP 5.6ff., that one could imagine someone saying that
actually each person talks only for himself, since only he *knows* what he
means. But then he ought really to say that actually everyone really talks
for *me*, since only I know how I understand the words!

Section 359

1   We do not say of a dog that maybe it speaks to itself, but what of a
machine? Can it think? Many philosophers and artificial-intelligence
scientists would claim that machines can think, or, alternatively, that we
are on the brink of creating such machines. W.'s response here is oblique.
Shelving the question of thinking until §360, he queries whether a

machine could be in pain. Rather than replying, as most of us would, with a simple negative response, he shifts the question subtly. Is the human *body* a machine which thinks or is in pain? Surely nothing can come any closer to being such a machine? But we do *not* say of the body that it thinks or is in pain: my tooth hurts — but *I* am in pain, not my tooth (cf. §281 and 'Men, minds, and machines', §5.).

2   Vol. XIII, 129 contains the draft of §359 in the context of a long discussion of thinking and believing. Our philosophical unclarity about thought and belief, and more generally about what is problematic in psychology, is manifest in the picture we have of a hidden mechanism, whether in the brain or, ethereally, in the mind. We think that our difficulties would be resolved if only we knew more about the processes in these mechanisms. But it is not undiscovered processes which concern us here; rather it is the use of familiar 'processes' of belief, such as saying 'I believe . . .'. The mechanism which we do not understand is not in our minds or in our brains, but in our lives, where this expression is at home.

This is followed by PI §359, which is succeeded by the remark that the word 'I' in 'I have a pain' does not refer to a body, hence it does not stand for a machine either. This observation, one might say, is the mature wine from the reflections of PG 105, which pursued a different line of attack, closer to the strategy of PR, Ch. VI.

2.1   'It surely comes as close as possible to being such a machine': but not all that close; see Z §614: 'But you would never talk like that if you were examining the behaviour of a machine. — Well, who says that in this sense a living creature, an animal body, is a machine?' (My translation; cf. 'Behaviour and behaviourism', §4.)

.

SECTION 360

1   This applies §281 to the question raised in §359. It makes no more sense to anticipate the construction of machines that can think than to attempt to make machines to investigate the colours of numbers. Of course, that is not to say that we may not one day make thinking beings in laboratories, with or without organic material! (Cf. 'Men, minds, and machines', §5.)

1.1   (i) 'of dolls and no doubt of spirits too': these are 'secondary' uses, whose intelligibility is parasitic on the primary use.
       (ii) 'Look at the word "to think" as a tool': cf. §421.

SECTION 361

1   This probes deeper the observation of §360 that we say only of a
human being and what is like one that it thinks. *If* someone were to say
that the chair is thinking to itself, we would wonder *where* it is thinking.
And that is highly significant, for when we are told that a human being is
talking to himself, we do *not* wonder where he is doing this (save,
trivially, where he is when he is doing it). Why does the question of
where the chair is talking to itself seem to demand an answer? Precisely
because if the contention that the chair is talking to itself is to make even
remote sense, we need to bring the chair within the ambit of the human
form, as it were. We must see it as a potential agent that could manifest
thought in action and expression. So, in a Disney film in which chairs are
animated, they have faces and mouths. Here, if we are told that the
armchair said something to itself, the question of where it did so would
not arise.
     §361(c) belongs together with §362. One wonders, when doing
philosophy, what it is like to say something to oneself. It seems as if the
answer lies in careful introspection, careful observation in one's own case
of what happens when one says something to oneself in the imagination.
But, of course, that is not so at all. For typically, nothing *goes on*, save
that I said to myself that . . .; or if anything *else* goes on, it is irrelevant.
So to explain what it is *like* to say something to oneself is not to describe
an 'inner' event or process, but rather to explain the circumstances in
which one uses the expression — as, indeed, when one explains the
meaning of the expression. (The only thing that 'goes on', one might
say, is that one does *not* say anything aloud for a moment, as one reflects
and says to oneself that . . .)

1.1   (i) 'im Innern': 'inwardly', i.e. in his imagination.
     (ii) 'What is it like to say something to oneself?': W. does not explore
here the contours of the concept of saying things to oneself (cf.
'Thinking: the soul of language, §2); he is concerned primarily with the
point that it is not a concept of *an experience*. One does not teach someone
what 'saying something to oneself' means by directing his attention to an
experience.
     (iii) 'was da vorgeht': since this alludes to 'was geht da vor' in the first
sentence of (c), it should be similarly translated.

2   This derives from MS. 165, 204 and 211f., but its remote ancestor is
Vol. XII, 227ff. Apropos the private linguist who keeps a diary of his
experiences, it is noteworthy that it is not wholly clear what is meant if

one says that when he reads his diary, certain images come before his mind. So is it a mistake to talk, without more ado, of the private linguist as having, or as *perhaps* having, mental images? W. takes a round-about route. One cannot assume, without more ado, that a table has mental images. If that is because one does not assume that it has a mind, then why not assume that it does? It is surely because there must be both body *and behaviour*, for it is action that is the criterion for whether a being has a mind. After all, if asked to entertain the thought that the table sees an image before it, one wouldn't rightly know what one was meant to suppose, how to apply the expression 'to have an image' to a table in this context. Why can one do so in the case of a human being? It is important that when we conceive of a human as having an image before his mind, we look at his face and demeanour, not at his feet or his stomach. Is that because we think the image is *in* his head? That is the metaphor we use; but look at its application!

So one cannot imagine a table's seeing or having an image ('with what part?' one might ask), but only a human being doing so. But then the *objection* to the private linguist's imagining things in association with his diary-entry collapses, for we *can* suppose that this man sees an image before him! Not so: for 'we *can* suppose that . . .' really amounts to the fact that this is a well-entrenched English sentence with a use, that we can *ordinarily* get around with it. But then ordinarily we never stop to wonder how states of mind, like having an image before one, *adhere* to people (and not to tables); rather, we make use of our expression. (Just as we pay our bills with banknotes and don't stare at them trying to see how their value adheres to them.) This is not because we aren't thinking, but because we *are* thinking, and our thought is not in a cramp!

One's qualms over talking of the private linguist's having mental images stem from not knowing how to apply the expression correctly in these (non-ordinary) circumstances; hence the feeling that one does not know how the images *adhere to* this person! But what mental imagery 'adheres to' is what a person *says* and *does*, i.e. to his actions.

2.1   'where': for a discussion of the location of thought, see BB 7f. and 'Thinking: methodological muddles and categorial confusions', §4.

SECTION 362

1   As with so many psychological terms, we are prone to think that we teach the meaning *indirectly*, as it were guiding the pupil by remote control until he homes in on the private experience which *is* speaking to oneself in the imagination. Then he can give himself a private ostensive definition! This illusion was exposed by the private language arguments.

In this context the supposition would be doubly erroneous, since, in addition, speaking to oneself is not an experience.

2.1   'without telling him directly': cf. BB 185; LPE 285f.; PI p. 194; Z §545, all of which discuss aspects of the direct/indirect contrast in relation to learning, teaching, and understanding psychological expressions. But 'indirect' makes *sense* only if it is *intelligible* that what is done indirectly be done directly.

CHAPTER 3

Imagination

(§§363–97)

INTRODUCTION

The tenth 'chapter' runs from §363 to §397, but there is no sharp break separating it from the previous discussion. §361(c) argued that the concept of saying something to oneself is not linked with 'what takes place' when one says something to oneself, and §362 emphasized that this concept is not acquired by engendering an inner happening which then functions as a sample for a private ostensive definition. §363 switches to the example of imagining, but the example is incidental to the point of the remark, and the subject of the imagination only gradually comes to the forefront of the discussion.

§363 is linked to previous remarks via the idea that imagining (or having a sensation) is something that *happens*, an inner event, which one then communicates to others by means of speech. W. focuses upon a misconception of communication that characterizes the philosophical tradition, a theme he has touched on earlier in the book (§§6, 304, 317). That picture distorts the diversity of the language-game of telling someone something and mischaracterizes it as the transference of something mental (the sense of one's words) from the mind of the speaker to the mind of the hearer.

§364 reverts to the opening move of §363, for it seems as if W. is denying that there are any mental processes. The interlocutor takes up an example which seems to refute W. decisively, viz. calculating in the imagination. Surely this is an inner process, exactly like the outer process of calculating on paper, only without paper! This W. disputes, and it seems as if he is denying that calculating in the head is real calculating. But, of course, it is real calculating-in-the-head (as opposed to pretending to calculate in the head), just as characters in a drama may play a real game of chess (as opposed to pretending, in the play, to be playing a game of chess (§365)). Calculating in the head is neither more nor less real than calculating aloud, but it is not a mental process corresponding to a physical process, as one physical process may correspond to another (§366). Such a correspondence can obtain only when it makes sense to talk of a method of projection from one process to another, but the mental image of a sign is not a *representation* of the sign imagined.

§§367–8 digress: we think of a mental image as an inner picture, but to describe one's mental image is not to describe something visible to oneself alone. It is rather to describe what one imagines, and that is altogether different from describing what one sees. The criterion for what a person imagines is what he says and does.

§369 reverts to the matter raised in §363 (viz. what happens when one imagines something) and focuses on the special case of calculating in the head. Clarifying what is called 'calculating in the head' cannot be done by explaining that one adds one number to another, etc., *in one's head*. The correct method of conceptual clarification of concepts of the imagination is to describe how the word 'imagination' (or 'doing such-and-such in the head') is used (§370). This looks as if it bypasses the philosophical concern with the nature or essence of the imagination in favour of mere lexicography, but it does not. §§371–3 briefly pursue this issue: essence is expressed by grammar, and an investigation into the essential nature of this or that *is* a grammatical one. §374 picks up the methodological remark in §370: the claim that one cannot explain what images are by pointing (even in one's own case) or by describing what happens when one imagines something makes it sound as if there is something one cannot do, viz. display one's mental images (whereas in fact one is pushing against the bounds of sense). The best therapy here is to yield to the temptation to use the picture of a private object off which one reads a description and to investigate its application. Then it will become clear that it is incoherent.

A tree-diagram of the structure of Part A (§§363–74) is given on the next page.

The structure of Part A:

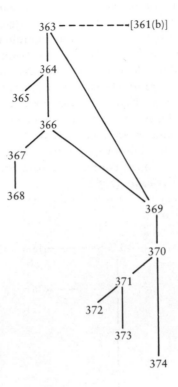

Part B (§§375–82) examines features of the conception of a 'private object' from which one derives a description. §375 opens the discussion with the old example of reading to oneself (cf. §156). One can teach someone to read to himself only if he can read; and one says that he can read to himself only if he can say what is written on the page he purports to have read. But he does not derive a description of what he has read to himself from scrutiny of the 'inner process' of reading to himself. §376 switches to the example of saying something to oneself (cf. §§361–2): what is the criterion of identity for two people to say the same thing to themselves or to have the same image? No inductive correlation with laryngal or brain-processes is possible in the absence of a non-inductive criterion. §§377–8 explore the question of the criterion of identity for mental images. In the first-person case no criterion at all is employed, either for characterizing one's mental image or for its identity with another's image (or a previous image one had oneself). One's avowal and behaviour, however, are public criteria for third-person statements about mental images and their identity. It is tempting to suppose that an avowal is justified by reference to one's recognition of the image one has. This futile manoeuvre is examined in §§379–82. Recognition presupposes the intelligibility of misrecognition. It only makes sense to speak of recognizing something *as* such-and-such if what is recognized can be picked out in some other way. It is unintelligible to interpose a 'process of recognition' between an experience and its expression, for then the question of how one identifies the process of recognition would, absurdly, arise. One is tempted to invoke a private ostensive definition as a rule to guide one in characterizing one's experience, but that is unintelligible. The ability to say what colour one has in view involves mastery of the technique of using colour-words, but rests on no grounds (§§380–1). Equally, the ability to say what colour one is imagining rests on no grounds, although, of course, it is parasitic upon mastery of the public vocabulary of colours (§382).

The structure of Part B:

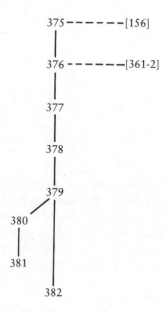

Part C (§§383–9) reverts to the theme of mental concepts and their analysis. §383 picks up the methodological remark of §370 and wards off a further misunderstanding. It may appear as if W. is propounding a form of nominalism and so denying that there are essences; but nominalism interprets all words as names and fails to describe their use — which is what is necessary for the clarification of a concept and hence for elucidation of an essential nature. §384 reminds us that describing the use of a word does not fall short of clarifying the concept it expresses. §385 resumes the discussion of §369 concerning calculating in the head. The concept of calculating in the head is parasitic upon the concept of calculating, and the criteria for calculating in the head are internally related to the criteria for calculating. §386 raises a worry parallel to that of §364: there it was queried whether, on W.'s account, calculating in the head is really calculating; now the interlocutor misinterprets W.'s qualms about the relation between the concepts of calculating and calculating in the head as qualms about whether he might not be mistaken in thinking that he calculates in the head. But this mislocates his qualms, which arise precisely because such doubts are excluded by *grammar*, not by the unmistakable similarity between images and what they are images of. §387 is an aside; §388 explores the correct observation that someone who has mastered the colour-vocabulary knows that he can pick out a given colour on sight. That capacity does not rest on having a mental image which one compares with the colour one sees. §389 concludes the discussion by locating a source of confusion in the thought that an image of X is a super-likeness of X (it looks so like X that one *cannot* mistake it for anything else!). But this confuses the absence of recognition or identification in the case of one's avowal of what image one has with the presence of an unmistakable criterion of similarity.

The structure of Part C:

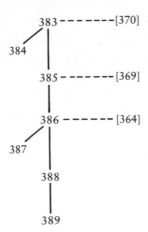

Part D (§§390–7) is concerned with the relation between imaginability and the bounds of sense. For someone to imagine something and for what he imagines to make sense (as Lewis Carroll's imaginings deliberately do not), it must be possible to give an account of what it would be for things to be as he imagines. Hence someone who insists that he can imagine stones being conscious can be dismissed, in the light of §§281 and 284, as indulging in nonsensical image-mongery (§390). §391 gives a contrasting example: one can imagine people in the street being in frightful pain, but concealing it. However, merely saying so does not suffice. And attributing pain to the mind, i.e. something which is conceived as having no essential connection with the body, merely compounds the confusion. Rather, one must fill in a story, imagine artful concealment, etc. Then one can be said to be imagining this. §392 cautions against an error: that I imagine this or that is not a matter of *what goes on in me* but of the story I tell. §393 emphasizes that one can imagine (it makes sense to imagine) pain without pain-behaviour; but even here it would be wrong to suppose that a *picture* or *paradigm* of pain is involved (cf. §300). This becomes clear when one reminds oneself of natural contexts in which one might tell someone to imagine something. What goes on in his mind is irrelevant to whether he does imagine what we tell him to. That would be relevant only to empirical investigations into the heuristics of the imagination and the accompaniments of imagining (§394). §§395–7 conclude the investigation by emphasizing the shaky relation between imaginability and sense. That one cannot imagine anything in connection with a certain proposition does not mean that one does not understand it (§396), and that one can imagine something in such a case does not necessarily indicate the use of the sentence in question, for in some cases what one imagines is simply the expression of a misleading picture.

The structure of Part D:

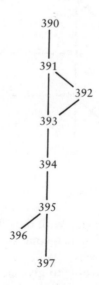

Correlations

PI§	PPI(I)§	MS. 129	MS. 124	MS. 165	Vol. XII	Others
363	278	49–50	262–3[1] 280[2]	127–8[2]		
364	279–80	74–5	247–9			
365	281	75				
366	282	75–6	250–1			
367					207	MS. 164, 166
368						MS. 162(b), 97–8
369	283	76–7				
370					319	
371					340	
372						Vol. VI, 144; Vol. X, 157
373					340	
374					243–4	Vol. XVI, 133–4
375		125	281	131		
376					242	
377		115–16	281[3]	131[4]		MS. 180(a), 66[5]
378		118–19				MS. 180(a), 65–6
379		119				MS. 180(a), 71
380		116–18; 182				MS. 180(a), 65[6], 71[7], 74[8]
381		179–80				MS. 180(a), 68
382					120	Vol. V, 199[9]
383	284	190–1				
384		114–15	284	150		
385	285	77	252			
386(a)	286	77–9	272–4			MS. 179, 41
387	286[10]	79	273			
388					27	
389					28	
390		90		59		
391	288	13–14		53		
392	289	14				
393	290	14–15; 80–1; 131–2		54		MS. 179, 61–2
394	291	80–1; 132		54–5		
395	292	16				MS. 179, 63
396		194				
397	no known source					

[1] PI §363(b) only.
[2] PI §363(a) only.
[3] PI §377(a) and first sentence of (b) only.
[4] Only last sentence of PI §376 and first sentence of PI §377(b).
[5] PI §377(b) only.

[6] PI §380(b) only.
[7] PI §380(a) only.
[8] PI §380(c) only.
[9] PI §382(b) only.
[10] Two remarks have the same number in TS.

Images and the imagination
   1. Landmarks   2. Seeing, imagining, and mental images
   3. Images and pictures   4. Visual images and visual impressions
   5. Imagination, intention, and the will

EXEGESIS §§363–97

SECTION 363

1   This opens the long series of remarks on imagining, but multiple strands connect it with antecedent discussions. One does not learn the use of the expression 'to say something to oneself' by learning to identify an inner process which is called 'saying something to oneself' (PI §361) and which constitutes a defining sample for a private ostensive definition (PI §362). Perhaps so, the interlocutor reasons, perhaps saying things to oneself is peculiar, but surely when one imagines this or that, something *happens*! And it is surely *that something* which one communicates to another when one tells him what one imagines! W. defers for a moment the consideration of the irrelevance of what happens when one imagines something to what it is that one imagines (cf. PI §§369–70). Instead he probes one very general feature which informs the interlocutor's picture. Given that something happens and that one then emits a noise (utters words), what for? On the interlocutor's conception of language and its use, it is to tell someone what has happened, viz. what image has come before one's mind. For does not language always function in one way, always serve the same purpose: viz. to convey thoughts — in this case thoughts about what happened when one imagined whatever one imagined (PI §304)? Is not the purpose of a proposition to convey to another how it is with one (PI §317), what is before one's mind? This uniform conception of communication (*Mitteilung*) by means of language, of telling someone something (*etwas mitteilen*), is now brought under fresh attack. For how is telling done? What is called 'telling someone something'? Is there only one such thing, only *one* technique of communicating, telling, something to someone?

(b) sharpens the critical focus of the remark: we take discourse for granted and operate with a primitive picture of interpersonal communication by means of speech. That primitive picture has roots in the Augustinian conception of language, according to which sentences are essentially descriptions of states of affairs. It can, as we have seen, be variously elaborated. A Fregean conception would argue that language typically functions 'to convey thoughts — which may be about houses, pains, good and evil, or anything else you please' (PI §304). A more psychologistic elaboration, characteristic of the British empiricists, German psychologism (including Husserl), and linguists following in de Saussure's footsteps, conceives of communication as a matter of encod-

ing ideas in the speaker's mind into words that will stimulate corresponding ideas in the mind of the hearer. ('Uttering a word is like
striking a note on the keyboard of the imagination' (PI §6).) Either way,
we conceive of the words uttered as a mechanism for producing in the
hearer a certain mental state, viz. that he should grasp the sense of those
words, entertain the thought that was in my mind, have the same
(exactly similar!) ideas I had. If this upshot has been achieved, then the
hearer has understood what the speaker has told him. What he then does
with the thought he has thus grasped is a further matter!

This compelling preconception distorts the heterogeneity of the roles
of sentences, misconceives both the range and the diversity of what can
be called 'a description', and misrepresents the concepts of thought and
idea, and *a fortiori* of thinking and having or entertaining an idea.
Equally, it twists out of all recognition the concept of *understanding* what
the speaker told one, and (in all its elaborations) misconstrues what it is
for the speaker to mean what he says. Accompanying and reinforcing
these logico-linguistic misconceptions is a rich variety of misapprehen-
sions of psychological concepts and of their linguistic expression: of what
it is to tell someone that one is in pain, to communicate to another one's
fears or anxieties, to divulge one's intentions or motives, to recount one's
memories, or to elaborate what one imagines.

(c) shifts the example from imagining to pain, and elaborates with
respect to this example one absurd consequence of the picture delineated
in (b). If we think that the purpose of the proposition is to let another
know how it is with us (PI §317), then we will conceive of telling
someone that one has a toothache as aimed at inducing in him the
knowledge that one is in pain. And with all due philosophical humility,
we may leave the nature of the 'mental state or process' of knowledge
undecided (PI §308) — sometime we shall know more about this queer
phenomenon of knowledge. But this is not admirable caution; rather it is
already to have erred. For, on hearing someone groan 'I have a
toothache', knowing that he is in pain is not a mental state or process that
mediates between his utterance and one's response (e.g. 'Can I get you an
aspirin?'). The purpose of telling someone that I have a toothache is
misrepresented if conceived as a matter of inducing a 'mental state or
process of knowing' in the hearer, and the criteria for whether the hearer
has understood what I communicated to him lie in his *responses* to what I
said, not in a queer and as yet indeterminate mental process.

1.1   (i) 'to tell what happened', 'communication through language': note
that the translation masks the fact that 'mitzuteilen' and 'Mitteilung' are
cognates. The peculiarities of the English verb 'to tell' are not at issue
here.

(ii) 'Mitteilung durch Sprechen': 'communication through speech', in contrast with communication by means of gesture and non-linguistic behaviour (cf. MS. 124, 261f.). For does the child who has hurt his hand and cries and shows his bruised fingers to his mother for commiseration *not* communicate the fact that he is in pain to his mother? But would anyone conceive of this as the conveying of a thought from the child's mind to the parent's? Yet the linguistic avowal of pain grows out of, and in appropriate contexts may have the same function as, the primitive pain-behaviour the point of which is to solicit sympathy or aid (as in the above example).

(iii) 'etwas Seelisches': this characterization of the sense of one's words would seem to restrict the target to psychologistic conceptions of sense or meaning. Such a restriction is unnecessary, since the same picture informs Frege's model of communication through speech, save that sense is conceived Platonistically. MS. 124, 262 and MS. 129, 50 have here 'ein ätherisches Ding' ('something ethereal'). The explanation perhaps lies in MS. 165, 9ff. which examines the idea that a sentence has a sense because the speaker is conscious and *means* it. This meaning, it seems, is something mental ('dieses Meinen ist natürlich etwas Seelisches') and private. So one is inclined to wonder what *happens* when one means a sentence — for an act or process of meaning is conceived of as what connects the mere words (sounds) and the facts. Subsequently W. anatomizes the confusions implicit in this conception. It may be that he had this, rather than the equally confused Fregean picture, in mind in §363(b).

(iv) 'that he *knows* that I am in pain': the switch from the example of imagining to having pain disrupts the flow of the argument, and is not obviously significant. It is perhaps explained by the disparate MS. sources, §363(a) being derived from a discussion of imagining in MS. 165, 127f., and (b) – (c) from MS. 124, 262f., which focuses on the communication of the fact that one is in pain. MS. 129, 49f. brings the two together in the final MS. draft, and opens equivocally 'Wenn ich mir etwas vorstelle // etwas empfinde // . . .' ('When I imagine something // have a sensation // . . .').

(v) 'Die Uhr zeigt uns': *zeigt*, not *teilt mit*, hence better 'shows us the time', since the concept of telling the time is not a special case of the concept of telling someone something.

2   PG 39 and 107 observe that though we distinguish between a thought and its expression, we must not conceive of signs as a potion that will produce in the hearer the same kind of condition as in the speaker.

MS. 165, 9ff. is a remote ancestor: one is inclined to think that a sentence has a sense because I *mean* it, that my meaning it effects the connection between the mere words and the facts (cf. PI §358). This is, to be sure, confused. We talk of meaning a sentence we utter in contra-distinction, for example, to uttering a sentence as an exercise in a language class. In the former case we intend to tell someone something. What *happens* when we mean it? Is it always the same? And how does it *accompany* the utterance: word by word or by enveloping the whole sentence? Certainly there is a difference in the surroundings and accom-panying circumstances of the two cases. But meaning the sentence is not an accompanying mental process comparable to a pain — that is not how 'to mean' is used.

MS. 165, 126ff. has the first draft of PI §363(a). It occurs in the context of a discussion of whether it makes sense to talk of someone imagining things who has not learnt a language, i.e. who cannot give expression to his imaginings. §363(a) here encapsulates the picture of one who contends that imagining is an inner process which is independent of its expression. If one *can* speak, one can then tell another about this inner event! W.'s queries in this passage therefore challenge this picture of telling someone what one is imagining. He adds: is the language-game of telling the same whether one tells someone about a physical process or a mental one? Of course, one wants to say that one means by one's words just that which happens, that one's words refer to a very specific inner event, a process analogous to an outer process which one's words describe. (This remark was then transcribed into MS. 124, 280.)

MS. 124, 261ff. has the first draft of §363(b) – (c) in the context of a discussion of someone who has not learnt a language trying to elicit help or sympathy for his pain from another by means of gestures and facial expressions. Is this not a case of communicating to another the fact that he is in pain? It may sound as if such an account bypasses the very pain itself — for where in the gestures and grimaces is there a *reference* to the pain? But if it sounds so, W. responds, that is only because one has a wrong conception of what it is to communicate or tell someone something. That wrong conception is then spelled out in a draft of §363(b) – (c).

SECTION 364

1   It seems to the interlocutor as if W. is denying that anything at all goes on when one imagines something, as if he were suggesting that the mind is a complete blank. (Cf. MS. 165, 132: 'A complete blank?', W. retorts there, 'God forbid! what I am saying is the complete opposite of that.') The interlocutor switches to what seems an irrefutable example of something going on: calculating in one's head. Here, surely something *happens* – a calculation goes on, for the result does not just spontaneously

come to one, one works it out! Indeed, how would we *explain* how the calculator got the right result if not by reference to an inner process of calculating, an inner process that must be just like the outer process of calculating on paper, except for the fact that it takes place in the mind.

The objection misfires, for it misconstrues the thrust of W.'s argument and rests on a distorted view of the concept of calculating in the head. In the first place, W. is not denying that various things may occur in one when one does a mental calculation ; rather, what he is denying is that they constitute the calculating, that they are necessary or sufficient conditions for performing a mental calculation. If we were to hear what went on in the mind of a calculating prodigy, 'it would perhaps seem like a queer caricature of calculation' (Z §89).) Secondly, the interlocutor's citing this example as an instance of something's happening (§363) or taking place (§361) in the mind *as he understands these expressions* rests on a categorial confusion. Just as saying something to oneself *in foro interno* is no more an instance of saying something than an imagined experiment is a kind of experiment, so too, calculating in the head is not an instance of calculating *in the sense in which* calculating out loud or in a pocket notebook are. And when W. tries to disabuse him of his misconception, he interprets W.'s objections as a form of behaviourism. But W.'s point is to clarify the fact that the move from talking of calculating out loud or on a blackboard to talking of calculating in the head involves a grammatical transformation as radical as that involved in moving from talk of marrying women to talk of marrying money.

The interlocutor conceives of calculating in the head as a process precisely analogous to calculating on paper (PI §366), only without the paper. But this is absurd; it is akin to: 'Saying something to oneself is precisely analogous to saying something aloud, only without making a sound'. We do not have here an analogy resting on a correspondence of processes, as we do with calculating aloud, calculating on paper, calculating on one's fingers, and calculating on an abacus. Rather, we have a new *grammatical articulation* which introduces a *secondary*, parasitical use of 'to calculate'. For one can only learn what 'calculating in the head' is by learning what 'calculating' is (PI p. 220); and only if one has learnt to calculate, on paper or out aloud, can one come to grasp what calculating in the head is (PI p. 216). This observation is a grammatical one, not a hypothesis belonging to learning theory, for the impossibility is a *logical*, not a psychological, impossibility. By contrast, one can learn to calculate with an abacus, even if one has not learnt to calculate on paper. This new grammatical articulation (viz. calculating *in the head*) was not forced upon us by the phenomena (no move in grammar is *forced* upon us). Instead of saying to someone 'Calculate the result in your head!', we might have adopted the form of words: 'Now get the result *without* calculating!' (RPP I §655). And if someone found himself naturally inclined to say 'I did the sum inwardly', we might correct him, saying 'You don't calculate *inside* anything! You calculate *unreally*', and he would thenceforth use this form of representation (cf. RPP I §657).

The interlocutor hypostatizes an 'inner process of calculation' analogous to an outer one in order to *explain* how it can be that the correct result was arrived at. But he fails to see that his explanation is no more comprehensible than the explanandum; in fact it is incoherent! It is, to be sure, extraordinary that human beings, having learned to calculate aloud or on paper, should then be able to produce the correct result of a calculation without writing or saying a word. That is a fact of our natural history. But to hypostatize an inner process of calculation, just like an outer one only inner, provides no more than a mirage of an explanation.

'Neurophilosophers' may postulate neural circuitry as a surrogate calculator, for, they may insist, it must be possible to explain calculating in the head. But all that neurophysiology could ever hope to explain is not the 'mental process' of calculating in the head, only the neural prerequisites for it. For neural activity, even if causally necessary for the exercise of one's capacity for mental arithmetic, is not *calculating*, any more than electrical current's moving through circuitry of silicon chips in a pocket calculator is calculating! Is this to argue that the phenomenon of calculating in the head is inexplicable? Not at all; it is, rather, to suggest that the request for an explanation *thus construed* takes what is in effect a conceptual confusion as the locus of an explanandum calling out for an empirical explanation. One can, of course, investigate the psychological and neurophysiological prerequisites or concomitants of doing calculations in one's head, but the only explanation of what calculating in the head is consists of a *grammatical* explanation, a description of the circumstances in which this expression is to be used. To be sure, if we were to discover such-and-such neural concomitants of calculating in the head, we would be able to infer from the fact that we had just done a mental calculation that such-and-such a neural process had just occurred (PI p. 220).

§364(b) raises a consequent, natural worry. Is W. suggesting that calculating in one's head is in some sense less real than calculating on paper? The question is confused: really calculating in one's head is real calculating-in-one's head, in contrast with pretending to calculate in one's head and blurting out any old number, just as real calculating on paper may be contrasted with pretending to do a calculation on paper. But it makes no sense to ask whether mental calculation is more or less real than calculating aloud or on paper (cf. Exg. §366). The interlocutor attempts one further gambit: is calculating in the head *like* calculating on paper? For it is obviously tempting to think that we call *this* 'calculating in the head' *because* it is an inner process resembling an outer one. W. replies with an analogy: is a drawing of a person, a piece of paper with lines on it, *like* a human body? One might say that a dog is much more *like* a human being than any drawing could be! But one also says that this drawing is a good likeness! Calculating in the head is like calculating on paper in so far as one gets such-and-such a result in both cases, that, if interrupted, one can say how far one has got, etc. And it is also wholly unlike calculating on paper in as much as there is no paper, one writes nothing down, etc. One might say that calculating in the head is much more like humming a tune in one's head than it is like calculating on paper!

1.1   (i) 'That it has, say, just "come" to him . . . ': that, of course, W. does not want to say. It is characteristic of calculating in the head that if interrupted, one can say how far one has got ('I've added the first two columns, but not yet subtracted the sub-total'), that one can explain the steps of the calculation. If, however, someone can always produce the right answer spontaneously, but cannot say how it is arrived at ('It just comes to me'), we might, at least in some cases, *not* say that he calculates in the head, does mental arithmetic (cf. PI §236), but rather that he can just tell you the answer without doing any calculation.

        (ii) 'But what if I said: "*It strikes him as if* he had calculated"': he can tell us steps of the calculation, even though he does not make any perceptible calculations, and he can tell us the result of the sum, just as if he *had* calculated. So it is almost as if he had calculated somewhere, somehow, and told us about it. Moreover, he is inclined to say 'I did it in my head'. But, of course, his utterance is not a report of a process visible only to him, and what he is inclined to say does not have to be (although it has been) adopted as a model for a form of expression in our language (RPP I §657).

2   MS. 124, 247ff. elaborates at greater length. Three further points are noteworthy. (a) The phrase 'there must have been a calculation going on' means something like: there surely must be a calculating-machine at work there, otherwise getting the result would not be intelligible. That is indeed how we are disposed to view things. W.'s response is ironic: if it is not intelligible, what difference does it make (i.e. would we cease calling this 'calculation in the head' if it turns out that there is no 'calculating-machine' in the head?)? (b) W. tries another gambit: instead of 'explaining' that the person got the right result by reference to the inner process of calculating, tacitly conceived of as an inner calculating-machine, why not turn things upside down and say that it is because the result is the same as that obtained by calculating that we say that he calculated *in his head*? A later addition cancelled this: one could rather say this in cases in which we calculate 'unconsciously'. The point is further clarified by PI p. 220 (see below). (c) W. adds a methodological

suggestion: instead of hypostatizing mysterious inner processes, clarify the inclination to indulge in such hypostatization and then explain the *inclination*!

PI p. 220 elaborates the tie-up between 'saying' and 'saying to oneself', and by implication 'calculating' and 'calculating in the head'. One can tell another what one has said to oneself or calculated inwardly, and one can accompany one's inward speech or calculation with overt actions (e.g. jotting down the number to be 'carried' in adding or ticking off columns of figures), just as one may beat time with one's hand as one sings inwardly.

A further point is added: we are tempted to insist that, nevertheless, calculating inwardly is surely a certain activity which one has to learn! All right, W. concedes, but what is 'doing' and what is 'learning' here? 'Doing something in one's head' and 'learning to do something in one's head' are as different from doing and learning to do something overtly as calculating in one's head is different from calculating.

RPP I §655 illuminates further: one need not look at calculating in the head under the aspect of *calculating*, although it has (as clarified above) an essential tie-up with calculating. Indeed, one need not even conceive of it under the aspect of doing, for doing is something one can show or demonstrate (*vormachen*) to another.

SECTION 365

1   An aside on the peculiar context-dependence of 'real'. Adelheid and the Bishop are, of course, playing a real game of chess, not just pretending to play a game of chess *in the play*. Similarly, calculating in the head is doing a real calculation-in-the-head.

1.1   'Adelheid and the Bishop': in Goethe's *Götz von Berlichingen*, Act II, scene 1, in which the scene opens towards the end of the game (which does not mean that the game had no beginning!). In MS. 129, 75 W. contemplated a different dramatic example, viz. the game of chess in *Nathan the Wise*.

2   MS. 166, 51ff. has a long discussion of 'real' and 'pretend' as used in discourse about a drama apropos the question of whether when one imagines something, one has a real image before one's mind. The criteria for someone dying in a play (e.g. Lear) differ from the criteria for someone dying. But that is no reason for denying that Lear really dies at the end of the play. Similarly, the criteria for someone having a vivid mental picture (image) differ from the criteria for someone seeing a

picture, but that is no reason for denying that someone may really have a vivid mental image of something.

Section 366

1   This continues the theme of §364(b): one is inclined to think that the mental, or 'subjective', is less real than the physical, or 'objective' (since one cannot *touch* it!); but it is noteworthy that in the appropriate idealist or phenomenalist frame of mind, one can talk oneself into the opposite point of view. Both conceptions, MS. 179, 55 comments, signify just as little! For both rest on a mistaken apprehension of the function of language and of its relation to a reality that corresponds to it (MS. 124, 250, interposed between §366(a) and (b)).

   If one is beset by the idea that multiplying 24 by 16 in one's head is less real than doing the calculation on paper, one should reflect on the fact that if a competent calculator says 'I have multiplied 24 by 16 in my head, and the answer is 384', one does not doubt his word. Is this really a multiplication, without writing anything down? To be sure; it is not merely *a* multipliciation, but this very one — although in the head, not on paper. Convinced by this point, however, one is inclined to think that if it is a genuine multiplication, then multiplying in the head must be a mental process corresponding to multiplying on paper. It must have the same logical multiplicity as the written calculation and corresponding mental constituents, just as multiplying on paper and multiplying on an abacus might be said to have the same logical multiplicity and corresponding constituents. But this is incoherent, for it presupposes the intelligibility of a method of projection (a rule) which determines the mental image of a sign (e.g. the image of '2' or of '+') as a representation of the sign itself. And that is precisely the presupposition underlying the idea of a private language (MS. 124, 250). For it involves the notion of a private experience (having a mental image of '2') and of our words having a private meaning ('The mental image of '2' is *this*'). And that in turn drags in its wake all the confusions raked over hitherto; for it would be intelligible to wonder which *is* the mental image of '2' or how I know that *this* image I now have is a mental image of '2', etc. But these questions make no sense.

1.1   'it would then make sense . . .': the objection applies equally to the conception of the psychical constituents of a *Gedanke* implicit in the *Tractatus* (see R 37).

2   MS. 124, 251 continues with a remark on the 'reality' of the subjective and the objective. The idea that one is more or less real than the other is

absurd. We represent *both* in our language, and our ordinary discourse about the subjective is perfectly in order as it is, and no more needs correction by philosophers than our talk about chairs and tables. But one point must be stressed, viz. that the *grammar* of propositions about subjective things is not the same as that of propositions about objective ones; i.e. the language-games are different.

SECTION 367

1   A difficult remark, rendered even more difficult in translation. At first blush, it seems in flagrant conflict with §301: 'An image [*Eine Vorstellung*] is not a picture, but a picture can correspond to it.'

The conception of calculating in the head that is under attack in §366 is that of a mental process that corresponds to doing a calculation on paper. So what corresponds to a sign on paper, say '2', is a mental image or picture of the sign (cf. MS. 124, 249). We are prone to think of a mental image of an object as a representation of the object in the manner in which a literal image (a picture) of an object is a representation of it. Of course, in the case of such a genuine representation, it *does* make sense to talk of a method of projection according to which the picture is a representation of that of which it is a picture.

A *mental* image (*Eine Vorstellung*) or picture (*Vorstellungsbild*), however, is *not* a representation, and there can be no method of projection determining it as a representation of what it is an image of. It is the imaginer's *avowal* that determines it as an image of this or that, and *that* is not based on his observation of his image or on a method of projection, since it is not based on anything (cf. PI §377). One does not determine what object one is imagining by reference to a resemblance between it and the mental image, as one may sometimes determine what a picture (portrait) is a picture of (Z §621). One cannot compare one's mental image with what it is an image of in the way in which one can, e.g., compare a portrait with its subject for verisimilitude. It makes no sense to talk of *knowing* or of being *mistaken* about what one's mental images are images of, whereas one may well know, be ignorant, or be mistaken about what a picture is a picture of. In short, 'The image [*die Vorstellung*] is not a picture [*ist nicht ein Bild*], nor is the visual impression one. Neither "image" nor "impression" is the concept of a picture [*ist ein Bildbegriff*], although in both cases there is a tie-up with a picture, and a different one in either case!' (Z §638).

The grammatical observation being made here (PI §367) is that to describe my mental image of . . . *is* to describe what I imagine. The words with which I describe what I imagine can typically also be used to describe what a picture is a picture of. Indeed, one can often, given the appropriate facility, paint what one imagines. In such a case, the verbal description of what one imagines and the verbal description of the picture one has painted may well be identical. So one might say that what one's mental image is an image of is what the picture one has painted is a picture of. Hence a description of what one imagines is also a description of a possible picture which would represent what one imagines. But one must not confuse the description of a possible picture with the description of a private, mental picture which only the owner can see. For the mental image is not a picture, its owner cannot see it, and his description of what he imagines is not the description of a private object. (See LSD 136f.)

1.1   (i) 'Vorstellungsbild': the English cannot capture the multivalence of the German. 'Vorstellungsbild' is *mental image*, but also *mental picture* in the sense in which we say 'I have a vivid picture of that long-gone scene in my mind's eye', and further intimates an *imagined picture*.

(ii) 'Wenn Einer seine Vorstellung beschreibt': it is important for this remark that it is *not* phrased 'Wenn Einer beschreibt was er sich vorstellt', although, of course, the whole thrust of the remark *is* that to describe one's mental image just is to describe what one imagines.

2   Vol. XII, 207 has this scrawled in the top margin, not as a constituent part of an argument, but as an epitome of the long discussion (pp. 206 – 8) of the misleading picture (conception) we have of a private object which only its owner can see. It is important, W. stresses, to realize that this is just a simile (*Gleichnis*). It is of the nature of this conception that we can make further assumptions about this inner object and about what a person does with it; for we cannot merely say that he has a private something and does something with it. But if we conceive of someone's mental image as something which only he can see, if we say gravely that we cannot really know what his (mental) picture looks like, then we strip any assumptions about this 'object' of their sense.

MS. 164, 164ff. has a parallel discussion. We may say of someone that he has played chess with another in his imagination. But how does he know that it was chess? Has he learnt chess-in-the-imagination? We could point at a real game of chess and ask him whether *that* was what he imagined, and, if he agrees, say that he did indeed have a mental picture (*Vorstellungsbild*) of a game of chess. But what kind of picture is that? What kind of projection of a game of chess is it? There is no answer to this, and it is not a significant question, for a mental image (*eine Vorstellung*) is not a picture (*ist eben kein Bild*). If one compares it with a picture, it would have to be a picture which no one, not even its owner, knows what it looks like! For in answer to the question of what I am imagining, I too, even for myself, can point only to objects perceptible to others. For me to imagine further a pointing finger within my mental image would be a redundant farce, and merely concentrating my attention is not a kind of pointing for me. The mental picture, W. concludes punningly, is the picture which corresponds to my image ('Das Vorstellungsbild ist das Bild, das meiner Vorstellung entspricht').

MS. 124, 282 notes that one says that one imagines, e.g. a tree falling, that one sees it clearly before one. One has a clear picture before one's mind's eye. But why a picture? And if a picture, why not a tree?

SECTION 368

1   This provides a parallel or analogy for the relation between the mental image and the picture which is described when someone describes his image (*seine Vorstellung beschreibt*). The relation is not determined by a method of projection. If it were, it would make sense to say that a person's sincere description of his image (i.e. of what he imagines) is mistaken. That makes no sense, for the criterion for what image someone else has is what he says and does (cf. §377(b)).

Suppose I describe a room to someone with the intention of conveying the impression which the room makes, e.g. that it is eery or sinister. I then get him to paint an *impressionistic* picture from this description to show whether he has understood the description and grasped the impression, the 'atmosphere', of the room. He now paints the room, transposing colours dramatically (one might think of Van Gogh's painting of the café at night in Arles). This is the impression he got of the room from my description. Now what determines whether he has correctly represented the impression of the room (which he has never seen), understood my description of its atmosphere? It is not that he has used a method of projection of green onto dark red and yellow onto blue. It is *my avowal* that that is indeed what it looks like, that that is how it impresses one. (Note that my utterance 'Yes, that is what it looks like' does not rest on comparing my 'private impression' with the picture that he has painted (cf. PI §280). The criterion for whether I have conveyed to him (and he has understood) the impression which the room makes is not whether his painting matches 'my private impression' which 'only I can see', but whether I *react* to his painting with such an avowal.)

2   The sole source for this obscure remark is MS. 162(b), 96–9. Since the above interpretation may be thought debatable, and since the role of the remark in the argument of PI is unclear, the complete context is given below:

'Beschreiben' heisst ein Beschreibungsspiel spielen. — Wie sieht so ein Spiel aus?
Wir geben dem Andern eine Beschreibung, und er soll irgendwie nach ihr Handeln;

und dadurch zeigen, dass er die Beschreibung verstanden hat. — Da gibt es sehr verschiedene Fälle! Beschreibungen einer Anordnung von Körpern, Beschreibungen von Farben, Beschreibungen von Körperempfindungen, von Stimmungen, etc.

'Beschreibe Deine Empfindungen bei der Zeile: "In allen Wipfeln . . . !".' Ist es klar, was hier gemeint ist? Was hier als Kriterium dafür gilt, dass der Andere es aufgefasst hat?

('To describe' means to play a describing game. — What does such a game look like?

We give someone a description and he must act on it in some way, and thereby show that he has understood the description. — There are many different cases! Descriptions of an arrangement of bodies, descriptions of colours, descriptions of bodily sensations, of moods, etc.

'Describe your impressions of the line [of the poem]. "In all the treetops . . . !"[1] Is it clear what is meant here? What counts here as a criterion that someone has understood?)

Then follows a draft of PI §368 which is virtually identical with the printed version. The discussion continues as follows:

'Aber kannst Du die Atmosphäre beschreiben, die diese Farbe (diese Zeile) umgibt?' — Warum soll ich nicht die Atmosphäre zur Farbe rechnen und sagen: Wenn ich die Farbe beschreibe, beschreibe ich damit, was Du diese 'Atmosphäre' nennst. Will ich sie 'ohne diese Atmosphäre' beschreiben, *dann* muss ich der Beschreibung etwas hinzufügen.

Aber die Frage ist: In welchem Falle sage ich, ich *habe* die Atmosphäre *vermittelt*, und in welchem Falle, ich habe nur die Worte (Farbe), aber nicht ihre Atmosphäre vermittelt? Ich meine: in welchem Fall sage ich, die Vermittlung sei // ist // gelungen? Oder: Wie unterscheiden sich die Fälle, in denen das eine und in denen das andere (ich sage nicht: '*nur* das andre') vermittelt wurde?

('But can you describe the atmosphere that envelopes this colour (this line)?' — Why shouldn't I count the atmosphere as part of the colour and say: if I describe the colours, I thereby describe what you call this 'atmosphere'. If I want to describe them 'without this atmosphere', *then* I must add something to the description.

But the question is: in which case do I say: *I have conveyed* the atmosphere, and in which case: I have communicated only the words (colour) but not their atmosphere? I

---

[1] This is the third line of Goethe's poem 'Wandrers Nachtlied II':

> Über allen Gipfeln
> Ist Ruh,
> In allen Wipfeln
> Spürest du
> Kaum einen Hauch;
> Die Vögelein schweigen im Walde.
> Warte nur, balde
> Ruhest du auch.

(Over all the hill tops it is still, in all the treetops you can hardly feel a breath stirring. The little birds are silent in the forest. Wait! Soon you too will be still.) Prose translation by David Luke in Goethe, *Selected Verse* (Penguin Books, Harmondsworth, 1964).

mean: in which case do I say that I have conveyed this successfully? Or: what distinguishes the cases in which the one and those in which the other (I don't say: '*only the other*') is conveyed?

Section 369

1   This picks up the unfinished business of §363. We have a picture of imagining or calculating in the head as an inner process analogous to an outer one, in which certain things happen which are then described when one describes what one imagined or how one calculated. To understand what 'calculating in the head' means, one should observe what happens when one does a sum in one's head. Then one can give oneself a correct ostensive definition (§362)!

W. concedes that *in a particular case* the answer to the question 'What goes on when you calculate that sum in your head?' might be 'First I add 17 and 18, then I subtract 39 . . .'. But that kind of answer does not explain what calculating in the head means; it presupposes it. If there is unclarity about the general concept of calculating in the head, it will not be eliminated by invoking the concept of doing a specific calculation in the head. For in response to the answer given, we will now ask 'What on earth is it to add 17 and 18 *in the head*?' Moreover, the answer 'First I add 17 and 18, then . . .' can be given in response to the question 'What is it like — what happens when one does a calculation on paper?' So this description cannot characterize the difference between calculating in the head and calculating on paper, any more than the description of what one imagines can serve to differentiate between a picture before one's mind's eye and a picture before one's eyes.

1.1   'In a particular case': it is not a general feature of calculating in the head that each step be thus gone through (cf. Z §89, quoted in Exg. §363, 1).

Section 370

1   This methodological remark elaborates, for the special case of imagining, the point already made about thinking in §316 and about sensation in §314. 'What are images?' and 'What happens when one imagines anything?' are questions about the nature or essence of the imagination, and it seems that they are to be answered by careful introspective scrutiny of the phenomena. But a question about the nature of imagination (or thinking, sensation, etc.) is a question about a concept, and concepts are clarified by describing the use of words. Hence the examination of the use of the words 'to imagine' and 'imagination' is not

a study of 'mere words' *as opposed* to an investigation into the nature of the imagination; it *is* a study of its nature. (Indeed, this investigation, unlike a lexicographical one, will not confine itself to words, but will also examine the human behaviour, reactions, and responses associated with imagining which, in appropriate circumstances, constitute criteria for saying that a person imagines this or that.)

The question 'What are images?' appears to invite us to 'look and see'. If we carefully observe what happens when we imagine things, then we will apprehend the nature of images and of the imagination! But, contrary to the empiricist and phenomenological traditions,[2] the question of the nature of the imagination (like the question of the nature of thinking previously examined) cannot be resolved by ostension, let alone by 'private' ostensive definition, or by describing what happens when one imagines anything.

1.1   (i) 'dem Wesen der Vorstellung': 'the essence of imagination' would be preferable in order to preserve continuity with §371.

(ii) 'zu erklären ist': 'to be explained'.

(iii) 'nor yet by a description of any process': the failure of answers to the question of what happens when . . . to shed light on the nature of what is signified by a psychological expression is elaborated in numerous other remarks, e.g. §§34–5, 661, 675 (for meaning and interpreting), §§139, 152–5 (for understanding), §§305f. (for remembering), §§316, 321f., 327, 332, 339, 361, 427 (for thinking), §§392, 394 (for imagining), §§417f. (for consciousness), §545 (for hoping), §§591–2, 659 (for intending).

2   BB 24 has a parallel remark about knowing. 'What is it like to know?' is misleading in as much as it invites a description of a process, whereas the point of the question (in a philosophical context) is to clarify the grammar of the verb 'to know'. The question is: what do we *call* 'getting to know'?

SECTION 371

1   An investigation into the essence or nature of the imagination *is* an investigation into the use of the word 'imagination', for *essence is expressed by grammar*. Given that W. clearly does not think that 'imagination' is definable by an analytic (*Merkmal*) definition, how can he suggest

---

[2] Hume, *Treatise of Human Nature*, Bk. I, Pt. i, Sect. 1, and Bk. I, Pt. i, Sect 3; James, *Principles of Psychology*, Vol. II, p. 46; Russell, AM 144ff.; Husserl, *Logical Investigations* (Routledge and Kegan Paul, London, 1970), Essays 1, 5, and 6.

that imagination has an essence or nature? There is, in fact, no conflict here, as is evident from PI §92 (cf. exg. §92, 1.1(i)). The nature of imagination is clarified by a surview of the grammar of 'imagination'.

This brief remark crystallizes a *leitmotif* of W.'s later philosophy. Superficially it applies to the philosophy of the *Tractatus*, for there the logical syntax of empirical propositions *shows* the essence of things. An immediate difference, however, consists in the fact that according to the *Tractatus* one can only speak about objects, one *cannot express* their essential nature, for propositions can only say how things are, not what they are ('Ich kann nur *von* ihnen sprechen, *sie aussprechen kann ich nicht*' (TLP 3.221)). This difference, one might claim, merely reflects the narrowness of the *Tractatus* conception of a proposition, since what W. later calls 'grammatical propositions' do *not* count as genuine propositions in the *Tractatus*. And since, in the later philosophy, grammatical propositions are said to be expressions of *rules* (and hence fundamentally unlike empirical propositions with a sense), the shift in view might (wrongly) appear to be minor. A more fundamental difference, however, is the fact that in an important sense the *Tractatus* held logical syntax to be responsible to the language-independent essences of things since it *mirrors* the logical form of reality (TLP 4.121). The internal properties of things cannot be described in genuine propositions, but are *shown*. Even in the *Philosophical Remarks* W. still cleaved to this conception in a modified form: 'the essence of language is a picture of the essence of the world; and philosophy as custodian of grammar can in fact grasp the essence of the world, only not in the propositions of language, but in rules for this language which exclude nonsensical combinations of signs' (PR 85). By the time he wrote the 'Big Typescript' however, W. had freed himself from this misconception. According to the later philosophy, grammar is autonomous. Far from grammar reflecting the nature of things, what we conceive to be natures or essences are merely the shadows cast by grammar. This conception is diametrically opposed to that of the *Tractatus*.

2   This remark should be related to the observation 'Like everything metaphysical the harmony between language and reality is to be found in the grammar of the language' (PG 162 = Z §55). The *Tractatus*, a culmination of the high metaphysical tradition, explained this harmony in terms of the necessary relations between language and the world. That misconception, resting upon a confused view about the essential nature of a symbolism, projected an intra-grammatical articulation onto an imaginary, essential, extra-grammatical one.

LSD 20 distinguishes two ways of talking about 'the nature' of an object: (a) by specifying its properties which are *not* defining criteria of the object, (b) by specifying its defining criteria. In the latter case, the differences in the 'nature' of different things, e.g. space and colour, are not determined by the properties which we can attribute to them truly as opposed to those we cannot, but rather by the grammar of the words that signify them. The grammar of '1 foot' does not differ from the grammar of 'green' *because* the nature of one-foot length differs from the nature of the colour green; rather the difference in their nature *is* the difference in the grammars of the respective expressions.

RFM 63–5 elaborates critically upon Platonist conceptions of necessity. Geometrical propositions about shapes seem to articulate the essence of such forms; but, W. responds:

> I say, however: if you talk about *essence*, you are merely noting a convention. But here one would like to retort: there is no greater difference than that between a proposition about the depth of the essence and one about — a mere convention. But what if I reply: to the *depth* that we see in the essence there corresponds the *deep* need for the convention. (RFM 65)

Section 372

1   The quoted sentence to be considered appears to allude in a generalized way to the position delineated in the *Tractatus*. At that stage, W. firmly believed that there *are* intrinsic necessities. The possible occurrences of objects in states of affairs 'must be part of the nature of the object' (TLP 2.0123), determined by the internal properties of objects that conjunctively constitute their logical forms (TLP 2.0141). However, it is impossible to describe in genuine propositions the existence of internal properties and relations (TLP 3.221, 4.122, 4.124); rather, they are manifest in empirical propositions that are concerned with such objects occurring in (contingent) states of affairs.

What, then, is the correlate in language to such intrinsic necessities? In one sense, it is the logical form of the symbols that symbolize the relevant objects, the variable for which names sharing certain features are substitution instances. But what is shown by the forms of names, of course, is not something that can be expressed in any proposition, not even a meta-linguistic one. In another sense, to which W. is apparently alluding here, it is the arbitrary grammatical rules for the use of signs. For while the ordinary grammatical rules for the combinations of signs are indeed arbitrary and the correlations of signs with their meanings are arbitrary, the *form* of the resultant proposition is not arbitrary, but corresponds to a logical form (TLP 3.315). '*When* we have determined one thing arbitrarily, something else is necessarily the case. (This derives from the *essence* of notation.)' (TLP 3.342).

If this *is* what W. is here alluding to (see also LWL 57), then obviously we are being invited to consider the quoted remark by way of *contrast* with the conception of necessity or essence that characterizes W.'s later philosophy. Grammatical rules are indeed, in one sense, arbitrary. They are not accountable to any reality (PG 184), and the propositions constructed in accord with grammatical rules do not *mirror* the objective, language-independent, logical forms of things, as the *Tractatus* supposed (TLP 4.121). On the contrary, what appear to be intrinsic necessities are themselves merely illusory reflections of grammar. 'It is not the property of an object that is ever "essential", but rather the mark of a concept' (RFM 64); for all our talk of *essence* merely notes conventions (RFM 65). Far from the common rules that govern the construction of 'p', '$\sim\sim p$', '$\sim p \vee \sim p$', '$\sim p. \sim p$' mirroring negation (TLP 5.512), they *constitute* it.

For a discussion of W.'s later account of necessity, see Volume 2, 'Grammar and necessity', pp. 262–347.

1.1   (i) 'naturnotwendigkeit': a necessity in the nature of a thing, i.e. an intrinsic necessity, not a natural, causal necessity.

   (ii) 'abziehen': better 'derive', to preserve continuity with §374, or (excessively literally) in both remarks 'pull off' (as one pulls off a proof in printing) or 'take an offprint'!

2   This derives from Vol. VI, 144, where it occurs in the context of a discussion of negation, viz. that it lies in the nature of negation that double negation cancels out. It reappears in Vol. X, 157 without the prefix 'Überlege' but in quotes. An added note in square brackets says 'Perhaps apropos of the paradox that mathematics consists of rules'. Its context here is as in PG 184 (= BT 235). It was typed into the 'Big Typescript' without prefix or quotes, but these were added in pencil, together with a note on p. 234v. 'Bezieht sich auf Sätze wie $\sim\sim p = p$' ('Relates to propositions such as $\sim\sim p = p$').

The context in the 'Big Typescript' (= PG 184) is significant. It seems as if an ostensive definition could come into conflict with other rules for the use of a word. (This illusion is exacerbated if one thinks of syntactical, combinatorial rules as antecedent to an ostensive definition which gives content to the form determined by syntax. For then it appears as if one might erroneously try to 'inject' the wrong content into that predetermined form!) But this is mistaken, for grammatical rules cannot collide, unless they contradict each other. They are not answerable to a meaning (a content, such as a *Tractatus* 'object' in the world); they *determine* a meaning (which is not an object, but the use of a word). In that sense, grammatical rules are arbitrary; they are not accountable to any reality. There can be no question is to whether these or other rules are the correct rules for negation, i.e. whether they accord with the meaning of 'not'. For without the rules, the word has no meaning; and if we change the rules, the word will have a different meaning, and we might just as well change the word too (PI p. 147, note (b)). Then occurs PI §372, followed by an explanation of the arbitrariness of rules of grammar (like the rules of chess), which are constitutive, in contrast with the non-arbitrariness of rules of cooking, which specify means to a logically independent goal.

Section 373

1   The nature or essence of anything is given by rules of grammar which determine the application of an expression, for they fix the concept in question.

1.1   '(Theology as grammar)': an allusion to a remark W. attributes to Luther, that theology is the grammar of the word 'God'. AWL 32 interprets this to mean that an investigation of the word would be a grammatical one, clarifying what it makes sense to say about God. What counts as ridiculous or blasphemous here would also show the grammar of the word.

2   The contention that grammar tells us what kind of object anything is is heir to PR 54: 'Grammar is a "theory of logical types"'; i.e. what a theory of logical types endeavoured futilely to do is already done in, laid down by, the grammar of a language.

2.1   (i) 'kind of object': PG 463f. warns against two different uses of 'kind'. We say that infinite numbers are a distinct kind of number from finite ones, and assimilate that remark to such a claim as 'Coxes are a different kind of apple from Bramleys'. But whereas in the latter case we distinguish objects (apples) by their properties, in the former we distinguish different logical forms. BB 19 amplifies: distinctions between kinds of numbers, kinds of propositions, kinds of proofs, are distinctions between different *grammatical structures*.
    (ii) '(Theology as grammar)': Z §717 gives an example: 'You can't hear God speak to someone else, you can hear him only if you are being addressed.' That is a *grammatical* remark.

Section 374

1   After the three remarks about natures or essences, W. reverts to the main theme, viz. the characterization of a mental image (or of calculating

in the head). The picture that we have here is of a 'private object', something which only its owner can see, but which he cannot show to others. It seems that one derives ('abziehen' as in §372) a description, takes an offprint, from this object when one describes one's mental image.

One is almost irresistibly tempted to represent the matter as if there were something one *couldn't* do — as if one were prevented from showing other people one's mental image and so had to make do with a second-best, viz. giving them a description taken from the object which they cannot see. One way to combat this misleading picture is to yield to it and to investigate the incoherences that follow from trying to apply it. This task is undertaken in the next sequence of remarks.

2   This derives from Vol. XVI, 134, from which it was copied, with modifications, into Vol. XII, 243f. The context in both sources is the remark 'I can't *know* whether he says the ABC to himself in his mind'. But, W. replies, does *he* know? What if we were to say: he can't know either, he can only *say* so? One might say that he can no more check whether what he has is what is called 'pain' than I can, for there is no check. The language-game begins with his *saying* that he has pain, not with his *knowing* (Vol. XII, 243 modifies this: he can no more check whether what he imagines is really the sound we call 'a' than I can. But, of course, it would be equally wrong to say that he does *not* know whether he imagines the sound 'a', for that would mean that he was uncertain whether it was 'a' that he imagined. It would be more correct to say that there is here neither knowledge nor doubt. The language-game begins with his *saying* that he imagines . . .) So the language-game begins, as it were, with a description that does not correspond to a descriptum (though this grammatical remark, Vol. XII adds, could also be completely misleading). Then follows a draft of PI §374. In Vol. XVI, instead of the last sentence, we have:

Als finge das Sprachspiel also in Wirklichkeit *nicht* mit der *Äusserung* // dem Ausdruck // an, sondern mit dem 'privaten Gegenstand', nur könne ich diese Wurzel meines Ausdrucks nicht vorzeigen.

(As if the language-game did not really begin with the utterance // expression //, but with the 'private object', only I could not display this root of my expression.)

In both manuscripts the sequel applies these reflections to the conception of remembering as an inner process. All that really means, Vol. XVI, 134 notes, is that the language-game begins with the expression of remembering.

Z §134 (see Exg. §248) pursues a different strategy. Rather than yielding to the temptation to use the picture of a private object, with its corollary that one cannot do something here (viz. one cannot show it to anyone), W. insists that we should not say 'one cannot', but 'it does not exist in this game' or 'there is no such thing here'. One must not confuse the bounds of sense with limitations or constraints. It only makes sense to talk of being prevented from doing something or being unable to do something (constrained not to do it) if something *counts* as doing it. Otherwise the 'can't' merely registers a grammatical convention (cf. BB 54, 56).

3   A perfect target for this remark is given in Frege's 'Thoughts', which W. read:

> it is impossible to compare my sense-impression with someone else's. For that, it would be necessary to bring together in one consciousness a sense-impression belonging to one consciousness and a sense-impression belonging to another consciousness. Now even if it were possible to make an idea disappear from one consciousness and at the same time make an idea appear in another consciousness, the question whether it is the same idea would still remain unanswerable. It is so much of the essence of any one of my ideas to be a content of my consciousness, that any idea someone else has, is, just as such, different from mine.[3]

Here we have, with a vengeance, the picture of the private object which no one else can see and off which I read its description. How then does one compare images, in Frege's view? Very poorly — 'If two persons picture the same thing, each still has his own idea. It is indeed sometimes possible to establish differences in the ideas, or even in the sensations, of different men; but an exact comparison is not possible, because we cannot have both ideas together in the same consciousness.'[4]

SECTION 375

1   This opens the investigation of the application of the picture of the mental object accessible only to oneself, off which one reads a description which communicates to another what one imagined, said to oneself, or calculated in one's head. How does one teach anyone to read to himself? *Not* by inducing in him an inner process called 'reading to oneself' and bringing him 'to the point of giving himself a correct ostensive definition' (PI §362). One does not teach someone what 'reading to oneself' means by telling him 'what takes place' when one reads to oneself (cf. PI §361). One teaches a person to read to himself only after he *can read*, just as one can learn to calculate in one's head only if one can already calculate (PI p. 220; Exg. §364, 1). Moreover, one cannot intelligibly teach a

---

[3] G. Frege, 'Thoughts', in *Collected Papers on Mathematics, Logic and Philosophy*, p. 361.
[4] G. Frege, 'On Sense and Meaning', ibid., p. 160.

person (who has just learnt to read aloud) how to read to himself by telling him to do just the same as he does when he reads aloud, only without making a sound. But one might say, 'Now look at what is written here without reading it aloud, close the book, and tell me what it says!' If he does so, however, he does not derive a description of what he has read to himself from scrutiny of a 'private process' of reading to himself, but from looking at the written words without reading out loud! How does one know if he can read to himself? By his reports of what he has read, by whether he is 'afterwards able to repeat the sentence word for word or nearly so' (PI §156). But, to be sure, this is not a report of an inner process which only he can see. How does he know that what he is doing is reading to himself? Here too (cf. Exg. §374, 2; Vol. XVI, 134) one might say: he does not *know*, he can only *say* that he has read the passage to himself. There is no question of either knowing or being uncertain, for 'I think I am reading to myself, but I'm not sure' is senseless.

SECTION 376

1   One cannot explain what it is to calculate in the head, read to oneself, or say something to oneself in terms of the idea that what one does is just the same as what one does when one calculates, reads, or speaks aloud, only in the head. *That* explanation by means of identity does not work here (cf. PI §350), although, of course, if A calculates 17^3 on paper and B calculates 17^3 in his head, then one may say that B did in his head the same calculation as A did on paper. But that *presupposes* and does not give a criterion of identity for calculations in the head. Pursuing further the application of the misbegotten picture of the 'private object' which I cannot show to anyone but from which I derive a description, W. now examines the question of the criterion of identity of images, silent sayings, etc. Since they cannot be shown to another, they must, it seems, be identified 'indirectly'.

What is the criterion for two different people *doing the same* 'in their heads' (e.g. reciting the alphabet)? W. addresses in the first instance the Watsonian behaviourist position, and only obliquely the view, more popular today, that the same neurological processes must be going on in the brains of the two people. Watson wrote: 'I should throw out imagery altogether and attempt to show that all natural thought goes on in terms of sensory-motor processes in the larynz.'[5] It is *possible*, W. concedes,

---

[5] Quoted by Russell, AM 153, from J. B. Watson, 'Image and Affection in Behaviour', *Journal of Philosophy, Psychology and Scientific Methods*, 10 (July 1913).

that identical laryngal physiological processes go on in two people who are saying the ABC to themselves or thinking or wishing the same thing. But we do not teach the use of 'saying . . . to oneself' by reference to the identification of such a laryngal process, *nor by reference to any brain-process*. The occurrence of any such process is therefore only inductively correlated with inward sayings, calculatings, etc., and hence the inductive correlation (if one is found) *presupposes* a distinct criterion for identifying silent speech or calculation. And, of course, it is perfectly possible, even if there are such correlated processes, that my imagining (saying to myself) the sound 'a' when reciting the alphabet in my mind and someone else's doing so correspond to *different* processes in each of us. And that shows that the *concepts* of identity or difference of mental images cannot be determined by reference to physiological processes.

2.1   'a process in the larynx or the brain': PI p. 212 observes with respect to aspect-seeing that the psychological concept hangs out of reach of any physiological explanation. *Mutatis mutandis*, this remark applies to imagining, saying to oneself, etc. (cf. PI p. 220).

Z §§608ff. remarks that no supposition is more natural than that there should be *no* process in the brain correlated with thinking, so that it would be *impossible* to read off thought-processes from brain-processes. We are inclined to think that there *must* be a corresponding process, but that merely indicates that we are in the grip of a picture. For why the 'must'? — Otherwise, we might reply, one could not *explain* thinking; it would be utterly mysterious! — Not at all. We could not explain thinking *in that way*, but who says that it must be explicable thus? And if there were such a psycho-physical parallelism, would that be any *less* mysterious than its absence?

SECTION 377

1   The 'logician' in (a) echoes the view criticized in §350 ('It is 5 o'clock on the sun' means simply that it is just the same time there as it is here when it is 5 o'clock). But that manoeuvre has been shown to be futile. It is a mistake to think that the concept of X is given independently of the criteria of identity for X's. What counts as the same X or a different X is a contribution to the grammar of the expression 'X', not a further (epistemological) question that can be subsequently settled once the concept of X is determined (cf. PI §353). An analogous absurdity to severing a concept from the criteria of identity for things falling under it is the idea that the concept of being high is determined independently of the manner in which we establish that a building is high on the one hand or that a musical note is high on the other — as if this were merely an

extraneous psychological or epistemological question and not part of the grammar of 'high building' or 'high note'.

(b) follows §350 in taking the criterion of sameness of two images (parallel to the identity of time here and on the sun) as parasitic upon the criterion for an image being an image of such-and-such, e.g. red. (In §350, of course, there *is* no criterion for its being 5 o'clock on the sun, and *therefore* no criterion for its being the same time on the sun as it is here.) In the third-person case, the criterion for the redness of his image is that he says, e.g., 'I am imagining the colour red' or points at a poppy and says 'That is the colour I imagined'. But in my own case, *I have no criterion*. I do not say 'I am imagining red' on the grounds of my
· behaviour, any more than I say 'I am in pain' on the basis of my behaviour. So too, if someone says how he imagined the colour of the wall to be (e.g. that ↗ colour), and I respond that I imagined it the same, I employ no criterion of identity.

Does this finally explode the idea that I 'derive the description' of what I imagine from a private object, read it off the facts which are accessible only to me? No, not yet. For the wayward philosopher may try yet another avenue, viz. that in one's own case one *recognizes* one's mental image as an image of, say, red. One might then rightly say that the description is read off the facts. This is explored in the next remarks.

1.1   'wie ein Mensch sich von der Gleichheit überzeugt': 'how a person satisfies himself of identity'.

2   LPE 281 raises with respect to mental images a question parallel to PI §253 on sensations: viz. *can* two different people have the same mental image? Here too we are tempted to argue that I cannot have your image, therefore I cannot have the same image as you, but only one exactly similar. But for precisely the same reasons as in §253, this is confused. If A and B have an image of X characterized in the same way, then they have the same image.

2.1   (i) 'For myself, when it is my own image, none': MS. 166, 29f. observes that in such cases we are misguidedly tempted to transpose the grammar of physical objects to the mental domain. But

we can't apply any such criteria in our own case, and that's what we mean by talking of the privacy of the objects. Privacy here really means the absence of means of comparison. Only we mix up the states of affairs when we are prevented from comparing the objects with that of not having fixed a method of comparison. And in the moment we would fix such a way of comparing we would no longer talk of 'sensations'. (In English)

Of course, one is inclined to object that in one's own case too, one distinguishes between pretending to have . . . and really having . . .; for 'surely I must make this distinction on some grounds! Oddly enough — no! — I do distinguish, but not on any *grounds!*' (MS. 166, 44).

(ii) 'And what goes for "red" also goes for "same"': MS. 180(a), 60f. explains: when two impressions (or images) are like *this* ↗ (and I can *show* you in the course of explaining what it means to be the same), then we call them the same. I don't recognize that they are the same in any different way than that they are red. For I say that my image is red, i.e. an image of something red, if it is this ↗ colour; and I say that my image is the same as the one I had yesterday if both were images of this ↗.

3   It is tempting to think that distinguishing between sameness and difference (independently of the concept of what it is that is identical or different) is the most fundamental and simple of the mind's operations. This was nicely articulated by James:

> the mind can always intend, and know when it intends to think of the same.
> This sense of sameness is the very keel and backbone of our thinking.[6]

and subsequently:

> Any fact, be it thing, event or quality, may be conceived sufficiently for purposes of identification, if only it be singled out and marked so as to separate it from other things. Simply calling it 'This' or 'That' will suffice.[7]

Section 378

1   In response to §377, the interlocutor shifts to a judgement of identity of two mental images in one's own case, e.g. saying that I now have the same image as I had yesterday. Surely, before I can rightly say this, I must *recognize* them as the same, just as before I can rightly say that *this* is the same letter as the one I saw yesterday, I must recognize it as the same. Similarly, one is inclined to think that if I conjure up an image of A and an image of B, then *before* I can say that I imagine them as being the same colour, I must *recognize* the two images as being of the same colour.

The claim is confused. If recognizing were a mental event or process that occurs prior to saying that the two images are the same, then how is one to know that once this has occurred, the word 'same' describes one's

---

[6] James, *Principles of Psychology*, Vol. I, p. 459.
[7] Ibid., p. 462.

recognition; i.e. how is one to know that this event is 'recognizing them as the same'? Does one also have to recognize the recognition? That is evidently absurd. But if I say 'I imagine A (or: My image of A is) *this* ↗ colour' (pointing to a red apple) and then add 'And I imagine B (or: My image of B is) *this* ↗ colour' (pointing again to the apple), then someone could indeed say, 'So you imagine them as being the same colour' or 'So your mental images of A and B are of the same colour'. In this case, one might say, 'I express my recognition in some other way', viz. by pointing at a sample (cf. Exg. §379).

Justification, it has already been argued (PI §265), consists in appealing to something independent (the measure, as it were, must not shrink or expand at the whim of what is measured). Now, in conformity with the previous discussion of rules, W. stresses that a justification must be (potentially) public. For just as there can be no 'private' (i.e. unshareable) rule, so too there can be no 'private' justification, otherwise there will be no distinction between being justified and thinking that one is justified. So if I need a justification for using a word, it must also be one for someone else. (A rule which I can follow must be one which it *makes sense* for another person to follow.) But my characterization of my mental image as being red or as being the same as the one I had yesterday neither needs nor admits of justification. It is neither justified *nor* unjustified; but, of course, 'to use a word without a justification does not mean to use it wrongfully' (PI §289).

1.1   'dass das Wort "gleich" meine Erkenntnis beschreibt?': should this be translated 'that the word "same" describes what I recognize (or am aware of)' or 'that the word "same" describes my recognition (awareness)'? It might be said that it makes no difference, since 'to describe my recognition', if it means anything in this case, means to describe what I recognize. But perhaps the more cumbersome version, as well as being a more literal translation, also captures better the philosophical bafflement. (Cf. 'eine Vorstellung beschreiben' in §367.) Note that 'recognize' does not distinguish 'erkennen' from 'wiedererkennen'.

2   This derives from MS. 180(a), 65f., which is part of an extended discussion of recognition of mental images (pp. 57–72). W. explores, and rejects a variety of avenues:

(i) What does one call 'comparing one's own images'? Well, I say, e.g., that I have the same image of red as previously. So how do I compare them? One is inclined to say that one directs one's attention to whether they are the same or different. But how do I do that? Isn't it just twaddle? Isn't it rather that if asked in appropriate circumstances whether they are the same (and it is that which is the directing of attention), I react with words?

(ii) How does one compare heights? — with the unaided eye or with the aid of a theodolite, etc. How then does one compare two sense-impressions in the course of comparing heights with a theodolite? There seems to be no 'how' about it. One wants to say 'I look', 'I direct my attention', etc. And when that happens? Then I simply see that they are the same or not the same.

(iii) So should one say that I 'see immediately' that the impressions are the same? That too would be nonsense. MS. 180(b), 2 elaborates this: it only makes sense to talk of immediate recognition (or of discerning immediately) if it also makes sense to talk of mediate recognition (or of discerning mediately). There are language-games with this contrast: e.g., I can recognize or discern immediately that this is N's handwriting; I don't need M's testimony. But this possibility of contrast does not apply here.

LSD 110ff. focuses more sharply on the fact that it makes sense to talk of recognizing only where it also makes sense to talk of misrecognizing. We can speak of recognition only where we can also talk of correct and incorrect. But if there is no criterion of recognizing something correctly or incorrectly, then there is no room for talk of recognition at all. We say: It is the same *and* he recognized it; but if the criterion of its being the same is that he 'recognized it', then, again, we do not have a case of recognition at all. If the criterion for having the sensation or image is that one sincerely says so, that means that there is no such thing as misrecognizing it. And that means that there is no such thing as recognizing it either.

3   That recognition lies at the heart of first-person discourse about, e.g., memory and imagination is a fundamental tenet of empiricism, clearly articulated in Hume's explanations of the relations between impressions and ideas. Russell was heir to that tradition: 'It is this fact, that images resemble antecedent sensations, which enables us to call them images "of" this or that. For the understanding of memory, and of knowledge generally, the recognizable resemblance of images and sensations is of fundamental importance' (AM 155).

Section 379

1   In §378 the interlocutor supposed a process of recognition to mediate between having a mental image and describing it, e.g., as the same as an image one had yesterday. W.'s response was: once the recognition has occurred, how is one to know which word applies? Now he probes further. One wants to say 'I recognize it as *this*, and then I remember what it is called'. This makes sense only if *it* and *this* are distinct and,

moreover, only if I can point to *this* (cf. §378: 'Only if I can express my recognition in some other way'). In a psychological experiment, for example, I may recognize the picture on the screen as a picture of *this* geometrical figure on the table. Then I may remember that this figure is called 'an icosahedron'. But in the case of a mental image, neither of these two conditions is satisfied. (Of course, I might say 'I had a vivid mental image of that curious figure on the table — what is it called?')

1.1   'Ich erkenne es . . . ': to preserve uniformity with §§378, 380–1, better 'I recognize it'.

2   This derives from the long discussion in MS. 180(a); see Exg. §§201, 2(i), and 202, 2(i).

SECTION 380

1 'How do I recognize that this is red?' The question is an expression of succumbing to the temptation to interpose an act or process of recognition between seeing and saying 'This is red'.[8] Note that W. has broadened the scope of the discussion; for now, it seems, he is no longer concerned only with characterizing one's mental image as an image of red, but also with characterizing a colour one sees as red (cf. MS. 180(a), 61ff.). For in respect of the confusion that is here in question, viz. of the interposition of a *private* transition from what is seen to saying what is seen, seeing red and imagining red are similar.

If we suppose that when I see something red I recognize that it is red, and if we think that recognizing that it is red is an event or process antecedent to saying that it is red, what should we say that we see *before* we 'recognize' that what we see is red (MS. 180(a), 61)? The interlocutor is tempted to say 'I see that it is *this*' and then he remembers what 'this' is called. But what is the 'this' that he sees it to be? Of course, he could say that he sees that the object is the colour, pointing to something *else*, which functions as a sample. That is correct, but now we note that he must see that the object before him *is* the colour of the sample. Does he also *recognize* the identity of the colour of the sample and the colour of the object before him? And does he now need a sample for this identity, and so on *ad infinitum*?

---

[8] This is parallel to the thoughts that I must understand an order *before* I can obey it, know where my pain is before I can point to it, etc. 'We are treating here of cases in which . . . the grammar of a word seems to suggest the "necessity" of a certain intermediary step, although in fact the word is used in cases in which there is no such intermediary step' (BB 130).

Evidently that is not the trap into which he has fallen. Rather, in seeing that the object is *this*, he wants to point to the object itself, in fact to its colour! Or, more accurately, to his impression of its colour. And he wants to point with his attention! This is spelled out in BB 175: one wants to let what one sees speak for itself, as if the colour seen were its own description. In fact, W. argues, one is merely going through the motions of attending to a sample, although there is no sample. For an object cannot be a sample of itself, and an ostensive definition says nothing about the object which is functioning as a sample. One seems to be pointing out to oneself what colours one sees, whereas all one is doing is staring at a coloured object, as it were contemplating a possible sample which is not used as a sample but seems to be its own description.

Why does W. contend that the interlocutor is steering towards the idea of a private ostensive definition? One reason is this: one wants to say 'I see *this*, and then I know what it is called'. But what is 'knowing what it is called'? Well, I must be able to justify saying that it is red. An ostensive definition, a rule for the use of 'red', is a justification (LSD 16). But I do not employ a public sample here. I recognize that what I see is red; I remember that that is what it is called. And now it must seem as if

recognizing always consisted in comparing two impressions with one another. It is as if I carried a picture of an object with me and used it to perform an identification of any object as the one represented by the picture. Our memory seems to us to be the agent of such a comparison, by preserving a picture of what has been seen before, or by allowing us to look into the past (as if down a spy-glass). (PI §604 = PG 167 = Vol. XI, 7)

But an *impression* is not a rule (LSD 17), and there is no such thing as a private sample.

§380(c) clarifies: one wants to invoke a rule to justify the transition from 'I see *this*' (which really amounts to 'I see what I see', i.e. it amounts to nothing at all) to 'I see red'. But no rule can justify the *private* transition from seeing to words, i.e. to giving expression to what I see. One has to *do* something, viz. *say* 'This is red'. In the first place, even where there *is* a genuine rule, it has to be applied. And although there can be rules for the application of rules, explanations come to an end, and then a rule must be applied, without *further* guidance. In the second place, a 'private ostensive definition' is not a rule. The very idea of a rule mediating between a subjective impression (seeing *this*, for example) and words is incoherent, for there can be no technique of application here, no institution of use of a rule; there would be no objective regularity in the use of this putative rule and hence no distinction between applying it correctly and thinking that one is applying it correctly. (Cf. Volume 2, 'Following rules, mastery of techniques and practices', pp. 178–9; Exg. §§201–2).

2   This derives from MS. 180(a), 67–74. It is noteworthy that this discussion of recognition led up to a draft of what is now PI §§201–2 (cf. Exg.). A more polished, re-ordered version occurs in MS. 129, 116ff., and a more compressed re-drafting of that, approximating to the final draft, occurs later in the same MS. at p. 182 (see Volume 2, p. 148).

W. discussed recognition extensively. A number of further points bear on the remark here. The concept of recognition is far more specialized, variegated, and context-sensitive than one supposes. It would be quite wrong to say that I recognize familiar objects in my room everyday when I see them or familiar faces of my friends whom I see daily. One context in which we speak of recognizing something or someone *as* such-and-such is if we initially do not know, or do not realize, that it is such-and-such (MS. 180(a), 62). But if a philosopher were to ask whether we recognized the furniture in our room this morning, we would probably say 'Yes'. If so, we mean no more than that on seeing it, we did *not* ask ourselves what it was. Here we conflate absence of lack of recognition with presence of recognition (cf. LSD 17f.; PG 165ff.) Only in very special circumstances does it make sense to talk of recognizing a colour (e.g. 'That brilliant yellow reminds me of something . . . Ah, yes — it is the colour Turner used in his painting of . . . '). But when I look at the sky and see that it is blue, I cannot be said to go through a process of recognizing the colour (cf. MS. 180(a), 61–3). Of course, I may look at a coloured object and see its colour, but not remember what it is called. But then I can tell someone later and point at a sample, saying 'It was this ↗ colour', and he may say 'Ah, yes — that's eau-de-Nil'. It does not follow that when I look at a red poppy and say that it is red, I first recognize that it is red and then remember what that colour is called.

SECTION 381

1   The interlocutor persists: if I do not recognize that the colour of this tomato is red by first seeing *this* and then knowing what it is called, how *do* I recognize it? The question is misleading, but one might answer 'I have learnt English'. Of course, that is not a *way* of recognizing, nor is it a justification for saying 'This is red'. It merely reminds us that 'knowing' here consists in mastery of a technique of the use of a word. Someone who knows what 'red' means can *say* when confronted with a red object in daylight that it is red. But nothing mediates between his seeing and saying.

1.1   'Wie erkenne': to preserve uniformity with §§378–80, better 'How do I recognize?'

2   This derives from MS. 180(a), 68, where it is followed by:

Wie weisst Du, dass diese Worte hier passen? — Nun, ich habe sie gelernt. Und wie weiss ich, wie ich diese Lehren hier anzuwenden habe?

'Die Lehren lassen mich im Stich; ich muss jetzt einen Sprung machen' heisst: Ein 'Sehen, dass dies rot ist' nützt mir nichts, wenn ich doch erst noch Worte finden muss // zu den Worten oder Handlungen übergehen //, die zu der Situation // Lage // passen. (MS. 180(a), 68–9)

(How do you know that these words fit here? — Well, I have learnt them. And how do I know how I am to apply this teaching here?

'The teaching leaves me in the lurch; I must now make a leap' means: A 'seeing that this is red' does not avail if I must still find words // make the transition to words or deeds // which fit the situation // circumstances.)

That is to say, mastery of the technique of using 'red' cannot intelligibly be thought to fall short of being able to apply it. The use of a word is guided by a rule, but *given the rule*, one must *apply* it.

BB 148f. observes that the temptation to say that something *happened*, e.g. an act of recognition, between seeing and saying that such-and-such is red, something which makes one say 'That is red', stems from the fact that one can look at an object and say a word, viz. 'red', and still not be naming the colour. But, by implication, knowing what 'red' means is not something that happens. Nothing *makes* me call what I see 'red'; rather, I exercise my capacity to name colours.

It is noteworthy that throughout the numerous discussions of colour-recognition there is a perhaps unavoidable equivocation on 'justification'. On the one hand, W. insists, one may say that there is *no* justification, no *reason* for saying that something one sees is red (LSD 126; RFM 406). One has no *ground* or *criterion* for an ordinary, immediate colour-judgement. On the other hand, he insists, an ostensive definition, which is a rule for the use of a word, *is* a justification (LSD 17). Though confusing, there is no inconsistency here. An ostensive definition is not an evidential or criterial justification. Moreover, our ordinary colour-judgements are typically made in the absence of any sample (although they make sense only because they belong to a language-game which is essentially played with samples). But one may point to a sample to determine agreement in definitions, and that one points to a correct sample is a criterion of one's understanding of the colour-name in question. One may also justify one's calling A 'red' by pointing to a sample of red and saying 'That ↗ colour is red, and A *is* that colour'. This justifies one's application of the word to A; i.e. it vindicates one's use of the word, but not by way of evidence or justifying grounds of judgement. Moreover, it does not answer the question of how one *knows* that what one sees (viz. A) is red. For there is no answer to that question save 'I know what "red" means, I have learnt English'. Finally, though appeal to a sample can, *in this sense*, justify the application of a word, the agreement of the colour with the sample cannot be further justified — that, in the practice of the language-game with colours, is what is called 'being red' (cf. RFM 406).

SECTION 382

1   After generalizing the problem of recognizing the colour of one's mental image to recognizing a colour *per se*, W. now reverts to the mental image. The picture that is being explored is of a 'private object' from which one derives a description (PI §374). Part of the conception is the idea that understanding a word is associating it with a mental image, and also that uttering a word and meaning it is having a mental image and, as it were, transcribing it into words. It is these ramifications of the primitive picture that are now under attack.

Suppose I hear the word 'blue' and an image comes to mind. How can I *justify* this occurrence? For if I cannot justify it, it is mere coincidence and belongs to the natural history of the use of the word. *That* I associate the word with a mental image does not determine correct from incorrect uses of the word, for I must associate it with the *right* mental image. Whether it is right is determined by the rule for the use of 'blue', and that is not, and does not involve, a mental image. But if so, then the mental image, even if it is 'right', is irrelevant to whether I understand the word.

Of course, I was taught how to use the word 'blue', but not by being shown a mental image of blue (LSD 39f.). Rather, I was shown samples and told that *that* ↗ colour is blue. But a mental image is not a sample. One cannot point at a mental image, even in one's own case; and the phrase '*This* mental image' has no ostensive, but only anaphoric, use.

2   Vol. XII, 120 has a draft of this in the context of a long discussion of knowing what the word 'blue' means. The salient points are: (a) I cannot test whether I understand what 'blue' means by calling a blue mental image to mind. For how can the word 'blue' show me which colour I should select from my mental colour-box, and how can the colour which I imagine show me that *it* is the right one? Do I *choose* which image fits the word 'blue'? And can't the *wrong* one come (p. 114)? (b) The criterion for whether I understand the word is the agreement of others to my applications of it (i.e. that this is what is called 'blue'), not the image of a colour that comes into my mind (p. 115). (c) It is tempting here to try to distinguish between objective and subjective understanding. One might conceive of my subjective understanding as a matter of associating an image with a word heard or read (as if one turned a knob and a little card

with a picture on it pops up). So subjectively understanding a word would mean associating it with a picture; objectively understanding it would mean associating it with the *right* picture. One might then say that a language, in so far as it is understood only subjectively, is not a means of communication with others, but a tool-box for one's own private use. But the question is whether this is still to be called a language. It is to be so called only if one plays language-games with oneself; and that is indeed possible, as in Robinson Crusoe's case. Yet what he does counts as a language-game only in so far as it displays an appropriate regularity of behaviour. If someone makes noises, yet displays no such regularities, we could not say 'Perhaps he is speaking a purely private language in which he associates each noise with the same mental image' (pp. 116–8).

On p. 120 is a draft of PI §382(a) – (b), followed by

Was heisst denn hier: '*diese* Vorstellung'? Kann ich denn auf sie zeigen? Kann ich etwa *in mir* auf sie zeigen, wenn sie *meine* Vorstellung ist? Wenn ich mir einen blauen Kreis und einen Pfeil vorstelle, der auf ihn zeigt — zeigt der Pfeil auf meine Vorstellung? Könnte ich mir auf diese Weise private hinweisende Definitionen geben? (Denke immer an den *Gebrauch* der Zeichen!)

(Yet what is here called '*This* image'? Can I point at it? Can I perhaps point at it *in myself*, if it is *my* image? If I imagine a blue circle and an arrow which points at it — does the arrow point at my image? Could I give myself private ostensive definitions in this way? (Think always of the *use* of signs!))

To imagine an arrow pointing at a blue circle is not to point, nor to imagine anything pointing at an image of a blue circle, any more than to imagine something rotating is to rotate a mental image!

SECTION 383

1   Having provided an antidote to the temptations of the private object off which one reads its description, W. reverts to the methodological point raised in §370: one ought to ask not what images are or what happens when one imagines something, but how the word 'imagination' is used. This makes it appear as if we are interested only in words, not in the nature of imagination; but that, W. urged, is an illusion. Now he examines a further source of confusion. To be sure, we are not analysing a phenomenon, i.e. describing what happens when, e.g., we think (understand, imagine), but a concept, e.g. the concept of thinking (understanding, imagining). We are indeed concerned with describing the use of a word. But now this may appear like a commitment to a form of nominalism. Nominalists repudiate the Platonists' idea that words stand for universals, abstract essences in reality, and insist that there are

only words. (Similarly, the formalists in mathematics deny that numbers are abstract objects, and insist that there are only numerals.) But this crude dichotomy is misleading. One is led to impale oneself on the horns of this dilemma through a misguided commitment to the Augustinian picture of language, according to which all words are names, which either name something or name nothing. The nominalist is right to think that there are no *entities* corresponding to abstract nouns, adjectives of quality, or numerals. The Platonist is right to insist that qualities or numbers are not just words. The dilemma is avoidable once the idea that all words are names which stand for some entity is abandoned. The description of the *use* of words will clarify the concepts that bewilder us, illuminate the difference between numerals and numbers, bring to light the nature or essence of thinking (cf. PI §§370–3). The essence of thought is not to be found by analysis of the phenomena of thinking, but by clarification of the use of the words 'think' and 'thought'.

SECTION 384

1   This emphasizes the general point of §383. It is a fundamental misunderstanding to think that I must study the headache I now have (the phenomenon) in order to clarify philosophical problems about pain (cf. PI §314). But it is no less misleading to suppose that clarifying the use of a word falls short of analysing, rendering perspicuous, the concept it expresses. When one learns the correct use of the word 'pain', one learns the *concept* of pain. Hence, if an investigation into the essence of thinking is a conceptual investigation, it is to be pursued by describing the use of the relevant words.

SECTION 385

1   After the lengthy detour, W. now picks up the thread of §369. The concept of calculating in the head is parasitic on the concept of calculating. Does it follow that being able to calculate in the head is parasitic on *having done* calculations out loud or on paper? W. does not answer the question here, but only raises the further question: what would be the criterion here for being able to calculate in the head? Is the implied conclusion that it is *not* imaginable. for someone to learn to calculate in his head unless he does calculations aloud or on paper?
     MS. 124, 252 suggests that that would be wrong.

Wäre es denkbar, dass Einer im Kopfe rechnen lernte, ohne je schriftlich, oder mündlich zu rechnen? Nun warum nicht. 'Es lernen', heisst nur, dazu gebracht werden, dass man's kann. Aber könnte man dazu *abgerichtet* werden? — Es könnte uns Einer Rechnungen schriftlich vormachen, wir würden nie welche schreiben, oder aussprechen; aber nach und nach kämen wir dahin, das Resultat ohne Fehler hinzuschreiben.

(Would it be conceivable for someone to learn to calculate in the head without ever calculating on paper or aloud? Well, why not? 'Learning it' means only: being brought to the point of being able to. But could one be *trained* to do it? — Someone might demonstrate written calculations to us, although we would never write any down or say them aloud; but by and by we would come to the point of writing down the result without mistakes.)

What would be the criterion here for being able to calculate in the head? Well, giving the correct answer and giving the right justification for it when challenged, as well as indicating how far one had got if interrupted, etc. — in short, the same criteria as in ordinary cases.

So far, so good. But is it also conceivable that a whole society might be acquainted only with calculating in the head? That is obviously more doubtful. What would the teaching and the training look like. The criteria for calculating in the head would not interlock, as they do in the previous case, with calculating aloud or on paper. It would make no sense for someone to say 'Wait, I've added the first two columns, but not the third', for the concept of a *column* of figures is parasitic on written notation. And so on. One might conceive of such beings asking one of their kind to multiply 123 by 794, and him then answering '97,662'. The others might pause a moment and then say 'Yes, that's right': and so on. But is this *calculating in the head*? For remember, they *have no concept of calculating* (unlike the previous case). One might, given further details, conceive of this as a limiting (degenerate) case (as a point is a limiting case of a conic section). But equally, one might deny that the concept of *calculating* had any role to play here at all. Instead, one might say of these beings that they know the answers to sums, *without calculating*. (Would that be 'intolerably mysterious'? No more so than knowing the answer by doing a calculation in the head! (cf. §364))

1.1   'gravitate towards another paradigm': viz. that of the mathematical prodigy who can answer without calculating.

2   In MS. 124, 247ff. this occurs in a consecutive sequence of remarks incorporating PI §364 and §366, all on mental arithmetic.

It might seem at first blush that the above interpretation conflicts with the later remarks 'Only if you have learnt to calculate — on paper or out loud — can you be made to grasp, by means of this concept, what calculating in the head is' (PI p. 216) and 'You can only learn what "calculating in the head" is by learning what "calculating" is; you can only learn to calculate in your head by learning to calculate' (PI p. 220). There is no conflict, however, for in the envisaged scenario (MS. 124, 252) the learner *is* taught what calculating is; it is demonstrated to him. True enough, he *does* no calculation aloud or on paper, but one may presume that he corrects the overt miscalculations of others, checks his calculations in the head against his teacher's written calculations. Here one might well say that he *can* calculate on paper, but does not. Not so, however, in the 'limiting case' of a tribe who 'calculate only in the head'.

SECTION 386

1   W.'s investigations into the concept of calculating in the head look like qualms about whether he really calculates in his head. (In §364 the interlocutor interpreted W. as suggesting that doing a sum in one's head is not really calculating; to which the reply was 'It is real calculating-in-the-head!') Hence the interlocutor says, quite rightly, that if one knows what it is to calculate, then if one says that one has calculated something in one's head, one will have done so. For if one had not so calculated, one would not have said that one had. And, by parity of reasoning, if one says one has a red mental image, then one's mental image is red. And so on.

This is all true, but it mislocates W.'s qualms, which are not qualms over whether he may not be *mistaken* in saying that he has calculated in the head or over whether his mental image might be not red but some other colour. For, to be sure, it makes *no sense* to suppose that one might make such a mistake. And here is the nub: for how is it *possible* that all doubts and uncertainties are excluded? The interlocutor supposes that the inward calculation and the mental image of red are private processes or objects from which one derives their description (cf. PI §374). Hence his exclamation 'You always know well enough what it is to calculate' and 'You know what "red" is elsewhere'; if one knows when to call an apple 'red', surely one can be confident about calling one's mental image 'red'!

But that is precisely mistaken. However good my eyesight, it makes *sense* for me to make a mistake about the colour of an object in view (the light may be poor; the object may be in the shade or in the vicinity of other objects whose colours induce a deceptive appearance; or I may have been looking at very bright objects whose effect is to distort my perception for the moment). But does my confidence that I have imagined *this* colour stem from my knowledge that my mind's eye is not bedazzled or from the fact that the light of the mind casts no distorting shadows? If my assertion that my mental image was *this* ↗ colour were read off a 'private object', then it might be supposed that I *look* at my mental image and look at this patch of cloth and see that they are the same colour. But that makes no sense. There is no such thing as *looking* at my mental image (it does not matter, e.g., whether the light is poor), and my mental image cannot be said to *look like* the colour of the cloth. The representation of the image in reality, by, for example, painting a patch and saying '*That* is the colour I imagined' is not done by comparing the image with reality (the patch) for match in the manner in which a representation of the colour of the curtains in a painting is done by collating.

The interlocutor objects that one can recognize a man from a drawing straight off, so why not a colour one has imagined from a splash of paint? Well, one can — one can say: that is the brilliant yellow I imagined. But in the case of the subject of a portrait, I can say what he looks like (youthful, with humorous eyes, unruly hair, etc.), and can say that he looks as the drawing represents him as being. But if I represent my mental image by a patch of paint, I cannot say that the coloured patch tells you what my image *looks like* or say what my image *must look like* if it is to be an image of this colour. There is no such thing as *teaching* someone to have a mental image of precisely this colour, although he may indeed have one and say so.

1.1   (i) 'das Abbilden der Vorstellung in die Wirklichkeit': 'representing the image in reality'.

(ii) 'Sehen sie sich denn zum Verwechseln ähnlich?': 'Do they look so alike that one might mix them up?'

(iii) 'I cannot accept his testimony . . .': the interlocutor is inclined to say that he *knows* that his mental image is red. If asked how he knows, he will insist that he can see the colour before his mind. Asked whether he is certain that it is precisely this shade of red, he will reply that he is quite certain, that he has no doubts. Does this not refute W.'s case? Does it not show that the mental image is a private object off which one reads a description? No, not at all. For this is not *testimony*. It is not a *report*, which is very probably true. Rather, it is an expression of the pictures we use in this domain. It shows what we are inclined to say, what figures of speech come naturally to us when we talk about the imagination. (But it does not show that they are only figures of speech. And it does not reveal the peculiar application of these turns of phrase; *that* requires the philosophical skill in noting grammatical differences which W. is trying to teach us.) Cf. PI §594(c).

(iv) 'what he is *inclined* to say': and what he is inclined to say is, of course, not philosophy or a theory, but the raw material for philosophy, something for philosophical treatment (cf. PI §254).

2   MS. 124, 274 follows this with a draft of PI §316. What goes hand in hand with this misconception of imagining is the idea that the concepts

of the 'inner', e.g. thinking, can be clarified by 'introspective observation', by noting 'what happens' when we are thinking.

2.1   'But it is *this*: that we should be able . . .': MS. 124, 73f. is more explicit:

> Sondern dies: Gefragt, welche Farbe ich mir vorgestellt habe, zeige ich auf sie, oder beschreibe sie; aber wie kommt es, dass ich das ohne weiteres tun kann; dass mir das Abbilden der Vorstellung in die Wirklichkeit so wenig Schwierigkeit macht? Sehen sich denn Vorstellung und Wirklichkeit zum Verwechseln ähnlich?

> (But it is this: if asked what colour I imagined, I point at it or describe it; but how is it that I can do this without more ado; that representing the image in reality gives me so little difficulty? Do image and reality look as alike as two peas?)

SECTION 387

1   What then is the 'deep aspect' of the matter? It is, presumably, the logical character of avowals of the inner, that something which has the form of a description of an object visible only to its owner is not one, that two language-games should be homologous, yet so utterly different. And further, that a mental image, which seems a picture *par excellence*, a 'super-likeness' of that of which it is an image (PI §389), is not a likeness at all and is not a picture.

SECTION 388

1   We can, without more ado, point out or describe the colour we have imagined (§386). We can also, without more ado, say that we can show someone what colour violet, for example, is. In the former case we are tempted to give a pseudo-explanation of how it is possible that we should be able to do this, viz. that we *copy* our mental image (when we paint what colours we imagined) or read off its description by observing it. A parallel illusion besets the latter case, for we are inclined to think that our confidence that we can show someone what violet is (i.e. that we *know* that we can show it) rests on the fact that we conjure up a mental image of violet. If we can do *that*, we think, then we can surely show someone what violet is: if we are given a paintbox, we simply point at the pigment which is the same colour as our violet mental image!

Both pictures are misconceived. That I am able to show (or say) what colour I imagine is not a capacity distinct from — logically independent of — being able to imagine a certain colour; for showing (or saying) what colour I imagined is a *criterion* for having imagined that colour. And conversely, an inability to show (or say) what colour one is imagining (given, e.g., a comprehensive colour-chart) is a criterion for not, or not clearly, imagining a specific colour at all.

Similarly, knowing that I can tell you what colour violet is does not rest on conjuring up a mental image of violet (although one may do so). For, (a) one would then ask how one knows that the mental image one has conjured up is a mental image of violet rather than of some other colour. One cannot say that one 'recognizes' it (PI §378), and if one falls back on the simple assertion that one can conjure up an image of violet at will, one might as well simply insist (probably rightly) that one can pick out violet on sight. (b) If one can conjure up a mental image of violet, how will that enable one to identify the violet paint in the paintbox? There is, after all, no technique of laying an image alongside reality as a measure. A mental image is not a sample and cannot be compared with reality; i.e. there is no such thing as comparing my mental image with a coloured object to see if they are the same colour. For a mental image of violet does not *look like* the pigment in the paintbox, and no one, myself included, can *look at it* (cf. Exg. §386).

How then *do* I know that I shall be able to do something? W. reduces the question to its right, farcical proportions: how do I know that the state I am in is that of being able to do that thing? But against *this* muddle we have been forewarned: being able to do something is not a mental state, as being excited, depressed, or (perhaps) being in pain are (Exg. PI p. 59n.; BB 117f.), and an avowal of ability is not an avowal of being in such a state. (And if it were, should one argue: I am in such-and-such a state now, and in the past I have always found that when I am in such a state, I subsequently succeed in doing so-and-so?) So do I *know* that I can show you what violet is? Of course, just as I know that I can recite the ABC. How do I know? Well, I might say again, 'I have learnt English', I know what 'violet' means (and a criterion for my knowing that is precisely that I do pick out violet on sight). But what justifies my claim to know this? One might reply 'I have used this word correctly countless times in the past', but also 'that we don't need any grounds for *this* certainty either. What could justify the certainty *better* than success?' (PI §324).

2   These reflections originate in PR 57f. My assertion that I can point out a certain colour may express the expectation that I shall recognize it on sight in the same sense that I expect a headache if I am hit on the head. This is an expectation that 'belongs to physics', i.e. has inductive grounds. Or it may not have such grounds and, W. here suggests, would not be falsified if I fail to recognize the colour. 'Instead, it is as if the proposition is saying that I possess a paradigm that I could at any time compare the colour with.' But both interpretations, he continues, are suspect. For, regarding the first, if I do give a sign of recognition when I

look at a colour, how do I know it is the colour I *meant*?[9] And with regard
to the second, 'we are still forced to say that the image of the colour isn't
the same as the colour that is really seen, and in that case, how can one
compare these two?' Nevertheless, W. concludes, 'the naive theory of
forming-an-image can't be utterly wrong.'

His position at this stage was clearly unstable. The seeds of suspicion
grew; the 'naive theory' *is* utterly wrong. In the sense in which a mental
image has a colour (is an image of a colour) it *is* the same colour as the
object one points at when one says 'That ↗ is the colour I imagined';
but, of course, the image is not a sample, and the criterion for its being
such-and-such a colour is not its *match* with a public sample, but the
speaker's avowal, which rests on no criteria at all (PI §377).

SECTION 389

1   W. concludes this part of the discussion by pin-pointing one deep
aspect of the illusions that beset us here. We think of our mental images
as pictures which only we can see, in fact as 'super-pictures' which
cannot be misinterpreted. For an ordinary picture, though it is a picture
of X, may look like (and be wrongly taken to be) a picture of Y. But it is
essential to a mental image of X that it is of X and nothing else. So it
comes to seem like a super-likeness. Yet this is confused, for that the
mental image of X *is* an image of X is not determined by its likeness to
X. We are prone to think that it is a picture which needs no interpretation, so closely does it resemble what it is a picture of. It is true that it
needs no interpretation and also that it makes no sense to suppose that I
might be mistaken in my characterization of my mental image. But that
is not because it looks more like its object than any picture. It is rather
that it neither looks like nor fails to look like its object. It is not a picture
at all. How does one *know* that one's image is of X and not Y (which
looks like X)? One does not *know*, nor can one be mistaken. One *says so*,
without grounds, as one says what one means or what one thinks.

2   The relation between an image and what it is an image of is
comparable not to the relation between a portrait and its subject (where
the portrait may resemble someone or something else), but to the
relation between an expectation and what fulfils it (BB 36), a thought (or
proposition) and what makes it true (PG 161), or a possibility and what it
is a possibility of (PI §194). It is not an image *of* X in virtue of a method

---

[9] Well, I said I can pick out *violet* and *this* is what is called 'violet'. So my characterization
of my image presupposes my mastery of the use of the word.

of projection or in virtue of a similarity, let alone a 'super-likeness'. (Cf. LA 67.)

Section 390

1   This opens a fresh sequence of remarks on the imagination which are concerned with the relation between imaginability and the bounds of sense. §281 and §284 gave ample reasons for dismissing as irrelevant image-mongery anyone's insistence that they *can* imagine a stone's being conscious.

1.1   'And if anyone can do so': since W. clearly holds that there is no such thing as a stone's having consciousness or being conscious, how should this be understood? Not — that perhaps someone really can imagine this, but it is of no interest. For 'a stone's being conscious' is a senseless concatenation of words, and there is here nothing *to* imagine. So either (a) someone can conjure up a certain mental image in connection with these words, but that is just irrelevant image-mongery; or (b) someone *says* he can imagine it, but that is of no interest (cf. MS. 179, 58, quoted below).

2   This originates in MS. 165, 59. Its context is an exploration of the different language-games with 'image', which illustrates the categorial diversity of the use of distinct psychological verbs, a diversity that necessitates the careful investigation of particular cases. After a fragmentary draft of PI §§391, 393–4, W. observes that here, as always, the first mistake we make in a philosophical investigation is the question itself. Then

> Aber hat nicht Spinoza gesagt, wenn ein Stein Bewusstsein hätte, würde er glauben, er fiele zur Erde, weil er fallen will? Das ist die Art von Fiktion, die in einer Fabel am Platz sein kann, aber in der Philosophie gar nichts leistet. Erstens: Wie haben wir uns das vorzustellen, dass ein Stein Bewusstsein hat? Zweitens: Welchen Grund haben wir zur Annahme, ein Stein, wenn er etwas glauben könnte, würde eher das als das glauben? Drittens: Wenn wir, die wir doch Bewusstsein haben, von einer Höhe herabstürzen, sind wir der Meinung, wir fallen, weil wir fallen *wollen*?[10]

> (But didn't Spinoza say, that if a stone were conscious, it would believe that it falls to the earth because it wants to fall? This is the sort of fiction which has a place in a fable, but in philosophy achieves nothing. First: how are we supposed to imagine a stone's being conscious? Secondly; what reason do we have for the supposition that a stone, if it could

---

[10] There are three different drafts of this remark, of which this is the most polished. W.'s information about Spinoza is probably derived from Schopenhauer. *The World as Will and Representation*. (Dover, New York, 1966), Vol. 1, p. 504.

believe something, would believe this rather than that? Thirdly: when we, who are
conscious, fall from a height, are we of the opinion that we fall because we *want* to fall?)

Then, one remark later, occurs a draft of PI §418(b), followed by §390.

In a fairy-tale, we can talk of pots and pans seeing and hearing (PI
§282), but this is a special game with language that we play, a kind of
nonsense. If someone says that he can imagine a conscious stone, this is a
similar nonsense, an idle play of the imagination that traverses the
bounds of sense to no purpose.

MS. 179, 58 supposes someone saying 'I'm not sure whether I can't
imagine that this chair is in pain'. So what! In what way is that of any
interest? What connection does it have with our ordinary life? This
remark is followed by a draft of PI §391.

Section 391

1   Someone who insists that he can imagine a stone's being conscious is
indulging in mere image-mongery. Unlike the narrator of a fairy-tale or
fable, his putative imagining has no consequences, save to stir up
philosophical clouds of dust. What does his imagining amount to, save
mere words which lead nowhere? By contrast, one might actually
imagine that the people in the street are in frightful pain, but are artfully
concealing it. But if this is really to be a case of imagining, I must not
merely say to myself 'His soul (mind) is in pain, but what has that to do
with his body?' for that would again be mere image-mongery (*Vorstelle-
rei*), motivated by confused philosophy. Rather, I must suppose *artful*
concealment, strength of will not to show the pain. I might even imagine
sympathizing with them, but not showing my sympathy out of respect
for their insistent self-control. And so on. Here, unlike the example of
§390, I can really be said to be imagining and not just idly playing with
words.

1.1   (i) 'I as it were play a part': analogously to the actor in §393 below.
       (ii) 'Wenn ich das tue, sagt man etwa . . .': 'When I do this one might
say . . .' Note the connection drawn here between imagining and action
(see §393).

Section 392

1   So I can imagine people in the street being in frightful pain, but
concealing it. On the other hand, to say that I can imagine a stone's being
conscious is merely idle words. Is the difference, then, a matter of what

goes on in me when I am asked to imagine the one or the other? Does imagining so-and-so consist in such-and-such going on in my mind when I imagine it? But then someone might reply, 'I can imagine it too, but *without* such-and-such going on.' For example (cf. §391), he might insist that he can imagine one of the people in the street being in frightful pain yet artfully concealing it, but *without* saying to himself 'It must be difficult to laugh when one is in such pain'.

However, whether one can or cannot imagine something is not determined by what goes on in one's mind when one tries to imagine it. A report of what *went on* when one imagined . . . is 'natural science', whereas to say *what one imagined* when one imagines . . . is a criterion for having imagined it. But these may appear similar, and then the analysis fluctuates misleadingly between empirical correlation and grammatical description of what counts as 'imagining such-and-such'.

SECTION 393

1 The interlocutor still insists that a *picture* of pain or a paradigm of pain must be involved in imagining someone who is laughing to be in pain (cf. PI §300). For, obviously, I do not imagine any pain-behaviour, I imagine pain — which he has. But that route has been blocked, since imagining pain is not picturing pain (ibid.). So what do I imagine when I imagine someone who is laughing to be in pain? Well, just that! But then, what is the process of imagining? Why should imagining be a *process*?

W. endeavours to relieve the philosophical pressure by reminding us of a context outside philosophy, i.e. a context in which language is *not* idling, in which we tell someone to imagine something. Thus we might tell an actor to imagine that one of the other characters is in pain and concealing it, but we do not tell him what he must do. (Nor do we describe to him what must 'go on in his mind'.) We tell him what he is to imagine and then see how he now interprets the role. Outside philosophy, imagining something interlocks with *action* (cf. §391).

1.1 (i) 'And I do not necessarily imagine *my* being in pain': of course, one might, for one might say to oneself 'If I were in such dreadful pain, I should find it fearfully difficult to laugh like that; it would need great self-control'.

(ii) 'For this reason the suggested analysis is not to the point': the analysis of imagining so-and-so in terms of a 'process' of imagining. The addition of the word 'either' in the translation is both unnecessary and misleading.

2 Vol. XII, 146 makes clear what primitive picture stands in the way of a perspicuous representation of the concept of imagining. We conceive of

someone imagining a red circle in terms of a picture of the person with a red circle floating, as it were, in a cloud above his head, just as artists represent a person dreaming by painting him lying asleep with a cloud hovering over him in which the 'dream picture' is painted, or again, as films represent recollections by a round image surrounded by darkness and blurred at the border. Is that what a memory 'looks like'? And yet everyone understands what this image signifies. Here one sees the primitive pictures of processes in another person's mind that correspond to forms of expression in our language.

SECTION 394

1 Having reminded us of the kind of context in which we say 'I imagine that . . .' or tell someone to imagine something, and hence having clarified the irrelevance of 'inner processes', W. now reminds us of the contexts in which one might ask someone what actually went on when he imagined something. These are, for example, the contexts of empirical investigations into accompaniments of imagining or into the heuristics of the imagination. And the answer we would expect would not be a description of *what was imagined*. ('When I imagine someone in frightful pain but not showing it, I always think of a scream cut off suddenly.')

SECTION 395

1   This draws what is, by now, an obvious conclusion. We are inclined to think of imaginability as a criterion of sense, but *many* unclarities surround that thought. There is unclarity over what *counts* as imagining, e.g. whether someone who says that he can imagine a stone's being conscious has actually imagined any such thing (although clearly, if we say that he has, it is no criterion of sense). There is unclarity over the role of mental imagery in imagining: does the absence of any mental image imply unimaginability? Moreover, does the presence of mental imagery guarantee sense? And does its absence imply lack of sense? Finally, in cases where one *can* imagine such-and-such, where 'such-and-such' makes good sense, does the fact that one can imagine it *explain* what the expression means? The answer to all these questions is 'No'.

2   MS. 129, 16ff. follows this with a long remark enumerating a variety of unclarities. 'I can imagine someone in frightful pain, but not showing it' would be followed by a description of *how* one imagines this (e.g. 'It must be difficult to laugh, . . . etc.' (PI §391)). 'I can imagine a society in

which it is indecent to calculate except to pass the time'; here 'I can imagine' means roughly 'I can elaborate this picture'. 'I can imagine an endless row of trees' means, more or less, that I can associate a picture with this phrase. But it does not give an explanation of the infinite. And so on.

SECTION 396

1   If imaginability is not a criterion of sense, is not imagining something in association with a sentence a criterion of understanding? Not at all; the criteria of understanding lie in behaviour, in explanations, and in the use one makes of a word or sentence, not in accompanying mental imagery (PG 73; cf. PI §449).

SECTION 397

1   It is a crucial feature of the imagination that one can say or otherwise exhibit (e.g. by a drawing) what one imagined and how one imagined it. For the criterion for someone's imagining something is that he says or portrays what he imagined. Hence the question of whether imaginability ensures sense (§395) amounts to the question of whether representability by those means of representation by which one describes what one imagined ensures sense. One can, for example, draw what one imagines, and this *may* illuminate the use of a sentence and clarify its sense. But in other cases, e.g. those of imagining another person dreaming (Exg. §393, 2), a wholly misleading picture may obtrude itself.

1.1   'Mittel der Darstellung': 'means of representation'.

CHAPTER 4

The self and self-reference

(§§398–411)

INTRODUCTION

This sequence of fourteen remarks deals with the self or, more perspicuously, with aspects of the use of the word 'I' and 'my' which generate certain kinds of philosophical confusion. It is linked to the antecedent discussion of the imagination in as much as the example with which scrutiny of the concept of 'the visual room' ('the subjective world') begins is that of imagining. This, however, is incidental, for 'the visual room' just is personal experience in general.

Part A (§§398–403) opens with the interlocutor's exclamation 'Only I have got THIS', apropos his imagining or seeing something. But this is illusion, since one cannot see one's mental images or visual impressions, one does not 'have' something that one's neighbours may not equally have, and the experience upon which one concentrates incorporates no owner and no object to which 'I' might refer. But when one's gaze is idling, when immersed in philosophical reflection, it is easy to generate such representational idealist, and ultimately solipsist, illusions. The 'visual room', W. emphasizes, has no owner in the sense in which the material room has.

§399 embroiders on the absence of any 'owner' of 'the visual room'. §§400–1 ward off misunderstandings. The absence of an 'owner' (a 'visual owner' of the 'visual room') is not a physical discovery or a phenomenological one, but a feature of the grammar of descriptions of what is seen or imagined, etc. So too, the 'visual room' itself is not a discovery but a new grammatical articulation making possible new kinds of descriptions (of how things strike one perceptually), new ways of looking at things.

§§402–3 elaborate the absence of any role for 'I have . . .' in the description of *what* I imagine or how I see what I see ('I have the impression that . . .'). Rather, this phrase pin-points *for others* the grammatical character of the ensuing description. Once this feature is noticed, one is tempted to accuse ordinary language of misrepresenting the facts; but this temptation stems from our failure to apprehend the different *uses* which expressions of similar *form* have, viz. 'I have . . .' and 'He has . . .'. For a form cannot be false to the facts. This confusion lies at the root of metaphysical disputes, in which a *representational form* is attacked (by solipsists or idealists) for misdescribing the facts and defended (by realists) as if it correctly described the facts.

The structure of Part A:

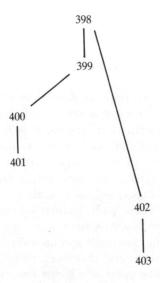

Part B (§§404–11) focuses on the use of the first-person pronoun and possessive pronoun. §404 reminds us that in saying 'I am in pain' I neither name nor point to a particular person, any more than when I groan. Indeed, in a sense, I do not *know* who is in pain. I do not find out *who* is in pain by identifying a person, viz. myself, and attributing pain to the person thus identified. Rather, in giving verbal expression to my pain, I draw attention to myself (§405). §406 examines a natural objection: granted that in drawing attention to myself I do not *name* myself, surely when I say 'I am in pain', I want to *distinguish* between myself and others. This, too, subtly distorts the role of 'I have . . .'. §407 further explores the kinship between a groan and an avowal of pain. It is *saying* 'I have a pain' which is a criterion for who is in pain (like groaning), but *what is said* does not identify who is in pain. §§408–9 examine a final objection designed to save something of the apparent referential role of 'I'. Surely when I say 'I am in pain' I have no doubt about *who* is in pain, i.e. I *know* that *I* am. But this is nonsense (cf. PI

§246). An analogy illuminates the absence of any function for 'Now I know who is in pain — I am'. §410 summarizes the source of the confusions. It lies in misconstruing the role of the first-person pronoun and in distorting its peculiar relation to names. §411 notes differences in the use of the first-person possessive pronoun.

The structure of Part B:

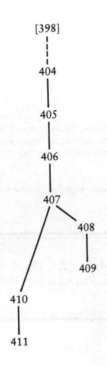

Correlations

PI§[1]	Vol. XII	Vol. XVI
398	211–13	62–7
399	221	88
400	221	91
401	222	92–3
402	213	68;[2] 78–80[3]
403	154	
404	155–6	
405	157	
406	158	171
407	165	36; 174
408	169	
409	169–70	162–3, 230[4]
410	332–3	
411	183	174–5, 223, 242–3

[1] Note that this sequence of remarks, unlike some of the subsequent ones, did *not* occur in the Intermediate Version. The decision to interpose this brief discussion of the first-person pronoun was therefore taken only while compiling the final draft.
[2] First six lines only.
[3] Remainder of PI §402.
[4] An early draft of the last six lines, together with a note 'For p. 169' which refers to Vol. XII.

I and my self
  1. Historical antecedents 2. 'The I, the I is what is deeply mysterious' 3. The eliminability of the word 'I' 4. '"I" does not refer to a person'

SECTION 398

1   W. here reverts to the theme of §253, viz. the illusion of unique possession of experience that is rooted in the fact that we employ the representational form of ownership when we talk of experiences. We say that we *have* mental images, *have* pains, and *have* visual (or other perceptual) impressions. In the grip of this illusion one is inclined to think that another cannot *have* what one has, and one is then disposed to employ the indexical expression 'this' to emphasize what it is that another cannot have; for one will insist 'At any rate only I have got THIS' or (as in §253) 'But surely another person can't have THIS pain'. But one forgets that there can be no deictic use of 'this' in respect of one's experiences, but only anaphoric or cataphoric reference. 'Only I have THIS' serves no purpose, for one cannot point, either for others or for oneself, at the mental image or visual impression one has. To be sure, one can *say* what one has, e.g. a vivid image of such-and-such or a splitting headache. But, of course, someone else may have that too.

What one *has* when one imagines something or when one sees something is not something which others, by contrast with oneself cannot see. For one does not see one's mental images or visual impressions. We do indeed speak of *having*, but this having is not a kind of *possessing* at all; and in having a certain image one does not possess something that others cannot possess, since one does not *possess* it oneself. (That of which one cannot be dispossessed, one cannot possess either.) Furthermore, if one excludes others from having what one has, e.g. a vivid image of such-and-such, then one thereby renders it senseless to talk of *having* in one's own case. It makes sense to talk of oneself as having a visual impression or mental image only if it also makes sense to talk of someone else having the same impression or image (cf. BB 55).

If the interlocutor's insistent remarks make no sense, how can W. say that he understands them, that he knows what the interlocutor means? It is not that he understands their sense, but rather that he is familiar with the circumstances in which the temptation to say such things becomes irresistible (cf. Exg. §275 and 'The world of consciousness', §1) and has anatomized the phenomenology of philosophical illusion in such cases, e.g. how one thinks to point at the 'private object' *with one's attention* (§§274f.), how one *immerses* oneself in a colour-impression that seems to belong to oneself alone (§277), and how one stares motionless at what one sees (BB 66). So what is the interlocutor speaking of? W. clarifies: he is speaking of personal experience, of the perceptual impression an object gives one. If the interlocutor is sitting in a room, one might say that he is speaking of 'the visual room'. But he projects upon his discourse about his visual impressions the grammar of the actual visible objects he sees, and it is precisely here that he goes wrong. One can walk about, look at, point at the actual room; it may belong to one, to someone else, or to no one. But one cannot walk about, look at, or point at one's visual impression of the room; there is no such thing. We do indeed use the same form of expression in characterizing our visual impressions as in describing what they are visual impressions of, but the visible room and the 'visual room' are categorially distinct. The visible room may contain its owner, may have or lack an owner. But the grammar of our discourse about the 'visual room' excludes any *owner*. I do not enter into the characterization of how what I see strikes me, any more than the eye is part of the visual field. And my 'ownership' of the visual impression is not a *feature* of the impression, but consists in *my* giving expression to how the visible room struck me.

§398(c) gives a parallel case of a shift in the grammar of 'ownership'. The grammar of the visual room is as different from the grammar of the visible room as the grammar for characterizing a picture of an imaginary landscape is from the grammar of descriptions of a landscape. (One can say 'The farmer is just about to enter the house', but one cannot add 'Wait a moment and you'll see'! What it makes sense to say of what is depicted does not always make sense to say of the depiction.)

1.1   (i) 'Was ist dann das, wovon du redest?': 'But what then are you talking about?' W. is not suggesting that he is familiar with this private object (*diesen Gegenstand*), but rather with the confusion that leads to such ideas.

(ii) 'Es gehört insofern nicht mir an . . .': better 'In so far as it cannot belong to anyone else, it doesn't belong to me either!' or 'In so far as I want to apply the same form of expression to it as to the material room in which I sit, it does not belong to me.' For in the sense in which the visible room may be mine, the 'visual room' is not.

2   This derives from Vol. XVI, 62 – 7, preceded by a remark connecting it with the subject of PI §253, for the idea that another cannot have the mental image before his eyes which I have before my eyes is parallel to the idea that another cannot have the same pain as I have. It is only a metaphor to say that one 'sees' it 'before one', a simile of inner sight. And, of course, another can imagine what I imagine and can have the same mental image as I do.

Then follows a draft of PI §398. In the sequel, W. explores at length the confusion of genuine ownership with the representational form of ownership. In the former case, but not the latter, it makes sense to ask 'Does it really belong to you; doesn't it perhaps belong to someone else?' (Vol. XVI, 70). When I say that I have a certain mental image, I don't have to know *who* has it! Indeed, it makes no sense to say 'I *know* that I have this (or, a certain) mental image'. Does it mean that I know that I have *this* one rather than some other one? Or that I know that *I* have it? Both are senseless. What would it be like if I had a different mental image, which I mistook for this one, or none at all, but just fancied that I did? What would it be like if someone else had this mental image, viz. a mental image of X? That, of course, is possible. One wants to say, not 'This, which I describe thus-and-so', but rather, 'This, which I see before me' or just 'This' (pp. 71f.). But there is no deictic use of 'this' in respect of one's sense-impressions or mental images.

2.1   (i) 'the "visual room"': the 'visual room', as is evident from the previous quotation, is a particular case of the 'room' of personal experience. LPE 296f. talks here of *the world* (of experiences) that lies behind words ('the world as representation', *Die Welt als Vorstellung*, as Schopenhauer called it); but, W. stresses, 'if the *world* is idea, it isn't any person's idea. (Solipsism stops short of saying this and says it is my idea). But then how could I say what the world is if the realm of ideas has no neighbour?' (This harks back to the Schopenhauerian ideas of W.'s youth (NB 72 – 91).)

        (ii) 'I can as little own it as I can . . . point to it': BB 71f. remarks, 'If, however, I believe that by pointing to that which in my grammar has no neighbour I can convey something to myself (if not to others), I make a mistake similar to that of thinking that the sentence "I am here" makes sense to me (and, by the way, is always true) under conditions different from those very special conditions under which it does make sense.'

        (iii) 'But then he cannot for example enter his house': Vol. XVI, 62 has instead, 'Aber hier hat "gehören" eine andre Grammatik als gewöhnlich, denn der Bauer kann z.B. sein Haus nicht benutzen' ('But here "belonging" has a different grammar than ordinarily, for the farmer cannot, e.g., make use of his house'). The picture is a picture of the owner sitting before his house, but the painted house does not belong to the painted owner.

SECTION 399

1   This explores further the picture of the 'visual room', the 'world as idea' (cf. LPE 297). If the 'visual room' had an owner, the owner would

have to be a possible constituent of the 'visual room', an object of 'visual experience'. But one cannot locate oneself in one's visual field, and the 'visual room' is not *a part* of a larger space wherein its owner might be located. I can stand in front of the stove I see, but I cannot stand in front of my visual impression of the stove (Vol. XVI, 89f.). The first-person pronoun in 'I have a visual impression of the room' or 'I imagine the room thus: . . .' does not designate anything I see or imagine. (Of course, I might imagine myself looking at the stove, but my 'visual body' cannot see (Vol. XVI, 90).) Philosophers who find themselves in these dire straits have argued that 'the I', or 'the self', is therefore merely a bundle of perceptions (as it were, a collection of visual furniture) or a logical construction out of sense-data or a transcendental subject or, as W. himself argued, the limit of the world (TLP 5.641). But this is merely to compound confusion with mystification.

1.1   'There is no outside': visual space has no limits, for it is not *part* of a space. That is why it is absurd to try, as psychologists have done, to *draw* a visual image or visual field (in this peculiar sense of the term). Cf. PR 267. And it is not a part of space, for whereas one can ask where in one's visual field the stove is located, one cannot ask where one's visual field is located (BB 8).

2   This derives from Vol. XVI, 88, which further comments on the quite different use of spatial expressions in the domain of mental and visual images, by contrast with physical space. One speaks of having a visual image, mental image, or after-image *before* one, but not *behind* one. One cannot see *another part* of one's visual space. And so on. These remarks are not phenomenology, however, but grammar.

SECTION 400

1   Our discourse about visual impressions and mental images sounds like the description of a discovery, as if the introduction of these forms of expression were in response to finding that apart from the physical world there is also the world of imagination and of subjective experience. But this is illusory. To talk of things being blurred at the edge of one's visual field (unlike talk of images on a photograph being blurred), of conjuring up an image of something revolving (which is not to revolve an image!), is to introduce a new way of speaking. We thereby add new articulations to our language (Z §425) which make possible not descriptions of new objects (objects in the world of sense-data), but new descriptions of, or descriptions essentially related to, familiar objects (e.g. descriptions of

how objects strike one, impress one), new language-games (e.g. of describing how one imagines things).

1.1 (i) 'a new comparison': we compare our visual impressions to objects of vision and use the language of visible objects to describe our visual impressions of objects.

(ii) 'a new sensation': Why so? Because the substratum of such visual experiences is mastery of a technique (cf. PI p. 208), the *concept* of seeing is modified here, as it is in the case of aspect-seeing (PI p. 209). Hence the introduction of new forms of description itself modifies our visual experiences — we can see things in a sense in which, in the absence of these conceptual techniques, we could not (cf. §401). The term 'sensation', however, jars here.

2 BB 57f. compares the confused disagreement between realists, idealists, and solipsists with the confusions over unconscious thoughts and feelings. Psychoanalysts 'were misled by their own way of expression into thinking that they had done more than discover new psychological reactions; that they had, in a sense, discovered conscious thoughts which were unconscious'. But in fact what they had done was primarily to introduce a new grammatical movement, a new way of speaking.

SECTION 401

1 This amplifies §400: we think of the introduction of a new articulation in grammar as heralding the discovery of new objects, as if 'There are sense-data' were on the same level as 'Material objects consist of electrons' (cf. BB 46f., 64, 70).

§401(b) suggests that saying that one has *merely* made a grammatical movement is misleading, for this grammatical articulation makes it possible to describe what previously was not describable, viz. how things appear to us to be (even though they are not so). So we have a new way of looking at things (*eine neue Auffassung*) and can record not only how they are, but how they strike us as being, how they impress us. One might compare this to the introduction of an impressionistic style of painting, as opposed to a purely naturalistic one.

It is unclear what W. means by a mere new grammatical movement which does *not* introduce a new way of looking at things.

1.1 'Du deutest die neue Auffassung . . .': 'You interpret the new way of looking at things as . . .'.

SECTION 402

1   The 'visual room' has no owner, and it is readily viewed (wrongly) as
a discovery. Now W. warns against a further misinterpretation. It is
indeed true that the words 'I have' in 'Now I have such-and-such an
image' are merely a sign to someone else. They do not signify anything
in the image that I entertain. In this respect they function rather like
prefacing one's remarks by 'I say!' (or by loudly clearing one's throat).
The utterance 'I say! Such-and-such is the case' does not *tell* one's hearer
who is saying something, but rather draws the hearer's attention to
oneself (Vol. XII, 171).
    One may recognize this feature and misinterpret it. For one is now
inclined to say that ordinary language is here defective, that it *misdescribes
the facts*. One might then entertain the thought of a more accurate
language in which one did *not* say 'I have such-and-such an image', but
rather made a special sign with one's hand and merely gave a description
of the image. So too Lichtenberg suggested that instead of saying 'I
think', we should say 'It thinks', as we say 'It rains'[1] (M 309). Similarly,
the author of the *Tractatus* proclaimed as a metaphysical insight that
'there is no such thing as the subject that thinks or entertains ideas' (TLP
5.631; see Exg. §402, 2.1, below). But this is immensely misleading.
Such philosophers achieve a partial insight into the different *uses* of
expressions with grammatically similar *form*, but misconstrue it. 'I have
such-and-such an image' performs its role perfectly satisfactorily; it is
used to tell another what I am imagining.[2] It has the same grammatical
form as 'John has such-and-such an image', but a very different use. The
latter is asserted on the basis of behavioural criteria, whereas the former
is groundlessly avowed. The latter involves reference to a person and the
possibility (intelligibility) of misidentification of the person, as well as
mistaken description of what he is imagining, whereas the former does
not. They can both be said to be descriptions; but if so, then descriptions
of logically different types.
    Philosophers who criticize the first-person mode of expression have a
picture, viz. a picture of 'unowned data', which conflicts with the *picture*
of our ordinary mode of expression, viz. the subject as owner of the
image. But they fail to notice that the conflict is one of *form*. Noting
correctly that 'I have' is not here fulfilling the same role as 'He has', they
infer that 'I have such-and-such an image' misdescribes the facts. But that

---

[1] Of course, this is confused; for 'thinks' is not a feature-placing predicate. Moreover,
Lichtenberg never clarified what, if anything, we should say instead of 'He thinks'.

[2] Although, of course, this language-game of telling is altogether different from telling
someone what happened in Parliament yesterday (cf. Exg. §363).

is quite wrong. The role of 'I have such-and-such an image', unlike that of 'N has such-and-such an image', is not to identify a person who has a certain image, but to describe what image *I* have. (Those who hear what I say will identify who is imagining without more ado.) And what expression could *more correctly* describe what images I am entertaining than 'I have such-and-such an image'? The philosophers' complaint is one about the misleading similarity of form between sentences which fulfil very different functions; but they misconstrue their grievance. For the *form* of an expression cannot say something false; it is what the expression *says* which is true or false. I would indeed be misrepresenting things if I said 'I have such-and-such an image' when I have a different image or when I am not actually imagining anything at all. But the form of an expression cannot say something false when what the expression says is true; the only way for 'He has pains' to be false is for him *not* to have pains. (Does 'It is raining' misrepresent the facts because one cannot ask 'What is raining?'?)

The confusion is instructive and of quite general import, for metaphysical disputes are typically enmeshed in this very confusion. Idealists and solipsists attack the normal form of expression as if the mere form stated how things are; whereas the only cogent case that can be made out in their favour is a recommendation to adopt a different form in which the very same facts are represented in different guise (see Exg. §403). For when the idealist tells us that material objects are *really* only collections of ideas, he does not mean that one will not hurt oneself if one scrapes one's shins against a table; and when the solipsist argues that only the present is real, he does not mean that he did not have breakfast this morning. Rather, they misconstrue what they are doing, conflate different forms of representation, and think they have achieved an insight into the true nature of things. Similar confusion is evident in those realists who in effect defend our normal form of expression against idealism and solipsism, but do so by stating facts we all know, as Dr Johnson did in 'refuting' Berkeley by kicking a stone, or (less crudely) G. E. Moore did in 'proving the existence of the external world' by demonstrating that he had two hands.

1.1   (i) 'Vorstellungswelt': 'world of representation', though quasi-technical, might better capture the Schopenhauerian picture involved here, as well as implying greater generality than 'the imagined world'.

(ii) 'ist wie ein "Jetzt Achtung"': 'is like an "Attention now!"' i.e. it is like the heralding of an announcement the function of which is to draw attention.

(iii) 'As if, for example the proposition "he has pains" . . .': why the shift from 'I have an image'? Perhaps because it is potentially misleading to talk of avowals as false, rather than as untruthful or insincere. But then why not 'He has an image'?

2   Vol. XII, 213ff. adds further points:

(i) One wants to say that when one has pains, there are just pains, and there is no question of a person entering into the experience. So wouldn't simply 'Pains!' describe the whole fact of the matter? But, first, is that a description? And secondly, what purpose does it serve? One misguidedly compares the situation with one in which a description is to be given. So one thinks of the imagination (or the domain of experience) as a *world* that is to be described, as a geography book describes the earth. But how far is the expression of pain the description of a world, and what is it for? The contrast is comparable to the difference between (a) 'At such-and-such a place there is a house which has such-and-such features . . .' and (b) 'Once upon a time there was a wealthy man who lived in a house which . . .' (or 'Imagine a house which . . .'). The application of these 'descriptions' in the various cases is altogether different.

(ii) In saying that 'I have . . .' is only for others and not for myself when I describe my images, one may still be misled. Is it only for others because I *know* that the image is mine?

(iii) One is inclined to say 'What more can he know than how things are? And he comes to know that by means of the description of the image.' Here one does indeed conceive of the description as a description of 'a world'. But this obscures what such a description is for, what one does with it.

By implication we are invited to reflect on the language-games with 'I imagined things thus', on the contexts in which one tells someone how one imagines something, and the consequences in the language-game of giving such a description. Here too, one might emphasize, the language-game *begins* with the description of what one imagines.

One might compare the 'I have . . .' to the direction-arrow on a map. It too belongs to the map, only not to the map as a picture. (Rather, it shows what one can do with the picture.)

2.1   (i) 'the description of the image is a *complete* account of the imagined world': this was the view taken in TLP 5.63–5.634, esp. 5.633.

> Where *in* the world is a metaphysical subject to be found?
> You will say that this is exactly like the case of the eye and the visual field. But really you do *not* see the eye.
> And nothing *in the visual field* allows you to infer that it is seen by an eye.

Vol. XII, 235 (mis)quotes the final remarks:

> 'Nichts im Gesichtsfeld deutet darauf hin etc.' (Log. Phil. Abh.). Das heisst sozusagen: Du wirst vergebens im Gesichtsraum nach dem *Seher* ausschauen. Er ist nirgends im Gesichtraum zu finden. — Aber die Wahrheit ist: Du *tust* nur, als suchtest Du nach einem Etwas, nach einer Person im Gesichstraum, die nicht da ist.

('Nothing in the visual field indicates, etc.' (Tract. Log. Phil.). That means, as it were: you will look in vain in visual space for the *viewer*. The viewer is not to be found in visual space. — But the truth is: you only *pretend* to be looking for a something, for a person, in visual space, who is not there.)

The Kantian (Schopenhauerian) observation of the *Tractatus* presented an insight into the bounds of sense as a metaphysical discovery. But the truth is that there is no space *in grammar* for an owner in the visual field, not no space in the visual field. And confusion over this point leads naturally to the further two ideas, first, that the description of the *Vorstellung* (image or representation) is a complete account of the *Vorstellungswelt* (world of representation) and second, that ordinary grammar misrepresents the facts. But what seems like a description of a private world is not a description of a *world*, but of what one imagines (or of how what one perceives strikes one) — a description which has various uses, all of which are *unlike* descriptions of the world.

(ii) 'the words "I am having" are like "I say!. . ."': as noted above, this is an inaccurate translation, although it does make the right point. Coincidentally, W. did comment on this use of 'I say!' Vol. XII, 170 observes that if one prefaced every sentence with 'I say!', the role of which was to attract attention (like clearing one's throat), it would be absurd to claim that every sentence says who is talking. Applying this reasoning to 'I have . . .', it would be absurd to interpret a person's description of his images as saying whose they are. Their role is to introduce a description of what one imagines.

(iii) 'we are tempted to say that our way of speaking does not describe the facts as they really are': BB 69 compares our confusion here with one which might arise among philosophers in whose language, instead of saying 'I found nobody in the room', one said 'I found Mr Nobody in the room'. They would probably find the similarity between 'Mr Smith' and 'Mr Nobody' disturbing and might wish to abolish it, as philosophers have recommended abolishing the 'I' in 'I have a pain'. But, W. stresses, 'We are inclined to forget that it is the particular use of a word only which gives the word its meaning'. '*Mr* Nobody' is misleading, since 'Mr' is standardly used to introduce a singular referring expression. But, of course, 'Mr Nobody' is *not* used like a singular referring expression. One cannot ask where Mr Nobody is, and there is no Mrs Nobody. The sentence 'Mr Nobody is in the room' in the envisaged language no more misdescribes (falsifies) the facts than Alice's 'I see nobody on the road'.

3   Many empiricists from Hume onwards fit the bill of this remark. Russell may serve to exemplify the style of thought:

It is supposed that thoughts cannot just come and go, but need a person to think them. Now, of course it is true that thoughts can be collected into bundles, so that one bundle is my thoughts, another is your thoughts, and a third is the thoughts of Mr. Jones. But I think the person is not an ingredient in the single thought: he is rather constituted by relations of the thoughts to each other and to the body . . . It would be better to say 'it thinks in me', like 'it rains'; or better still 'there is a thought in me'.[3] (AM18)

Section 403

1   This amplifies §402. W. once envisaged a language of an oriental despot in which, instead of saying 'I have a pain', the despot said 'There is pain', and instead of saying 'N.N. has a pain', he said 'N.N. is behaving as the Centre [the despot] behaves when there is pain' (cf. WWK 49; PR 88f.). Of course, this would not imply that the facts of the matter were being overlooked or distorted. If N.N. behaved as the Centre behaves when there is a toothache, the dentist would treat him, etc. Equally, the *concepts* differ, so the objection to this mode of expression that other people have the same as the Centre is incorrect; for no one *has* anything (in this form of representation). But, of course, people with serious injuries and diseases behave in the same way, viz. as the Centre does when there is pain.

So this new mode of representation does not describe or misdescribe the facts 'as they really are' (§402), for a grammar can neither conflict with nor conform to the facts. It is the application of a grammar in statements that is answerable to the facts. So nothing would be gained by adopting this novel notation. But equally, the solipsist (coherently construed) was not suggesting that only he should be treated at the hospital. Rather, he was under the *illusion* that an alternative notation would describe the facts better (as if 'There is pain' would be more accurate than 'I have a pain'). Whereas all he has really noted is that the use of 'I have a pain' is very unlike that of 'He has a pain'.

1.1   (i) 'Art der Darstellung': 'mode of representation'.

(ii) 'As long as a notation were provided . . .': we would have to distinguish between being in pain and pretending to be in pain, for example. This could be done thus: 'N.N. is behaving as the Centre does when there is pain' = 'N.N. is in pain', and 'N.N. is behaving as the Centre does when it looks as if there is pain, although actually there is not' = 'N.N. is pretending to be in pain'. Other moves can be imagined for concealing pain, having pain but not showing it, etc.

(iii) 'Other people have just the same as you': this would be no objection, since the envisaged grammar would make no room for this

---

[3] To which one wants to reply 'Who's me?'

grammatical articulation. But again, analogues for sameness of pain can be envisaged in terms of relations between patterns of behaviour.

2   Vol. XI, 154 has this preceded by one of the very few remarks in which W. reflects on the fact that our language *does* provide an alternative form of expression to that of ownership. What is it, he queries, that rebels against the form of expression 'I have . . .' here? Well, there is available a different form of expression in which the question of 'mine' does not arise — indeed, is quite senseless. We would simply say 'It hurts now'. But it is remarkable, he adds, that in such a discussion we are inclined to say of our ordinary mode of expression: 'Really what this means is . . .' (as if the form of an expression were *wrong*). It is noteworthy that we do *not* ordinarily rebel against the form of an expression, but only when doing philosophy.

2.1   'neither does the solipsist *want* any practical advantage': BB 58f. explores this at length. One cannot reply to the solipsist by appeal to common sense (e.g. 'Why do you tell us this if you don't believe that we really hear you?'). Rather one must remove the temptation to attack common sense. The source of the solipsist's puzzlement is dissatisfaction *with a notation*, which presents itself in the guise of an insight into the nature of things. Three points must be borne in mind, however: (a) The new notation (e.g. that resembling the oriental despot's above) is not justified by the facts. The rationale for the solipsist's notation is not that *his* body is the 'seat of all life'. (b) By a new notation no facts are changed (cf. BB 57). One symbolism is as good as another and no one symbolism is necessary (AWL 22). (c) The solipsist does not actually go through with the shift of notation, but mixes up the new notation with the old one (AWL 23). He generates incoherence by proclaiming 'Only *my* pain is *real*' for 'my pain' belongs to the same system as 'his pain', and 'real pain' to the same system as 'pretended pain'.

SECTION 404

1   Having clarified the nature of the 'visual room', W. now turns to the 'owner'. We naturally conceive of the first-person pronoun as fulfilling a similar role to the third-person pronoun. So 'I' seems to signify the owner of the visual room, the *res cogitans*. This idea, however, rests on a confusion of form and function.

§404(a) opens with the paradoxical remark 'When I say "I am in pain", I do not point to a person, since in a certain sense I have no idea *who* is'. Despite its air of paradox, W. insists that it can be justified (cf. PI p. 195(f)). Of course, it does not mean that I do not know who I am, know that my name is N.N., etc. (although that too is possible in cases of amnesia). But does it follow from the fact that I know that I am N.N. and the fact that I have pains that I know who has pains? After all, 'I, who am N.N., know I am in pain' makes no more sense than 'I know I am in pain' (PI §246).

W. does not focus on this point here (see §408), although it partly explains the phrase '*in a certain sense* I have no idea *who* is' (my emphasis). Rather, he concentrates on 'the main point', viz. that in saying 'I am . . .' I do not point to, pick out, or identifyingly refer to a person. I do not name a person, as I do when I say 'N.N. is in pain', but others can discern who is in pain from my utterance, as indeed they can from my groans of pain. One might say that the difference between 'He is . . .' and 'I am . . .' here corresponds to the difference between pointing and raising one's hand.

§404(b) explains one aspect of the difference in role between 'I am . . .' and 'He is . . .'. To know who is in pain is to know that a certain person satisfying a certain description or specifiable by ostension fulfils the criteria for being in pain. One may specify very many criteria identifying a person, but in saying '*I* am in pain', one invokes no criteria, for one does not *identify* a particular person as he who is in pain, nor does one *point at* a particular person, as one does with 'He is in pain'.

1.1   'Personal "*identity*"'/'my saying that "I" am in pain?': the rationale for *both* scare-quotes *and* italics is not clear. It is evident that W.'s concern here is not with the link between the notion of identification and the criteria of sameness and difference of persons, but with the fact that in saying 'I am in pain' one does *not* identifyingly refer to a person. (For discussion of personal identity, see BB 61f.; AWL 60 – 3; PLP 214 – 16.)

2   Vol. XII, 155f. has this followed by a remark which throws light on the independence of 'I have a pain' from criteria of identification of a person. For 'I have a pain' is not replaceable by 'L. W. has a pain' if, for example, a radical change of bodies occurs (cf. LPE 308). The function of 'I have . . .' is altogether unlike that of 'L.W. has . . .' as this expression is used by others.

2.1   'someone else sees who is in pain from the groaning': Vol. XVI, 25 elaborates. I experience pain, but not that *I* have it. For myself, I groan with pain; for others, I say 'I am in pain'. The groan corresponds to 'pain', perhaps, but not to 'I'; rather, my groan shows another that I am in pain in as much as I groan. But when I groan with pain, it is not as if I choose *this* mouth in order to express the fact that it is *I* and not someone else who is in pain (cf. BB 68). Later (Vol. XVI, 170) W. remarks that to say 'I have a pain' is *to complain*. He who thus complains is said to *have* a pain. Hence one can't call the complaint the *statement* that so-and-so has a pain.

SECTION 405

1   Granted that the role of 'I' in 'I have a pain' is very different from that of 'N.N.' in 'N.N. has a pain', and granted that by using it I attract the hearer's *attention* to myself, then surely when one uses it, one wants to draw his attention to *a particular person*? Of course, I am a particular person, say N.N., and not someone else. And when I groan 'I am in pain' I do draw the attention of others to a particular person. But does it follow that I use 'I am in pain' because I want to draw attention to a particular person, namely N.N.? No, that may still be misleading, distorting the distinctive role of the first-person pronoun here. I need not mean *any* person when I groan 'I am in pain', any more than when I just groan. (But when I say 'He is in pain', I mean *him* ↗.) I do not *single out* a particular person from among others by any referential device (I do not choose the mouth that says 'I am in pain'); I get *others* to single out *me*. (Who is me? No matter, let them find that out, as long as they help me!) And when they single me out, they do not do so in the way in which I have, since I have not done so at all. Their identification does not rest on a proper name, definite description, or ostension that I have supplied, but on a signal I have evinced.

Note that 'I say!' similarly functions to draw the attention of others to myself, without singling me out in any particular way. Pointing serves to draw attention to a particular person, namely . . . (and here one gives an identifying description), but raising one's hand draws attention to oneself (and there is no 'namely' about it, any more than when one groans). If the teacher asks 'Who knows . . .?', and I raise my hand, *he* can supply an identifying description if he pleases.

1.1   'The answer might be': presumably because it is not *incorrect*, but potentially misleading with respect to the distinctive role of 'I'.

SECTION 406

1   The interlocutor grants that when I say 'I am in pain' I want to draw attention not to a particular person satisfying some description, but to

myself. Nevertheless, he now objects, with 'I have . . .' I surely want to distinguish between myself and other people! Clearly this is sometimes true, e.g. when the teacher asks 'Who can . . .?' or 'Who knows . . .?' But equally obviously it is not so when I merely groan with pain; rather, I just manifest my suffering. And does that not apply also when 'Oh! Oh! I've hurt myself!' is wrenched from my lips? Nevertheless, even in those cases where it might be said that I do want to distinguish between myself and others, does it follow that I want to distinguish between myself characterized by name and others similarly characterized?

2   Vol. XVI, 171 has:

'Aber Du gebrauchst doch "ich" im Gegensatz zu "er". Also, unterscheidest Du doch dadurch zwischen Personen.'

. . . Aber es ist nicht, als zeigte jetzt gleichsam derselbe Zeiger auf mich. 'Ich' and 'er' haben eben (*ganz*) verschiedene Funktionen in der Sprache.

('But you do use "I" in contrast to "he". So you do distinguish thereby between persons.'

. . . But it is not as if the same pointer, as it were, is now pointing at me. 'I' and 'he' have after all (*wholly*) different functions in language.)

Vol. XII, 158 has the first sentence of §406, followed by the explanation:

— Das heisst also: ich will nicht sagen, der Andre habe Schmerzen, *sondern ich.* — Ich will die Worte sagen, die ich sage, und nicht andere. Aber das Wort 'ich', obgleich es an derselben Stelle im Satz steht, wie 'er', funktioniert anders. Weiss ich denn, wer redet, wenn ich weiss, dass ich rede?

(— That means: I don't want to say that the other person has pain, *but that I have.* — I want to utter the words I utter and not others. But the word 'I', even though it stands in the same position in the sentence as 'He', functions differently. Do I then know who is speaking when I know that I am speaking?)

Six pages later W. reworks the material from Vol. XVI, 171:[4]

'Aber Du gebrauchst doch "ich" im Gegensatz zu "er". Also unterscheidest Du doch zwischen Personen.' Nun, ich sage in diesem Fall 'ich', und sage nicht 'er'. Und 'ich' steht allerdings an der gleichen Stelle im Satze, an der in andern Fällen 'er' steht. Aber es ist nicht, als zeigte *der* Zeiger jetzt auf *mich* (d.h. hier: auf meinen Körper), der sonst auf einen Andern zeigt. (Denn nicht darin besteht es, dass *ich* Schmerzen habe: dass sie

---

[4] For the complex dating of Vol. XII and its parts, see G. H. von Wright, 'The Wittgenstein Papers', in his *Wittgenstein* (Blackwell, Oxford, 1982), pp. 50f., and S. Hilmy, *The Later Wittgenstein* (Blackwell, Oxford and New York, 1987), ch. 1.

jetzt in *meinem* Körper sind.) Denn ich bin ja eben versucht zu sagen: vom Andern wisse ich, dass er Schmerzen habe, weil ich sein B<u>enehmen</u> // ihre Wirkung // b<u>eobachtete</u>, von mir — weil ich sie *fühle*. Aber das ist eben sinnlos, weil 'ich fühle Schmerzen' dasselbe heisst, wie 'ich habe Schmerzen'. Es scheint hier so, als hülfe mir in einem Fall der *eine* Sinn, im andern Fall der andre, den Besitzer des Schmerzes finden, wie ich etwa einen Gegenstand einmal mit den Augen suche, einmal mit den Ohren. Und man kann wohl sagen, dass mich in einem Fall der Gesichtssinn zum *Ort* der Schmerzen leitet, im andern Fall der Sinn des Schmerzgefühls; aber mein Schmerzgefühl leitet mich nicht zum *Besitzer* des Schmerzes.

Wenn jeder dieser Leute 'weiss', dass er Schmerzen hat — weiss dann jeder etwas anderes? Weiss nicht jeder dasselbe, nämlich: '*ich habe* Schmerzen'? — Anders aber, wenn es heisst: 'er hat Schmerzen' — denn 'er' bezieht sich auf einen Namen, eine Beschreibung oder (e<u>ine</u>) hinweisende Gebärde; ohne eine solche Beziehung ist der Ausdruck ohne Sinn.

'Ich' und 'er' dienen // haben eben // in unserer Sprache nicht gleichartigen Zwecken // gleichartige Funktionen //. (Vol. XII, 164f.)

('But you do use "I" in contrast to "he". So you do distinguish between persons.' Well, in this case I say 'I' and don't say 'he'. And, to be sure, 'I' stands in the same place in the sentence where, in other cases, 'he' stands. But it is not as if *the* pointer, which otherwise points at others, is now pointing at *me* (that means here: at my body). (For that *I* have pains does not consist in this: that they are now in *my* body.) For I am indeed inclined to say: I know that another has pains because I <u>observe his</u> <u>behaviour</u> // their effect //, that I have pains—because I *feel* them. But that is actually <u>senseless</u>, for 'I feel pains' means the same as 'I have pains'. It seems here as if now *one* sense, now another, assists me in finding the owner of the pain, as if, for example, I look for an object now with my eyes and now with my ears. And one can indeed say that in the one case I am led to the location of the pain by the sense of sight, in the other case by the sense of feeling (-pain);[5] but my feeling of pain does not lead me to the *owner* of the pain.

If each of these people 'knows' that he has pains — does each one know something different? Doesn't each one know the same, namely: '*I have* pains'? — But it is different in the case of 'He has pains' — for 'he' is connected with a name, a description, or an ostensive gesture: without such a connection the expression is without sense.

'I' and 'he' do not serve // have // the same purpose // function // in our language.)

Section 407

1   It is the *expression* of suffering (the *Äusserung*) that identifies the sufferer, not a self-reference or self-identification. One might imagine the heroic officer referring the stretcher-bearers to someone else scream-

---

[5] This seems a wholly mistaken assimilation of sensation to perception. I do not *find out* where my pain is by feeling it in my arm, as I find out where a pin is by feeling it in the armchair. However, this does not affect the point W. is making. W. rectifies it some pages later in Vol. XII; cf. Exg. §408, 2.

ing in pain further down the trench. He says, through clenched teeth and
with a groan, 'Someone is in pain — I don't know who.' So the
stretcher-bearers help him too, for he is clearly in pain himself.

2   It is unclear from the MS. sources (Vol. XII, 165; Vol. XVI, 174)
whether this is what W. had in mind here. Other possibilities are (a) an
amnesiac (but then the phrasing is very poor and misleading; however,
Vol. XVI, 36 may intimate some such case); (b) a different form of
representation, in which 'someone', which is obviously not a referring
expression, does service for 'I'. This is illuminating, but then 'I don't
know who' is wrong, and misplaced.

Section 408

1 The interlocutor tries one last move to preserve his picture of the
functioning of the first-person pronoun in avowals. Surely 'I' *is*
employed to distinguish between myself and others. For do I not know
something to be true of myself and not of others when I say 'I am in
pain'? I am not, after all, in danger of making a mistake through
ignorance of who is in pain. So when I am in pain I surely know *who* is in
pain (contrary to §404).

   This is to no avail. A constituent of 'I don't know whether I or
someone else is in pain' is 'I don't know whether I am in pain' (the 'or
not' is redundant), and that, as argued (cf. §246), is not a significant
proposition.

2   Vol. XII, 169 has this, preceded by the observation that 'I know that *I*
have pains because I feel them' seems like 'I know that *I* have the
"Plumpsack" because I feel it' (as opposed to seeing it). W. is referring
here to a children's game of this name. The 'Plumpsack' is a knotted
handkerchief and also the player who holds it. The children stand in a
circle, facing inwards, while the player holding the 'Plumpsack' moves
around behind them until he touches one of them with it, drops it and
runs round the circle, chased by the person he has touched, trying to
obtain the vacated place without being hit with the 'Plumpsack'.

'Du weisst doch insofern, wer den Schmerz hat, als Du weisst, dass *Du* ihn
hast' — scheint etwa zu sagen: 'Du weisst doch jedenfalls, dass der Schmerz jetzt bei
Dir ist' — so wie man sagt: 'Ich weiss jetzt, wo der Plumpsack ist, — weil nämlich *ich*
ihn habe.' Das heisst aber *doch*: 'Jetzt bin ich nicht mehr im Zweifel darüber, wer ihn
hat, — weil ich ihn nämlich habe.' Aber kann man auch sagen: 'Jetzt bin ich nicht
mehr im Zweifel darüber, wer Schmerzen hat, weil ich sie habe'? Bin ich über die
Andern jetzt weniger im Zweifel, und war ich über mich vorher im Zweifel?

('You do know who has the pain in so far as you know that *you* have it' — perhaps seems to say: 'At any rate you do know that the pain is with *you*' — as one says 'Now I know where the *Plumpsack* is — because *I* have it.' But that *actually* means: 'Now I am no longer in any doubt about who has it — because I have it.' But can one also say: 'Now I am no longer in any doubt about who has pains, because I have them'? Am I in any less doubt about the others, and was I previously in any doubt about myself?)

SECTION 409

1   This gives an analogy to illuminate the point made in §408 and especially in Vol. XII, 169 (just quoted). In the game with the electrical shocks, it would indeed be odd to say 'Now I know who is feeling the shocks, it's me' — odd, but not, in this context, unintelligible, since it just amounts to 'I am the one who is being electrified'. If I feel a shock, at any rate I know that no one else is being electrified (*ex hypothesi*). But now suppose that I can feel the shock even when someone else is electrified. In this case 'Now I know who . . .' drops out of the game, for it *draws no distinction*. Pain is akin to this latter case. (The former is more akin to the game with 'Who has the "Plumpsack"?', wherein I can see whether others have it and feel on my back if I do.) Obviously I can feel pain whether or not another is in pain (pain is unlike the 'Plumpsack'). So the fact that I have a pain tells me nothing about whether others do or do not have a pain too. And equally, that I have a pain now gives no quietus to any doubts I might have as to whether I have a pain, since doubts are senseless.

SECTION 410

1   The indexicals 'I', 'here', and 'this' are not names (although Russell notoriously thought that each individual use of 'this' was a paradigmatic case of using a pure name, and W. once seems to have thought that 'this' incorporated the general form of a name as such (cf. NB 61)). But these indexicals are connected with names, and that in *various* ways. The peculiarities of the word 'I' that have been discussed in the previous six remarks are facets of the special use of this expression (and something different would have to be said of 'here' and 'this', not to mention 'now'). One feature common to these indexicals is that although they are *not* names, nevertheless they are used to explain names (that is one of

their connections with names). If asked who N.N. is, I may, if I am N.N., answer 'I am N.N.'. I may explain what a colour-word means by pointing at a sample and saying 'This is red'. And I may, while showing visitors around Oxford, stop before the Sheldonian and say with a gesture 'Here is the Sheldonian'.

1.1   'dass die Physik charakterisiert ist': i.e. it is a defining feature (*Merkmal*) of this science — the propositions of physics are *impersonal*, *ahistorical*, and typically *context-free*. Hence indexicals are excluded, like route maps in an astronomical atlas as opposed to a road atlas.

3   James argued that despite interruptions of consciousness by sleep, 'the consciousness' remains sensibly continuous and one. What now is the common whole? The natural name for it is *myself*, *I*, or *me*.[6] Russell characterized the first-person pronoun in a preliminary way as an 'ambiguous proper name' (LK 164). 'The word "this"', he wrote, 'is always a proper name' (LK 167). Further 'there is such a relation as "attention", and . . . there is always a subject attending to the object called "this". The subject attending to "this" is called "I", and the time of the things which have to "I" the relation of presence is called the present time' (LK 168).

Section 411

1   This concludes the discussion of the words 'I' and '*my* experience' by noting the diversity of uses of '*my*'. In particular W. is concerned with the distinction between what he called the 'reflexive' and 'possessive' *my* (Vol. XVI, 174).

In the case of 'Are these books *my* books?' we have an example of property ownership. An ostensive gesture can pick out which books are mine, viz. *these* ↗. That they are mine is determined by the fact that they are in my possession, that I purchased them, or was given them. (Of course, lawyers will distinguish possession from ownership and real property from, e.g., copyright.) Ownership of books is alienable, and there may be books that belong to no one.

Having limbs is different. It is not legal institutions or social conventions that make *this* foot *my* foot. Which foot is *my* foot? Well, I can point to it and say '*That* ↗ is my foot'. But note that the ostensive gesture here, unlike that with 'These books ↗ are my books', is *reflexive*. Can there be any doubt for me? Yes, in cases of paralysis or loss of sensation.

[6] James, *Principles of Psychology*, Vol. 1, p. 238.

For *my* foot is the foot that moves when I wiggle my toes; it hurts me when I hit my toe, but I don't feel a thing when I hit yours, etc. But in cases of paralysis or anaesthesia these criteria are of no use, and we obviously fall back on the co-ordinate criterion that my foot is the foot attached to my leg. Note that 'ownership' of limbs is in principle, and of organs is (now) in practice, transferable.

Having a body is different again. 'Which is my body?' can intelligibly be asked of mirror-images (perhaps in a Hall of Mirrors at a fairground) or of photographs. In these cases one can point at the image, ask whether *that* ↗ is me, whether *that* is what I looked like as a baby. But if one says '*This* is my body' with a *reflexive* gesture, this is only an *explanation* of the use of 'my body'. Hence, too, the only *practical* application of the question 'Is this body my body?', where it involves a reflexive gesture, is in teaching a child how to use 'my body' and 'his body' (Vol. XVI, 223). For it makes no sense for me to be mistaken over which body is mine (save in the case of mirror-images or pictures). I do not own my body as I own my books; if I sell myself into slavery, it is not 'just my body' that I sell, and I am not left bodiless. 'Does my body look like that?' means the same as 'Do I look like that?' (although, of course, 'I' does *not* mean the same as 'my body').

What, finally, of 'Is this sensation my sensation?' What practical application does W. have in mind? He gives no clue, save to note that an ostensive use of the demonstrative pronoun is here excluded, as in the pseudo-ostention of directing one's attention. Possibly what he has in mind is an anaphoric reference to a description of a sensation, perhaps when one is reading a medical book and trying to identify one's own illness from the description of the symptoms.

1.1   'Under certain circumstances, however, one might touch a body': it is unclear what W. is thinking of. One possibility is a rhetorical question accompanied by tapping oneself on the chest: 'Is this body my body?' one might exclaim, 'Then I am at liberty to abuse it as I please!' Another possibility is as an exclamation of delight as one looks in the mirror after a prolonged effort to lose weight; here one touches one's body, pats one's flat stomach, etc.

2.1   (i) '*my* books . . . *my* foot . . . *my* body . . .': Vol. XII, 183 notes that 'my' can be defined as *possessive* or as *reflexive*.

      (ii) 'mine': Vol. XII, 185 remarks that 'mine' is what I *have*. If you want to find out what is mine, look to see who owns it, e.g. who bought this house, who dwells in it, etc. But what if one asks 'Look to see whether this is *my* face'? (Of course, this too has a use if I refer you to a photograph of my class at school thirty years ago.)

(iii) 'Does my body look like that?': Vol. XVI, 242 notes that this is equivalent to 'Do I look like that?' Further, in saying 'This is my body' and 'This is me' ('Das bin ich'), one makes the same indicative gesture, but of course 'me' ('ich') does not mean the same as 'my body'. One must beware, however, of the idea that the two expressions 'I' and 'my body' signify different things, for that idea tempts us to give our form of speech the primitive interpretation that 'I' dwell in my body.

———————

CHAPTER 5

Consciousness

(§§412–27)

INTRODUCTION

Part A of this 'chapter' runs from §412 to §421. It consists of a brief discussion of a limited range of questions about the nature of consciousness. W. does not attempt here to survey the grammar of this expression, but only to relate it to the antecedent preoccupations of the book. Some confusions and bogus mysteries surrounding the concept of consciousness exemplify philosophical diseases hitherto diagnosed, and these can be dispelled by therapies that have already been explained.

§412 opens the discussion by noting the feeling of an unbridgeable gulf between consciousness and brain-processes. The illusion of a mystery, of a gulf between wholly disparate, unconnectable phenomena, is a projection of a categorial distinction, of a difference in the grammatical character of certain expressions. The sense of mystery afflicts us only in philosophical reflection, when language is idling.

§413 draws attention to one source of our confusion, viz. the idea that we can examine the nature of consciousness by introspection. But the attempt to do so, like James's attempt to investigate the 'central nucleus of the Self' by introspection, reveals only the state of the philosopher's attention when, in such circumstances, he thinks of consciousness and tries to analyse the meaning of the word. §414 gives an analogy for the vacuousness of seeking to uncover the nature of consciousness thus, and §415 is a general methodological remark.

§§416–21 focus on a pair of suppositions implicit in the illusion of a mysterious gulf between brain-processes and consciousness. When we thus project a category distinction in grammar onto reality, we think that consciousness is an object of experience, that we are witnesses in our own case to the fact that we are conscious. Hence we imagine that the proposition 'I am conscious' is used to record an item of indubitable Cartesian knowledge. But that is not the role of this sentence (§416). One does not, as the Cartesian supposes, observe or perceive one's own consciousness, and the experience which occasions one's saying 'I am conscious' is not an experience of being conscious (§417). The idea that we are witnesses to our own consciousness conceives of our consciousness as a fact of experience, something we witness in our own case and report for the benefit of others. But this leads to a peculiar incoherence (§418). For consciousness is then conceived to be a curious, perhaps indescribable, experience that contingently accompanies human activities, but not those of trees. If so, it would have to be possible to describe the lives of human beings (including myself) who lacked this peculiar experience of consciousness. But this makes no sense.

That human beings are conscious (or unconscious), whereas trees and stones are not, is a grammatical remark, not an empirical observation. This point is ironically highlighted in §419. §420 explores the supposition that other human beings, though behaving as normal, nevertheless lack consciousness. The supposition is meaningless, although it may produce an uncanny feeling as when one views something (the crosspieces of a window) as a limiting case of another (a swastika). §421 concludes this part of the discussion by endeavouring to dispel the feeling of paradox that may beset us when philosophizing about states of consciousness.

The structure of Part A:

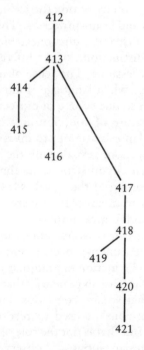

§§422–7 explore the status of pictures that are embodied in our forms of representation. We have a picture of the soul (as an ethereal being within the body), of blindness (as a darkness in the head) or of a benzene molecule (as a hexagonal ring). In all these cases the picture is prominent in the expressions we use. It is important not to dispute the correctness or validity of these pictures (§§422–4), but equally important not to be misled by the pictures into thinking that they represent the facts as if they were proto-theories. What must be investigated is the *application* of these pictures, the uses of these expressions in human life. For whereas pictures, literal or verbal, are typically surveyable at a glance, have an immediately obvious application, and hence fulfil a useful role in guiding us in the application of an expression, in the philosophically bewildering cases this is not so. In the domain of the mental, for example, pictures force themselves upon us, for they are built into our forms of representation; but their application is unclear and difficult to survey, and they exacerbate our conceptual confusions when philosophizing (§425). Indeed, the picture associated with mental concepts (like those associated with certain concepts in set-theory) suggests an ideal use for a god, which we cannot achieve (§426). But this is an illusion. When we say that we would like to know what is going on in someone's head, this typically means that we would like to know what he is thinking; and the way to find out what he is thinking, even for a god, is not 'seeing into his consciousness' (§427).

The structure of Part B is linear.

Correlations

PI§	PPI(I)§	MS. 129	MS. 124	MS. 165	Vol. XII	Others
412	294	81–3	263–6			
413	295	84–5	266			
414					221	Vol. XVI, 88
415						MS. 157(b), 80; Vol. XV, 1
416	296	84	275			MS. 179, 48–9
417	297	85	275–6			MS. 179, 50–1
418	298	86	277			MS. 179, 53
419		126	238			
420	299	86	277–8			MS. 179, 53–4[1]
421	300[2]	87	285			MS. 165, 158–9
422					282	
423					324	
424					325	
425					159	
426					162	Vol. XVI, 29f.
427					340	

[1] PI §420(a) only.
[2] This is the final remark of PPI(I).

The world of consciousness
1. The world as consciousness   2. The gulf between consciousness and body   3. The certainty of consciousness

EXEGESIS §§412-27

SECTION 412

1   The idea that there is an unbridgeable gulf between something as *material* as a brain-process and something as immaterial, *as diaphanous*, as consciousness comes naturally to the mind of a philosopher or a psychologist, or indeed of anyone caught in the trammels of the abstract noun 'consciousness'. Brain-processes can be observed in laboratories, monitored by inserting electrodes in the brain, traced through complex neural networks in the cerebral cortex. How can these result in something so categorially different as *consciousness*? At what point in the innumerable electro-chemical interactions in the brain does consciousness arise? Indeed, how could something like consciousness arise from the firing of nerve-cells? The questions induce vertigo.

W. begins with the phenomenology of this particular bafflement. First, he draws our attention to the fact that this bemusement does not arise in the ordinary stream of life. Secondly, he notes that this sense of vertigo is characteristic of logical legerdemain. We have a similar feeling when we are told that one infinite set is *larger* than another, that there are *more* reals than rationals. Thirdly, what produces this feeling in the present case is the illusion of 'turning my attention on to my consciousness'. It is noteworthy that this phrase has *no* use in ordinary life. But when reflecting on the nature of consciousness, instead of examining the way the words 'consciousness' and 'conscious' are *used*, we think to investigate the phenomenon by, as it were, watching ourselves while we are conscious (cf. PI §316). And since we are attempting to isolate 'consciousness itself', not consciousness *of* what we see, hear, or feel, we are prone to 'concentrate' on vacant staring or gazing, which seems to give us the pure consciousness uncontaminated by particular objects of which we might be conscious. It is not surprising, then, that the phenomenon should appear singularly elusive.

§412(b) is a reminder for the particular purpose at hand (PI §127), bringing words back from their metaphysical to their everyday use (PI §116). For one might indeed say 'This is produced by a brain-process' in a neuropsychological experiment in which electrodes are being inserted in one's brain. 'This *what*?' — 'This flashing of lights that I am now experiencing at the periphery of my visual field.'

1.1   'Was ich so nannte . . .': the translation has omitted the parenthesis
'(for these words are after all not used in ordinary life)', 'these words'
being 'turning my attention on to my own consciousness'.

2.1   (i) 'an unbridgeable gulf between consciousness and brain-process':
MS. 124, 263 remarks that the strongest expression of this idea is the
thought that both are different aspects of the same thing. This is
exemplified by the claim, remarked on elsewhere (MS. 165, 145), that
states of consciousness are neural processes 'seen from the inside' (cf.
Exg. §270, 2). James quotes C. Mercier, *The Nervous System and the Mind*
(1888), p. 9.:

> Having thoroughly recognized the fathomless abyss that separates mind from matter,
> and having so blended the very notion into his very nature . . . the student of
> psychology has next to appreciate the association between these two orders of
> phenomena. . . . They are associated in a manner so intimate that some of the
> greatest thinkers consider them different aspects of the same process.[1]

   (ii) '(The same giddiness attacks us)': MS. 129, 81 remarks instead that
this feeling, as in set-theory, is a sign of confusion, not of the *difficulty* of
the object.
   (iii) 'which I uttered as a paradox': Vol. XII, 325 remarks on Pascal's
characterization of man as a weak, thinking reed. If one said that man
was a talking reed, the remark would resonate quite differently. But
'thinking' here should mean *being conscious*. The tone suggests the
paradox that a piece of matter should be conscious. And yet, of course,
there is no paradox here at all. As W. observes elsewhere (TS. 229, §735),
'Only when we disregard its use is a proposition paradoxical.'

3   James wrote:

> Mental and physical events, are on all hands, admitted to present the strongest
> contrast in the entire field of being. The chasm which yawns between them is less
> easily bridged over by the mind than any interval we know. Why, then, not call it an
> absolute chasm, and say not only that the two worlds are different, but that they are
> independent?[2]

SECTION 413

1   The attempt to discover the nature of consciousness by introspection,
by 'turning my attention on to my own consciousness', is quite futile.

[1] James, *Principles of Psychology*, Vol. I, pp. 135f.
[2] Ibid., p. 134.

For the question as to the nature of consciousness, like the question as to the nature of imagination (PI §370), is to be answered by examining the use of a word. For we are not analysing a phenomenon, but a concept (PI §383). W. has already shown (PI §§316ff.) that observing what goes on in one's own mind while one is thinking will not clarify what thinking is, but only what goes on while one is thinking. Here the introspectionist commits an even more grievous error. For while one can attend to what goes on in one's own mind when one is thinking, there really is nothing to attend to when one purports to 'turn one's attention on to one's own consciousness'. Here one has a case of introspection akin to James's endeavour to discern the character of 'the self'. What he discovered was not a peculiar inner object which is 'the self' or 'the Self of Selves', but rather the state of his own attention when he says 'self' to himself. In both cases one is searching for a pseudo-object.

1.1   (i) 'William James': James's announced goal was to settle for himself 'how this central nucleus of the self may *feel*'.[3] He concluded:

> the '*Self of Selves*', *when carefully examined, is found to consist mainly of the collection of these peculiar motions in the head or between the head and throat.* I do not for a moment say that this is *all* it consists of, for I fully realize how desperately hard is introspection in this field. But I feel quite sure that these cephalic motions are the portions of my innermost activity of which I am *most distinctly aware*.[4]

(ii) 'so far as it means': the qualification is necessary, of course, because the truncated reflexive pronoun is itself the source of conceptual illusions concerning the nature of a person or human being.

(iii) '(And a good deal could be learned from this)': e.g. about the phenomenology of philosophical illusion (cf. PI §§274–7).

Section 414

1   An analogy for such cases of introspection: the loom is one's mind; going through the motion of weaving is attending to it; and the weaving of a piece of cloth is clarifying the nature of consciousness or 'the self'. The emptiness of the loom corresponds to the absence of any inner object of awareness called 'consciousness' or 'the self'.

---

[3] Ibid., p. 298.
[4] Ibid., p. 301.

SECTION 415

1   A methodological remark (associated with PI p.56n.). It is not obvious why W. located it here. Its MS. context is not this (see also RFM 92).

What are the 'remarks on the natural history of human beings' which we do not notice because they are omnipresent? Presumably such elemental facts as that we cry out in pain when we stub our toes, flinch when another person near us hurts himself, that a mother nurses a child who cries in pain and does not think that maybe the child is pretending; and more generally that our own attitude towards others (whom we recognize as human beings) is an attitude towards a person, and that this attitude does not rest on an inference from observations of their behaviour (cf. PI p.178). And why are these (and many other) remarks pertinent to philosophy? Because in countless ways the facts to which they draw attention condition our language-games.

Some commentators have seen in this remark (and in its consequences in W.'s philosophy) an affinity with Humean naturalism. But this can be misleading. Hume invoked general facts of nature to disarm sceptical qualms of any practical consequences. In his view the voice of Reason deprives us of any *grounds* for repudiating scepticism about the 'existence of the external world', the 'unity of the self', etc., but Nature comes to our aid:

> If belief, therefore, were a simple act of thought without any peculiar manner of conception, or the addition of a force and vivacity, it must infallibly destroy itself and in every case terminate in a total suspense of judgement. But as experience will sufficiently convince anyone who thinks it worthwhile to try, that though he can find no error in the foregoing arguments, yet he continues to believe and think and reason as usual, he may safely conclude that his reasoning and belief is some sensation or peculiar manner of conception which 'tis impossible for mere ideas and reflections to destroy.[5]

All rational argument speaks in favour of sceptical conclusions. They not only *make sense*, but are supported by justifying reasons. Mercifully, however, Nature has not left the matter to Reason, but 'has doubtless esteem'd it an affair of too great importance to be trusted to our uncertain reasonings and speculations'.[6]

But this is far removed from W.'s strategy and argument. He invokes facts of natural history to remind us of the context in which our language-games are played; he draws our attention to the backdrop of

[5] Hume, *Treatise of Human Nature*, Bk. I, Pt. iv, Sect. 1.
[6] Ibid., Bk. I, Pt. iv, Sect. 2.

regularities of human behaviour which give point to the grammatical structures we employ. These sceptical doubts which Hume conceived of as well supported are vacuous, not because we cannot bring ourselves to believe them to be justified, but because they are *senseless*. What look like good reasons supporting such doubts involve subtle violations of the bounds of sense, and they are repudiated neither because we cannot, as a matter of fact, believe them, nor because they are false, but because they make no sense.

Hume and W. concur in the idea that there is a dramatic gulf between philosophical theory and human, natural practice. Hume, however, holds that gulf to be harmless because of our inability to give credence to philosophical theory even though it is true. W., on the other hand, argues that the philosophical theory is nonsense, that the doubts can be stated only by violating the rules of grammar that give the constituent expressions their meaning. They are *idle* doubts, not because of a natural inability to hold them to be true, but rather because they are mere houses of cards, illusions generated by grammatical confusion.

SECTION 416

1   In philosophical reflection it can readily seem as if the fact that human beings are conscious is the one indubitable fact before which scepticism must come to a halt. We surely agree that we enjoy perceptual experiences, and in as much as we are in a position to do so, are we not witnesses to our own consciousness? But, W. objects, we misconstrue here the possible role of 'I am conscious'. Saying this to myself is vacuous; saying it to another, if it is conceived as registering a piece of Cartesian knowledge (something known to myself alone by the mere 'experience' of being conscious), would not be understood. For so conceived, 'consciousness' would have to signify *this*, which I have. And that, as has been shown, is not intelligible. But, of course, propositions such as 'I see', 'I hear', 'I am conscious' do have their uses, only not as reports of Cartesian *indubitabilia*.[7]

1.1   'sie haben *Bewusstsein*', 'Ich habe Bewusstsein': 'they are *conscious*', 'I am conscious' — and so too in §§418, 419.

2   In MS. 179, 48 and MS. 124, 275, which is derived from it, this passage is preceded by a draft of PI §316. This makes it clear that the

---

[7] For the Cartesian, of course, it is not 'I see' or 'I hear' that registers an item of indubitable knowledge, but 'I seem to see' or 'I seem to hear'. 'I am conscious', however, is viewed by the Cartesian as equivalent to 'I think' as he conceives of thinking.

interlocutor here imagines that to get clear about the nature of consciousness we must observe ourselves while we are conscious, and that what
we thus observe will be what the word 'conscious' means.

Z §§401f. elaborates the thought in a more explicitly Cartesian
direction (see 'The world of consciousness', §3).

SECTION 417

1   The interlocutor, who thinks that we are witnesses to the fact that we
are conscious, conceives of consciousness as an object of introspective
observation in which one *perceives* one's consciousness. But, W. responds, there is no room for *observation* here. (Could I *fail* to discern my
consciousness? Could I *make a mistake* in my observation? Could I keep a
record of my consciousness? Well, I might keep a diary when in hospital,
and write 'Today I recovered consciousness after being in a coma for a
week'. But is that a record of *an observation*?)

Similarly, there is no question of *perception* here. For I do not see, hear,
etc. my consciousness. One is tempted to say that 'perceive' here
signifies the fact that I am attending to (or even, am aware of) my
consciousness. W. does not repeat the objection, canvassed in §412, that
'attending to my consciousness' is a form of words with no ordinary use
at all. Instead he raises a fresh one, viz. that the interlocutor wanted to
report an indubitable fact, viz. that he is conscious, but now finds himself
reporting a quite different one, viz. that he is in a state of attending to
something. Is this meant to be equally fundamental and indubitable? And
is it independent of being conscious?

It is clear enough why the interlocutor wishes to insist on such inner
perception or attention. For he thinks of consciousness as an *experience*,
hence something to which one may attend. But that is a mistake. To
have *any* experience, one must be conscious; i.e. if X is unconscious (or
asleep), we do not say 'X is having such-and-such an experience'. (Note
that dreaming is not an experience!) It is not *an experience* of being
conscious that occasions my saying 'I am conscious again', but rather the
experience of noticing someone tiptoeing around my bedroom in the
evident belief that I am asleep.

2.1   (i) 'but that my attention is disposed in such-and-such a way': MS.
179, 51 has 'sondern, dass ich mich in einem bestimmten seelischen
Zustand befinde, wie wenn ich sage "Ich bin aufgeregt"' ('but that I find
myself in a certain mental state, as when I say "I am excited"').

(ii) '*What* experience?': MS. 179, 51 and MS, 124, 276 move in a
slightly different direction. This question must be answered, W. emphasizes, and in a way that will be intelligible to others (i.e. not by

reference to a mythical inner object known only to myself). For I learnt the language from others, and what they cannot understand, I cannot either.

SECTION 418

1   The Cartesian interlocutor takes the fact that he is conscious to be a fact of experience. Of course, it is an empirical fact that he is now conscious, yet might have been unconscious if the anaesthetic had not worn off. But that is not what he means. His conception is that a particular inner experience occasions (§417) and makes true his statement 'I am conscious', and further, that the inner experience is what 'consciousness' means. As he sees things, human beings are their own witnesses that they are conscious; this is a fact that they experience, each for himself, and can then convey to others. This, W. implies, is to confuse a grammatical remark with an empirical observation. We say of human beings and of what behaves like human beings that they are conscious or unconscious (PI §281), but we apply neither concept to trees and stones. This is a rule of grammar, which determines what it makes sense to say, not an empirical observation.

The interlocutor, who conceives of the proposition that human beings are conscious creatures as an empirical fact, must be able to give an account of what it would be like if they were not. Of course, he does not mean that all human beings might fall asleep (as in *Sleeping Beauty*). So his supposition that other human beings might lack consciousness does not mean that they would, in the ordinary sense of the term, be *unconscious*. No — they would *behave* just as they normally do; for, after all, behaviour is not consciousness! But they would 'really' be automatons — a point explored in §420. Hence the supposition that others might lack consciousness would make no *perceptible* difference. But what about oneself? Here one is forced to say that one would not be conscious — there would be, as it were, no light in one's soul. One would not have all *this*, which is now before one's mind's eye! And yet one's behaviour and speech would not differ one jot! One imagines that one would be, as it were, an empty shell, but one that was nevertheless exactly like a full one, except from the inside. But here one is trying to imagine a coin with only one side!

2   Ms. 179, 53 has this, preceded by a further pair of remarks that follow the draft of PI §417. The interlocutor exclaims 'But I am conscious!', and W. replies ironically: 'How curious that I know that this is called "consciousness".' The obvious implication is that on the interlocutor's conception 'consciousness' is the name of a 'private experience'.

3   Russell articulates (without fully subscribing to) the empiricist confusion upon which W.'s remark is targeted:

> If there is one thing that may be said in the popular estimation to characterize mind, that one thing is 'consciousness'. We say that we are 'conscious' of what we see and hear, of what we remember, and of our own thoughts and feelings. Most of us believe that tables and chairs are not 'conscious'. We think that when we sit in a chair, we are aware of sitting in it, but it is not aware of being sat in. It cannot for a moment be doubted that we are right in believing that there is *some* difference between us and the chair in this respect: so much may be taken as fact, and as datum for our inquiry. (AM 11).

Section 419

1   An ironic remark apropos §418. There are circumstances in which it is correct to say that a certain tribe has a chief, but are there any circumstances in which one might add 'and the chief is conscious'? Is there any such thing as fulfilling this social role and *not* being conscious? Clearly 'The chief must surely be conscious' is not an empirical observation resting on the fact that one has never come across chiefs who run the affairs of a tribe but who lack consciousness.

2   Z §394 pursues the same point more explicitly:

> What would is mean for me to be wrong about his having a mind, being conscious? And what would it mean for me to be wrong about *myself* and not have any? What would it mean to say 'I am not conscious'? — But don't I know that there is consciousness in me? — Do I know it then, and yet the statement that it is so has no purpose?
>
> And how remarkable that one can learn to make oneself understood to others in these matters!

These remarks exemplify one aspect of the dependence of sense upon the context of use. 'I am conscious' does have a use — in very special circumstances. But it has none to register an item of indubitable Cartesian knowledge.

Section 420

1   This explores the thought introduced in §418, viz. what it would be like if (other) human beings lacked consciousness, where being conscious is conceived as an 'inner experience'. Can't one imagine it? Here we have a case of a picture obtruding itself upon us and yet being of no use at all (PI §397). We can entertain the idea when alone; we then imagine people

as automatons, hence going about their business with a vacant stare as in a trance. Whether this picture can be filled in intelligibly is debatable; but the idea that they are automatons is doing *some* work in so far as they differ from normal human beings in their gaze. (Nothing, as it were, lies behind their eyes.) But, in contrast with the case of imagining that the people one sees in the street are in frightful pain but artfully concealing it (PI §391), to imagine that those very people one sees behaving normally are mere automatons runs up against the limits of sense (see 'Behaviour and behaviourism', §4). For after all, neither an automaton nor a human being can pretend to be conscious (Z §395). At most, one can induce in oneself a strange feeling of alienation in this case.

1.1   'seeing one figure as a limiting case . . . .': and by so doing we can alter the impression it makes on us (cf. MS. 179, 55).

2   Vol. XII, 234 (= Z §251) explores a similar line of thought. One is inclined to think that the supposition that this person, who behaves quite normally, is nevertheless blind makes sense. 'After all', one wants to say, 'I picture it.' But the picture here does no work; it is all there is to the bogus assumption.

   PI p. 178 examines a related thought. It is just as misguided to suppose that we *believe* that others are *not* automatons (or indeed that we are *certain* that they are not).

Section 421

1   This identifies one source of our confusions when we drift into the Cartesian seas of doubt. We think of the physical as material, extended in space, public, and tangible. The mental seems to belong to a different domain, a different 'order of being'. It is private, accessible directly only to its owner, intangible, even ethereal; it is the 'inner', hidden from the sight of others, correlated only causally with the physical behaviour of bodies. When in the grip of this picture, innumerable mundane sentences suddenly seem paradoxical, mixing up two different ontological realms in a way that appears to distort the facts of the matter. We say 'He suffered great torments and tossed about restlessly', but can that which suffers torments be the same as the body which tosses about? Isn't it the mind or soul that suffers torments and the body that tosses about? Is there not an unbridgeable gulf between states of consciousness and physical states? Would a better language not *analyse* such sentences on this model: instead of saying 'He embraced her joyfully', should we not say that his body embraced her and his soul was joyful?

   W. tries to defuse the bogus paradox by drawing our attention to an analogous case of 'mixing the tangible and the intangible' which does not induce in us any sense of paradox. *The number three* and *stability* are not tangible either; but no one feels any logical impropriety in the sentence 'These three struts give the building stability'. Once we notice this, our intellectual unease may be lessened. Then we may be able to see the sources of our confusion, which are manifold.

W. does not here identify them, but merely gives us a methodological reminder, steering us away from the Augustinian picture (which is one root of our troubles). Instead of thinking of the sentence as a description (and of its constituents as names of entities, tangible or intangible), we should conceive of the sentence as an instrument for certain purposes and of its sense as its employment. By implication, we should not conceive of 'He suffered great torments . . .' as naming three objects (viz. a mind, suffering, and torment) which must be 'ontologically homogeneous', and he 'He tossed about restlessly' as naming another three objects which by, contrast, must 'belong to a different domain'. Rather, we should think of the circumstances in which it is appropriate to use such a sentence, e.g. a nurse's report to a doctor on how a patient fared in the course of the night, and of the purposes it serves, its possible roles in a language-game.

2   This was the concluding remark of the intermediate version of PI, completed in late 1944 or early 1945. If W. thought of this, for a short while, as a finished work, then §421 must presumably be viewed as concluding the series of remarks on consciousness, and the final sentence as epitomizing a methodological *leitmotif* of the book.

2.1   'But does it worry you if I say . . .?': the method exemplified here is analogous to that described in PG 212: 'we must describe a language-game related to our own. . . . Such a contrast destroys grammatical prejudices and makes it possible for us to see the use of a word as it really is . . . .'

Section 422

1   This and the following five remarks explore the fact that we have, laid up in the forms of our languages and in the metaphors and similes we use as a matter of course, a *picture* of the mental and of its relation to the physical, of the soul and of its relation to the body. It is one of the great strengths of W.'s approach that he does not dismiss these pictures as false proto-theories. Philosophical theories grow out of these pictures, but only through their misinterpretation. The pictures themselves are, as it were, emblematic illustrations of concepts, iconographic representations of grammatical structures (cf. PI §295). And just as we should look at the

sentence as an instrument and at its sense as its employment, so too we should view these word-pictures as illustrations and learn their point by examining their applications.

To believe that men have souls or minds is not *per se* to believe in a Cartesian dualist metaphysics. Rather it is to cleave to a certain form of representation of human experience, human relations, and human values. This readily seems mysterious, even mystery-mongering. Hence W. appositely invokes a scientific picture to place beside it. For when we are taught about carbon rings, we do not typically feel metaphysical qualms; nor do we think that we are being hoodwinked. But this involves a picture too, and its sense is difficult to discern. In both cases we need to examine the application of the picture.

1.1   (i) 'What am I believing in when I believe that men have souls?': not, to be sure, that somewhere within the body there is an ethereal object called 'the soul'. PI p.178 discusses the religious doctrine that the soul continues to exist after the disintegration of the body:

> Now do I understand this teaching? — Of course I understand it — I can imagine plenty of things in connection with it. And haven't pictures of these things been painted? And why should such a picture be only an imperfect rendering of the spoken doctrine? Why should it not do the *same* service as the words? And it is the service which is the point.

Here the picture, e.g. of the soul (represented by a homunculus) leaving the body, is on the same level as the words. In such cases, understanding consists in noting the role which words and picture play in a form of life.

(ii) 'this substance contains two carbon rings': PI p.184 remarks of the proposition 'The carbon atoms in benzene seem to lie at the corners of a hexagon' that 'this is not something that seems to be so; it is a picture'. To unpack this picture, to survey its application, involves extensive explanations of chemical theory.

2   Something similar can be said of certain literal pictures, e.g. Michelangelo's depiction of God creating Adam in the Sistine Chapel (LA 63). A picture of a plant in a botanical handbook is a picture by similarity. Its role is to enable us to identify the plant; it tells us what the plant looks like. This sort of picture therefore has a familiar, straightforward application and a readily understood technique of comparison. Not so the depiction of God: it does not purport to tell us what God *looked like* when he created Adam, and it would be absurd here to say 'Of course, I can't show you the real thing, only the picture' (as one might say of a historical painting). The role of such a picture is of a totally different kind, and to describe its application is a far more difficult and subtle

matter than in the case of the picture of a plant; and so too with our word-pictures of the soul.

Section 423

1   It is unclear what the expression 'these things' refers to here. Presumably W. is alluding to such psychological turns of phrase as 'A thought flashed through his head', 'He said in his heart . . .', 'In my mind I saw . . .'. In such cases we use expressions into which a certain picture (not a theory) is built. It is not in dispute that these things happen, that thoughts flash through people's minds, that they see things before their mind's eye. These are the pictures we use, and their validity is not in question. But when doing philosophy, it is important that the applications of these pictures be clarified, lest we be misled by the pictures into constructing philosophical theories or, worse, into criticizing our ordinary ways of expressing ourselves as embodying false theories.

2   Vol. XII, 324 has this in a different context. W. discusses the remark 'It is fate'. What information does one convey to another by saying this? None at all, and yet it is not empty chatter. It gives a picture, a comparison; and it would be wrong to suppose that it is replaceable by a literal interpretation. For only by means of *that* simile and no other can one articulate, give expression to, one's response or attitude. PI §423 follows this remark, and is followed by.

Denk wir drückten die Absicht eines Menschen (<u>immer</u>) so aus, indem wir sagen: 'Er sagte gleichsam zu sich selbst: Ich will . . .' Das ist das Bild. Und nun will ich wissen: wie verwendet man den Ausdruck 'etwas gleichsam zu sich selbst sagen'. Denn es heisst nicht: etwas zu sich selbst sagen.

(Imagine that we (<u>always</u>) expressed a person's intention by saying: 'He as it were said to himself: I want . . .' This is the picture. And now I want to know how one applies the expression: 'As it were saying something to oneself'. For it does not mean: saying something to oneself.)

This is then followed by a draft of PI §424.

Section 424

1   This repeats the point of §423 and adds an illustrative example. There is nothing wrong with the picture of blindness as darkness in the soul or in the head of the blind man. One can represent blindness thus: ,

as opposed to thus: ; but this pictures does not dictate its own application, any more than does the explanation 'He is blind who cannot see'. The question is, what are the criteria for saying of a person that he is blind? And similarly, when do we say of a person that *this* is how it is in his head (cf. Vol. XII, 232)?

2   RFM 142 observes: 'You cannot survey the justification of an expression unless you survey its employment; which you cannot do by looking at some facet of its employment, say a picture attaching to it.'

Section 425

1   Typically pictures, both literal and verbal, can illuminate the use of an expression in as much as we find the application of the picture obvious and unproblematic. An example is given in §425(b): the picture does not *explain*, but its application is perspicuous, surveyable at a glance. (And this, indeed, is characteristic of illustrative diagrams in mechanics or instruction manuals.) So the picture can illustrate the application of an expression.

However, in the case of the pictures we have of the mental, things are quite different. The pictures are readily available; indeed, they force themselves upon us. We think of sensations as especially private property, something which we *have* and which we are intimately *acquainted* with (like a beetle in a box that no one else can see). We conceive of imagining as akin to sitting in on a private viewing, that we 'see' our own mental images, which our neighbour cannot see (cf. PI §398). We are captivated by the idea that thinking is a mental activity, just like a physical activity, only mental! In all these cases the picture not only does not help us out of the difficulties we have *when philosophizing*; it exacerbates our difficulties and is often one of their causes. For *these* pictures, typically derived from the physical domain, are *not* applied in the way which we naturally anticipate; i.e. they are not applied as the corresponding pictures of physical objects, processes, and activities are.

Section 426

1   The picture we have, e.g., of pain, the picture that forces itself upon us at every turn because it is built into our form of representation, seems utterly perspicuous. I have a pain; you have a pain; i.e. you have exactly the same as I have when I have a pain. What could be clearer? But when we compare the actual use of 'He has a pain' with that suggested by the picture of *having an object*, it seems muddied, a kind of second best. If

only, as Hume put it, 'we could see clearly into the breast of another, and observe that succession of perceptions, which constitutes his mind'![8]

Here, in the philosophy of psychology, we have a predicament analogous to something we find in set-theory, viz. a form of expression which seems to be designed for a god who can see, for example, the whole of each of the infinite series of natural numbers, rationals, reals, etc. and see that the set of reals is greater than the set of natural numbers. Hence too, it seems that, while we cannot 'see clearly into the breast of another' but must make do with an indirect route, a superior being would be able to 'see into human consciousness'.

We cannot do what this superior being can, for we lack his cognitive powers. So when *we* use these expressions, our technique of application, relative to that suggested by the picture embodied in their *form*, is a detour, an indirect route. The form of our expressions suggests a straight highway (viz. peering into the mind of another person, correlating the members of one infinite set with another, just as we correlate cups and saucers, etc). But that highway is closed off to us.

Of course, there *is* no such highway, only the picture of one. And it is permanently closed to us only in the sense in which we cannot walk down the painted highway in a picture. For the bounds of sense do not prevent us from venturing into territory in which someone *can* walk; they fence us off only from the void of nonsense.

2   Vol. XII, 162 has this in the context of a discussion of 'ownership' of experience and of the transition from 'I have . . .' to 'He has . . .'. The difficulties we encounter here stem from the fact that we have a picture which makes us expect an application of our expression which is quite different from its actual one.

2.1   'designed for a god': cf. PI §352, where it is said that God can *see* whether there are four consecutive sevens in the expansion of π, whereas we cannot. In PG 484, W. pin-points the incoherence: if we say that we cannot, but that a 'higher intellect' can, grasp an irregular infinite decimal, then we must describe the *grammar* of the expression 'higher intellect'. We must specify what it can grasp (what can intelligibly be specified as being so grasped) and what it cannot; and further, in what circumstances it is correct to say 'It has grasped . . .'. But then it will emerge that describing grasping here *is* itself grasping. And in the only sense in which a higher intellect can grasp, so too can we!

[8] Hume, *Treatise of Human Nature*, Bk. I, Pt. iv, Sect. 6.

SECTION 427

1   This concluding remark makes clear the sense in which the picture associated with thinking is in order, but does not have a straightforward application. When we wonder what is going on in someone's head, we are expressing not our ignorance of neurophysiology, but our ignorance of what someone is thinking. The picture of an inner process in the cranium is, of course, misleading when doing philosophy; for the use of the phrase 'He is thinking of . . .' is not to describe any such process. But in ordinary discourse this very picture *is* applied unproblematically, only not in the way in which we apply 'I wonder what is going on in his stomach'. Moreover, even if a god could 'peer into' the consciousness of another, he could not see there, for example, what the person was intending (cf. PI p. 217) or indeed thinking, but only what goes on when someone intends to do such-and-such or is thinking of so-and-so.

2.1   'going on in his head': LW §978 remarks that one does not *have* to see the external as a façade behind which mental powers are at work. And when someone talks about himself quite sincerely, one is not tempted by that picture.

> Criteria
>   1. Symptoms and hypotheses 2. Symptoms and criteria
>   3. Further problems about criteria 4. Evidence, knowledge, and certainty

INDEX

(Since the exegetical part of this book corresponds exactly to PI, this index should be used in conjunction with the original text and its index.)

Index
313

subject (owner) of 48, 51f., 94, 98, 99,
  100, 124–5, 126
Pascal, B. 296
patience 34
Pavlova, Anna 105
Pepys, S. 18n.
perception 203f., 205f.
person (see also Human Beings) 282, 283–5
philosophical confusion 53, 137–9
philosophical illusion 85–7, 297
philosophical temptation 54
philosophical therapy/treatment 55–7
philosophy 54–7, 85f., 184f.
  and psychoanalysis 56f.
pi (π), expansion of 198–200, 308
picture 88f., 108, 116f., 119–21, 121–3,
  230–32, 260
Platonism 253f.
Plumpsack example 286f.
pointing 'privately' 62
pretence 35, 36–40, 41
privacy 34f., 244
  epistemic 30–5
  of ownership 46–52
private language 17, 18, 19, 21, 22, 57f.,
  61f., 63, 66, 67, 71, 74f., 76, 82
  machine analogy for 64
private object 73, 81f., 112, 113, 114, 117,
  141, 240f.
private ostensive definition (see also
  Ostensive Definition) 29, 62, 63, 65,
  67, 73, 77, 249
private picture 113, 114, 116
private samples (see also Samples), 28,
  62–7, 69f., 74, 82, 85, 101f., 116f.,
  119
process 133–7, 172f., 183f., 263f.
  inner/mental 107, 130–2, 134–7, 183f.
proposition 109f., 157f., 198, 201f.
  a priori 43, 44, 45
  'genuine' 201
  grammatical (grammatical statement/
    remark) 33f., 34f., 42–6, 98f., 109,
    114f., 133, 236–9, 301
  picture theory of the 108
psycho-analysis 56f., 275

Quirk, R. 183n.

rage 28
Ramsey, F. P. 137
realism 122
reading to oneself 241f.
reason 103
recognition 66, 69f., 78, 80, 245–7, 248,
  250, 251, 259
referring (expression) 25–7, 85, 281f., 283
Reid, T. 84
remembering (see Memory)

report 156f., 242
right, being/seeming 63f., 74, 82f.
rule, 18, 19, 62, 67, 110, 249
Russell, B. 131, 137, 198, 235n., 247, 279,
  287, 288, 302
Ryle, G. 137, 174

samples (see also Private Samples) 28, 63,
  67, 74, 82, 101f., 110, 248f., 259
Saussure, F. de 160, 221
scepticism 66, 110, 298f.
Schlick, M. 86f.
Schopenhauer, A. 261n. 273, 277, 279
secondary uses of words 90, 92f., 225
self 85f., 297
sensation-names/words 17, 23, 24, 57f.,
  59, 78, 100f.
  learning the meaning of 23f., 25, 26, 27
  naming 24, 26, 27, 61–4, 71
  teaching 24, 27, 94, 99, 100
sensations (see also Pain) 23–8, 34f., 70f.,
  73, 77–81, 83, 90, 91, 108, 142f.
  criterion of identity of 70, 71, 72, 79,
    80, 96, 100, 102
sense-impression (see also Visual
  Impression) 67f., 83–5, 87, 117, 203,
  205, 241
Shanker, S. 199n.
Siamese twins 47f., 124
sincerity/insincerity 40, 104
solipsism 19, 35, 86, 111f., 139, 273, 277,
  280, 281
  semi 95, 111
'something' 71, 111, 112, 113f., 117f., 129
soul 93–5, 133, 206f., 305
speech-acts, reflexive 16, 18, 23
Spinoza, B. 261
state, mental/of mind 37, 133–7, 160
surmise 31
Svartvik, J. 183n.
symptom 202–4

talking to oneself 17, 19, 21, 68f.
talking to oneself in the imagination 20,
  189f., 191, 192, 206f., 210
technique 61, 72f., 102, 112, 249
thinking 33f., 135, 156f., 181–4, 185
thought
  communication of 223f.
  criterion of identity of 187f.
  dual-process conception of 161f.,
    168–81
  expression of 157f., 159, 160, 177f.
  and language 171, 186f., 189, 191f.
  privacy of 34, 35
  speed of 161, 162, 163
  thought-reading 160f.
topic neutrality 189, 190f.

8483